# THE NEW FRONT PAGE

## A NEW ERA IN COMMUNICATIONS

The Early Bird satellite roars into space.

# THE
# NEW FRONT PAGE

*John Hohenberg*

COLUMBIA UNIVERSITY PRESS

*New York and London 1966*

John Hohenberg, with a background of twenty-five years of newspaper experience in New York, Washington, at the United Nations, and abroad, is Professor of Journalism at Columbia University's Graduate School of Journalism and Secretary of the Advisory Board on the Pulitzer Prizes. He is the editor and commentator for *The Pulitzer Prize Story* and is the author of *The Professional Journalist* and *Foreign Correspondence: The Great Reporters and Their Times.*

Copyright © 1966 John Hohenberg
Library of Congress Catalog Card Number: 65-26341
Printed in the United States of America

IN GRATEFUL MEMORY OF
THE JOSEPH PULITZERS,
FATHER AND SON

# INTRODUCTION

Joseph Pulitzer's front page glowed with satisfying news in the closing years of his turbulent life. The new century was showering the marvels of a blessed age on a proud and self-confident America. As the old publisher's secretaries softly read to him from his New York *World*, he could meditate on the endless surprises that were the lot of mankind.

Andrew Carnegie had set aside a million dollars to create an Endowment for International Peace, a princely sum for the noblest of causes. In that happy time, enduring peace not only seemed possible; it was almost at hand. Carnegie, in fact, was so hopeful of the abolition of war, "the foulest blot on our civilization," that he instructed his trustees to select the next most noxious evil to be banished from the earth.

True, a few zealots here and there warned of the coming of war, but they were without influence. No sensible American wanted a large army and navy; the founding fathers, in their wisdom, had cautioned against a powerful military establishment. As for those militants who wanted to spend money on armaments, they could always be silenced with a British quip of another century—that if military men could do so, they would fortify the moon.

American power, in any event, was sufficient. It was a sturdy rock in the morass of international affairs. Had not President Theodore Roosevelt proved it? While he had outraged Pulitzer with his conduct of the Panama Canal business, he had later sent a thrill of pride through the nation by proclaiming, "I took Panama!" And who could fail to be impressed with a President who was so outraged by the abduction of an American merchant in North Africa that he threatened to send the Marines after a Berber bandit chieftain? The nation thoroughly approved of the menacing ultimatum from the White House: "Perdicaris alive or Raisuli dead!"

It was, on the surface at least, a time when men could look forward to universal brotherhood. Booker T. Washington still had enormous prestige in a white-and-black civilization that was theoretically separate but equal. He was much admired for his doctrine, which he propounded to his white neighbors, that in all things "that are purely social we can be as separate as the fingers, yet one as the hand in all things essential to mutual progress."

Now and then, of course, labor seemed to be getting out of hand despite the placidity of Samuel Gompers and his American Federation of Labor. The Los Angeles *Times* was dynamited in the midst of a dispute; elsewhere, the Wobblies were making trouble. Moreover, the Socialists were waving the Red flag under the leadership of such radicals as Eugene V. Debs. But most people thought that all this, too, would pass and some dreamers talked of factory wages rising to as much as $1 an hour.

Everywhere, the miracles of science were being felt and observed. The age of flight was dawning. Soon after the Wright brothers proved that man could fly a rickety craft that was heavier than air, Glenn H. Curtiss hurtled the 132 miles from Albany to New York City in the astonishing time of 152 minutes. In doing so, he won the *World's* $10,000 prize for continuous flight.

But there were other scientific achievements of even more consequence to Pulitzer's front page. The wireless, Marconi's lusty infant, was being used to span the seas. Already, it had proved its usefulness by bringing rescue ships to the side of the sinking White Star liner *Republic*, thus saving all but six of her 1,600 passengers. With such an instrument, how could the whole world fail to be drawn together?

Yet, there were many things that Pulitzer could not find on his front page; in the classic definition of journalism, they were not news. During the year of the great publisher's death, a solemn-eyed little professor at the German university in Prague, Albert Einstein, was forging the key to the atomic era by perfecting his special theory of relativity. Mme. Marie Curie was isolating a gram of pure metallic radium in France. And in the New England hills, Professor Robert H. Goddard was experimenting with rockets, not knowing all the while that an engineer in France, René Lorin, was working on the theory of jet propulsion. Thus, when Pulitzer died on October 29, 1911, the future was taking shape slowly under the crowded surface of events.

Today there is a new front page. Its headlines cast long, bleak shadows in an age of desperation when man has found the means to destroy himself and all the world about him. Its news would scarcely be comprehensible to the readers of Joseph Pulitzer's day, only a little more than a half century ago. A cataclysmic change, wrought by a social and scientific revolution without parallel in history, has spread throughout the earth in the wake of two world wars, a great depression, and the generation of terror that has become known as the Cold War.

The news of the new front page puts an enormous burden on editor, reporter, writer, and reader alike, a strain that can scarcely be lessened by the development of the electronic media that Pulitzer knew only as code signals that crackled through a rotary spark gap aboard his yacht. For today the news is of the harnessing of the atom, whether it is used for war or for peace; of the conquest of space and soon, perhaps, of time itself; of an era when an astronaut in his space capsule can cross the nation in ten minutes and orbit the earth in less time than it took Curtiss to fly from Albany to New York City; when Americans and Russians are racing for the moon.

Then, too, on the new front page is news of fifty billions a year for the defense of the United States, not of a single million for peace; of a sorely divided world torn between the doctrine of a free society, as represented in the American dream, and the closed Communist societies of the Soviet Union and China; of bringing that dream to realization at long last for the American Negro, who rightfully demands the exercise of his birthright as a citizen in all parts of the land.

There is still more to that new front page: the dilemma of how to provide aid for tens of millions of people in the underdeveloped areas of the world, and still meet the more pressing needs of millions of underprivileged Americans; the imperative necessity for better education, better housing, better highways, better facilities for health; the conquest of disease and the extension of the benefits of improved medical care to those who are most in need of it and least able to afford it; the urgent requirement for more modern government, a more adequate safeguard against crime and other breaks in the social fabric, a wiser accommodation in an industrial society to the coming of an automated work force.

Over the course of a year, all these facets of life in the latter part of the twentieth century loom large on the new front page. From the fainthearted, always ready to give up on the democratic ideal, there are the inevitable cries, "The people don't care, the people don't want to understand, the people want to be left alone. Give the people a Leader." It is a sickeningly familiar gospel, which was heard so often in the Europe of the 1930s, and even in the home of free society, Britain itself.

It is true that there must be a desire to learn before knowledge can be imparted; today, the new front page of a superior newspaper is compounded of such knowledge. And it is these newspapers, the New York *Times* being an example, whose circulation is steadily rising, while rising costs are forcing others to merge or suspend publication. The net effect on the nation is sobering.

There is more than enough evidence that people *do* want to know something more than the bare events of the day; otherwise, they would be satisfied with five minutes of sketchy radio news rattled off by a singsong announcer in a bored voice. Instead, despite a measurable drop in the number of daily newspapers from a half century ago, the sales of daily newspapers have exceeded 60,000,000 copies, news magazine and current book sales are soaring, and the time given to network news telecasts has more than doubled in five years. The effect appears to be an information explosion rather than an information glut. In any event, there is no sign that the sources of supply are drying up. Instead, more seem to be opening up each year. And that has created a problem.

Archibald MacLeish has expressed it as follows:

"That we live in a context of crisis we all know, but too many of us react to our knowledge as firemen react to the bell on the station wall: we go shrieking off in the big red truck wherever. Some of us think the crisis is military—the Russians. Some see it as political—the Communists. To those of one opinion it is politico-economic—the Under-Developed Areas. To those of another—the great majority of mankind—it is military-moral-scientific—the Bomb.

"But to all of us or almost all the crisis is a crisis in the sense that a fire is a fire: something to get at fast, something that has just now befallen us, something which, if only we will deal with it quickly enough and definitively enough, can be put out—eliminated. . . .

"Our crisis, in other words, like all historical crises, is a crisis in the human situation, not a crisis in a laboratory or on a launching pad, or even in the office of a chief of state. Human intelligence has made certain discoveries culminating, over the course of forty years, in fantastic acts of mind which have changed everything including—and this is the most crucial and most critical of all the changes—the human mind itself. In altering the universe which mirrors us we have altered ourselves as figures in the mirror. And it is this alteration of the universe and of ourselves which has produced the problems which bedevil our time." [1]

This volume is devoted to an examination of the change in our national posture as it is reflected, not in a mirror, but on the new front page of our daily newspapers. It coincides roughly with the five decades of the Pulitzer Prizes in Journalism, first awarded in 1917, a good point from which to look forward as well as to look back. As might be expected, the Prizes themselves have developed into a barometer of journalistic change.

While the computer now sits in the newsroom and the long overdue process of mechanical and electronic change has taken firm hold of the newspaper, typography and production are less important than what has happened to the substance of journalism. After all newspapers, like men, are conservative in dress and change slowly in outward appearance; the inner transformation, when it occurs, counts for much more. For convenience's sake, I have discussed the substance of the new front page under nine rather arbitrary headings, but in each of these there are gradations of change that are readily apparent. Had I chosen to do so, I might have used a score or more without exhausting the subject. But in no case could I have approached the richness and the fascinating variety of the mass of American newspapers themselves, as reflected in the hundreds of exhibits that pile up each year before the Pultizer Prize juries at Columbia University.

Instead of covering the whole span of the Prizes, as was done in *The Pulitzer Prize Story*, what I tried to do here was to emphasize the newest and most meaningful aspects of American journalism. Under each heading will be found selections that illustrate the growth of a particular body of journalistic practice or an important trend.

Necessarily, the base of the selection process was an exhaustive reading of newspapers from all parts of the country, plus the large number of Pulitzer Prize nominations that are made each year. Added to this was the work of staff members of Pulitzer Prize-winning newspapers and

[1] Archibald MacLeish, *New York Times Magazine*, Dec. 25, 1960.

of Pulitzer Prize winners themselves, although relatively few are represented here by the efforts that won them their awards. Much of this is available in the previous volume.

For those who are interested in the standards of selection, they were entirely my own. I used what I liked, within the space that the Columbia University Press provided, and hereby absolve the University, the Advisory Board on the Pulitzer Prizes, the Pulitzer judges, and my faculty colleagues of all responsibility for what appears here. After a dozen years in the Prize administration, I was finally able to exercise the privileges of a judge and accepted the responsibility with alacrity. While this volume appears on a ceremonial occasion, therefore, nothing about it is ceremonial. The pieces herein are offered as superior examples of American professional journalism.

With that, I conclude. I thank my wife, Dorothy Lannuier Hohenberg, for her cheerfulness and patience with a nighttime and week-end writer, and her willingness to criticize that part of my work which appears here. My thanks, also, go to Robert J. Tilley and Joan McQuary of Columbia University Press, who have seen me through another difficult exercise. I am particularly indebted to my efficient associates in the Pulitzer Prize Office, Andrea Stevens Flynn, Murray MacDonald Hellenberg, and Juris Pirvics, and to the pillar of the Columbia University Journalism Library, Wade Doares, and his assistant, Jonathan Bryan May.

Finally, to President Grayson Kirk of Columbia University, Joseph Pulitzer Jr., and the other members of the Advisory Board on the Pulitzer Prizes, and to Dean Edward W. Barrett of the Columbia University Graduate School of Journalism, I express my gratitude for the privilege of being associated these many years with the Pulitzer Prizes.

JOHN HOHENBERG

*Columbia University*
*in the City of New York*
*June, 1965*

# CONTENTS

# ILLUSTRATIONS

# I. THE CIVIL RIGHTS STRUGGLE

Hodding Carter, the eloquent editor of the *Delta Democrat-Times* of Greenville, Mississippi, proposed an article on Mississippi to a national magazine editor shortly before the Supreme Court's school desegregation decision of 1954.

"I don't think Mississippi is ready for an article yet," was the editor's lofty reply.[1]

Ten years later a courageous Negro couple, Samuel Adams, a reporter for the St. Petersburg (Fla.) *Times*, and his wife, Elenora, drove through a dozen Southern states. Their purpose was to report on compliance with the Civil Rights Act of 1964. They found many Souths—and many different kinds of Southerners—with a certain amount of progress everywhere, the smallest in Louisiana, Alabama, and Mississippi.

On a o-to-100 scale denoting progress toward compliance with the Civil Rights Act, he rated West Virginia, North Carolina, Kentucky, Florida, Tennessee, Virginia, and Georgia at 50 percent or better. He put South Carolina and Arkansas just above the three most recalcitrant states of the Old Confederacy.

"Racial prejudice," Samuel Adams wrote, "isn't going to evaporate because Congress passed a law. It will be many, many years before a Negro driving through the South can forget his fear. But the Negro has hope now. The law is important to him. And steadily increasing acceptance of the law throughout the South can only ease tensions." [2]

[1] Hodding Carter, *Where Main Street Meets the River* (New York, Rinehart, 1952, 1953), p. 331.
[2] Samuel Adams, *Highways to Hope*, a booklet reprinted from the St. Petersburg (Fla.) *Times*, Nov. 13, 1964, pp. 10–11.

Nevertheless, no journalist could foretell the end of the crisis—and it was the journalists who were telling this story to a worried nation and to the world. A measure of the change that had been made on the mind and heart of America by a decade of racial turmoil could be gauged by the difference between Hodding Carter's experience in 1954 with a surpassingly blind Northern editor and the Adamses' experience in 1964.

There was another measurement that meant even more to journalists. Just before World War II, Ray Sprigle of the Pittsburgh *Post-Gazette* cropped his hair, acquired a suntan, and posed as a Negro while touring the South with a representative of the National Association for the Advancement of Colored People. His widely syndicated pieces were mild by today's standards, but Hodding Carter called them "distorted, prejudiced, and frequently erroneous" and made fun of them in a piece for *Look* magazine, describing the adventures of a mythical reporter, Ol' Fearless, in the North.[3]

Twenty-five years later, humor was in short supply whether reporters went South to cover the racial crisis or plunged into the Negro ghettos of the North. Moreover, a single reporter's sortie into the South could scarcely have attracted national attention, for there were literally dozens of them at every point of crisis. At about the time of the Adamses' trip, for example, Mississippi was swarming with reporters from the North, all of them unwelcome. While the Chamber of Commerce of Philadelphia, Mississippi, greeted visitors with a brochure of welcome headlined in Choctaw, the highway police were under no illusions. They told the reporters, "Don't wander around the streets. Stay close to the hotel." [4]

The community was in an uproar at the time over the discovery of the bodies of three murdered civil rights workers, and the accusations originally made in the case against twenty-one townspeople including the sheriff. A young reporter, Joseph Lelyveld of the New York *Times*, was at work with a photographer when he was surrounded by a gang and told to leave town. The reporter displayed a statement from Mayor Ab Davis Harbour, requesting courtesy for strangers.

"I didn't like the damned mayor's statement," the gang leader said,

[3] Carter, *Main Street*, pp. 316–17.
[4] *AP Log*, June 25–July 1, 1964.

"and I know a lot of other people who didn't like it. No mayor is going to tell us what to do."

Lelyveld and his photographer asked for protection at the sheriff's office, but didn't get it. They were advised to leave town.[5] Since he was on special assignment for the Sunday section, it wasn't too much of a problem because he didn't have to stay long. But for other reporters, the threat of violence here—as in other critical areas of the South and some of the Northern ghettos—remained a grave problem. Constant intimidation, blows, and broken cameras were commonplace in the South wherever Northern newspapermen went. Tom Kendrick of the Washington *Post* was forced out of one town, threatened in another. As for foreigners, there was an extra hazard. Nobody could forget that Paul L. Guihard, a 30-year-old correspondent for Agence France-Presse, had been shot and killed during the 1962 riots at the University of Mississippi.

Long before 1964, the South had been well aware of what was coming, as its journalists could testify. With remarkable insight, W. J. Cash wrote well-nigh a decade and a half before the Supreme Court's decision on what he believed to be the South's failings:

"Violence, intolerance, aversion and suspicion toward new ideas, an incapacity for analysis, an inclination to act from feeling rather than from thought, an exaggerated individualism and a too narrow concept of social responsibility, attachment to fictions and false values, above all too great attachment to racial values and a tendency to justify cruelty and injustice in the name of these values, sentimentality and a lack of realism—these have been its [the South's] characteristic vices in the past. And despite changes for the better, they remain its characteristic vices today.

"In the coming days, and probably soon, it is likely to have to prove its capacity for adjustment far beyond what has been true in the past." [6]

Hodding Carter, too, had no illusions about the temper of the South toward any who would disturb its own notions of proper race relations. As a leading Southern moderate, he had received thousands of letters

[5] Joseph Lelyveld, "A Stranger in Philadelphia, Miss.," *New York Times Magazine*, Dec. 27, 1964, p. 36.
[6] W. J. Cash, *The Mind of the South* (New York, Vintage, 1941), pp. 439–40.

annually long before the Supreme Court decision from angry critics
of his position in favor of broad civil rights for Negroes. "In respect to
granting these rights," he warned, "a majority of white Southerners
will not easily be led or driven, and there is more to their stubborn
resistance than simply a susceptibility to demagogic oratory. Determination on continued political mastery is near the center of this hard
core of resistance to change." [7]

Ralph McGill, then editor of the Atlanta *Constitution*, also sensed
the inevitable conflict. On the eve of World War II he wrote that
"only a handful of persons" had noted preparations to file suits to
test the segregation laws that kept Negroes out of universities in certain states. And a year before the high court's decision, he wrote a
column, "One of These Days It Will Be Monday," a warning that the
school decision was coming on one of the Mondays when the court
customarily announced its rulings.

When that Monday came on May 17, 1954, the great Georgian
mourned that "none of those whose duty it was to cope with the effect
of it had done any preparatory educating or planning." He added sadly,
"It could be seen, too, that we were all caught in it, white and colored,
the haves and the have-nots." [8]

There were few in the North or the West who could match such
realism. The predominant mood of the white liberals outside the
South who wrote for publication was more like that of Hodding Carter's
magazine editor. One example was Oswald Garrison Villard, who had
been editor of the New York *Evening Post* and founder of the *Nation*.
As early as January 17, 1908, he saw profound changes in the South's
racial attitudes, for on that night he heard Marse Henry Watterson,
the editor of the Louisville *Courier-Journal*, proclaim at New York's
Carnegie Hall, "I want nothing for myself or for my children which
I am not ready to give to my colored neighbor and his children." Villard
called it "the most important utterance ever made by a Southern white
man in the North on this subject." [9] By 1929, consequently, Villard
was writing in *Harper's* that the whole color line in the South was in

[7] Carter, *Main Street*, pp. 225, 315.

[8] Ralph McGill, *The South and the Southerner* (Boston, Little, Brown, 1959,
1963), pp. 24–25, 170–71.

[9] Joseph Frazier Wall, *Henry Watterson: Reconstructed Rebel* (New York, Oxford University Press, 1956), p. 286.

rapid process of disintegration.[10] But he was not alone in his wishful thinking, by any means.

The record of the Pulitzer Prizes, often a fever chart, indicates the extent to which journalists were preoccupied with the racial problem before and after the Supreme Court's desegregation decision. In the thirty-nine annual awards announced from 1917 to 1955, there were five prizes for newspaper crusades against racial extremism in both the South and the North. In the nine annual awards between 1956 and 1964 there were eight prizes for distinguished journalism dealing with the racial crisis—one for public service, one for reporting, and six for editorial writing.[11]

All the pre-1955 prizes were public service gold medals, awarded to newspapers for their opposition to the Ku Klux Klan. They were the New York *World*, 1922; Memphis *Commercial Appeal*, 1923; Columbus (Ga.) *Enquirer-Sun*, 1926, and Indianapolis *Times*, 1928, with a shared award in 1953 for two North Carolina weeklies, the Whiteville *News-Reporter* and the Tabor City *Tribune*, during an upsurge of Klan sentiment there. Of course, there were numerous other instances of journalistic interest in racial problems over that period, but the attention of the Pulitzer juries and the Pulitzer Advisory Board was diverted elsewhere.

How different it was as the South began its massive resistance to the enforcement of the desegregation decision! As mobs rioted for four days in February, 1956, and forced the withdrawal of the first Negro student to be admitted to the University of Alabama, Autherine Lucy, only the Tuscaloosa *News* tried to give the hysterical community a different kind of leadership. For his moderation and his courage, Buford Boone, the editor, was awarded the 1957 Pulitzer Prize for editorial writing.[12]

When the first Negro students sat in hitherto all-white classes at Central High School in Little Rock, Arkansas, and federal troops patrolled the city, Harry S. Ashmore, then the executive editor of the *Arkansas Gazette*, wrote on October 20, 1957:

[10] Cash, *Mind of South*, p. 308.
[11] Records of the Pulitzer Prizes. See also John Hohenberg, ed., *The Pulitzer Prize Story* (New York, Columbia University Press, 1959), pp. 329–56. The Pulitzer Prize records are also published in the *World Almanac*.
[12] Examples of his work and that of other Prize winners, may be seen in the Pulitzer Prize exhibit, Special Collections, Butler Library, Columbia University.

"The false hope is that the rest of the United States, by persuasion or force, can be brought to abandon the declared public policy of the nation and let the South alone. The presence on our streets of a detachment of the 101st Airborne Infantry, ordered here by the most conciliatory President in modern times, should disabuse us of that notion. The point is that sooner or later we have got to make some adjustment of our legal institutions to comply with the public policy of the United States—or once again secede from the Union, which no one seriously contemplates."

The White Citizens' Councils, the lineal descendants of the Klan, boycotted the *Gazette* and threatened Ashmore. Yet, he maintained his call for the support of the law in Arkansas. Even more important, he retained the backing of his 85-year-old publisher, John Netherland Heiskell. There were two Pulitzer awards that year, one to Ashmore for editorial writing and another to Heiskell's *Gazette* for public service, the only double prize of its kind in Pulitzer annals. Ashmore, laden with honors, joined the staff of the *Encyclopaedia Britannica*. Heiskell, surviving a cumulative loss in revenue of more than $2,000,000, was still running the *Gazette* in 1965 at the age of 92, and accepting still more honors for his steadfastness.[13]

The first Pulitzer Prize awarded to a reporter for coverage of the deepening racial crisis went to Mary Lou Werner of the Washington *Evening Star* in 1959. She did more than report the day-to-day news and the rising tensions over the closed schools in northern Virginia. By the very nature of her work and the interpretation which she placed on it in specially written articles, she contributed to public understanding and a calmer approach to an eventual solution of the crisis in the area.

In the same year the Pulitzer Prize for editorial writing went to Ralph McGill. Technically, the award was for his year's work and his leadership in the *Constitution's* unremitting efforts to keep the peace in Georgia and move along the moderate path toward increased civil rights for Negroes. Actually, it recognized a lifetime of service in the cause of racial understanding. Much the same rationale was behind the 1960 Pulitzer Prize for editorial writing to Lenoir Chambers of the Norfolk *Virginian-Pilot*.

[13] New York *Times*, Dec. 9, 1964. See also Hohenberg, *Pulitzer Prize Story*, pp. 101–6.

The focus of segregationist opposition shifted to Mississippi where in 1962 the rioting mobs demonstrated against the admission of the first Negro, James Meredith, to the University of Mississippi. Once again, a journalist stood up when most others in the state were bowing to public clamor in an unrighteous cause. This time it was a young small-town editor and publisher, Ira B. Harkey Jr., of the Pascagoula *Chronicle*. He opposed the mobs and the government of the state to support Meredith's cause when larger and more powerful newspapers did not dare. He was rewarded with the 1963 Pulitzer Prize for editorial writing and a bullet hole through his front door. As a result of the harsh pressures that built up against him, he had to sell his paper and leave the state.

Still another small-town editor and publisher, Hazel Brannon Smith, held out after ten years of unrelenting opposition by the White Citizens Councils. Because she pleaded the cause of civil rights and argued for moderation in Mississippi at a time when church burnings, midnight shootings, and murder stained the state, she won the Pulitzer Prize for editorial writing in 1964. Yet, her Lexington *Advertiser* and her three other weekly papers were badly hurt by the backlash of boycotts. She was made the victim of unholy smears, two court actions (both reversed, after initial judgments against her), and the bitter hatred of all segregationists. In 1965, she still was able to hold out.

Considering the temper of the vast Southern majority of those years and the viciousness that was abroad, the surprise to a Northerner was not that there were so few brave Southern voices, but that there were so many. The McGills, Carters, and Hazel Smiths were not alone. Even in the Deep South, a tiny weekly, the Coushatta (La.) *Citizen*, could and did take on the Ku Klux Klan's rabble and run an editorial addressed to the Klan: "Get the Hell out of Red River Parish." Elsewhere in the South, in Chattanooga and Louisville and Nashville, in Charlotte and Norfolk and Wheeling among others, there was decency and an effort to lead. In large part because of the work of the Norfolk *Ledger-Star* and John A. Hamilton, the 1,700 Negro children of Prince Edward County, Virginia, were able to go to school after four years without education. And in the Selma crisis, in 1965, the Birmingham *News* appealed for moderation. Of course this did not make up for the failures of the press elsewhere in the South, but it provided a challenge that was vitally necessary.

The national crisis had its impact on the press outside the South, too. In the roster of Pulitzer Prize exhibits for 1963, 1964, and 1965, more were devoted to integration than to any other subject. A special Pulitzer citation, given to the Gannett Newspapers in 1964 for their use of success stories in integration, was a partial recognition of the importance, the volume, and the quality of the special coverage of the most important social problem of the era.

There were others who made a calculated effort to piece together the complicated mosaic of an emerging pattern. Some of the most significant were a Chicago *Daily News* team report, "The Negro in Chicago"; a series by staff writers and Negro leaders in the St. Louis *Post-Dispatch*; the articles of Claude Sitton in the New York *Times*; a series of "in depth" interviews with Negro leaders by Robert S. Bird of the New York *Herald Tribune*; the New York *Post's* special report on Negro education; the Washington *Post's* detailed coverage and analysis; the Washington *Star's* massive report on the Negro march on Washington; and extended commentaries and campaigns in the Des Moines *Register*, Denver *Post*, Cincinnati *Enquirer*, and Boston *Globe*.[14]

Out of the avalanche of newsprint that poured from the presses, there was one that was unfamiliar because it was new. It was a flimsy little publication, the bi-weekly *Citizens' Appeal* of Vicksburg, Mississippi, which began regular appearances on November 2, 1964, with no assurance of how long it would last. It was put out by Negroes from Vicksburg and visiting civil rights workers. And it published news that was suppressed by segregationist papers—the bombing and burning of offices, libraries, churches, and schools.

The *Citizens' Appeal* represented a calculated risk for its editors and reporters. But as it announced in a front page editorial in its first issue:

"Those who are afraid to risk their safety forget that they have no real safety to risk. If we are going to be beaten and bombed anyway because we are black, why not at least be beaten and bombed because we are doing something for our race?"[15]

Such was the story of the journalist and the racial crisis in the mid-1960s, the most significant social development in American life. In the pages that follow, he and his newspapers are shown in the midst of the struggle.

[14] *Columbia Journalism Review*, Summer, 1964, p. 10.
[15] *Columbia Journalism Review*, Winter, 1965, p. 40, letter dated Sept. 3, 1964.

## 1. *HOW IT BEGAN*

In Relman Morin's four decades as a reporter, he saw the best of peace and the worst of war. Wherever there was action, he was generally in on it. If anyone could be said to have participated in the writing of a first draft of history, it was he. For it, he won two Pulitzer Prizes and many other awards and was still active in his sixtieth year.

Morin was born in Freeport, Illinois, on September 11, 1907, took his A.B. from Pomona College in 1929, and promptly set out for the Far East. He had begun work on the Los Angeles *Times* in 1923 and by that time knew his way around a newsroom. But after a year in Shanghai on the old *Evening Post*, he was back in Los Angeles, this time on the *Record*. In 1934, he joined the Associated Press, where he remained as foreign correspondent, war correspondent, Paris and Washington bureau manager and, finally, roving correspondent.

On the morning of September 23, 1957, he was in a glass-enclosed telephone booth outside Central High School in Little Rock, Arkansas, and dictated the story of the wild mob scene as the first Negro children went to class there. To his first Pulitzer Prize, won in 1951 for his Korean War reporting, he thereby added a second. He also acquired a deep interest in the integration story, which he covered from time to time. The following account, written on May 17, 1964 as part of a historical survey for the AP, goes back to the beginning of a great social uprising in the United States.

### LINDA GOES TO SCHOOL

#### *By Relman Morin*

On a spring day in 1951 a Negro clergyman in Topeka, Kansas, went to school with his 9-year-old daughter.

Linda Brown attended Monroe Elementary, an all-Negro school, twenty blocks from her home. She rode the school bus most of the way. But on that day the Rev. Oliver Brown did not take his daughter to Monroe. Holding Linda's hand, he led her to an all-white school, Sumner Elementary. It was four blocks away. They walked.

In the building, the Rev. Mr. Brown attempted to enroll Linda.

The request was denied. He told her to wait in the hallway. Then he took the request to the principal of the school. Again it was denied.

This brief sequence was soon to go into American legal and social history as part of the monumental decision by the United States Supreme Court in the case of "Brown vs. Board of Education."

In seventeen states segregation was mandatory.

All this, of course, was beyond the understanding of a 9-year-old girl. Nor did Linda Brown understand why her father had taken her that day to the school for white children.

Today she says: "My father felt strongly for the whole Negro race. And he was upset because I had to go so far to school. He felt that we paid taxes the same as anyone else and there was no reason for this inconvenience."

Linda Brown's father could have told her that much more than "inconvenience" to Negroes was involved in his action. Segregated public schools had been a fact of American life for a century before he and other Negro parents challenged it in 1951.

It began in the North, in Boston in 1849, and lasted there until 1855. In San Francisco in the early 1900s Oriental children for a time were assigned to a separate school.

The Supreme Court, in its ruling of May 17, 1954, said: "It is apparent that such segregation has long been a nationwide problem, not merely one of sectional concern."

The scene in Sumner Elementary was one Negro's protest about a school. But what followed, as a result of the court's decision, was a social upheaval involving much more than the public schools. From this was to come the great drive for full equality for the Negro— voting rights, job opportunities, housing, public accommodations, the right to enter a public park, the right to read a book in a public library.

Every corner of America would feel it.

Who could have foreseen what lay ahead? Who envisioned federal troops again marching into Southern cities, police battling demonstrators in Northern cities, bloodshed and rioting, the multiplicity of law suits, "impeach Earl Warren" signs, the Black Muslims, shuttered schools, acts of courage and acts of cowardice?

A painful decade was beginning.

The racial picture in the United States today is mottled. It is a montage of sunlight and shadow. For example, the Justice Department maintains figures on what has taken place in 556 cities in Southern and border states. Statistics cover almost nine months.

They show that desegregation of some public facilities, or formation of bi-racial committees, went from 36 percent of the 556 cities as of June 21, 1963 to 69 percent as of February 11, 1964, when the last report was compiled.

In the field of Negro voting rights, the report cites Baker County, Georgia, where the department worked for two years to induce local officials voluntarily to change a long-standing pattern of discrimination. The county board of registrars permitted Negroes to register. Of 243 Negroes who applied, 200 were found qualified and were registered. They voted in a local election later in the same month.

Similarly, the report says, in Macon County, Alabama, Negro registration went from 13 to 42 percent in 1963, in Bullock County, Alabama, from 1 percent to 27.6 percent and in Washington Parish, Louisiana, from 4.6 percent to 23.9 percent.

These are barometers. Whether they are encouraging or discouraging depends on your point of view.

---

As time went on, strange things began to happen. Joseph A. Loftus telegraphed the New York *Times* on February 24, 1965 from Richmond, Virginia:

"Both major parties for the first time are openly courting the Negro vote in Virginia."

The Republicans had appointed a Negro assistant to the state chairman; the Democrats, not to be outdone, welcomed a dozen or so Negroes to their annual fund-raising Jefferson-Jackson Day dinner, presided over by the one-time leader of the "massive resistance" movement, Senator Harry Flood Byrd.

And in New York City, on February 21, 1965, the fanatical Black Muslim movement was split wide open when Negro gunmen shot dead a black nationalist, Malcolm X, in a Manhattan hall. Whether police could have stopped it, even if they had been forewarned, remains problematical.

Ten years after the start of integration, there were more problems than ever before.

## 2. RALPH MC GILL VIEWS THE SOUTH

"This is a harvest," wrote Ralph McGill after the bombing of a synagogue and a school in the South.

"It is the crop of things sown. It is the harvest of defiance of courts and the encouragement of citizens to defy law on the part of many Southern politicians.

"You do not preach and encourage hatred for the Negro and hope to restrict it to that field." [16]

In righteous indignation he attacked the governors, the lawyers, the judges, the civic leaders, the ministers—yes, even his own kind, the editors—who had been campaigning to halt desegregation in defiance of the law. He was one of the few in the South who had always dared the whirlwind, heedless of both personal comfort and safety. In twenty years as the executive editor and editor of the Atlanta *Constitution*, he had been the stouthearted champion of many a generous cause.

It was for a lifetime of such exemplary service that he was awarded the Pulitzer Prize for editorial writing in 1959 and later invited to become a member of the Advisory Board on the Pulitzer Prizes. Yet, these and all his other honors did not change him. In his sixties, when lesser men were reaching for their carpet slippers, he was more active than ever in a new role as the publisher of the *Constitution*, beginning in 1960, and a widely read national columnist.

The only hint of future greatness about Ralph McGill at his birth in the hamlet of Soddy, Tennessee, on February 5, 1898, was his middle name, Emerson, which he seldom if ever used from boyhood on. His eminence was scarcely based on a superior formal education, for his studies at Vanderbilt were interrupted by service in the U.S. Marines during World War I, and he never did graduate. Nor did he soar to fame at the outset in journalism. Like so many others, his earliest work and his best training came as a sports writer and sports editor, first for the Nashville *Banner* in 1922 and later for the Atlanta *Constitution* beginning in 1931. It wasn't until 1938, when he left the sports desk to

[16] Ralph McGill, "One Church . . . One School," Atlanta *Constitution*, Oct. 15, 1958.

be the *Constitution's* executive editor, that he glimpsed wider horizons
—a parade of robed and masked Klansmen around the newspaper's
building in an overt attack on him. In 1942, despite the Klan, he
became the *Constitution's* editor.

There was never anything of the sobersides or thin-lipped reformer
about McGill. He was a large-hearted, kindly man, a good companion
and a great story-teller who could lighten the chores of the dullest day
and make a humdrum evening gay and exciting. Yet, for all his social
and professional gifts, he was never satisfied with the comfortable life
of a Southern gentleman. Deep inside him there was an innate spirit
of fair play that drove him again and again to the defense of those who
were unable to defend themselves.

He would never have called himself a crusader, and yet, in a journalistic sense, he was one. Without intending to do so, he became one of
the bravest leaders of the cause of moderation in the South. Without
him, the beautiful city of Atlanta might well have found itself far
more a battleground of the civil rights movement than it actually was.
It cost him far more than he was ever willing to admit—a sense of
security and a peaceful home life. For when mad-dog crowds gathered
in the night, when shots were fired and obscene threats made regularly
by telephone, what family could feel secure?

The McGills' small brick home became the repository of garbage
that was dumped on the lawn. One night, someone emptied a six-
shooter into their mailbox as a gesture of warning. Another time, a
rifle bullet pierced their window pane and plunged into the back of a
chair. As for the menacing telephone calls, they came with such regularity that the family disregarded them until, because of Mrs. McGill's
failing health, the telephone was changed to an unlisted number.[17]

Together, the McGills endured all this and more—Ralph, his devoted
Mary Elizabeth, and Ralph Jr.—until Mrs. McGill's death in 1962.
Thereafter, McGill's devotion to the cause of a better and saner South
seemed, if anything, to increase. He had seen the University of Georgia
desegregated in January, 1961, despite the howling protest of a mob.
He knew it could be done.

When setbacks came, and they were inevitable, he took them deeply
to heart. In the following piece on Birmingham, which he wrote in

[17] McGill, *South and Southerner*, pp. 287–88.

1963 at the height of the rioting there over the Rev. Dr. Martin Luther King's desegregation campaign, he set down his shock and his horror in New York, where he was attending a meeting.

"A Southerner," he wrote, "felt an occasional near-compulsive wish to break suddenly into loud, despairing laughter. Birmingham was smoking with hate where once the stacks of her mills stained the sky with their plumes. Hate ran through Birmingham's streets."

The New York *Herald Tribune* was so impressed that it ran McGill's story of May 14, 1963 in the *Constitution* across the top of its own Page 1 under a headline, "A Sensitive Southerner's View of a Smoking City." In essential part, it is reproduced here.

## WHEN HATE FILLED BIRMINGHAM
### By Ralph McGill

Birmingham is not a Southern city.

It was born of coal, iron ore, and limestone. It never knew crinoline or lace. The chemical smoke and slag from its early furnaces made mock of magnolias and mocking birds.

It came into being just before the turn of the century, and it had a dramatic effect on the small farms of Alabama. Nowhere was the sharecropper and tenant evil so deeply and wretchedly fixed as in Alabama. The regular jobs at mine and smelter were like economic manna from heaven to men who had worked at heavy farm toil for a year and ended up deep in debt to the plantation owner.

The city drew them. They opened mines. They dug coal. They learned to make steel. The Negro, also freed from sharecropper peonage, came, too. But he was, by and large, a plantation field Negro. He had as little learning as the whites, and he had even less sophistication.

One of the wells from which hate and prejudice are drawn in the South, or anywhere else for that matter, is fear of economic competition. The poor white man, escaping from his tenant farm, or from the few worn-out acres where his father had worn out a life, had no more skills than the Negro. The fingers of both were curved to fit the handles of plows and hoes. But, one had a white skin. And that was a symbol of being better and of deserving more.

So, the Negro, as he came to Southern cities from being a cropper or a tenant, was kept in his "place" there as rigidly as he had been on the cotton farm.

The new and magic city of Birmingham was made to grow and her night skies to glow with the pourings of steel by those persons, white and black, who hurried in from the poor, inadequate, segregated schools which, in the early days of the city's development, were open for only a few months each winter. Their stamp has been on it ever since.

The managerial class came and built on the slopes of Red Mountain and other hills that rim the city. Business came. The city began to read books, to go to college, to furnish audiences for concerts and art festivals. But the stamp of her beginnings is on her, and the prejudices, and the mores born with her continue.

There was something else, too, that helped condition the city and bring her to riots and bloodshed that shocked the world of our friends and delighted our enemies. Birmingham was a stronghold of anti-union strength. The battle of the Steel Worker's CIO Union, and more particularly, John L. Lewis' United Mine Workers, produced violence and men willing to commit it. Nowhere were the hard-won union victories more fiercely held. No Southern unions, in the beginning, more thoroughly saw to it that those Negro members whom the CIO said they must admit kept their place.

The Negroes, grateful for the union, were content then to sit on the back rows and listen. Dynamite blasts are nothing new to Birmingham. The union wars heard a lot of them.

One more thing—

Alabama is still a rural state. There is Montgomery, sleepy since Jefferson Davis took the oath there. Birmingham is the only really industrial city in the South. Here of late, hard times have come a-knocking at her door.

The governor of the state, George Wallace, was a Horatio Alger sort of boy. He worked his way through college and law school. But like Bull Connor, the Commissioner of Safety, he had that inexplicable feeling that the Negro, somehow, didn't have the same rights as a white man and should be barred from all associations in schools.

Alabama has had a long, uninterrupted line of such guidance—from Jeff Davis' day of oath-taking to now. The newspapers, in the writer's opinion, largely abdicated their responsibility. Birmingham and Alabama have many wonderful people who would have been willing to go with reform. The churches had enough big givers with opinions and attitudes to match those of Mr. Connor and Governor Wallace, and so they did not join actively in the dialogue.

So all roads led inevitably to the demonstrations and the prayer meetings begun by Dr. Martin Luther King Jr. There have been some who criticized his tactics, saying he should have waited. This is not, in the writer's opinion, valid. There has been enough waiting. Dr. King's tactics had to be cut to fit the cloth. And the cloth was Bull Connor and Governor Wallace. Dr. King didn't have much choice.

It is significant that the Black Muslims, an extremist group pledged to destroy the white man and to build a new, glittering ghetto for the Negro, also hate Dr. King. They, too, were critical of his tactics— presumably because they succeeded. It should not be overlooked here that the Negroes have used neither guns nor dynamite. The hate has been lately one-sided. Dr. King's preachings and passive resistance ideas have won a great following. One of these days the South, even Birmingham, will be grateful to Dr. King.

Elsewhere, the Southern leadership is moving ahead. The Negro will have what the Constitution guarantees. The ugly clamor and shrieking hate out of Birmingham should not blind us to the promise of our nation being fulfilled.

———

But the hate in Birmingham did obscure the promise of the civil rights movement for many a day. Claude Sitton, the New York *Times*'s great correspondent in the South, wrote that few in Birmingham were untouched by terror after the bombing of the 16th Street Baptist Church on September 16, 1963, in which four little Negro girls were slain.

"The shock waves from the bombing," Sitton reported, "were felt across the nation. Southerners feared that others might come to regard Birmingham as the measure of the region's race relations and thus intensify the pressure for a change. Northerners knew . . . that the re-action of Negroes would create new racial unrest in their communities.

"Americans everywhere turned toward Birmingham and asked why, what was it that made it seemingly impossible for whites and Negroes to live together here in peace."

But if the Birmingham of 1963 was the shame of America, Ralph McGill's Atlanta represented its hope for something better. As McGill wrote: "The greatest of all compensations was to be one of the many who worked long and patiently at the arduous job of seeing to it that the people of Atlanta knew the facts and the alternatives. To see the golf courses, transportation, eating places, libraries, and schools desegregated without an incident but rather with understanding and good manners was a warm and rewarding experience. There is almost an ecstasy which is quite indescribable, in seeing, and feeling, a city slowly but surely reach a decision and act on it. For a time, one lives a shared existence which is deeply rewarding." [18]

On the basis of that decision, Atlanta in 1965 became the first city of the South to honor one of its most distinguished citizens, the Rev. Dr. Martin Luther King, Jr., upon his receipt of the Nobel Peace Prize. He mourned at his brilliant bi-racial gathering that the "good people" didn't do more.

## 3. THE ADAMSES TOUR DIXIE

Samuel Adams, a 38-year-old reporter for the St. Petersburg (Fla.) *Times*, and his 35-year-old wife, Elenora, drove their leased compact auto out of St. Petersburg along Interstate Route 4 on a chilly but bright October morning in 1964.

"We were middle-class tourists with no serious money problems," he wrote, "and we normally would stop at top quality motels and seek out fine restaurants. We were to forget, if we could, our color. We were to report what happened to us, but to precipitate no trouble."

Within an hour, an attendant turned them away from the Hillsborough River State Park. But after they published their experience, a press agent said it shouldn't have happened because all Florida state parks were desegregated. That's the way it went for fifteen days, during which they drove 4,300 miles through twelve Southern states.

Samuel Adams was no ordinary reporter and the St. Petersburg *Times* was no ordinary newspaper. He was Georgia-born, held three college degrees, and had worked on a variety of topflight assignments for the *Times* and other papers for ten years. The *Times* had won a

---

[18] McGill, *South and Southerner*, p. 297.

Pulitzer Prize for public service in 1964, a hallmark of quality. Both the editors and the reporter agreed that it was time to make a test of the first effects of the passage of the Civil Rights Act of 1964. As for Mrs. Adams, the mother of two children and the assistant projects director of the Community Service Foundation in St. Petersburg, she bravely went along for the ride.

There were rebuffs and there was danger. But, they found that there was a bright side, too. Savannah was a model city, as far as they were concerned, and at once-segregated Albany, Georgia, they found that they were welcome. In South Carolina, they saw that most business people were "swallowing the public accommodations law, but they don't like it," and their experiences in North Carolina, Virginia, and Kentucky were somewhat better. Except for West Virginia, however, they were scarcely comfortable elsewhere in the South. And in Mississippi, the danger signs popped up on every side. Here was the report from Mississippi, first printed in the St. Petersburg *Times*, November 13, 1964, later reprinted as a pamphlet, *Highways to Hope*.

## "THEY DO THEIR DIRT AT NIGHT"

### *By Samuel Adams*

A police car drove slowly down the street, stopped, turned around, and headed back toward us in the dusty midday sunlight.

"No need to fear anybody now," explained Mrs. Aaron Henry, our hostess. "They do their dirt at night."

We were sitting in the Fourth Street Drug Store in Clarksdale, Mississippi. A ragged rectangular hole in the ceiling over our heads had been ripped by an explosion a few weeks earlier.

The store is owned by Dr. Aaron Henry, head of Mississippi's Freedom Democratic Party and president of the State Conference of the National Association for the Advancement of Colored People.

This was the second time police had passed the store since our arrival. The officers peered into the store as the car crept past. Mrs. Henry and a woman working with her had told us that visitors with out-of-town license tags are often arrested after they leave.

Mrs. Henry and a woman employee at the drug store sat rattling off a list of "don'ts" to two neophyte Negroes in Mississippi:

DON'T travel on the highway after dark.

DON'T use white rest rooms at a certain oil station, for the attendant would have police follow and arrest us further down the road on some traffic charge.

DON'T be out in Clarksdale after the midnight curfew if you are a Negro or a "freedom" worker.

DON'T get arrested on a traffic charge or our car would be impounded, I would be jailed, and my wife left on the street without transportation.

Spurning Mrs. Henry's offer to house us, we went to Holiday Inn. We circled to keep from being followed. But a short time later we were back at Mrs. Henry's, and we slept that night in the Henry home under the shotgun protection of the Rev. Willie Goodlow, who had guard duty that night.

We accepted Mrs. Henry's hospitality after being permitted to register at the Holiday Inn. Even as I had started to register, a slightly built, dark-haired man had pointed out our car to a burly individual wearing a plaid shirt. They had talked briefly in full view of my wife, and she was frightened.

The matronly desk clerk gave me a registration card after a lengthy telephone conversation with someone about me. The telephone rang again before I finished registering. The clerk said, apparently to someone on an extension, "Yes, I've got to take him. That's what the boss said."

Back at the car, Elenora told me that we were being watched from a window over the club lounge by a man and a woman. I drove to Room 31 with my lights off, making it more difficult for them to see my tag or car from their lighted room. I backed in, obscuring my license tag against a low hedge. The car was left loaded, and facing out.

The room was next to the end of a wing, at the rear of the complex a stone's throw from a road. A fence about three feet high separated the motel property and the public roadway.

Soon after we were settled in the room, the click of leather heels on the paved walk claimed our full attention. The sound stopped at our door. I opened the door and faked conversation with my wife: "Are you sure we have everything you want out of the car?"

Outside was a Negro restaurant porter writing on a pad and trying to appear interested in something other than our car or room. He left, but we heard similar sounds of heels clicking our way fifteen minutes later. We suspected he was getting our car tag number.

Just as Elenora was beginning to feel more secure, she discovered an inside door leading to the room adjacent to ours. It was locked from the other side. I tried, but couldn't lock it from ours.

"That does it. It's better to be a live coward than a dead hero. Please take me back to Mrs. Henry's and let's accept the room she offered us," said my wife.

On the way out, I went into the motel office for my receipt and told the clerk we thought we'd look for a restaurant away from the motel. Seconds after we left, Elenora told me a policeman was behind me. We stopped at a gasoline station and he made a U-turn and drove past the other side of the station.

Early Saturday we took Mrs. Henry's advice. We mailed the motel key instead of returning it—one of several precautions taken to avoid being followed. We headed our compact car south into the cradle of the racist White Citizens Council—Sunflower County, home of James Eastland and of Fannie Lou Hamer, the rotund Negro whose story of her arrest and flogging for registering to vote shook the Democratic National Convention in Atlantic City.

I stopped to photograph a trio of cotton pickers harnessed in bags six feet long. It was then we discovered that the car that had been trailing us was being driven by a policeman. We were between Parchman State Prison and Drew, Mississippi. The unmarked police car kept moving.

At Drew the police car was waiting. We stopped at a gasoline station as he pulled out and headed into town. No rest rooms were open to us at most places where we stopped. It was no better in Ruleville and in Tallahatchie County.

At a large Gulf station in Greenwood, the rest rooms were locked and the attendant said he didn't have the key. At other stations the rest rooms were "out of order" or "not for y'all." Denials of rest room use caused Elenora to become ill before we reached Jackson. At Jackson we stopped at a large Sinclair station with four rest rooms—two for both races. Jackson also offered some limited restaurant and motel service, according to Mrs. Thelma Sanders, a Negro businesswoman whose home was bombed earlier in the year.

Up to this point our experiences in Mississippi had indicated no hope. Now, suddenly, we found tiny islands of hope in Jackson, the state capital. A pleasant white woman volunteered to send us to a white cafeteria, and we learned later that Negroes also are served at one other white restaurant.

The sun was setting when we reached Vicksburg's Holiday Inn. "I'm sorry, we got tours coming in," the woman said. We suspected there actually was room at the inn and telephoned back after driving two miles. "I'm about 30 miles away," said Elenora, telling a little white lie. "Can you house us when we get there?"

"Sure we can," was the reply.

She had neglected to say that we were Negroes.

We also telephoned to Vicksburg's Magnolia Motel and were offered a room. The offer was withdrawn and we were referred to a Negro hotel when they learned our racial identity. We spent the night in Louisiana and it was the next afternoon when we returned to Mississippi at Natchez. Some Natchez service stations offered a "colored" rest room while others refused us altogether.

Where U.S. 98 splits off from U.S. 84 west of Budef, we ordered gasoline from a slightly built white boy who directed me to the rear of the station. I went to a door marked "Men." The boy, aged about 17, met me coming out.

"Didn't I tell you the nigger room was round back?" he asked.

I smiled as if I didn't hear, and asked a question of my own.

Summit, McComb, and Magnolia are three unyielding segregationist strongholds famous for violence against Negroes. They are in a cluster midway between Jackson and New Orleans. Nearby is Philadelphia, where three civil rights workers were murdered.

Also nearby is the murky Pearl River, like the Tallahatchie, famous as a watery grave of Negroes who "forget their place." We found the McComb Freedom House where COFO (Council of Federated Organizations) conducts Negro voter education and other civil rights activities. It had a gaping bomb hole big enough to drive a truck through.

To mislead the police car which trailed us, we stopped a few doors down the street and drove to Freedom House after the officers had left. It was late Sunday afternoon and Freedom House was buzzing. A citizenship class was being carried on in the back. Two college students who were to share night watch duties Sunday night were asleep in a front bedroom.

A late-arriving doctor-nurse team from New York drove up just as a search team was being organized to look for them. They go into jails, examine civil rights workers and, in effect, say to law enforcement authorities, "This prisoner is in good shape now. We will be back. If he is injured, you will have to answer for it."

We were told, "Nothing in McComb is desegregated." The rights workers said unless we were prepared to submit to arrest, search, and seizure, we should not attempt to use public accommodations in Southeast Mississippi.

We asked to use their pay telephone and were warned to talk in coded language because "the telephone is bugged." Handwritten lettering on the instrument read, "This telephone is *still* bugged."

I picked up the receiver and after a few clicks got my party in St. Petersburg. Our carefully planned departure for New Orleans brought no unpleasantness. We finally obtained service without regard for race in Mississippi while on the way from New Orleans back to Florida. In the Gulf Coast resort town of Biloxi, Mississippi, we used rest rooms which have no racial markings. Many Biloxi service stations, however, have segregated rest rooms.

———

The St. Petersburg *Times* concluded editorially, after publishing the Adams' story, that the old ways of the South were dying. "In some areas," the newspaper said, "there is open defiance, with violence just beneath the surface. In others, there is evasion and subterfuge. But almost everywhere there are heartening signs of progress. . . . The winds of change are blowing through the South and this is the big story —the real story."

The last word, however, belonged to Elenora Adams. As her husband reported: "Looking back, we're glad we made the trip. Elenora wouldn't want to do it the same way again, but a year from now or two years from now it probably would be genuine fun for both of us."

## 4. HODDING CARTER HELPS A LADY

During a weekly dinner of the Nieman Fellows at Harvard early in 1940, Hodding Carter heard a most persuasive editor argue that a newspaper could survive without advertising. Having had some experience to the contrary in Greenville, Mississippi, the equally persuasive Carter contended that it could not. The newspaper was *PM*, the Brooklyn waif; the editor was Ralph Ingersoll, who once ran *Time*. Such was Ingersoll's charm that Carter actually worked for him on *PM* for a few months, but left for practical reasons. Yet when *PM* died after a less than useful and effective life, there was no joy in Greenville.

Back at the *Delta Democrat-Times*, which at that juncture had finally become solvent, Carter wrote: "No newspaperman likes to see a newspaper die; no believer in a free press wants to see that press shrink; and no one who ever birthed a newspaper of his own or helped to breathe life into any other inanimate composite of white newsprint and black ink can be indifferent to the tragedy of *PM*." [19]

This was no mere pious expression of regret. Fortunately for newspapers, there are rare and warmhearted men like Hodding Carter who love newspapering, take a strange kind of pleasure out of all the abuse that goes with it, and would devote their lives to nothing else even if they had the chance.

Carter had had the chance often enough. Born in Hammond, Louisiana, on February 3, 1907, he gravitated to the North for his higher education and was graduated from Bowdoin in 1927. During the following year, he studied at the Columbia University School of Journalism, and from then on journalism was the most important part of his life. He was a reporter for the New Orleans *Item-Tribune*, a bureau manager for the United Press and the AP, and at the very bottom of the depression, in 1932, started the Hammond *Daily Courier* in the town in which he had been born. With him he took his bride of a year, Betty Werlein Carter, who helped him survive. From then on, he was a publisher and somehow he muddled through, first in Hammond and from 1936 on in Greenville. Not even his service in World War II entirely separated him from his work, for he contributed to both *Yank* and *Stars and Stripes* while he was in the Army.

There are few who have started newspapering with so much against them and come out on top with so many honors—a Nieman Fellowship, a Guggenheim Fellowship, the Southern Literary Award, a hatful of honorary degrees, and, in 1946, the Pulitzer Prize for editorial writing. Nobody could have blamed Hodding Carter for sitting back and enjoying life, but he wasn't the type. Seeing four small weeklies in trouble nearby in Mississippi, he gallantly took on somebody else's battles, as

[19] Carter, *Main Street*, pp. 116–17.

well as his own. That somebody else was Hazel Brannon Smith, who looked like a moviegoers' version of a Southern belle but handled her four weeklies with the skill of a true professional.

The Smiths and the Carters were neighbors. They both were in the Domesday Book that was kept for all Southern moderates by the White Citizens Councils of Mississippi. But while Hodding Carter and his *Delta Democrat-Times* were strong enough to fight off the opposition, Hazel Smith's papers were not. And so, despite trouble with his eyesight, Carter did battle to save the Smith papers from destruction by threat and by boycott in 1961. Heartened by his support and the attention it brought to her newspapers, Hazel Brannon Smith fought with superb courage against the sinister forces that threatened to overwhelm her.

This is the main part of Hodding Carter's story about her as it was published in the St. Louis *Post-Dispatch*, November 26, 1961.

## THE FIGHTING LADY

### By Hodding Carter

Until a few years ago Hazel Brannon Smith's career made an enviable success story. She came breezing into Holmes County, Mississippi, in 1936, a high-spirited, energetic, and joyful girl with a journalism degree from the University of Alabama and a loan of $3,000 to go toward the purchase of a broken-down weekly, the Durant *News*.

My wife and I had come to Mississippi to found our own daily in Greenville at about the same time. We remember meeting Hazel at our first press association session and hearing her tell her dream of making something out of what was then almost nothing. We worried a little because we doubted that the execution could ever match the vision.

We were wrong. In less than ten years Hazel had transformed the Durant *News* and bought the larger Lexington *Advertiser*. Later she was to acquire a third and much smaller one and, in the recent past, acquire in Jackson a suburban weekly.

Working night and day, learning the art of printing as well as of publishing, tirelessly striving to make Lexington, Durant, and all of Holmes County better and more profitable places in which to live, Hazel wrought miracles in the old shop in Lexington in which the papers were printed.

Today, one of the most modern and complete weekly printing plants in the state is housed in a pleasant building; Hazel and Walter Dyer Smith, the talented and friendly Yankee husband from Philadelphia whom she acquired when on a round-the-world trip after her pioneering trials were over, live in a more than comfortable home on a tract of some twenty rolling, tree-shaded acres within the city limits of Lexington. Despite the economic setbacks caused by the implacable hostility of the Holmes County bosses, they have hung onto a small cattle ranch where she and "Smitty," as everyone calls her husband, have for seven years been trying to improve the quality of their beef cattle.

But that is only the material side of it.

Twenty or so years ago, people began reading each week's issue of the Durant paper with eagerness rather than with the long-accustomed boredom; for Hazel was making good her promise to let the citizens know what was going on, to crusade for law and order, which to a considerable degree were strangers to Holmes County, and to bespeak the rights of all citizens—the last named probably being the most dangerous notion that had ever been publicly voiced in the county.

With the purchase of the Lexington *Advertiser* in 1943, Hazel stepped up her fight against the slot-machine operators, liquor racketeers, gamblers, and conniving officials who were finding easy pickings and little opposition in the clique-ridden rural county. In 1946, thanks principally to her persistence, a grand jury voted sixty-four indictments after investigating organized crime in Holmes County.

But Hazel became one of the objects of court action herself when the trial judge found her guilty of contempt of court for interviewing a witness, the widow of a Negro for whose death by whipping five white men were indicted but not convicted. The Mississippi Supreme Court reversed his decision.

The judge fined her $50 and sentenced her to fifteen days in jail, but suspended sentence and put her "under good behavior" for two years. Hazel refused the gag and appealed to the State Supreme Court which later ruled in her favor. Hazel won the cheers of her fellow editors inside and outside the state. But she had made dangerous enemies.

Then in 1954, Hazel really got in bad with the other whites. On the July 4 week-end, incumbent Sheriff Richard F. Byrd, accompanied by three other peace officers, drove his car up to a group of Negroes who had gathered at a roadside cafe, probably for a few illegal drinks. He asked one of them, a 27-year-old man, why he was "whooping" so loudly.

When the Negro denied that he was guilty of this serious violation of the peace, the sheriff shouted to him to get going. As the Negro ran, the sheriff shot him in the thigh.

In her first news story reporting the affair, Editor Smith recounted that she had not been able to get a statement from the sheriff. In the next issue of the Lexington *Advertiser*, Hazel told the story of how the man had been shot by the sheriff when he hadn't violated any law and how the sheriff had not even threatened him with arrest before the shooting. In a front-page signed editorial she followed up the newspaper report with a denunciation of the sheriff for brutality in this and other cases involving Negroes.

Wrote the angry young woman:

"The laws in America are for everyone—rich and poor, strong and weak, black and white. The vast majority of the Holmes County people are not rednecks who look with favor on the abuse of people because their skins are black. Byrd has violated every concept of justice, decency, and right. He is not fit to occupy office."

The sheriff filed a libel suit for actual and punitive damages in the amount of $57,500. At the October term of court, a trial jury awarded Sheriff Byrd $10,000 after each juror allegedly dropped into a hat for drawing slips of paper upon which he had written down the amount he thought the sheriff deserved. The Holmes County grand jury adjourned without indicting anyone in the shooting of the young Negro.

The year 1954 was a tense one in Holmes County for another and more significant reason. In the wake of the United States Supreme Court's decision on school desegregation, the citizens of little Indianola, less than fifty miles from Lexington, organized the first White Citizens Council, the white supremacy group which, while abjuring violence or masking, pledged itself to hold down Negro voting, fight "moderates," and prevent school integration by economic and social pressures. A second unit was almost immediately organized in Holmes County. Among its leading members were men actively aligned with the sheriff in his feud with the editor and suspicious of her advocacy of equal justice.

That summer a respectable Negro woman, a teacher for twenty years, was shot in her own home by a leading Lexington white man after she had remonstrated with him for driving his automobile into her yard and damaging it while turning around.

White Citizens Council members and others tried to persuade Hazel Smith to kill the story. She printed it. Telling the story did no good, for no arrest was made. The wounded teacher was dismissed from the school and her husband was fired by the filling station operator for whom he worked. The pair then moved to Chicago.

The embattled editor won a round in 1955 when the Mississippi Supreme Court unanimously and caustically reversed the libel judgment and dismissed the sheriff's suit. But in January, 1956, a set of council-dominated trustees in the Holmes County Hospital fired her husband as administrator of the hospital, despite the medical staff's unanimous resolution asking that he be retained. One trustee said in a newspaper statement: "There is nothing against him or his record. But his wife has become a controversial person."

The White Citizens Council leaders began organizing a concerted advertising boycott. Her local advertising volume shortly fell off some 50 percent. She kept and even gained readership; but without the necessary advertising and commercial printing volume, her papers began to suffer. And in 1958 her enemies organized a new weekly paper at a meeting at which an officer of the local White Citizens Council presided and asked for stock subscriptions from those present, mostly Council members.

Hazel Smith, lacking subsidy, began to show the strain. A cross was burned on her lawn by a group of teen-agers, including the son of a man prominent in Council circles. Hazel herself descended upon them as the cross burned, and after they had fled, removed the license tag from their car so that proof of ownership and probable occupancy could be made.

So what will happen next?

There is no real wealth in Holmes County. It is unlikely that the other newspaper will survive if Hazel's friends begin to speak out, as some already are doing. Men get tired of indulging their prejudices at the expense of their pocketbooks. And this is exactly what is happening in the case of the *Holmes County Herald*, a travesty of a newspaper which is only an instrument devised to destroy a brave woman, who twenty-five years ago came to Mississippi with eyes shining and dreaming a dream that had to do with the rights of all men and the freedom of newspapers to speak their pieces.

Maybe the brave bigots will stop putting up. Maybe the now silent, decent people will begin speaking up. Maybe next year, the Lexington *Advertiser*, which is celebrating its 125th anniversary this year, will still be Hazel Brannon Smith's editorial voice. If not, another light will have gone out in a shadowed state.

--------

The Pulitzer Prize for editorial writing in 1964 was awarded to Hazel Brannon Smith, but that was in itself no guarantee of survival in Mississippi. The "fighting lady" pluckily carried on against great odds. Life, she said, was a series of crises, but in 1965 she was still demanding equal justice for all citizens.

"It is not moral or just," she wrote, "that any man should live in fear, or be compelled to sleep with a loaded gun by his bedside."

And while neither she nor Hodding Carter had any illusions about the quality of Mississippi justice, she was the first to cry out over the murder of Medgar Evers. The cynical may ask what good it did, when two separate trials of a suspect ended without a conviction. Hazel Smith herself gave the answer:

"But if we think the present situation is serious, as indeed it is, we should take a long, hard look into the future. It can, and probably will, get infinitely worse—unless we have the necessary character and guts to do something about it—and change the things that need to be changed." [20]

This is the editorial on the Evers slaying from Mrs. Smith's Pulitzer Prize-winning file, published in the Lexington *Advertiser* on June 13, 1963.

## THE MURDER OF MEDGAR EVERS

### *By Hazel Brannon Smith*

The shocking, hate-inspired murder of Medgar Evers, Mississippi field secretary of the NAACP, is not only a reprehensible crime against the laws of God and man. It was a vicious and dastardly act endangering

[20] "Arrest of Bombing Victim a Grave Disservice," Lexington (Miss.) *Advertiser*, May 16, 1963.

the personal safety and well-being of every citizen, white and Negro, in Jackson and throughout the state. It poses a serious threat to future race relations.

The criminal should be found and punished to the fullest extent of the law.

When the unknown assailant took a position under cover of night near the victim's home and cut him down with a high-powered rifle, he did not kill the civil rights movement, as he may have supposed. He did kill a man who was a living symbol of the freedom that Mississippi Negroes are determined to achieve.

But far from killing the freedom movement in Mississippi, the perpetrator of the crime only made certain it will be increased tenfold. New leaders will arise to take Evers' place—and they will not be as moderate in their views, or as patient, reasonable, and understanding of the white man's position and views.

The murder was committed by an ignorant product of our sick, hate-filled society. Thus far it has been only a segment of our white community that has succumbed to hate. God help us when the Negro starts hating in Mississippi.

It is imperative that each of us examine our own heart and conscience and determine what part we have played, either in things done or left undone, in acts of commission or omission, in creating a society which permits a man to be murdered because of his desire to be free and equal under the law—a man who fought Hitlerism in Germany for all our freedom.

Time is running out for us here in the Magnolia State. People of good will must act now if we are to avert total disaster in the entire field of human relations. Mayor Allen Thompson will surely recognize the urgent necessity of establishing immediately a bi-racial committee to try to achieve some degree of real understanding before it is too late—indeed, if it is not already.

------

Was it all futile? Did nothing matter in Mississippi? Was there no place for right, for decency, for justice—even for compassion? For all his inner doubts, Hodding Carter had this to say in 1965:

"Mississippi today is not the Mississippi of fifty or even twenty-five years ago, when lynching was commonplace and planter and redneck

alike could kill a troublesome Negro without anyone trying to make
something of it. Most district attorneys today are better educated and
more conscientious. There are jurors who do vote to convict white cul-
prits whose victims are Negroes. There are a few politicians who survive without blaming race murders on Yankee meddlers or the federal
government. Here and there are some ministers. Here and there are
some teachers. Here and there are some newspaper editors. Here and
there are other folk who speak out. Not many, but they exist. Here is
the Negro talking out and talking back.

"And here is a federal government whose law officers do point out
the members of the mob, which is something, even though the mobsters
go unpunished, and because of whose judicial decisions and legislation
the qualified Mississippi Negro may yet vote freely.

"Change will come because it has to come if ours is to be a nationwide democratic society. Meanwhile, any Mississippian who publicly
denounces or even decries the persistent popular indifference to the
slaying of a Negro by a white man is certain to be even more publicly
denounced by many of his fellow citizens; a conspiracy of silence dominates much of the Deep South, and especially Mississippi, in the futile
hope that if we keep our mouths shut—or open them only in defense
—the whole thing will somehow go away."[21]

Thus spoke Hodding Carter, of Greenville, Mississippi.


## 5. BOB BIRD COVERS A PARADE

When Robert S. Bird came home from the Eichmann trial in Jerusalem,
which he had covered for the New York *Herald Tribune* with distinction, he was asked whether he believed himself to be an objective reporter.

"No," he said, "I don't believe I am. I am not interested in objectivity. I am interested in truth."

This was no mere exercise in semantics by a theoretical journalist,
but a hardheaded exposition of reportorial principles by one of the
leading professionals of his time. For while Bob Bird was born in
Amesbury, Massachusetts, in 1907, only his accent was a faint reminder

[21] Carter, "A Double Standard for Murder?" *New York Times Magazine*, Jan. 24,
1965, p. 30.

of it; he was a New Yorker from boyhood on, and a journalist from the time he was able to run copy in a newsroom. True, he studied at Columbia University, but it was on the desk and on the street that he learned the meaning of a journalist's life.

With the exception of a year as an assistant on the New York *Times* city desk, he excelled as a reporter for the *Herald Tribune*. For thirty years he covered crime, politics, international affairs. And then came the civil rights movement, and one of the most important of all assignments for Bob Bird. He was not a dominant figure and never meant himself to be, for he was small, slim, mild-mannered, and soft-voiced and he had thinning blond hair shot with grey. But he was tenacious, and a man of great courage, and he favored the most modern of reporting methods. Wherever he went, the tape recorder went along. And whatever he did, he noted it down with care and pondered over it instead of slapping it out, any old way, on a typewriter.

It was Bob Bird's way to concern himself with the meaning of events —the inner truth, not merely the outer appearance. He knew the futility of publishing whatever was said or done, regardless of whether it was true or misleading or entirely false. After all, the false canon of objectivity had helped to create the McCarthy inquisition, whose every accusation was blazoned so widely as the truth.

And so, when he went to the outskirts of Washington on August 28, 1963, to cover the great civil rights march on the capital, it was not merely to report on a parade. This was a mass movement which, like the bonus march of three decades before, might have turned into disaster. That it did not made it all the more impressive.

Here, in essential part, was history as Bob Bird recorded it for the New York *Herald Tribune*, August 29, 1963.

## THE MARCH ON WASHINGTON

### By Robert S. Bird

WASHINGTON—The Negro march on Washington turned out to be a profoundly moving demonstration—so big, so orderly, so sweet-singing and good-natured, so boldly confident and at the same time relaxed, so completely right from start to finish, that America was done proud beyond measure.

President Kennedy bespoke the feelings of everybody who witnessed it when he said last evening: "The cause of 20 million Negroes has been advanced" by the wonderfully handled event. And the whole world was a witness to it, and to the thing it represented.

This was the right guaranteed under the Constitution for the people to assemble peaceably, and to petition the government for a redress of grievances. In this historic gathering, which police said was probably the greatest ever held in Washington from the standpoint of the number participating, more than 210,000 persons provided an awesome example of this constitutional, democratic, American right.

They came from every part of the country, and about 30 percent—as estimated by this reporter walking along the line of march—were white supporters of the Negro-organized demonstration. There was no disorder whatever. By the time the meeting reached its peak before the Lincoln Memorial, even the thought of disorder had altogether vanished from the minds of the authorities.

Rather, there was displayed a total sense of innate order and self-discipline. At the same time, there flowed from the marching, singing, chanting thousands a joyous, triumphant spirit—triumphant in the hope that Negro equality with white citizenship shall surely prevail soon in every part of this land. That's what the demonstration was all about —a petition mainly for civil rights and jobs, but including also the whole spectrum of rights up to the ultimate ideal of equality.

The demonstrators came to Washington all during the night and all morning in special trains and chartered planes and in thousands of buses and private cars. A few came on roller skates and by walking.

It was an astonishingly dressed up crowd, almost as well turned out as a Sunday church service congregation.

There was not a slack-looking person in the whole assemblage, and the only blue jeans to be seen were worn by some young workers from the Students Non-Violent Co-Ordinating Committee fresh from the danger areas in Mississippi. And because they wore their firing-line "uniform" of the Southern Negro field hand, they got tremendous applause from the others.

The power of this demonstration was felt by all the observers, and the root of this power was conspicuously the personal involvement of each individual who had traveled here from his home to demonstrate.

The idea of his own personal involvement in the struggle has become dramatically the most potent force moving on the American

## CIVIL RIGHTS MARCHERS

One of the highlights of 1963 was the civil rights march on the capital.
This view was taken from the top of the Lincoln Memorial.

scene. The feeling of immeasurable pride felt by these marchers shone from the faces of young Negro girls and old Negro men, and the sound of freedom soared over Washington as they sang out their hearts.

As you walked up from Lincoln Memorial against the tide of marching demonstrators on Constitution Avenue, you were quickly overwhelmed by the singing and the equality demands on the marching signs, and by the warm combination of good nature, good order, and utter determination.

What it added up to was a display of responsibility by the Negro people that will not only go down in history, but which, one cannot doubt, will affect Congress's handling of the Administration's civil rights bill and future legislation.

Picture the scene:

The gathering of the tens of thousands on the grassy, tree-shaded Ellipse behind the White House and on the slope of park near the Washington Monument, facing down that vista of unparalleled beauty, the rectangular reflecting pool set in a grassy plot and leading down to the marble edifice that is the Lincoln Memorial.

Then the acres of park all jam-packed with this orderly crowd waiting for the word to march, and then the streaming columns moving out with almost military efficiency into the two avenues bordering the reflecting pool—Independence Avenue on the Potomac side and Constitution Avenue on the other.

This was the march. It began at 11:15 a.m. and continued until 1:45 p.m., converging before the Memorial.

The happy hordes did not so much march as stroll along in loose-flowing formation. They sang old spirituals, they sang the new freedom songs, and they sang the "Battle Hymn of the Republic," which Julia Ward Howe wrote in the Willard Hotel a few blocks from the Memorial on one sleepless night early in the Civil War.

The shrine that was the assembly point was so entirely appropriate that you looked at it in a new way. This white marble edifice 80 feet high serves as a monumental canopy over Daniel Chester French's heroic statue of Abraham Lincoln, who is sitting as if in meditation in an armchair.

Picture 210,000 Negroes and whites standing in petition before the hallowed Lincoln who emancipated the Negro people exactly a century ago.

Picture the representation of this crowd—every state in the Union, hundreds of organizations, church groups with their ministers, and union locals with their shop stewards, boy and girl students, men in wheel chairs, women limping on crutches.

And seated before them, in front of Abraham Lincoln, the leaders of the Negro people of America, and the Negro heroes of the current struggle for civil rights, and the press and broadcasting representatives from all the countries of the world.

The lawn around the Reflecting Pool could not accommodate everybody, and so hundreds of marchers were deployed to grassy places under the big elms and oaks. There they lay down their marching signs and broke out picnic lunches while loudspeakers carried the platform program to them as they rested in comfort with their shoes off.

There was a picnic quality about the whole assemblage anyway, a kind of church picnic quality, and there was something that went with the picnic atmosphere. This was a feeling that is often hard for people to get in their everyday life.

A feeling for country. Tens of thousands of these petitioning Negroes had never been to Washington before, and probably would never come again. Now here they were. And this was their Washington, their very own Capitol, and this was their lawn and that great marble memorial was their own memorial to the man who had emancipated them.

Even while they were demanding, with their marching signs and freedom songs, the first-class citizenship that has been denied them they were, indeed, enjoying their rights as first-class American citizens by rolling out their picnic baskets on their own U.S.A. property and exuding a feeling of joy and comfort.

## 6. THE PULITZER WAY

In common with other leading newspapers in the United States, the St. Louis *Post-Dispatch* was well aware in the summer of 1963 that a social revolution had burst upon the land. Beginning with the eruption of Birmingham in the spring, the tension mounted. No city, no matter how well ordered its race relations, could consider itself safe in this tinderbox of emotion. A spark, whatever the cause, could set a whole community ablaze.

The great need was to maintain communication between the disparate elements of the community at all costs. Different newspapers attempted to meet their responsibilities in different ways. But Joseph Pulitzer's newspaper, under the leadership of his grandson, Joseph Pulitzer Jr., determined to leave nothing undone to guard against a major outbreak.

Five major series of articles were undertaken. Throughout the long, dangerous summer, they were published prominently through the use of all the newspaper's resources. Said the *Post-Dispatch* editorially on May 12, 1963: "The denial of equal opportunity and equal rights, countered by insistent efforts to win them, are the symptoms of a deeper social virus—the breakdown of the community into a white community and a black one, the two at dangerous odds and lacking free communication between them."

The first of the *Post-Dispatch*'s series traced the progress that had been made in St. Louis in interracial matters; the second, employment among Negroes and what was being done to improve the poor record; the third, the plight of the Negro in the state of Missouri outside St. Louis; the fourth, the Negro leadership in St. Louis.

Then, the *Post-Dispatch* opened its columns to a series of articles by the Negro leaders of the civil rights movement, entitled, "The Negro Speaks." It was, the newspaper soberly declared, "the greatest social crisis the United States has faced since the depression of the 1930s."

Thomas W. Ottenad, of the newspaper's Washington staff, wrote:

"After being persistently disregarded for nearly a decade, the Negro revolt in the United States exploded into the public consciousness this year. The police dogs of Birmingham, the deaths at 'Ole Miss,' the demonstrations, violence, arrests, and bombings in scores of other places, North and South, made it plain at last that social upheaval is shaking this country.

"Although no one can yet see how far the consequences will reach, it is clear that few persons or communities will be left untouched and that for many life will never be the same again." [22]

It was against this background that the leaders of the Negro revolution wrote for Pulitzer's paper in August and September, 1963. The series was republished by the St. Louis *Post-Dispatch* in pamphlet form under the title *The Negro Speaks*. The work of two of those who participated,

[22] St. Louis *Post-Dispatch*, Aug. 25, 1963.

Gwendolyn Brooks, whose "Annie Allen" won the Pulitzer Prize for poetry in 1950, and the Rev. Dr. Martin Luther King Jr., who was to win the Nobel Peace Prize in 1964, is presented here.

## "RIDERS TO THE BLOOD-RED WRATH"

### *By Gwendolyn Brooks*

I remember kings.
A blossoming palace. Silver. Ivory.
The conventional wealth of stalking Africa.
All bright, all bestial. Snarling marvelously.
I remember my right to roughly run and roar.
My right to raid the sun, consult the moon.
Nod to my princesses or split them open,
To flay my lions, eat blood with a spoon.
You never saw such running and such roaring!—
Nor heard a burgeoning heart so craze and pound!—
Nor sprang to such a happy rape of heaven!—
Nor sanctioned such a kinship with the ground!

And I remember blazing dementias
Aboard such trade as maddens any man.
. . . The mate and the captain fragrantly reviewed
The fragrant hold and presently began
Their retching rampage among their luminous
Black pudding, among the guttural chained slime;
Half-fainting from their love affair with fetors
That pledged a haughty allegiance for all time.
I recollect the latter lease and lash
And labor that defiled the bone, that thinned
My blood and blood-line. All my climate my
Foster designers designed and disciplined.

But my detention and my massive stain
And my distortion and my calvary

I grind into a little light lorgnette
Most sly: To read man's inhumanity.

And I remark my Matter is not all.
Man's chopped in China, in India indented.
From Israel what's Arab is resented.
Europe candies custody and war.

Behind my exposé
I formalize my pity: "I shall cite,
Star and esteem all that which is of woman,
Human and hardly human."

Democracy and Christianity
Recommence with me.

And I ride ride I ride on to the end—
Where glowers my continuing calvary.
I,
My fellows, and those, canny consorts of
Our spread hands in this contretemps-for-love
Ride into wrath, wraith, and menagerie.

To fail, to flourish, to wither, or to win.
We lurch, distribute, we extend, begin.


## THE NEGRO IN AMERICA

### *By Martin Luther King Jr.*

The mood of the Negro today is one of impatience. There seems to be
no more room in his soul to wait. He has waited one hundred years
and not very much has been accomplished.

Today he has awakened from the long sleep of quasi-freedom. Everything that he seeks now was his right and privilege by law on January
1, 1863. He was miserably short-changed and he is demanding immediate restitution. In all fairness, it must be said that his mood is not
one of vengeance and bitterness, but he will not be put off any longer.

The strength and determination of the American Negro are waxing,
not waning. Realism impels me to admit that if some immediate relief
is not found to ease the compound frustration of the Negro community,
there is the terrible possibility of incidents of violence.

PAUL CONRAD ON CIVIL RIGHTS

From the 1964 Pulitzer Prize cartoon exhibit.

I do not believe there is any danger of a violent race war as long as there are signs of tangible progress in areas that affect Negroes most.

What the Negro wants today is his equality. He needs a social revolution; every quarter of his life demands it. Consider his plight, particularly in the South, in public education, medical services, employment, voting rights, and public accommodations.

The whole structure of his moment-by-moment experience is marshaled against him in such a way that he is disadvantaged; his "high visibility" penalizes him at every turn. If he is to be included in society, nothing short of a revolution will change his circumstances materially.

The Negro's demand for "equality" means the untrammeled opportunity for every person to fulfill his total individual capacity without any regard to race, creed, color, or ancestry. His insistent demand for equality must be approximated if not totally fulfilled. It is the only hope for the soul of this nation. The Negro is the most glaring evidence of the white America's sin and hypocrisy.

What must the Negro and the nation do to meet his needs? I would underscore the need for the federal government to get out of the segregation business; that is, it should withdraw federal funds from projects and states where statutory segregation remains in defiance of the Constitution of the United States.

Despite the most comprehensive civil rights bill in history, the federal government has yet to launch an effective day-by-day program that strikes at the flesh-and-blood considerations of what segregation does to the Negro in Birmingham as well as in the Brooklyn ghetto.

The other side of the coin is positive. If the plight of race and color prejudice, with its attendant penalty to the Negro, is removed, then a vigorous program of implementation of already-existing laws must be conceived. New legislation must be enacted by the Congress, or executive fiat must be used. Parallel and supplementary programs in job training and adult education will also be needed.

It seems likely that race and color prejudice will have all but disappeared in its most obvious forms in the next five years. The present temper of the Negro demands for equality will not allow statutory segregation to survive more than another year or two.

Three stages seem reasonable. First, we are able to see that even in the Deep South, hard-core states, the overwhelming majority of white people say "later" instead of "never." Thus, massive resistance has been conquered. Secondly, though segregation is still with us in many forms, I believe that if the present trend continues—and it must—for the most part we shall have a desegregated nation within the five years that I mentioned earlier.

Thirdly, despite the realization of a "desegregated society," the goal we seek is integration—intergroup and interpersonal living with mutual understanding and respect. We long for the day when color aristocracy will give way to character aristocracy.

This will take considerably longer. I would hazard the guess that it could be a generation away. This might be called a period of "national adjustment."

I am persuaded that the use of nonviolent direct action is the most practical and useful vehicle to fulfill the normal dream and aspirations of the Negro or any oppressed people. More importantly it is at the same moment the most moral and the most powerful. It is a critical supplement to the traditional methods and has much to do with the pace at which the others move.

The nonviolent revolution in America, with all of its drama and conscience-searing, is just coming of age. It has moved the Negro a giant step forward while fifty years of traditional redress through the courts have brought in many instances continued frustrations to the dilemma of his "Negro-ness."

## 7. PAUL MILLER'S SUCCESS STORY

During the tense and humid summer of 1963, when a racial crisis spread throughout the land, Paul Miller went looking for good news. It was a melancholy quest, at first, for few cities had hopeful reports. The news was compounded of shock and violence. The headlines fairly reeked of conflict.

Had Paul Miller conformed to the miserable stereotype of the news-paper editor, as he exists in the movies and television, he would have played the story for all it was worth and left the soul-searching to the rating agencies. But the headlines left him cold. And the news made him angry. He wasn't satisfied merely to print the sorry processional of events. As the president of the Gannett Group of twenty-five newspapers in the northeastern United States, he wanted the other part of the story—the extra dimension—the successes as well as the failures in this massive American social revolution.

And so, in his office in Rochester, New York, he wrote a memorandum to his principal associates:

"Every city has the same problem. If it has not, it soon will have. Every city is trying to find answers. Have any cities found answers that might be useful in Rochester and elsewhere? If so, what are they?"

Miller was bucking the tide and he knew it. However, it wasn't a new experience for him. He'd been doing it most of his life. Up from Diamond, Missouri, where he had been born September 28, 1906 into a clergyman's family, he had worked his way through school as a newspaperman and in 1931 had received his B.S. from Oklahoma Agricultural and Mechanical College. Then had come a long, patient struggle through the ranks of the AP—Columbus, Ohio, in 1932; Kansas City, Salt Lake City, Harrisburg, Pennsylvania, Philadelphia, and finally, in 1942, chief of the Washington bureau, a post he held through World War II and until 1947. Then, he joined the Gannett Newspapers; ten years later, he was the group's president. And in 1962, he became the president of the AP.

Now in 1963, Miller was a cheerful, broad-shouldered six-footer who scarcely looked his 57 years. With his friend and associate, Vincent S. Jones, the group's executive editor, he mobilized his forces for what eventually became a continuing assignment for all the Gannett Newspapers under the general title: "The Road to Integration." What Miller and Jones wanted was a whole series of reports of constructive accomplishment in civil rights, job opportunities, better housing, and better education for Negroes; in effect, progress, wherever it has been made and in whatever guise. Nor were all the reports to be from cities in which Gannett Newspapers were published. "The Road to Integration" led all over the nation.

Before the year's end, nearly a hundred articles had been contributed by three dozen editors and reporters, most of them being published throughout the group with an average circulation of 750,000. In 1964, as a result, the Gannett Newspapers won a special Pulitzer Prize citation for their work—the first such recognition ever given for distinguished public service performed by an entire newspaper group. The series was republished in pamphlet form.

It should have been the climax of Paul Miller's success story, but it wasn't. In newspaper work, the story—like life itself—goes on and has a way of taking an unexpected turn. That's the way it was with "The Road to Integration." For very soon, one of the finest of all the success stories, that of Rochester itself, was threatened in an appalling and brutal and entirely senseless manner.

Another summer came, and with it even greater tensions. On June 22, 1964, the case of the three young civil rights workers—two whites and one Negro—broke in Philadelphia, Mississippi, when their disappearance was reported. Soon afterward they were found murdered. On June 25, the St. Augustine riots flared in Florida. Disaster struck in the heart of Harlem in New York on July 18, and while the rioting kept up there it spread to Brooklyn two days later. Without warning, rioters led by hoodlums created havoc for three nights in Rochester beginning July 24.

The people of Rochester were stunned by what had happened to them. It made no sense. Nor did it seem to them to be a part of the tragic pattern of outbreaks that surged through Jersey City on August 2–4; Elizabeth and Paterson on August 11–14, the Chicago suburb of Dixmoor on August 16–17, and Philadelphia on August 28–30.

Paul Miller saw that "The Road to Integration" had reached a turning point. Quietly, but with great conviction, he wrote as follows in the Rochester *Times Union* on August 8, 1964.

## CIVIL RIGHTS

### By Paul Miller

Lessons have been learned from the Rochester riots that could mark a turning point for the better in the enormous problems of race relations in the United States. This conjecture grows out of a review of letters and telephone calls from many states. It springs also from what has been observed here at home.

What was different about Rochester's riots and the reaction to them in the city?

It was promptly understood by most that they sprang from senseless lawlessness—period. Few attempts were made to rationalize the riots as a legitimate protest, which they were not. The *Times-Union* expressed the view of the great majority of all groups and races, official and unofficial, when it said editorially at the time:

"Civil rights for any minority group has nothing to do with it. Rather, the rights of all 600,000 residents of this county are at stake. Police brutality has nothing to do with it, either. Rather, brutality *to* police is involved."

As the nation knows, Rochester has been at the forefront in good works of all kinds, including efforts to help disadvantaged newcomers. The effort here has been acclaimed in many ways, including the awarding this year of a Pulitzer Prize citation to the Gannett Newspapers for their continuing series of reports on constructive approaches to racial problems.

Against this background the nation was shocked at the insane violence here. Note this from an editorial in the Tulsa *World*:

"Rochester is a city that has gone out of its way to improve race relations. It has one of the best records of the country, and was proud of its progress. But a minority of malcontents trampled all the good that had been done. In a few hours a gang from the gutter tore down the work of years."

Solid progress will be resumed here, despite the riots. It will be because it must be. Progress has been slowed, no doubt about that. But Rochester knows that the community was working hard, officially and unofficially, to meet recognized problems. It would not let bums and hoodlums take over for long. It will not now let the wounds of their violence leave permanent harm.

This, it seems to me, is a lesson that is being drawn nationally from what has happened and what is happening in Rochester.

Legitimate grievances and protests by any group must be anticipated if possible, be sympathetically considered in any case—and acted on. But violence must not be tolerated, ever.

---

Paul Miller's editorial on the tragedy of Rochester in 1964 might have been written for the tragedy of Los Angeles in 1965.

Out of all the shock and violence, as contrasted with the many fine and heartening instances of progress; out of the senseless victories of the screeching demagogue, and the less dramatic but far more important triumphs of conscience; out of the outcries and speeches of protest, the moving editorials, and the terrifying newspictures and television footage, a nationwide consensus appeared to be emerging—

a determination that this civil rights struggle was not to be waged in vain. In creating that determination, many a journalist played his role with professional skill, in good conscience and with honor. If there were some journalists who were indifferent, and others who still feared the inevitable confrontation, they felt the sting of rebuke from those who were willing to move with the spirit of the times. Such things would scarcely have been dreamed of fifty years ago in a comfortable world which assumed, quite wrongfully, that the Negro "knew his place." That was the measure of progress.

# II. CRIME REPORTERS, NEW STYLE

Billie Sol Estes, a local boy who made good, was the ruler of a fabulous West Texas business empire worth many millions of dollars in 1962. Oscar O'Neal Griffin, Jr., was just a struggling newspaperman. The only thing they had in common was the explosive energy of youth and residence in a small town called Pecos, a Texas community of 12,000 that sat in the center of an arid, sun-scorched plain.

Estes was 37 then, a pudgy and boastful fellow with curly dark hair, an arrogant manner, and a moonface dominated by awesomely large spectacles. He lived in the grand manner, as befitted an up-and-coming Texas tycoon. His home was luxurious, his business activity far-reaching. He traveled in a private plane and talked airily about his powerful friends in Washington. He was, among other things, a member of President Kennedy's Cotton Advisory Committee.

Griffin, strong-faced and determined in manner at 29, was the editor of the Pecos *Independent and Enterprise*, with a circulation of only 3,400. Like Estes, he was a native Texan, born in Daisetta, educated in Liberty through high school, and graduated from the University of Texas in 1958 with a journalism degree. Unlike Estes, he wasn't much of a talker.

They had already clashed, these two. With the support of Alan Propp, general manager and part owner of the paper, Griffin had attacked Estes' candidacy for the school board in the *Independent* and had helped defeat him. Estes played rough. He started a rival paper, the Pecos *Daily News*, and tried to drive the *Independent* out of business. Soon Griffin found that he was working with a staff of only three persons.

It was at this unhappy juncture that the *Independent* began digging into Estes' background and the many rumors that had begun to circulate about his financial manipulations. These were complicated matters. Estes, moreover, was a powerful man.

Consequently, on February 12, 1962, when Griffin wrote his first exposé for the *Independent* and slapped it on Page 1 he did not sign it. Nor did he name Estes. But everybody in West Texas knew that the *Independent* was going after Billie Sol, although few gave Griffin much chance of bringing him down. After all, the man had friends in Washington!

Griffin's first piece charged in effect that somebody was making a lot of money from farmers and finance companies by the sale and subsequent mortgaging of 15,000 tanks for agricultural purposes in Reeves County, none of which actually existed. By March 1, the accusations had extended to a total of 33,500 tanks worth $34,500,000 in eleven Texas counties, also allegedly mythical. That was enough for the Federal Bureau of Investigation.

By March 30, Estes was under arrest on federal fraud charges and a national scandal had burst in Washington. Three officials of the Department of Agriculture resigned in the investigation that followed. An assistant secretary in the Department of Labor also left office after it became known that he had accepted a gift from Estes. A reorganization of the Soil Conservation Service was forced when it was shown that Estes' operations had extended from tanks to cotton allotments. And Senate and House investigating committees for weeks raked over Estes' shattered business empire, demanding to know just how it had been possible for Billie Sol to launch so many questionable undertakings.

Griffin had done his work well. No longer a mere small-town editor but the talk of newspapermen everywhere in the country, he moved from the *Independent* on June 1, 1962 to the staff of the Houston *Chronicle*. And on November 8, 1962, he had the satisfaction of covering Estes' first swindling conviction in Tyler, for which the ex-tycoon was sentenced to eight years in prison.

That, however, was only the beginning. During the next two and one-half years, investigators, who followed the trail Griffin had blazed, charged that Estes had obtained more than $20,000,000 from finance companies by fraud. He was tried in both state and federal courts on a series of charges growing out of these accusations and sentenced to a total of twenty-three years in prison upon being convicted.

While he was able to stave off prison for some time by filing appeal after appeal, Estes' freewheeling days were over. And Griffin, working at a variety of assignments on the *Chronicle*, looked forward one day to working in Washington. He had impeccable credentials: a 1963 Pulitzer Prize for local reporting.

He was not the first small-town Texan to distinguish himself for crime reporting in the modern manner. Roland Kenneth Towery, then managing editor of the Cuero (Texas) *Record*, exposed a scandal in the administration of the veterans' land program in Texas in 1954. In the same year Caro Brown, a reporter for the Alice (Texas) *Echo*, covered the downfall of a one-man political machine in Duval County with extraordinary courage. For their feats, both Mrs. Brown and Towery won Pulitzer Prizes in local reporting in 1955.

Their work, and Griffin's as well, illustrated the changes that had come about in the routine of the crime reporter. Once, he had been depicted as a devil-may-care fellow who hung out at police headquarters, waiting for a hot tip, and usually solved murders before the detectives did. It was an exaggerated portrait although, like almost everything else in the public's stereotyped image of the newspaperman, there was a little truth in it. After all, Alvin H. Goldstein and James W. Mulroy as cub reporters for the Chicago *Daily News* in 1924 virtually broke the murder of Bobby Franks and laid the basis for the subsequent Loeb-Leopold trial. There were others like them, although no reporter in recent newspaper annals ever resembled the sorry caricatures that appear in the movies and on television.

Once, crime reporting had meant primarily such unsolved Broadway murders as those of Dot King and Louise Lawson, both showgirls, and the equally violent and mysterious demise of Joseph Elwell, the bridge expert. Even the best newspapers in the land went all-out then to cover such spectaculars as the Hall-Mills and Lindbergh cases in New Jersey and the Snyder-Grey trial in New York. Much news space was given, also, to the exploits of such thugs as Gerald Chapman, John Dillinger, Lucky Luciano, and Dutch Schultz. The prohibition era was, by and large, an era of public irresponsibility, and it affected the press as much as any other institution.

If the great depression did not completely kill the old-time newspaper circus, World War II did. Mass killings on a scale that staggered the imagination and the coming of the atomic bomb, with the threat of the ultimate extinction of life itself, stripped the murder case headlines of whatever glamor they might once have had. In the postwar era, no. newspaper that ran boxcar-type and sob-sister nonsense over the Samuel Sheppard murder case was very proud of it. As for the sheet that published a movie actress' love letters to a gangster after he had been killed, the condemnation was well-nigh unanimous.

The public mood had changed, and the treatment of crime by responsible newspapers reflected it. It was no accident that the Chicago *Daily News*'s exposé in 1956 of a $2,500,000 theft by Orville E. Hodge, the Illinois state auditor, cast a romantic glow about the essentially unromantic work of George Thiem, the reporter who had done much of the checking of records in the case. He and his methods scarcely resembled those of Goldstein and Mulroy for the same newspaper thirty-five years before. There was a difference, too, between the methods of the Boston *Post* in 1920, which exposed an old-style swindler, Charles Ponzi, and the tiny Pecos *Independent* of 1962, which was able to uncover a nationwide scandal affecting the government by going after Billie Sol Estes. Both the newspapers and the newspapermen, as well as their targets, belonged to different worlds.

The world of the 1960s was one in which the Philadelphia *Bulletin* could expose a tieup between the police and the numbers racketeers by a first-rate example of modern photographic journalism. A cameraman, supported by two reporters, was able to take so many pictures of city police in front of a South Philadelphia numbers bank in 1963 that arrests and a wholesale departmental shakeup followed.

It was also a world in which the tiny Panama City (Fla.) *News-Herald*, with a staff of only six, could dare to accuse some officials in its local government of collusion with gamblers. The result was a change in the local administration and better law enforcement in 1962.

True, there were still newspapers in the 1960s that played crime for whatever shock and sensation they could squeeze out of it, but this was a discredited section of the press. The influential newspapers of the type of the *Wall Street Journal* and the Washington *Star* did not hesitate to report on crime when there was a substantial reason for it. They scarcely could be expected to bid for the juvenile penny-dreadful circulation; in fact, their crime stories were as sober and well-docu-

mented as anything that was of interest primarily to bankers. The
pieces that follow are examples of crime reporting, new style.


## 8. *THE END OF BILLIE SOL*

A few hundred words about an anonymous character in a country new-
paper in Texas, printed under a modest headline, could scarcely have
been expected to send Washington's blood pressure soaring in 1962.
And yet, in the light of subsequent developments, that article in the
Pecos *Independent* might well be considered a museum piece.

When Oscar O'Neil Griffin Jr., wrote it, he wasn't in much of a mood
to observe the niceties of journalistic style as it is taught in the better
journalism schools of the nation. There was no sharp lead, no disclosure
of sources, no documentation of charges beyond a reference to the
county clerk. Nor was there a single name in the piece.

It was just a vague inquiry and a few hints that something mighty
strange was going on in Reeves County, Texas. But it was enough to
light the fuse that blew up Billie Sol Estes, his business empire, and
those in government who had been unfortunate enough to befriend
him. Here is the essential part of that strange first story in the Pecos
*Independent* on February 12, 1962.


### THE GREAT TANK MYSTERY
*By Oscar Griffin*

Reeves County may well be the anhydrous ammonia tank capital of
the world—on paper, that is.

A recent tally of the number of tanks that exist on paper in this
county totals over 15,000. That appears to be a lot of tanks to use
for agricultural purposes when you realize that the allotment for cotton
is something less than 60,000 acres.

This means there's an ammonia tank available for every four acres
of cotton. Of course, the tanks are also used in the production of grain,
but cotton is the big user of the tanks. But if all these ammonia tanks
were in Reeves County it would mean an ammonia tank for every four
acres of cotton.

Put these 15,000 tanks, if they existed, end to end and they would
stretch from Pecos to Balmorhea via Highway 17 and 290.

## A SAD DAY FOR BILLIE SOL

Billie Sol Estes enters the lobby of Taylor County jail, Texas.

The location of the tanks is the big puzzler. The farmers who have signed chattel mortgages for the 500- and 1,000-gallon containers apparently do not have all of them on their property in Reeves County. And one agreement states that the tanks "shall be located at Pecos, Texas, and shall not be removed therefrom."

Fifteen thousand tanks are not to be seen in Pecos—or Reeves County for that matter.

But some farmers claim the tanks were never intended for use in Pecos or Reeves County. They further assert that this was understood when they signed for the tanks.

And the number of tanks some of the farmers have signed mortgages for borders on the fantastic. More fantastic, however, are the total liabilities assumed—some $13 million recorded in Reeves County alone.

Only a small percentage of the farmers in Reeves County are involved in the ammonia tank transactions. The actual number is less than 50. There are many other counties in West Texas and the Panhandle where the transactions are comparable. For the most part, only the names have been changed.

What do the farmers receive for "buying" the tanks, besides a chattel mortgage recorded at the Reeves County clerk's office? What does anyone gain by such financial transactions?

---

What, indeed?

Having raised the question, the Pecos *Independent* and Oscar Griffin proceeded to dig up some answers. There were three more articles, all unsigned, climaxed by one on March 1, 1962, which charged that since January, 1959, about $24.5 million worth of tanks had been mortgaged in eleven West Texas counties, with $14.5 million in mortgages filed in Reeves County alone. Someone, therefore, seemed to be raising quite a lot of money on mythical tanks.

Griffin signed his name to an article on March 30 in the Pecos *Independent* with good reason. It began:

"A Pecosite who fashioned a West Texas business empire from an ewe lamb he claims was worth $5 was arrested Thursday by FBI agents on charges of conspiracy to transport and transporting 'forged, altered and counterfeited securities' on anhydrous ammonia tanks in interstate commerce.

"Lodged in Reeves County Jail on the charges is Billie Sol Estes of Pecos, farmer, entrepreneur, and member of President Kennedy's Cotton Advisory Committee."

For nearly three years, Billie Sol fought through the courts to stay out of jail, and Oscar Griffin covered much of the story as a reporter for the Houston *Chronicle*. The ex-tycoon was convicted in a Texas Federal Court of mail fraud and sentenced to fifteen years in prison.

And so, in January, 1965, a brief news item from El Paso told how Billie Sol's $100,000 bail had been revoked, causing him to begin the day by putting on old clothes and mopping a cell he was sharing with four other prisoners. His lawyers were still trying, but it looked like the end for Billie Sol Estes.

As for Oscar Griffin, he had a piece of paper as a memento of the case. It was the Pulitzer Prize citation:

"For a distinguished example of local reporting in a United States newspaper, published daily, Sunday, or at least once a week, during the year, in which the pressure of edition time is not a factor, written in the form of a single article or a series, due consideration being given to the initiative and resourcefulness and to the constructive purpose of the writer.

"Awarded to Oscar O'Neal Griffin Jr., who as editor of the Pecos (Texas) *Independent and Enterprise* initiated the exposure of the Billie Sol Estes scandal and thereby brought a major fraud on the United States government to national attention with the resultant investigation, prosecution, and conviction of the culprit."

All this because a country newspaper in Texas wasn't afraid to ask a question and look for some answers.


## 9. THE SALAD OIL MYSTERY

The Allied Crude Vegetable Oil Refining Corp. filed a petition with the U.S. District Court in Newark, New Jersey, on November 18, 1963, for court protection under the Bankruptcy Act. The court next day appointed a receiver.

If anything at all was published in the newspapers, it amounted to a paragraph or so. After all, who cared?

The answer was nobody, at first, except for a mild-looking 29-year-old father of four children, Norman C. Miller, a reporter who had been assigned to the case by the *Wall Street Journal*. Miller had had only three years' experience, most of it in the San Francisco office of the *Journal*, and he had been in New York only since June, 1963.

Here, certainly, was no financial authority and he scarcely claimed to be one. He was a modest and quiet young man, born in Pittsburgh in 1934, the son of a physician, and graduated in 1956 from Penn State's Journalism School. He had worked for the *Wall Street Journal* but two months after graduation, then had spent four years in the Navy, being discharged in 1960 as a lieutenant, j.g.

What could such a young and inexperienced man do with the story of the bankruptcy of the Allied Crude Vegetable Oil Refining Corp.? Well, for one thing, he could work, which no other reporter seemed to be doing at the time; for another, he could ask questions. He did both.

Then he picked up the trail of the large, round president of Allied Crude, Anthony (Tino) DeAngelis, who at 49 had built his company into the largest supplier of edible oils for export in the United States only to see it fall apart. DeAngelis' story was written in rather elusive terms in many a government record and court case, a challenge to legal experts in the field.

Yet, by hard work and enterprise, Miller was able to begin unraveling the tangled skeins of high finance within two weeks. Under his byline, the *Wall Street Journal* published a blockbuster, a major Page 1 story, which it headlined "Outdoing Billie Sol." In it, for the first time, the astounded financial and business community learned that large quantities of nonexistent salad oil had been used to engineer a swindle that might go beyond $100,000,000.

Nothing like this had happened since Ivar Kreuger, the "match king," had been able to roll up a $500,000,000 swindle in the 1920s at the expense of his gullible friends in the international financial world. Truly, as the *Journal's* copyreaders pointed out, it made Billie Sol Estes look like a piker.

Miller followed up his first story with still more details, including the sad truth that, like the missing salad oil, the tanks in which it supposedly was stored in New Jersey also had never existed. But by that time the rest of the press was in full cry. It had a major scandal to report, thanks to Norman C. Miller and the *Wall Street Journal*.

This was the principal part of Miller's exclusive story in the *Wall*

*Street Journal* of December 2, 1963, which broke the case of the missing salad oil.

## OUTDOING BILLIE SOL

### *By Norman C. Miller*

BAYONNE, N. J.—Law enforcement authorities, investigating "the case of the missing salad oil" at a vast tank storage facility here, suspect they have stumbled on a swindle that will make Billie Sol Estes' escapades look like a kindergarten exercise.

Two weeks ago Allied Crude Vegetable Oil Refining Corp., the nation's biggest supplier of edible oils for export, filed a bankruptcy petition. It had made heavy purchases on credit of contracts for future delivery of soybean and cottonseed oil; when the prices of these products dropped on the New York Produce Exchange and the Chicago Board of Trade, and Allied's brokers demanded nearly $19 million to offset the decline in value of the contracts, Allied couldn't pay.

One result was the failure of a major Wall Street securities firm, Ira Haupt & Co., that had purchased some futures contracts on Allied's behalf. Another result was that major commodities dealers who believed that they had soybean oil, cottonseed oil, fish oil, and other edible oils stored here in Allied's tanks, or in the connected tanks of other companies, suddenly began to check their inventories—and found much of their commodities missing.

It is now clear that vast quantities of these "missing" commodities will never be found, and for a simple reason: they don't exist and never did.

Dozens of major companies dealing in commodities unwittingly bought phantom goods. They, in turn, borrowed millions from banks by unknowingly using as collateral the phony warehouse receipts issued to them.

The losses will be staggering. Claims already announced total $41 million and other claims still are coming in. Sources close to the investigation estimate final losses will reach $100 million and possibly more. By contrast, Billie Sol Estes' swindle, through loans obtained by using nonexistent tanks of fertilizer as collateral, is estimated at $22 million.

Insurance may not cover all of the losses. Policies covering commodities in storage usually rule out payments for losses due to fraud. Some of the storage companies that operate interconnected tanks here —but not all of these firms—will be pressed for huge sums by holders of worthless warehouse receipts. There also may well be substantial losses by some of the commodities dealers and banks that bought or loaned money on goods that now are nowhere to be found.

At the core of the massive mess is Allied, whose president, Anthony (Tino) De Angelis, has a history of difficulties with the Securities and Exchange Commission, the Internal Revenue Service, and the bankruptcy courts. Law enforcement authorities have uncovered information indicating that Allied sold nonexistent edible oils with the help of certain employees of some tank-storage companies here—employees who received payments from Allied in return for arranging the issuance of phony warehouse receipts. It should be noted, however, that most of the storage companies were not victimized by corrupt employees.

The tank-storage facility here, known as a tank farm, is the largest such facility in the East. Around 200 tanks—most of them grey and greenish blue—mass around the Bayonne port area as far as the eye can see. They are linked by a spaghetti-like tangle of pipes of all thicknesses. Inside the tanks are thick, amber vegetable oils and slimy fish oil that eventually wind up as salad oil, margarine, vitamin extracts, and as ingredients in other products, including paint.

Inspectors face formidable problems in determining the exact contents of some tanks. One surveyor, E. W. Saybolt & Co., reported to its client, an agent for some foreign bank, on its problems in measuring lard and tallow in some Bayonne tanks: "Solid materials in large shore tanks were not level so that accurate gauges could not be obtained. Some tanks that had solid material on top contained liquid underneath. This liquid may have been water. In several cases, it was not possible to break through the hard surface. . . . From our observations most tanks appeared to contain sludge on the bottom."

Thus far it is established that seven companies and financial institutions are pressing specific claims for various commodities at Bayonne, with an aggregate quantity of 500 million pounds and an indicated total value of about $41.1 million. But far more is involved. About two dozen other companies and financial institutions are known definitely to have investments in, or loans secured by, the Bayonne commodities, but their specific claims aren't on record.

Miller started something. The New York *Times* on December 8 characterized the sorrowful tale of Allied Crude "the most sensational Wall Street story of the past generation." Five days later, *Time* magazine called it one of the worst scandals in the history of Wall Street, which is not exactly peopled by Sunday School characters. *Newsweek*'s label on January 6, 1964 was: "The biggest financial intrigue in nearly half a century."

Thus, instead of rewarding superior reportorial performance on the local level in tracking down a murderer or covering a disaster, as had happened so often in the past, the Trustees of Columbia University in 1964 gave the Pulitzer Prize for general local reporting to Norman C. Miller for his expert work in the intricate field of high finance and crime.

When Tino DeAngelis pleaded guilty in Newark Federal District Court on January 8, 1965, the government's estimate of the extent of the losses in the Allied bankruptcy had reached $150,000,000 and were likely to go still higher. DeAngelis admitted to three charges of circulating forged warehouse receipts in interstate commerce and to a fourth charge that he had conspired to circulate $100,000,000 in forged warehouse receipts in interstate commerce.

"We've got the center of the web but there are still hundreds of strands we've got to follow," one lawyer said. "No one can tell where they are going to lead." [1]

Perhaps. But it was a pretty fair guess that a modern crime reporter like Norman C. Miller would be able to find out, sooner rather than later.

## 10. SCANDAL IN CHICAGO

George Bliss, a twenty-year man with the Chicago *Tribune*, uncovered a scandal in the spring of 1961. It wasn't a pleasant story, nor could there be anything very attractive about the telling of it. For it concerned the world's largest sewage disposal system, the Metropolitan Sanitary District of Greater Chicago.

An old-line reporter, intent on conflict and drama in the news, would

[1] New York *Times*, Jan. 9, 1965.

have thrown up his hands and torn up his notes. But to Bliss, then 44 years old, it was serious business, well worth engaging the interest both of his newspaper and the people of Chicago.

The net worth of the Sanitary District, which had been set up as an independent local government run by a board of nine elected trustees, was $3 billion. Its tax bill in 1961 was $71 million, its payroll $15 million. It covered 900 square miles, serving 107 communities with a population of more than 5,000,000 people.

Bliss knew his Chicago. As the son of a Chicago newspaperman, born July 21, 1918, in Denver, he had learned most of what he knew in the newsrooms. Like the New York *Times*'s great Meyer Berger, Bliss's formal education had not lasted many years but it didn't really matter. He had been exposing hoodlums and racketeers for years.

It didn't take him long to find out that there were "ghosts" on the payroll of the Sanitary District at $50 a day, that politicians had put some of their favorites to work there without bothering to see that they even reported for duty, and that other irregularities were costing Chicago's taxpayers a fortune. In all, he wrote more than eighty stories in the *Tribune* that May of 1961 about Chicago's scandalous Sanitary District, of which this was the first.

## "LAY OFF OR ELSE . . ."

### By George Bliss

In 1955 the American Society of Civil Engineers designated the Metropolitan Sanitary District of Greater Chicago as one of the "seven wonders of American engineering."

Few engineering experts doubt that the District's engineering feats are great. But there are many in government work, including District officials and engineers, who assert that it is truly a wonder that the District maintains any sort of efficiency under present conditions.

Frank Chesrow, District president, has ordered a private consulting firm to make three separate investigations of conditions that have led to a major payroll scandal. The state's attorney's office has been looking for possible criminal violations in charges of job cheating. Federal agents, including Internal Revenue and Labor Department investigators, have started inquiries into the operations of several firms and individuals who have had connections with the district.

The *Tribune* has found that the District payrolls are loaded with inefficient political favorites. There are men who receive paychecks they never earn. District workers have been paid for long periods without bothering to show up for work.

Contractors and firms doing business with the District are constantly being pressured into donating huge sums to political coffers. The Leyden Township Democratic organization has solicited the firms—and even District workers with civil service rank—for donations to build up its treasury.

A number of mystery men, some of whom have close ties to the crime syndicate, exert influence over District operations and are known to be key front men for firms wanting to do business with the District. The District employs 2,357 persons and its payroll is steadily mounting. Some officials, who have a thorough knowledge of its vast and intricate operations, claim that the District could be run efficiently with about 1,500 employees—if everybody put in a normal day's work.

Philip Furlong, District maintenance and operations engineer, charges that he has been warned to "lay off or else" whenever he attempted to crack down on loafers and keep up District efficiency. He said that several trustees told him he was "too tough" and was jeopardizing his career by cracking down on loafers. In several instances he was ordered to ignore the work habits of certain District employees because of their political influence. . . .

The *Tribune* has obtained copies of numerous memoranda and reports to top echelon officials in which department heads complained that tax money was being wasted by placing men with powerful political connections on advanced rate jobs where they were not needed. Political favorites, it was found, were "promoted" to higher paying temporary jobs after they obtained civil service rank. . . .

The District board is made up of six Democrats and three Republicans. They agree on almost all matters that come up at board meetings. There is some bickering on patronage but the big disagreements come when the District is criticized and no one wants to take the blame.

---

That was just the beginning. By the time Bliss was through, the $50-a-day "ghosts" were knocked off the payrolls. So were the grafters and the loafers. The next thing that happened was the opening of an inquiry by the Cook County Grand Jury, which led to a major reorganization of the Sanitary District. For his work, Bliss won a Pulitzer Prize for local reporting in 1962.

Three years later, he was still going strong. This time, he and the *Tribune* exposed gambling and vice in Gary, East Chicago, and Lake County, Indiana. On January 29, 1965, he published the address of East Chicago's gambling headquarters, where he estimated that $25,000 a day came pouring in from various rackets, and where at least 300 persons were employed. It is still big news in Chicago.


## 11. *CRIME AND MIRIAM*

The Attorney General of the United States signed a plaque in 1958 to express his gratitude to a crime reporter in Washington, D.C. The Attorney General, William P. Rogers, was not alone. Congressional leaders, judges, and police joined in this unique honor.

The reporter was something of a surprise, far more plausible in the society section than on Page 1—Miss Miriam Ottenberg of the Washington *Evening Star*. She was that rarity, a native of Washington; born October 7, 1914, she received her A.B. from the University of Wisconsin School of Journalism in 1935. Thereafter she became one of the keenest reporters in the nation's capital, and, later, president of the Women's National Press Club. She had been breaking crime stories on Page 1 of the *Star* for years—exposés of the narcotics traffic, the inner workings of gangland, and the like. She had done a praiseworthy series on mental illness, too. Her plaque from the Attorney General was well deserved.

Instead of resting on her honors, Miss Ottenberg looked around for greater challenges. She found one—the used-car market in Washington. In a series of articles entitled, "Buyer Beware," she showed that hundreds of men and women were being swindled by unscrupulous used-car dealers who acted within the framework of existing law.

As always, she got action. On April 22, 1960, President Eisenhower signed into law a bill approved by Congress which was designed to curb the abuses she had exposed. Buyers were protected. Maximum charges were fixed for installment plan buyers, and bonds were required both from dealers and finance companies. For the first time, used-car salesmen were licensed and controlled in the District of Columbia and used-car dealers were warned that they would lose their licenses for unscrupulous practices. The successful attack on the used-car racket won Miss Ottenberg a Pulitzer Prize that same year.

Three years later she broke a story that not only made Page 1 of the *Star* but also most other major newspapers of the United States. It was the first disclosure of an evil underworld empire called Cosa Nostra— "Our Thing." The exposé was like something out of the 1920s when the prohibition mobs were making their own laws and enforcing them with machine guns.

This was the first story, published in the Washington *Star*, August 4, 1963.

## COSA NOSTRA

### By Miriam Ottenberg

For the first time in the federal war on organized crime, a figure once fairly high in the mob hierarchy is telling all he knows about crime in America.

He has verified uncorroborated information previously developed by the Federal Bureau of Investigation as to the existence of a secret, nationwide organization that dominates a network of mobs in more than a dozen American cities.

He has put the finger on the top racketeers already under investigation. He has identified the bosses and explained exactly where they fit in the crime hierarchy. He has added new names and a flood of details on unsolved murders and mysterious disappearances. He has outlined the structure of a well-disciplined, terror-ridden, semimilitary organization dominating organized crime in America.

He has revealed the organization's name—hitherto an underworld secret. The organization is known as Cosa Nostra—Our Thing. The theory of a secret society at the hub of organized crime has been supported for many years by the Federal Bureau of Narcotics. It called it the Mafia. FBI agents had been collecting information indicating the existence of a close-knit crime syndicate.

Now, finally, someone has talked. His name: Joseph Valachi of New York, late of Atlanta Penitentiary; present address a closely guarded secret. Here are a few highlights from his story:

Vito Genovese, 66-year-old narcotics boss, is still kingpin of Cosa

Nostra, although he's now serving a fifteen-year sentence at Atlanta Penitentiary. It was Genovese and his henchmen who plotted the unsuccessful attempt on the life of racketeer Frank Costello, the slaying of gangster Albert Anastasia, and the crime convention at Apalachin, New York, on November 14, 1957.

The "delegates" to Apalachin were the bosses of the individual branches of Cosa Nostra and their bodyguards. Only slightly more than half the men who gathered at Apalachin were apprehended. The actual attendance was closer to 110 men than the 60 delegates rounded up by police.

It was at Atlanta that Valachi stopped being a blood brother of the mob and broke the conspiracy of silence—for his own desperate reasons. Now 60, Valachi had a record of arrests for robbery, extortion, burglary, gambling, and narcotics dating back to 1918. He had served time for a federal narcotics violation but had beaten most of the other cases. He was, in other words, an old-timer in the mobs.

In May, 1959, two men were arrested in New York as they were about to deliver heroin to a Federal Bureau of Narcotics undercover agent. One of those arrested turned out to be one of the largest interstate traffickers, and the trail led from him to Valachi as the man who had supplied him with the heroin.

Valachi went into hiding but was captured in November, 1959. He was convicted, jumped bond, but finally surrendered and was sent to Atlanta Penitentiary in June, 1960, to serve fifteen years.

On the morning of June 22, 1962, Valachi killed a fellow prisoner at Atlanta. After the killing, he sent for a Federal Bureau of Narcotics agent who had questioned him during the earlier narcotics investigation. He told the agent that the killing was a case of mistaken identity. He said he had learned via the prison grapevine that the mob had marked him for death and had assigned a killer to do the job on suspicion that he had informed on the giant narcotics ring. Ironically, Valachi had not talked—not yet.

Valachi told the agent that when a prisoner approached him, he thought it was the man assigned to kill him so he whacked him with a pipe and the man died. It was only afterward, when he saw the man's face, that he realized it was the wrong one.

A veteran FBI agent was assigned full time to the job of extracting from Valachi everything he knew. Valachi, meanwhile, had pleaded guilty to the murder of his fellow-convict and drawn a life sentence. He was spirited away from Atlanta, out of the federal prison system, and into a secret hiding place. As the months passed, FBI agents checked his stories. They began charting Cosa Nostra by "families," the tag given by the society to individual mobs.

Cosa Nostra is a terror organization, holding its members in thrall through blood oaths of fealty. Members of the organization are linked by blood ties and arranged marriages. The sons and daughters marry at their own social level in the tightly controlled structure. At the top is the ruling council, known as the "commission." Genovese is regarded as the nonelected but chosen overlord. Members of the "commission" are known as the "bosses," or heads of the "families" in cities across the country. The "families" control organized crime in their areas. The "boss" of the "family" decides who should be killed and by whom, usually in concert with his top lieutenants.

Valachi's stories of murder have been offered to local authorities to help clean up their cases although some of the perpetrators he named are already dead. As for the other crimes he has disclosed, the statute of limitations has already run out. His value, in other words, is not basically for purpose of evidence but for intelligence. He has confirmed much of what has been suspected for decades. He has shown the face of the enemy.

---

Cosa Nostra was news from then on. The Attorney General, Robert F. Kennedy, made it his No. 1 crime target. And when he ran for U.S. Senator from New York in 1964, the Cosa Nostra "families" and their sympathizers made an effort to defeat him but failed miserably.

If anyone could take satisfaction in the outcome of the exposé, it was Miriam Ottenberg. But at an age when most women are likely to consider a P.T.A. meeting or a luncheon for a local poet to be strenuous activity, the Washington *Star*'s crime reporter was on the trail of another exposé. Without crime exposés and Miriam, the nation's capital would scarcely have been the same.

## 12. A CRIME REPORTER'S LIFE

Edward Roger Cony is an authentic denizen of Wall Street—an editor of the *Wall Street Journal* in the heart of New York's towering financial community. As might be expected, he is a commuter. At the Manhasset stop on the Long Island Rail Road, he has a comfortable home, a wife, and four children.

It isn't precisely the kind of life one might expect a crime reporter to lead, but it suits Ed Cony. And if anyone were to doubt his credentials as a crime reporter, there is a Pulitzer Prize certificate in the Cony home that will silence any sharp tongue. All of which would be likely to cause mournful headshakings among the crime reporters of an older tradition and generations of movie fans who were brought up on stronger stuff.

Ed Cony's life has had its own quality of excitement. He is a thin, rather reserved Yankee with a strongly developed sense of morality, born March 15, 1923, in Augusta, Maine. He had the misfortune to enter Colby College just a year before Pearl Harbor and in 1942 was obliged to give it up after war came. In 1946, following his discharge from the Army, he attended Reed College in Oregon; in 1948, he received his bachelor's degree in political science. Three years later, he received his master's degree in journalism from Stanford.

Cony's reporting on the Portland *Oregonian* produced few sensations but gave him the solid training he needed. For when he joined the *Wall Street Journal* in 1953 as a reporter in the San Francisco bureau, he made good almost from the beginning. Two years later, he was Los Angeles bureau manager and in 1957 he was promoted to southeastern bureau director with headquarters at Jacksonville, Florida.

The big move to New York came in 1959. A year later, he was news editor of the *Wall Street Journal* at 37 years of age—a good record in itself. If he expected that a *Journal* editor would be chained to a desk except for two-hour lunches, he was mistaken. Within a short time, he was assigned to an intricate financial story that involved some of the most respected figures and corporations in the financial community in conflict of interest charges. No crime had been committed, yet the story had to be told.

After weeks of investigation which took him across the country, Ed Cony began his story this way: "Is it wrong for a corporation officer or director to profit personally from sideline transactions with the company he serves? The practice is not new; seldom does it violate public law; indeed, the intricate workings of the federal tax statutes almost seem to encourage it. Yet, this question of business ethics suddenly has been thrust into the headlines." [2]

Cony's piece for the first time dramatized the whole problem of conflict of interest for businessmen and brought about at least two shakeups in top managements. It won him a Pulitzer Prize in national reporting in 1961.

Having shown such talent as an investigatory reporter, Cony was kept on the job as often as he could be pried away from his desk. In 1963, he did an exhaustive study of the business dealings of Roy Cohn, the onetime chief counsel for Senator Joseph R. McCarthy's inquiries, which also was of subsequent interest to a grand jury. Soon afterward, he described, in "A Swindler's Legacy," how one of the largest financial institutions in the nation allegedly made possible a swindler's operations.

But one of the most difficult stories he had to write was a description of how the Cosa Nostra organization, first exposed by Miriam Ottenberg in the Washington *Star*, was able to penetrate the stronghold of legitimate business. He called his piece "Mafia and Business." In it, he alerted the financial community to the dangers of underworld financial dealings and thereby did more to blunt the power of the criminal organization than many a court.

Ed Cony's November 18, 1963 article in the *Wall Street Journal* was an example of modern crime reporting at its best.

## BUSINESS AND THE GANGS

### By Ed Cony

Who is putting the most new money into American business today?

Mutual funds, pension funds, insurance companies, and the trust departments of banks obviously are among the top sources of investment capital. But government officials are convinced another "institutional investor"—the underworld—also belongs near the top of the list.

Some businesses are old favorites of racketeers: vending machine con-

[2] *Wall Street Journal*, Aug. 15, 1960.

cerns, the wholesale distribution of liquor and beer, laundries and dry cleaners, bars and night clubs, hotels and motels, linen supply companies, garbage collection.

But the present-day list is much longer. J. Edgar Hoover, director of the Federal Bureau of Investigation, says it includes restaurants, bakeries, produce companies, and the entertainment industry, among others.

The McClellan committee has catalogued the business interests of the delegates to the Apalachin underworld convention of 1957. The catholicity of their interests can be seen by noting just a few of the entries on the committee's list—a Brooklyn funeral parlor, a Dallas food and liquor importer, a construction firm in Coral Gables, a Cleveland vending machine company.

The hoodlums do not operate just in the big cities, as the following entries in the McClellan committee directory suggest—a cheese company in a small Colorado town, a car wash in a Pennsylvania village, and a jukebox distributor in an Illinois city.

Though these businesses might be considered relatively small and obscure ventures, government authorities are convinced that Cosa Nostra leaders also finance and control some large industrial companies and real estate firms with nationwide holdings and reputations. But these links are difficult to prove because of the "front men" the racketeers use to hide their own connections with these companies.

Financial institutions, too, are not immune from penetration by leaders of organized crime. Gangsters attract a good deal of attention when they take money out of banks—at gunpoint. But it generally escapes public notice when they put money into banks. And not just as depositors.

One government official with a good deal of familiarity with this subject says: "As sure as I'm sitting here, two banks in New York City are controlled by hoodlums."

Why doesn't the government throw them out? "It's one thing to know it; it's quite another to prove in court a violation of the law," he responds.

Gangland figures and their associates—who frequently include lawyers, accountants, public relations men, and gamblers—are attracted to legitimate business for the same reason upright citizens are: They see it as an opportunity to earn a return on their money. "The racketeer has a lot of cash, and rather than let it lie fallow, he seeks to earn a profit with it," says a veteran federal law enforcement man.

Why is gangster penetration of business increasing? The basic reason is quite simple: The racketeers have more money to invest. They've pyramided their wealth through operations in narcotics, prostitution, gambling, and loan sharking. Law enforcement officials agree on this, although statistical proof is hard to come by.

There are some educated guesses, however, on the extent of the underworld's earnings. Professional gambling within the United States extracts about $25 billion annually from the customers, according to John Scarne, an author of three books on gambling, an adviser to the Hilton Hotels on the casinos in their overseas hotels, and a consultant to Puerto Rico on legalized gambling.

"About 90 percent of this gross win of 25 billions is from illegal gambling," Mr. Scarne estimates. The remaining slice comes from gambling at race tracks and such legalized operations as the Nevada casinos. Asked if illegal gambling is on the increase, Mr. Scarne replies: "It's not decreasing. That's for sure."

Probably the greatest source of illegal wealth, which eventually finds its way into legitimate enterprises, is loan sharking. Organized crime has been swift to exploit the great growth in the use of credit—although their lending operations can nowhere be found in government figures on consumer or business credit.

In New York, longshoremen are frequent victims of this consumer loan business of hoodlums. The longshoreman who can't get credit elsewhere and turns to the loan shark to borrow $100 may pay as much as $25 a week in interest. This is illegal under the usury laws, and such loans are not recorded in any legal document. The hoodlum relies on "muscle" to collect. From illegal loan sharking, organized crime has found it just a step to legal moneylending—through factoring.

A factor is a person or company which provides financing to business firms, usually by buying accounts receivable and collecting on them. Some factors, however, make loans against other collateral.

Hidden financing by hoodlums characterizes the liquor industry—including package stores, bars, night clubs, and restaurants with liquor licenses. In most states, a man with a criminal record cannot be the owner of a liquor store or bar. But Donald Hostetter, chairman of the

New York State Liquor Authority, puts his finger on a national problem:
"We're finding with regularity that the actual owners don't have their
names on the license." The racketeer "invests his money through a
nominee," he says.

And it's very difficult to discover who the man is fronting for. There's
a dearth of written records linking the criminal to his front. "Instead
of a note or some other legal document," notes Mr. Hostetter, "the
racketeer relies on a pistol for his security."

———————

Cosa Nostra was the most feared underworld organization of the
mid-1960s, but once its activities were pulled into the light of day its
power began to decline. The work of Ed Cony, Miriam Ottenberg, and
others was reminiscent of the crime reporters of another generation, led
by Meyer Berger of the New York *Times*, who dug into the somewhat
more messy career of Murder, Inc. Albert Anastasia, Buggsy Siegel,
Pittsburgh Phil Strauss, Frank the Dasher Abbadando, and their notorious lot are no more, and there are none to weep for them. In their day
they, too, ruled with machine guns. But they couldn't stand exposure
any more than the plug-uglies of Cosa Nostra.

## 13. "WHERE IS THAT $6,000,000?"

The first principle of reporting is to ask questions. Whatever else Gene
Goltz may know about his profoundly vexing and less-than-appreciated
art, he has never forgotten that. At the city offices of Pasadena, a suburb
of Houston, Texas, he began asking a single question in 1963. When
officials wouldn't pay any attention to him, he shouted it at them:

"Where is that $6,000,000?"

Goltz referred to a bond issue that had been voted by the citizens
of Pasadena in 1959 for municipal purposes. As a reporter for the
Houston *Post* and a citizen of Pasadena, he was doubly involved. As
he was fended off, given double talk, and denied access to city records,
his suspicions rose.

The phrase, "The people's right to know," so dutifully included in
the resolutions of every newspaper society for years on end, began to
mean something to him. He went to work.

Like George Thiem of the Chicago *Daily News,* who unmasked a $2,500,000 larceny in 1956 by the then State Auditor of Illinois, Orville E. Hodge, Goltz had to follow unorthodox methods in his search for the origin of the crimes he suspected had been committed.

This became no tale of reportorial derring-do, but a patient, resourceful search for access to records and witnesses who would tell the story. Goltz had no background for this kind of inquiry but he learned rapidly on the job. He was then 33 years old, having been born in Marquette, Iowa, on April 30, 1930. After service in the Air Force and attendance at St. Louis University and later the University of Missouri, he decided at the age of 27 to become a newspaperman. His first job was as a $42-a-week reporter on the weekly Tama (Iowa) *News-Herald.* Following a series of jobs in Iowa and Arizona on dailies and weeklies, he came to the Houston *Post* in 1961.

The Pasadena assignment was his first real challenge and he rose to it with remarkable skill. So often in these days of complicated finance at every level of government, the crime reporter suspects that he is part bookkeeper, part economist, part detective and part prophet. From the outset, that was destined to be Goltz's role and this is how he wrote about it, in substance, in his first article for the Houston *Post* on the Pasadena Story on November 4, 1963.


## "I'LL GET YOU!"

### By Gene Goltz

"Abandon all hope, ye who enter here." At least, abandon hope for information.

I sometimes think this sign should be erected in front of the Pasadena City Hall. The reason is that the ordinary citizen of Pasadena is not always welcome at the City Hall if he has come to look at the public records. He is likely to get a reception that ranges from a laughing brushoff to cold hostility.

I know. I have tried. And I am a citizen of Pasadena as well as a reporter. The right of the citizen to know how his city is being run is often flouted in Pasadena.

I found this to be true during a weary and hopeless search that lasted for six months. I was searching for the records that would show

how the city of Pasadena disposed of $6 million in bond money that the people voted in 1959.

I started looking last April when a man pulled me aside after a commissioners' meeting and said, "If you really want a story, why don't you try to find out where that $6 million bond fund went?"

He made two points: 1) That I would not be able to find out; 2) That the city commissioners didn't know themselves. He was pretty much right on both counts.

Before I was through investigating, however, it became clear that the bond issue had receded into the background. The thing that had become increasingly disturbing was the fact that it is harder for the citizen to examine records in the Pasadena City Hall than it would be for him to break into King Saud's harem.

There is no room here for me to detail the countless journeys I made to City Hall trying to get a look at bond fund records and later trying to get a look at the minutes of past commission meetings. There is room, though, to tell about two of those experiences.

In those first months, it was more of a joke than anything else. Often I would stick my head into one or another of the commissioners' offices and yell, "Where is that $6 million?"

After awhile, of course, it ceased to be funny. One time I went into the office of George Smith, the city engineer, and asked him. "I don't know if I should tell you," he said frankly.

In the Pasadena City Hall, all roads eventually lead to the mayor. Mayor James L. Brammer told me frankly once that the city's secretary would never let anybody see any records unless the mayor gave him permission. "If he did, I'd fire him and he knows it," the mayor said.

The bond issue was passed in 1959 and that was only four years ago. When I had some free time, I went back to Pasadena City Hall determined to get to the bottom of the bond records.

I was ushered into the mayor's office and we talked noncommittally for awhile. Then I mentioned the bonds and said I still wanted to look at the minutes. The mayor got up and closed the door. Then he told me that when somebody gets after him, he never forgets it.

"You might get me, but I'll tell you one thing," Brammer said. "I'll get you. It might cost me $3,000 but I'll do it."

He told me that he had friends in high places "reaching all the way to Washington" and that they wouldn't stand for the mayor of Pasadena being harassed by any newspaper.

---

That was the beginning of a two-year hunt, not only for the bond money, but for the source of wrongdoing in Pasadena. Goltz was harassed constantly. Once, he was punched in the nose outside a grand jury room by an infuriated city commissioner. But in 1964, numerous indictments were handed up against various city officials in Pasadena.

The Harris County Grand Jury report said: "The fact of this case is that Gene Goltz, a Houston *Post* reporter, through his diligent and devoted efforts to report the news, was the prime factor in triggering our investigation.

"The information developed by the persistent Mr. Goltz has comprised the basis for a substantial part of our total investigation. We highly commend Mr. Goltz for his courage and diligent reporting and we feel that he is deserving of commendation by all citizens for his endeavor to make this community a better place in which to live."

Gene Goltz was awarded the 1965 Pulitzer Prize in special local reporting for his work.

# III. THE DIGGERS

Martin Oliver Waldron roared at the governor of the sovereign state of Florida, which is scarcely what a well-behaved newspaper reporter should do. Governors are notoriously sensitive.

Nobody, however, had ever accused Waldron of being a coward. Nor had he ever been particularly distinguished for suave, Chesterfieldian conduct. He was a six-foot, 240-pound latter-day Falstaff who specialized in investigating the weak points of the state's government, then splashing his findings in the vigorous and highly independent St. Petersburg *Times*. It was a formidable combination.

Now Waldron was being asked by a proud and able governor, LeRoy Collins, for the sources of his information. Scant wonder that he roared! To an investigative reporter, a digger, sources were as sacred as a hair of the Prophet to a faithful Muslim. And a good deal more useful.

For hours, the governor and the digger fought it out in private in the executive offices at Tallahassee. But in the end, Martin Oliver Waldron's sources remained inviolate. His success should have been a warning to those who were to follow Governor Collins, but it wasn't. Besides being sensitive, most governors—and an assortment of other public officials as well—underrate the potency of a determined reporter who has the support of his newspaper.

So it developed that when Farris Bryant became governor of Florida, he paid scant attention at first to Waldron and his inquiries. But within a short time, political shock waves began radiating from the home of the St. Petersburg *Times*. The State House was shaken. On the basis of a telephoned tip from an anonymous official, Waldron had begun prying into the financial background of Florida's 211-mile Sunshine State Parkway. Worse still, he was digging into the activities of its chief administrative official, John Hammer, the chairman of the Florida Turnpike Authority.

It was the most difficult job the 39-year-old Waldron had ever taken on. But he had help. The small, tough, and equally determined publisher of the St. Petersburg *Times*, Nelson Poynter, backed him up with men, money, and some 4,800 column inches of news, editorials, interpretive articles, photographs, and charts. A somewhat startled public began learning things about the state's business that it had never known before.

Soon the *Times* was proclaiming in thick eight-column banner headlines that a road which should have cost $100,000,000 actually was soaking up some $400,000,000 in bonds financed by Florida taxpayers. Even for Florida, it was a scandal.

Moreover, Waldron and his fellow reporters produced documentary evidence to show that Chairman Hammer had spent $100,000 in two years on his official duties. Among the charges were $65-a-day hotel rooms, $30 a day for meals, orchids for secretaries, a chartered airplane, a chartered boat, and a generous amount of travel by more conventional means.

Chairman Hammer, a respected businessman, had a defense. He had been entrusted with the responsibility of selling state bonds and he argued that he couldn't "make money without spending money." At one point, he wrote Governor Bryant that Waldron had been "rude, discourteous, and ungentlemanly," and had "roared at my employees." After these and other disclosures, the governor flared: "I'm so mad I could pop."

Chairman Hammer resigned. The day of the unlimited expense accounts on state business ended. A state audit was ordered for the Turnpike Authority. New restrictions were placed on the financing of state bonds. And sufficient other reforms were made to provide substantial savings for both the state and its bondholders. The St. Petersburg *Times*, as a result, won the 1964 Pulitzer Prize gold medal for public service.

Waldron's work was, by and large, a superior demonstration of the art of the digger—the modern investigative reporter—as it is practiced today in an increasingly complex society. He is a member of a small, elite group of journalists—a creation of his time, born out of the intricacies of modern living and the sprawling, often outdated, processes of government. While the investigation of crime is a part of his function, it by no means limits his activity.

To be sure, there is nothing particularly new about the investigative function of a newspaper. It is almost as old as the newspaper itself, and it is scarcely confined to the United States, although the American press has exploited it more than others. After all, it was a great Irishman, William Howard Russell, who saved a British army in the Crimea more than a century ago with his exposés in the *Times* of London. And it was an even more illustrious Frenchman, Emile Zola, who published "J'Accuse!" in *L'Aurore* and thereby exposed the plot against Captain Alfred Dreyfus.

There is virtue, too, in the American example. Well-nigh a century ago, the grip of the Tweed ring on New York City was broken by the New York *Times*'s investigation. And the first Joseph Pulitzer, in the New York *World*, crusaded unremittingly against the varied larcenies of other crooked politicians. Nor can the magazine muckrakers at the turn of the century be forgotten—Lincoln Steffens and "The Shame of the Cities" in *McClure's*; David Graham Phillips and "The Treason of the Senate" in *Cosmopolitan*, and Samuel Hopkins Adams and "The Great American Fraud" in *Collier's*.[1]

As the muckrakers fell silent or died out, their places were taken by younger journalists on newspapers in a score or more of American cities, as the record of the Pulitzer Prizes testifies. But it was seldom, even on the New York *World* in Herbert Bayard Swope's era as executive editor, that the work of investigatory reporters was planned and organized on a systematic basis. Nor was any thought given to special training for them. When a specialist was needed for a particular inquiry, whether it dealt with the iniquities of a stockbroker or the shortcomings of the state's mental hygiene system, he was drafted from the ranks of general assignment reporters. The principal quality that was demanded of him was an infinite capacity for "righteous indignation," [2] seldom a dependable motivating force for journalists of scant sophistication and background. After the investigatory work was over, the reporter returned to the street to chase fires, report murders, and deal with the rest of the news grist as it then existed. It was an era of rugged individualism, and the reporter was expected to be the ruggedest of all. The remarkable part of his story is that he did such good—and frequently distinguished—work with so little preparation.

[1] F. L. Mott, *American Journalism* (New York, Macmillan, 1941), pp. 574–76.
[2] H. B. Swope to author, in conversation, 1957.

But with the emergence of a vastly changed society in the United States as a result of the upheaval that followed the great depression and World War II, the concept of the role of the journalist began to change, too. Within less than a generation, he had been forced to cope with such disparate subjects as social security and public housing, broadened programs of education and health, the rise of a stronger unionism, atomic energy, space rockets, civil rights, a whole new body of international organization, and a tremendous expansion in government at all levels. Even the Cro-Magnon type of editor began to understand that a university education was desirable for a journalist and that something more was needed for a specialist.

Almost through force of circumstance, the investigative reporter— the digger, in his latest manifestation—began to be set apart from his fellows. Those who were self-taught, and others who were university-trained, found that their efforts were being directed into areas of the news with which they were becoming increasingly familiar.

Of course, since first-rate reporters are never in great supply, the diggers could expect to be taken off investigatory work from time to time. But there were compensations. Some won Nieman Fellowships at Harvard and elected to study in areas of special interest. Others worked in advanced programs at the Columbia Graduate School of Journalism and elsewhere. The American Press Institute at Columbia, which is supported by American newspapers, began holding seminars solely for investigatory reporters and discussing their work as an entity in similar sessions for editors.[3]

In this give-and-take, which was conducted privately and without even the keeping of minutes, it became clear that the diggers and their discussion leaders were agreed that continuous and systematic checking had to be conducted, so far as possible, at key public offices at all levels. Check lists were prepared to point out common evils in local government and tell-tale symptoms that something wrong was afoot. Possibilities of fraud were scanned in the courts and in the police and finance departments. Nothing was overlooked—from marriage license bureaus to record-keeping offices. Even the attitudes of editors and reporters were examined to determine whether the diggers' efforts could be more efficiently directed.

Nothing like this had ever been done before. What it meant was that

[3] Records of the American Press Institute, New York, Apr. 1–12, 1963.

the watchdog function of the press, as exemplified by the work of its investigatory reporters, had become a matter of common interest to responsible newspapers throughout the country. It was also clear that an exchange of views and of methodology, once begun, probably would lead sooner or later to a decision to exchange information in advance of publication on inquiries that involved several communities or crossed state lines. Such exchanges already had been conducted between newspapers, notably in the St. Louis *Post-Dispatch*'s joint exposé with the Chicago *Daily News* of small-town Illinois editors who were on the Illinois state payroll in 1949. It was something new for investigatory reporters to be helping each other in the public interest.

The basic premise behind the development of the diggers as an independent force was explained best by one of them, Wallace Turner, who won a Pulitzer Prize with William Lambert in 1957 while they were investigating the Teamsters' Union for the Portland *Oregonian*.

"As modern political and economic life have become more complicated," he said, "the job of uncovering and publishing the meaningful truth has become harder and harder. It costs a publisher a lot of money to expose some evil that has become rooted in his state or city. He needs to have reporters who are capable of understanding what they find, lawyers who are able to weigh the evidence on which the stories are based. The publisher also needs personal qualities within himself—qualities of courage, dedication, motivation, and civic consciousness. . . .

"Another thing a newspaper has to do in investigative reporting is to be nonpartisan politically. . . . Because if you play politics with your investigations pretty soon your readers will get wise and refuse to believe you. When that happens, you've lost it all." [4]

It may fairly be asked, therefore, whether a press in which Republican publishers are in unquestioned majority will permit its investigatory reporters to act in a nonpartisan manner. The resignations during the Eisenhower administration, following newspaper exposés, would seem to indicate that the more responsible publishers place their newspapers above mere party interests or loyalties. Certainly, the New York *Herald Tribune* gave a large display in 1960 to a disclosure by David Wise, of its Washington staff, that Federal Communications Commissioner John C. Doerfer had taken a six-day Atlantic cruise on a yacht that belonged to a Miami Beach broadcasting station owner. When Doerfer resigned

[4] *Editor & Publisher*, May 10, 1958, p. 70.

following attacks on his position by all three Washington newspapers, the *Herald Tribune* gave prominence to President Eisenhower's remark that it had been a "wise decision."

The resignation of Sherman Adams as Assistant to the President in 1958 similarly followed a digging campaign in which Clark Mollenhoff, among others, helped establish that the Eisenhower "chief of staff" had accepted gifts from a New England industrialist. A number of other reporters participated in the Adams case, among them Robert G. Spivack of the New York *Post*, Robert Healy of the Boston *Globe*, David Wise of the New York *Herald Tribune*, David Kraslow of the Miami *Herald*, William Blair of the New York *Times*, and James Deakin of the St. Louis *Post-Dispatch*. Only the New York *Post* and St. Louis *Post-Dispatch*, of this group, have consistently supported most Democratic candidates.

The resignations of Richard A. Mack from the Federal Communications Commission, Hugh Cross from the Interstate Commerce Commission, and Robert Tripp Ross as Assistant Secretary of Defense all followed unfavorable disclosures by various investigatory reporters, mostly from Republican newspapers. The one resignation that could be attributed entirely to a paper with Democratic sympathies was that of Harold E. Talbott as Secretary of the Air Force. He resigned in 1955 following disclosures by Charles Bartlett in the Chattanooga *Times* that he had recommended a business associate to certain Air Force contractors.

Not without a bit of wry reflection on his role as a millionaire publisher and a distinguished Republican, John Hay Whitney of the New York *Herald Tribune* gave some thought to the principle behind such unhappy events. Then he reasoned out his own course as follows:

"To be fair is not enough any more. We must be ferociously fair, the way a computer can be on election night when it tells you facts you would rather not know—but tells them, nevertheless, with the emphasis they deserve. I am a man involved in more directorships and enterprises than many of my fellow citizens. I have political as well as other friendships. But the day my newspaper begins to cease troubling my nonjournalistic life, I will know something is wrong with it." [5]

To Whitney's advice to be "ferociously fair" must be added the injunction of the first Joseph Pulitzer to his successors on the St. Louis

[5] *Saturday Review*, Dec. 12, 1964, pp. 71–72.

*Post-Dispatch* to "never be satisfied with merely printing the news, always be drastically independent." [6] These are, obviously, statements of a publishing ideal to which many may aspire; however, only the most courageous and selfless can achieve it.

As an ideal, it sheds a somewhat different light on the role of the journalist in today's society. Certainly, he cannot be a mere fact-gatherer, an electronic stenographer, a messenger whose sole utility is that he can transcribe or repeat what is handed to him for immediate presentation to a mass audience. If that were the only purpose of the journalist, and there are still some in and out of government who would limit him to such a menial role, our newspapers would lose their influence as well as their independence and become mere shopping throwaways or government circulars.

Surely, it is clear that there can be no responsible and independent newspapers without reporters who are responsible and independent, no newspapers of integrity without editors of unquestioned integrity. In short, if the newspaper is to achieve the ideal which some envision for it as a public servant, it must be based very largely on the development of a wider array of journalists who believe, as do the diggers, that their first duty is to the public.

To some, such a notion may seem impossibly noble and utterly impractical when applied to the workaday journalist who, in James Reston's mournful phrase, can aspire to no more than a first draft of history. Yet, it is a pervasive theme in American journalism, one that is shared by a Martin Oliver Waldron of the St. Petersburg *Times* as well as a John Hay Whitney of the New York *Herald Tribune*. The first Joseph Pulitzer put it this way as long ago as 1904:

"What is a journalist?

"Not any business manager or publisher, or even proprietor. A journalist is the lookout on the bridge of the ship of state. He notes the passing sail, the little things of interest that dot the horizon in fine weather. He reports the drifting castaway whom the ship can save. He peers through fog and storm to give warning of dangers ahead. He is not thinking of his wages or of the profits of his owners. He is there to watch over the safety and welfare of the people who trust him." [7]

---

[6] First published in the St. Louis *Post-Dispatch*, Apr. 10, 1907.
[7] *North American Review*, May, 1904.

Some of the best in a vexing profession have aspired to measure up to the Pulitzer tradition. As evidence, a selection of the work of the diggers is presented here with a ceremonious bow to the few who have brilliantly succeeded and a salute to the courage of the many who have failed.

## 14. "MOLLENHOFF CAN DO IT"

"It is good to have a fellow like Clark Mollenhoff roaring around Washington," James Reston once said. "He keeps people honest." [8]

Clark Raymond Mollenhoff, the most formidable investigative reporter in Washington, may not win any prizes for popularity because of his activities, but he has a closetful of awards to testify to both his professional skill and his achievements. He is an intense, pugnacious lawyer-journalist who considers unwarranted government secrecy almost a personal affront and who, for more than a generation, has been waging a ferocious campaign against malfeasance, misfeasance, and nonfeasance in public office.

In fact, whenever the news of some developing scandal is particularly obscure or an accused government official has taken to hiding behind the screen of executive privilege, it has become a matter of routine in the Cowles Newspapers hierarchy to call on Mollenhoff. Because, as the saying goes both in Iowa and Washington and a number of way stations in between, "Mollenhoff can do it."

Mollenhoff has made his own way without much help from anybody, which is one good reason why he isn't afraid to tackle the most powerful of government officials or even his own kind, the ranking journalists of his day. He is never satisfied, either with himself or with anybody else. More often than not, he has gone into a highly competitive journalistic situation, in Washington, New York, and elsewhere, and immediately complained that nobody was doing a good job of investigating graft. A disgruntled rival once complained sourly, "Clark's like the Queen of Hearts. He's always yelling, 'Off with their heads!' "

There is a difference, of course. Mollenhoff is no figment of the

[8] James Reston, talk with students at International House, New York City, February, 1964.

imagination; when he cries, "Off with their heads," he generally gets action. For all the hand-wringing over what the timid call his "fanaticism," no one in Washington has ever been able to slow up his campaign for better government, and those who have tried generally have come to grief. His foes have been corruption and waste throughout his career.

While it may seem to some that Mollenhoff is always working, which is not too much of an exaggeration, he has managed somehow to lead a comfortable family life as well with his wife and three children in Washington. He came up the hard way from Burnside, Iowa, where he was born on April 16, 1921. In 1944, he was graduated from Drake University with a law degree, which was a considerable feat, since he also had been working as a reporter on the Des Moines *Register and Tribune* since 1941. Although he was admitted to the Iowa bar, his principal practice was as a kind of unofficial prosecuting attorney who dug into the wrongs of public office.

From 1950 on, when he was transferred to the Washington bureau of the Cowles newspapers, the nation's capital was his main scene of operations although he neglected neither Iowa, New York, Chicago, nor any other likely spot for official scandal. For his investigatory reporting, he won three awards from the professional society, Sigma Delta Chi, the Raymond Clapper and Heywood Broun awards, a John Peter Zenger award, three fellowships, and three honorary doctorates. In 1958, his persistent inquiry into labor racketeering won him a Pulitzer Prize and also helped establish the McClellan Rackets Subcommittee of the U. S. Senate. The Defense Department, the Internal Revenue Bureau, foreign aid, even the executive office of the President himself, were not immune from Mollenhoff's scrutiny. In one way or another, he was active in every major scandal that came to public attention and in some he was the prime mover. Nor did he play favorites between Republicans and Democrats. If he was like a tiger on the trail of President Eisenhower's "chief of staff," Sherman Adams, he was just as eager as a number of other Washington reporters to bring down Bobbie Baker, who had been a favorite of Lyndon B. Johnson's before he became President. Two of them, Paul Hope and John Barron of the Washington *Evening Star*, won a prize for their efforts.

This is Mollenhoff's portrait of Baker, put together from several accounts published in the Des Moines *Register* on September 29, and October 8, 11, and 14, 1963.

## "THE 101ST SENATOR"

### By Clark Mollenhoff

WASHINGTON—Robert G. (Bobby) Baker has resigned from his influential post as secretary to the Senate majority.

The 35-year-old politician-businessman submitted his resignation to Majority Leader Mike Mansfield rather than appear for a meeting to answer questions raised by Senator John Williams (R–Del.)

There is some Democratic hope that the resignation will end the investigation, for Baker had personal and financial ties over a broad area of the political front.

Vice-President Lyndon B. Johnson was majority leader in 1955 when Baker, then only 26, became secretary to the majority. He had been regarded as "Johnson's man" in the Senate, and because of his influence was referred to frequently as the "101st Senator."

He was a most accommodating young man, and tried to keep close personal ties with many persons on the Republican side as well as with the Democrats. However, he has long been a controversial figure.

Baker had his name on the door of a law office in downtown Washington, and was listed as vice-president of Don Reynolds & Associates, an insurance firm.

He admits he has piled up a fortune in outside businesses while holding his $20,000-a-year Senate job. His wife has had an $11,000-a-year job as records manager of the Senate Internal Security Subcommittee headed by Senator James Eastland (D–Miss.).

Baker came to Washington from South Carolina as a 14-year-old Senate page boy and has been employed by the Senate since then. He said he got his business start when he "scraped up and borrowed everything I could get" to invest in a stock that was selling for $1 a share.

"It went up to more than $50 a share," he said. "That was the best venture. I've had some that haven't turned out very well, and I had one stock just last year that was disastrous."

He asserted he had made a wise purchase of Maryland real estate for $1,000 an acre, and that he might be able to sell it for as much as $8,000 an acre. He has a small real estate holding in his home town of Pickens, South Carolina, and owns a large motel in his home state.

He branched out into a large luxury motel at Ocean City, Maryland, that was billed as the hideout for the "Advise and Consent" set, and in the last couple of years has been in the coin-machine vending business.

Baker owes his present troubles to another South Carolina boy who filed a law suit against him and others, seeking $300,000 in damages. The complainant, Ralph L. Hill, met Baker at a South Carolina society party several years ago. That, he says, was the start of their relationship.

Hill filed a suit against Baker on September 9, 1963, charging that Baker was the key figure in a conspiracy to take a coin-machine contract away from him.

Hill contends that, in early 1962, he was helped by Baker to land an agreement to furnish the coin machines to the Melpar Corp., of Falls Church, Virginia, a firm with contracts in the airplane industry. In his petition, Hill states that he paid Baker $250 a month for a year for using his influence, and that after a year he paid Baker $650 a month because of some additional use of the Baker influence in the vending machine business.

Hill alleges that in March, 1963, Baker came to him and demanded that he sell the stock in his Capitol Vending Company, Inc., to Baker for Baker's price. Hill states that he refused and that Baker then told him he would arrange to break Hill's contract with Melpar. Melpar 'has broken its contract with Hill in the last few weeks. Baker declares that Hill is "jealous" of him and his business and is involved in "a conspiracy to destroy me."

Baker's luxurious office has been a convenient place for carrying on outside business activities, and he has been able to find places for some of his relatives on the government payroll. Also, even under the Eisenhower administration, Baker was able to obtain a postmastership for his father in South Carolina with a helpful push from Minority Leader Everett Dirksen.

Baker says he did not consult the Democratic party leadership on his outside business activities. "It was nobody's business what I did outside of the Senate as long as it was proper and within the law," is his defense.

He has told the Register that he will submit his resignation without complaint if any substantial number of the Senate Democrats believe it is improper for him to hold his Senate job while engaging in his varied activities. Following his resignation, the Senate approved an investigation of his "outside interests."

The disclosure of Baker's activities cost him whatever interest the Senate had had in him, and President Johnson's friendship as well. The Senate committee investigating his dealings found in 1964 that he had been "guilty of many gross improprieties." But that didn't end the Baker case, by any means.

More investigations ground ahead, inside and outside the Senate, and Mollenhoff was active in many of them. As for the suit that started the whole unhappy affair, it was settled out of court in December, 1964, for about $30,000.

The case supported Mollenhoff's basic philosophy about the news of government:

"No single factor is more important to the strength of our democracy than the free flow of accurate information about the government's operations. The citizen in a democracy must know what his government is doing, or he will lack the soundest basis for judging the candidates and the platforms of our political parties.

"No administration enjoys admitting errors or mismanagement of government. Because the criticism is usually initiated by the political opposition, it is often harsh and overdrawn. An instinctive defensiveness springs up within the defending political party, and the battle rages.

"It is not my intention to argue that all government information should be made public immediately, for I am fully aware of the need for security on military matters as well as the need for some restrictions on release of information from personnel and investigative files.

"But any withholding should be done under specific grants of authority from Congress or under specific grants in the Constitution, and the authority should be carefully limited. The broad right of arbitrary withholding of information is not something that any officials should be permitted to arrogate to themselves." [9]

[9] Clark R. Mollenhoff, *Washington Cover-Up* (Garden City, N.Y., Doubleday, 1962) pp. 9–13 passim.

## 15. THE BIG SECRET

The city desk, that venerable institution of American journalism, is geared to accept murders, bombings, fires, political scandals, and natural disasters without wasting words. This is particularly true in Chicago, where a deskman, by tradition, is supposed to be shockproof.

However, in the spring of 1962, work at the city desk of the Chicago *Daily News* was interrupted. The gentlemen involved turned to a shy and pretty young woman reporter for the answer to a difficult and explosive question:

"Is it possible to write about birth control in Chicago?"

The reporter, Lois Wille, softly suggested that it was. John Stanton, the managing editor, joined the conference with Maurice Fischer, the city editor, and his chief assistant, Robert Rose. It was obvious that some of them had their doubts, but Mrs. Wille, as the resident expert, carried the day. With the eventual approval of Marshall Field Jr., the editor and publisher, the Chicago *Daily News* assigned her to prepare a series on birth control.

It may seem strange, in this anything but reticent era, that a great newspaper should be so careful about publishing the most commonplace and unsensational information about a fact of life. But in Chicago, birth control was one of the unspoken taboos of newspaper work up to that time. The powerful opposition of the Catholic Church, which was so important in Chicago, had caused political leaders to make birth control a secret to those who had the most need of it—the needy and the underprivileged. In the newsrooms, therefore, this became a "sensitive" matter.

Mrs. Wille, however, was told that it was her job to develop a series that would be fair to all sides, those who favored birth control, those who opposed it, and those who didn't know the first thing about it but would benefit through an end to secrecy. She was well equipped for such an investigatory report, the first of its kind in Chicago's less-than-inhibited daily journalism. For some time, she had had an interest in the social sciences. Now, all Chicago was her laboratory and the columns of one of the most influential newspapers in the nation were open to her, waiting for her conclusions.

Lois Wille, a native of Chicago, was 32 then. Her husband, Wayne, was feature editor of *Science and Mechanics* magazine. They had no children. In 1953, Mrs. Wille had been graduated from the Medill School of Journalism at Northwestern University, where she had been managing editor of the paper. In 1956, she joined the Chicago *Daily News* as a fashion writer, but she didn't linger in the perfumed world of the clotheshorse. It wasn't long before she was hiding in a laundry truck to get to Nikita S. Khrushchev for an interview during his visit to the city. She also managed to interview Prince Philip, using similar devices, when he and Queen Elizabeth came to Chicago. When it came to getting the news, her shyness disappeared.

At the beginning of her investigation of the big secret, birth control, Mrs. Wille ran into all the troubles she expected. Politicians, with one eye on the Catholic vote, didn't want to talk with her. They and others told her sharply that a newspaper had no right to print anything about birth control. All the archaic and outworn prejudices of centuries rose up against her, but she managed to surmount them all.

It isn't too long since the Chicago *Daily News* published Mrs. Wille's series, for which it won a Pulitzer Prize gold medal for public service in 1963. Even so, there is a rather quaint air about it today, and one wonders why anybody would have rushed into print to denounce it. Yet, many did; those, after all, were the days before the Ecumenical Council in Rome which represented a great turning point in Catholic thought on many problems.

A principal part of the first of Mrs. Wille's articles in the Chicago *Daily News* of 1962 is presented here as a matter of historical interest.

## WHY BIRTH CONTROL?

### By Lois Wille

On a hot Saturday morning in August, Mrs. Sandra Allmon, 26, walked into Newberry Settlement House just off Maxwell Street, waited in line with 100 other women and poured out her story:

"I asked about it at County Hospital when my youngest was born and everybody shut up like a clam. I've got seven now, I told the doctor. And he said, 'Well, you're healthy enough for seven more.'

"I asked my ADC man (Aid to Dependent Children) and he just said he didn't know anything about it. When I took my baby to the

Welfare Station, I asked them—and when you bring *that* up, why they act like they don't know you.

"I heard about you people from a neighbor. It was just like a miracle. I couldn't believe it. You're the only ones who will talk to me about it."

What Mrs. Allmon wanted was this: information and supplies to prevent her from having more babies.

She got it, as did 5,470 other women in the first eight months of 1962—from one of the dozen clinics in churches and settlement houses operated by the Planned Parenthood Association. Of these 5,470, at least 1,370 are supported by the Cook County (Chicago) Public Aid Dept.

They pay nothing for the services they receive at the clinic unless they choose a contraceptive pill, which costs them $2.50 a month. It is these free services for relief recipients that may break open the silent tug-of-war over birth control.

The key issue is: Should Planned Parenthood, a private agency with a $249,000 annual budget, be reimbursed with public funds for its services to welfare patients?

Or, stated another way: Should public funds be used for a purpose considered immoral by at least 40 percent of the population of Cook County? Of these the greatest numbers by far are the members of the Roman Catholic Church, joined in their views by the Greek and Jewish Orthodox Churches.

The most vocal proponents of the use of public funds for birth control service are members of the Planned Parenthood board of directors, an array of forty-eight civic and social leaders, rabbis, Protestant clergymen, and physicians. They are seconded by the Church Federation of Greater Chicago, representing twenty-seven denominations, the Chicago Gynecological Society, and the Chicago Institute of Medicine.

But so far Raymond Hilliard, director of the Cook County Public Aid Department, has not offered to pay the $15,070 Planned Parenthood says he owes them for the first eight months of 1962. And there the matter has rested until the arrival in Chicago of Harold Swank.

Before he was named executive secretary of the Illinois Public Aid Commission, Swank was never shy about discussing his views on birth control and public funds. As IPAC assistant executive secretary in charge of down-state, Swank often told his regional directors that he considered birth control services a legitimate public aid medical expense.

Now, after several weeks in the executive secretary's chair, Swank told the *Daily News*: "I want to do some further exploring to find out what other states offer. Assuming the facts I gather don't alter my position, I will go to the commission and ask them to authorize referrals to Planned Parenthood or any other private facility offering these services."

And what about reimbursement for the care of welfare recipients? "I would classify this as an appropriate medical cost," Swank said.

With these words, Swank gave a giant boost to a persistent band of Chicago area men and women determined to make birth control a part of public welfare policy.

---

Lois Wille started something.

In the Illinois legislature, there was a vigorous discussion of tax-supported birth control services which wound up initially in a strange compromise. The legislature itself took no action, resorting to a typical maneuver of the fainthearted. But it made no objection to the issuance of an administrative order providing state birth control services to all women on public assistance who live with their legal husbands.

A struggle began almost immediately to broaden the program, so that Chicago's Board of Health could offer birth control services. Mayor Richard J. Daley of Chicago, who had been inflexibly against birth control services in 1962, was beginning to change his mind by 1965. He was willing to discuss a study of family planning and suggest that the Chicago Board of Health look into it. "Even the Vatican is talking about it," he said.[10]

The big secret was a secret no more in Chicago.

## 16. THE MILLIONAIRES' DINNER

Representative Joseph W. Martin Jr., the Republican powerhouse from Massachusetts, was a fixture in Washington for more than two generations. He served successively from the 69th to the 89th Congress. For twenty years he was the Republican leader of the House and twice was its Speaker. With Bruce Barton and Representative Hamilton Fish, he also gained a curious distinction at the hands of Franklin D. Roosevelt

[10] Letter from Lois Wille, Jan. 22, 1965.

by being made the senior member of a firm of political isolationists in
1940—the mythical firm of Martin, Barton, and Fish.[11]

It was fitting, therefore, that a company of enthusiastic Texas millionaires should want to make him the guest of honor at a dinner in
1958. But when Edward T. Folliard heard about it, he raised the question of whether it was proper.

Folliard, like Joe Martin, was a Washington institution—the White
House correspondent of the Washington *Post*, a Pulitzer Prize winner
in 1947 for his exposure of a Southern "hate" society, the Columbians,
and a hard man to beat to a good story. Almost instinctively, he knew
the millionaires' dinner for Martin was worth investigating. When
Martin took off for Houston to enjoy his party, therefore, a surprise
was waiting for him. Folliard went to Houston, too, to cover the serving of the ceremonial meat and potatoes.

What happened is best told in the Washington *Post*, February 11,
1958, the essential part of which follows.

## A FAVOR FOR JOE

### By Edward T. Folliard

HOUSTON—Texas Republicans raised close to $100,000 last night with
a $100-a-plate "appreciation dinner" here for Rep. Joseph W. Martin
Jr., Republican leader of the House, from Massachusetts.

The Texans were showing their appreciation for past favors Martin
had done for them in Washington and for one they hope he will perform this year. They were counting on him to crack the party whip and
help put through a bill that would enrich many of them—a bill to ease
federal control over producers of natural gas.

Opponents of the bill in the House say that it would give the producers of natural gas an extra billion dollars a year, at the expense of
householders and other users of gas that is carried northward in pipe-
lines.

The 500 or so Texans at the dinner, held in the Crystal Ballroom of
the Houston Rice Hotel, were reminded in advance that "Joe Martin
has always been a friend of Texas, especially of the oil and gas produc-

[11] Robert E. Sherwood, *Roosevelt and Hopkins* (New York, Harpers, 1948) pp.
189–90.

ing industries." They were told how he lined up two-thirds of House Republicans behind the gas bill in 1952 and 1955.

They were told, too, that it will be up to Joe to rally his GOP forces behind the gas bill again this year, even if he has to put Northern and Eastern Republicans "on the spot" politically. H. J. (Jack) Porter, Republican National Committeeman for Texas, said that 1,000 tickets were sold for the dinner at $100 apiece. The $100,000 will be used in part to help elect Republicans to the Senate and House this year.

The extraordinary thing about the dinner, however, was the promise held out to those who were asked to attend. It was a promise that Martin again would throw his power and influence behind legislation that would help the Lone Star State in general and its well-heeled gas producers in particular. All of this was in letters sent out by Republican National Committeeman Porter.

One typical letter told of plans for the appreciation dinner and went on to explain how Martin had always been a friend of Texas and especially of its biggest and richest industries, those producing oil and gas. At the dinner there were as many multimillionaires among the guests as there were waitresses serving the $100-a-plate beefsteak dinner.

The so-called gas bill, which is really an amendment to the Natural Gas Act of 1928, is one of the most controversial measures in Congress and has been for a long time. Both the Senate and House passed such a bill in 1952. However, President Truman vetoed it, saying it was not in the public's interest. In 1955 President Eisenhower also vetoed the bill. He sent to Congress an angry message denouncing the "arrogant" activities of those who had lobbied for the bill. But he told Congress that he wanted to make it "quite clear" that there ought to be some legislation conforming to the basic objectives of the bill he was vetoing.

---

On the afternoon of the day that Folliard's account of the Houston dinner was published on Page 1 of the Washington *Post*, the gas bill was defeated. The great Texan, Speaker Sam Rayburn, gave the verdict for posterity: "The gas bill is as dead as slavery." Just what happened to the $100,000 was never formally announced, but the Republican National Commitee declined for the record to accept it. As for Joe Martin himself, his political fortunes declined. He was beaten for the

post of Republican leader of the House by Rep. Charles A. Halleck
of Indiana, a member of another celebrated Republican act, the "Ev
and Charlie" show.[12] The old Speaker, however, resumed his seat in the
89th Congress.

As for Ed Folliard, he went on to cover the thirty-sixth President,
Lyndon B. Johnson, following his election in 1964 to a full term in
office, but always took time out to observe a bit of ceremony. At the
opening of the 89th Congress, as at every other, Rep. Oren Harris (D–
Ark.), chairman of the House Committee on Interstate and Foreign
Commerce, introduced the same old gas bill. Nothing was expected to
come of it. Hadn't Mr. Sam himself said it was as dead as slavery?

"If Mr. Sam were alive today," Folliard commented, "he would probably say the same thing."


## 17. A MIGRANT AND HIS WORK

The plight of the migrant workers, who roam the eastern and southern
farmlands in season wherever they can find someone to pay them a few
dollars, has excited the compassion and the sympathy of many a newspaperman. But only a handful have tried to do something about it.

Allan Keller, for many years an outstanding reporter and feature
writer for the New York *World-Telegram and Sun,* wrote a scorching
series in 1953, documenting how the migrants were misused and cheated.
Keller succeeded in focusing public attention on their plight, and
remedial legislation resulted, but in a few years the problem was as
vexing as ever.

Howard Van Smith of the Miami *News,* visiting a migrants' camp at
Immokalee, Florida, in the winter of 1958, found 4,000 workers stranded
and at the point of starvation. A January freeze had wiped out crops
and there was nothing for the migrants to do. They lived in shacks, set
in filthy surroundings, and some were selling their personal belongings
for food. Smith's story resulted in immediate official action. Moreover,

---

[12] So called because Senator Everett McKinley Dirksen, the Republican leader of
the Senate, and Halleck gave periodic reports by radio and occasionally on television.
When Halleck lost his leadership at the opening of the 89th Congress to Representative Gerald R. Ford Jr., of Michigan, the "Ev and Charlie" show folded. Its notices
had never been too good.

the reporter's work attracted such wide attention that more than $100,-000 was raised to relieve the migrants' plight. He won a Pulitzer Prize in 1959, as a result.

In April, 1961, the New York *World-Telegram and Sun* again attacked the migrant problem. This time, a 36-year-old reporter and Marine Corps combat veteran, Dale Wright, was assigned to do the job. At his own suggestion, he went south that spring to work in the fields as a migrant to see for himself how bad the situation really was.

Wright was a first-rate newspaperman—husky, reserved, quiet-voiced, and studious in appearance. He had been born in Monongahela, Pennsylvania, and moved with his family to Canton, Ohio, when he was 15 years old. He was in the Marines for forty months, seventeen of them in the Pacific, beginning in 1943. When he returned to civilian life, he entered the Ohio State University School of Journalism and received his degree in 1950. Then came ten years as a reporter and editor on papers in Columbus, Ohio, and New York. He was associate editor of *Ebony* and the New York chief of bureau for *Jet* before joining the *World-Telegram and Sun* in 1960.

On his migrant labor assignment, he worked for twelve to fourteen hours a day in the fields under a pitiless sun from April until August 30, picking potatoes in Florida, corn in Carolina, peas in New Jersey, and potatoes in Long Island. Often, he ran into dangerous situations. Once, in Hastings, Florida, he found there was no crop and no job and left a dismayed gang of migrant workers to walk down the road toward town. The farm boss warned him, "Boy, I wouldn't do that. The police will work you over if you hang around town and make trouble. If they don't get you, I will myself."

As Wright put it, "Like everybody else, I was tired, depressed, and hungry. The only difference was that I could walk out and they could not."

He came home only once during his long effort with the migrants in order to see his wife, Dolores, and their small son. But whenever he could, he mailed his notes back to the office. In September, he began writing a ten-part series that shocked even hardened New Yorkers. This was one of his pieces from the New York *World-Telegram and Sun*, October 11, 1961.

## "I GOTTA KEEP PICKIN' TOMATOES . . ."
### *By Dale Wright*

On a warm, humid morning last April, a rickety old bus jolted along at its top speed between rows of carefully manicured estates along Route 1 from Miami south to Homestead, Florida. Although the vehicle had seats for thirty-five persons, it was crammed with sixty-four passengers.

I was one of them.

I was on my way to my first day of work as a migrant farm laborer in the lush tomato fields of southern Dade County. I had shaped up (reported for assignment) earlier that morning on a Miami street corner and was hired—with no questions asked—by a fat character known as a "labor contractor."

In the South, labor contractors round up crews of workers for transport and assignment to farms where crops are to be harvested.

"Everybody that gets on this bus," he promised reassuringly, "makes $10, $12, $15 today if you want to work. There's plenty of tomatoes to pick and there will be no cheating, nothin' taken out of your pay. And it will be clean work."

His pitch sounded good but I wanted to see for myself. The smirks on the faces of the seasoned migrant workers around me raised my doubts.

In a vast patch of ground outside Homestead our crew joined about 150 other farm workers. They were busy when we arrived gathering a crop of "red ripes," tomatoes ready that day for shipment to the markets and canneries. It was just after daybreak and a bright sun already had begun to broil the pickers as they stooped in the long rows.

The job was to pick and pack the tomatoes into baskets that contained five-eighths of a bushel. Each loaded basket weighed sixty pounds. When we had them filled we lugged them to the end of the row where they were loaded onto trucks. Pay promised was 12 cents a basket.

In the row next to mine, an emaciated man of about 40 coughed and spat incessantly as he bent to his task. When I noticed the blood and spoke to him about it, he muttered,

"Yeah, they say it's consumption. It don't make no difference. I gotta keep working. The doctor, he can't do nothin' for me. I got no money

## FOR THE MIGRATORY FARM WORKER

Dale Wright (center), then a New York *World-Telegram and Sun* reporter,
worked with the migrants to learn their problems at first hand in 1961.
He is shown here picking tomatoes on an eastern farm.

for medicine. I got a woman and a lotta kids. I gotta keep pickin' tomatoes."

Obviously, the man was seriously ill and belonged in a hospital. But he was trapped by the need to work for his family in the only job he knew how to do. Later, when we stood up to smoke a cigarette, he said to me:

"Been doin' farm work all my life. Don't know nothin' else. I can't go to a hospital. Kids gotta eat."

He said his name was Alonzo and that he lived in a tin and tarpaper shack near Goulds, Florida, for which he paid $10 a week rent. He added that three of his children—the small ones—had dry, hacking coughs and probably had caught the misery he had in his chest.

Medical treatment? No. None of the youngsters had ever seen a doctor.

Despite his illness Alonzo was a hard worker. As we worked along the endless rows of tomato plants, he loaded basket after basket of tomatoes and was soon far down the field from me. Later that day Alonzo told me he soon would be moving north from Homestead because the harvest was "going down." To keep living, he explained, he'd have to load his family and his belongings on a truck or bus going North, where other crops were ripening.

"It's the same," he said. "This job is just like the last one. Next be just like this one. Never no different. Never will be."

This sick, frustrated laborer, doomed long before his time, was summing up the lot of today's migrant farm worker. The back-breaking labor of stooping close to the orange-tinted Florida earth begins as soon as a picker can distinguish red tomatoes from green ones in the gray dawn of an endless day. His work ends when he no longer can see the tomatoes to pick them. At the promised rate of 12 cents a basket, a good picker can fill seventy to eighty baskets a day and earn—it says there— from $8.40 to $9.60 a day.

As bad as that kind of pay is, it generally worked out that the man in the fields received considerably less than the promised rate. Often the rate dropped on payday to 8 cents a basket and the field hand who actually "took home" $7 a day for his work considered himself lucky.

On my first day in the fields, I worked ten hours with only a fifteen-minute break for what they called lunch. It was the hardest, most punishing work I had ever done. In the first hours of that miserable day, my hands became grimy and encrusted with the green insecticide they spray on tomatoes. It covered my khaki pants and ate its way into my legs. It collected under my fingernails, covered my shoes and socks, and festered in the scratches I received.

But picking tomatoes was the easy part of the job. The hard part was lugging the heavy baskets to the end of the rows—often as far as 150 feet—to be loaded onto the trucks. All around me were men and women, all ages, dragging themselves along the rows on their hands and knees in near 90-degree heat.

Toilet facilities? There were none. The pickers, male and female, used the field whenever they found it necessary. It was more than a mile to the nearest clump of trees.

That lunch I spoke of? A little before noon a battered pickup truck drove into the fields. The meal consisted of greasy sausage sandwiches and warm soft drinks. The sandwiches cost 35 cents and the drinks 20 cents.

Drinking water was dispensed from a wooden barrel. We dipped our water with a sawed-off tomato can shared by some 200 other migrant laborers toiling in the fields. Because the barrel was in the middle of the field, thirsty workers had to walk as much as half a mile for a drink of water.

As I figured it that first day, we picked more than 5,000 baskets of tomatoes. After ten hours of stooping, squatting, crawling, picking, and loading, I'd earned just $4.32. Many of the men and women working with me had earned less.

---

These were the "forgotten people," as Dale Wright saw them. After the series was published, he said, "I hope it does some good. These people have nobody to speak for them." He won the 1961 Heywood Broun Award, later went into government work, and in 1965 was with the National Broadcasting Company in Washington. Like those who had tried before him, he knew that it would take many years and much more effort to bring about substantial reforms in the treatment of migrant workers.

## 18. INSIDE WELFARE

A new caseworker joined the Erie County Welfare Department in Buffalo, New York, in 1960. He gave his name as E. Prett May, his age as 30, and his previous employment as the Buffalo *Evening News*. Had his application been given a routine check, he would have been identified quickly as Edgar May, a reporter for the newspaper. But there was no check. Consequently, May worked for the department for three months and thus had a rare opportunity to study welfare problems from the inside.

The Buffalo *Evening News* did not want a stunt. Nor was May a stunt reporter. He was a serious, hard-working, naturalized American, born in Zurich, Switzerland, and educated at Columbia and Northwestern. He had obtained his B.S. in journalism from the latter university in 1957. During the following year, he joined the Buffalo *Evening News*.

May's experiences as a case worker became the basis for a fourteen-part series in his newspaper, entitled, "Our Costly Dilemma." Other members of the *News* staff, and its Washington and Albany bureaus, contributed information, as did veteran caseworkers and the local welfare commissioner. It was, therefore, scarcely an exposé in the familiar sense, but a well-documented study of a welfare department operating under enormous difficulties.

Overloaded caseworkers, relief recipients who hadn't been visited in three years, and deficient records were a part of the story. The rest showed how neglect had contributed to a departmental operation that was scarcely a credit to New York state. This is one of May's articles, slightly condensed, for the Buffalo *Evening News* in 1960.

### CAUGHT IN A PAPER JUNGLE
#### By Ed May

In a gray filing cabinet in the office of the Erie County Welfare Department where I worked there are supplies of forms that include a list of 65 different ones most frequently used by the caseworkers.

Each, used in duplicate or triplicate, serves a particular function in the paper empire that has grown with the administration of public welfare.

For example, it took 24 separate pieces of paper to give one of my relief recipients her first check. There are similar file cabinets and the same array of forms in welfare offices throughout the state.

Every form has a code number that has helped create a kind of numerical agency jargon. For example:

I had a case where the client didn't sign the K-173. This was spotted by the accounting department, and the clerk sent back the PA-14, the PA-16, the K-174, as well as the unsigned K-173 and a K-387 (a pink slip) telling me why the whole thing was rejected.

A caseworker may give away between $100,000 and $150,000 of your tax dollars in one year, but the bus tokens he uses for transportation in his work are individually recorded—including the name of the bus route. This is a two-stage operation which requires a bus fare report and then a bus fare claim. A trip to visit one welfare recipient is recorded like this:

| Date | From | To | Bus Line | No. of Fares |
|------|------|-----|----------|--------------|
| 1/13 | 200 Genesee | 200 Genesee | Genesee | 1 |
| 1/13 | 210 Pearl | 210 Pearl | Genesee | 1 |

Transfers are jotted down separately.

At the end of the month, the entries on the bus fare report (filled out in duplicate) are tallied and submitted on the bus fare forms. The department head then certifies that "the number of fares claimed in the account were actually and necessarily used by the claimant in the performance of his duties."

The claimant—i.e., the caseworker—then signs a 146-word certificate which begins:

"I, the undersigned, hereby certify that the labor or services, merchandise, materials, or articles changed in the within account or claim, payment of which is hereby acknowledged, actually have been performed, made, or delivered for the County of Erie," etc.

In a week or two your bus tokens are returned in a check.

The majority of forms are an outgrowth of federal, state, as well as county regulations which, caseworkers maintain, increase at a faster rate than garden weeds. All of these are collected in a 248-page single-spaced anthology called *The Public Assistance Manual.*

Two weeks after I was assigned to my unit I was asked to close a case because the client died. The rule book was very specific.

"Before the caseworker officially closes a case, he shall dictate a closing summary according to the following outlines":

It then listed eight points including these:

—Discussion of relief plans.

—Discussion of any social or health problems and treatment given.

—Any understanding with the client at the time of closing.

Remember, the client died.

Because there are five different categories of assistance, there are five different sets of rules and, sometimes, separate forms for each.

In January, for example, I was faced with this problem.

Mr. and Mrs. K., receiving old-age assistance to supplement their Social Security, notified the Welfare Department that on December 1 they moved to a new apartment where the rent was $8.80 higher. I had to change the address and give them $8.80 for two months because it wasn't included in their December and January grants.

Although Mr. and Mrs. K. are husband and wife, live in the same place, and receive identical grants of $25 a month, old-age assistance lists them as separate cases, so everything had to be filled out twice. This operation required 22 pieces of paper. Four checks (beside the regular monthly ones), four envelopes, and four 4-cent stamps are not counted in this total.

What is the result of all this maze of paper work?

My co-workers and I spent between 50 and 60 percent of our time in the office making out various forms. This left too few working hours to go into "territory" and visit clients.

"You've got to make up your mind," I was told when I first started. "You're either going to be behind in your paper work or in your home calls."

This paper jungle, combined with the high caseloads, has brought an air of hopelessness and has embittered more than a few who are charged with helping the needy. Because of the volume of paper work and the complexities that surround each client's budget, mistakes are easily made.

For example, a caseworker knew one of her clients was drawing $42 weekly disability benefits. But on the budget it showed up as $42 monthly. The "administrative error" cost the taxpayers $140 in one month.

One of my cases listed a food and clothing allowance of $39.95 monthly. It should have been $35.95. It continued for a year undetected and cost a needless $48.

Another included a special transportation allowance to a training school which was supposed to be in the budget for October, 1959, only. Last April, when all budgets received their semiannual review, the "one month" allowance was still part of the check although the client had quit school long ago.

What is the total of these wasted dollars? Some claim it runs into the thousands in Erie County alone. Across the state the figure has been pegged in the millions. One thing is clear: It takes only a handful of "administrative errors" to equal the $4,200 salary of an extra caseworker.

---

When the series was concluded, Commissioner Raymond W. Houston of the New York State Department of Social Welfare nominated May for a Pulitzer Prize.

"The Commissioner of the Erie County Welfare Department issued a 34-point reform program as a direct result of the series," Commissioner Houston wrote. "Many suggestions, such as increasing the number of caseworkers, lowering caseloads, and adding employment counselors have already been implemented. Distribution and interest in the articles caused them to be sent to schools, legislators, and Welfare Departments in all parts of the country."

May won a Pulitzer Prize in 1961. A member of the Pulitzer Advisory Board, in a completely unofficial pronouncement, suggested that Commissioner Houston deserved one, too, had he been eligible. It is a rare public official who appreciates criticism, however constructive, and takes immediate steps to implement it.

Four years later, May was in a position to know at first hand. He was a government official himself in the fight on poverty.

# IV. THIS IS
## PUBLIC SERVICE

When the news wires broke the Pulitzer Prize awards to the nation on May 2, 1960, the Atlanta *Constitution*'s Jack Nelson was among the winners. He was cited for his "excellent reporting on mental institutions in Georgia," received a handsome certificate for distinguished local reporting and a check for $1,000.

Normally, that would be the end of the story. But for the *Constitution*, it was the beginning. True, the newspaper had exposed shocking conditions at Milledgeville State Hospital, Georgia's enormous institution for the mentally ill. True, it had won the gratitude and the respect of physicians, psychiatrists, and the public at large and set in motion creaking state machinery for reform. But after the excitement over the Pulitzer Prize died down, it became clear that Milledgeville wasn't going to be reformed overnight.

The *Constitution* had a choice. A newspaper always has. It could have done something· more exciting, more pleasant, more beneficial to its circulation figures. It could have pointed to Jack Nelson's award as sufficient proof for its concern over Milledgeville. After all, every newspaperman knows an exposé isn't very exciting when it is done a second time, let alone a second year. The follow-up story, when and if it happens, therefore becomes a bored brush-off, as a rule.

That, however, was not what happened at Milledgeville. The *Constitution* sent Jack Nelson back to maintain public pressure for reform. And four years later, the newspaper and its editorial writers, its news executives, and its reporters were still hammering away at their thankless task, producing editorial headaches rather than sensations, columns of statistics rather than flaring headlines, painfully slow progress rather than wishful thinking that a major public responsibility can be met with a single crusade, no matter how brilliant.

In so doing, the *Constitution* underscored a growing feeling among responsible American newspapers that the problems of mental health—in common with other difficult areas of major public concern—could not be handled in the same old way. If there was to be reform, there had to be public understanding of the necessity for it. And that, inevitably, would take a long time, whatever the advantages of an initial exposé for its impact.

The theory and practice of the continuing campaign, as it developed in the *Constitution*, represented a profound break with much past newspaper practice in the handling of news of mental health. While other leading newspapers had made similar efforts, some with good results, few had been as effectively sustained, and none had begun in earnest with the award of a Pulitzer Prize.

For 250 years or more, the unmanaged or mismanaged institution for the mentally ill had been a happy hunting ground for the sensational journalist, and some of more sober mien, as well. As early as 1699, the rakish Ned Ward had written in the London *Spy* of appalling conditions at London's Bedlam, the worst mental institution of its time in England: "All I can say of it is this: 'Tis an almshouse for madmen, a showing room for whores, a sure market for lechers, and a dry walk for loiterers." [1]

In his *American Notes*, the fastidious Charles Dickens did not scruple to try to shock and titillate his readers with old-fashioned cliché-writing about the mentally ill that could scarcely find a place in a tabloid today. He wrote, with all stops out, about the "gibbering maniac with his hideous laugh and pointed finger; the vacant eye, the fierce wild face, the gloomy picking of the hands and lips and munching of nails."

In any event, since the days of Dickens, journalists in the United States have examined mental institutions from time to time, many for whatever sensation they could wring out of it, some with serious intent, a few for effective reforms. The story is still going around (and it is perfectly true) about the reporter who posed as a derelict, had himself voluntarily committed, announced after two weeks that he had re-

[1] London *Spy*, January, 1699, quoted in Louis L. Snyder and Richard B. Morris, A *Treasury of Great Reporting* (New York, Simon and Schuster, 1949), p. 8.

covered his sanity and wanted to leave, and was put at once in a strait jacket.

It took a long time for most editors to realize that the best-qualified crusaders for the reform of mental institutions were generally those who knew the most about it—the officials who had to live in them and administer them, generally with inadequate space, insufficient help, and woefully little money. That was the strength of the *Constitution's* position when it first began its inquiry.

For awhile, there was progress. But as public attention was permitted to slip away from Milledgeville, the reform movement lost its zip. Official attention wandered. And so, Jack Nelson went back to Milledgeville four years after winning his Pulitzer Prize award and learned that the job was far from finished. Once more, the newspaper and its editors and its investigatory reporter devoted their best efforts to a continuing examination of the great state hospital's problems. And once more, there was progress.

The *Constitution* was not alone in its development of the sustained campaign.

One of the most celebrated has been the long crusade against pollution of water and air in the New York metropolitan area, begun many years ago by the New York *World-Telegram and Sun.* During the campaign, Murray Davis, one of the city's veteran investigatory reporters, became an expert on pollution and wrote and lectured exhaustively on the subject before professional and lay groups. Even after Davis' departure from the staff the battle continued. The cause was taken up by others. Government agencies began emphasizing the seriousness of the problem in New York's waters. And at length, toward the end of 1964, Governor Rockefeller advanced a comprehensive program to combat pollution and asked the state legislature to do something about it.

The Nashville *Tennessean,* disturbed over what it considered the mishandling of absentee ballots for years, finally uncovered a major vote fraud in the Second Ward of Nashville in May, 1962. As a result of a continuing investigation, six men were convicted and sentenced for conspiracy and the state legislature enacted tighter election laws which took effect in 1964. Through a shorter but no less intensive investigation, the Charlotte *Observer* was able to convince the North Carolina legislature, too, that tighter absentee voting laws would have to be enacted.

## HELP CAME TOO LATE

William Seaman's 1959 Pulitzer Prize picture—a grim comment on the constant crusade for traffic safety.

In another area of importance, there was a notable advance in the willingness of newspapers to lead campaigns for civic redevelopment and advocate the issuance of bonds to help pay for the costs of such necessary urban renewal programs. One of the models for this type of activity was developed by the St. Louis *Post-Dispatch* with an impressive campaign for the adoption of bond issues. The newspaper's drive for public acceptance was notable because, when the bond proposal first was placed before the voters, it was defeated. Even so, the *Post-Dispatch* refused to give up. It renewed the campaign, demanding another vote on the same issue. This time, it put out a two-part Special Progress section, effectively printed in color, and carefully explored the need for each proposed public improvement. Each day it ran explanatory articles, with supporting editorials. The result was that the citizens of St. Louis were persuaded to adopt the bond program which they had at first rejected.

This kind of editorial leadership was also provided in a number of other communities with similar problems, notably Philadelphia, Baltimore, Detroit, Chicago, Louisville, Cleveland, Salt Lake City, Charlotte, Cincinnati, and elsewhere. It wasn't easy, by any means, for newspapers in these cities to take the lead in favor of unpopular urban renewal campaigns, particularly where the public was sharply divided. And it was also expensive, with no hope of any immediate return.

The field of legislative reapportionment, a forbidding one for the average newspaper of modest resources, attracted a substantial amount of sustained campaigning in various parts of the country. It could be expected that large, powerful papers in the big cities would support the U. S. Supreme Court's decision to eliminate the disparity that generally existed betwen the underrepresented cities and the overrepresented rural areas. But smaller newspapers such as the Hutchinson *News* in Kansas, the Monterey *Peninsula Herald* in California, the Asbury Park *Press* in New Jersey, and the Hartford *Times* in Connecticut also played key roles in the redistricting efforts in their respective states. As time went on, it was certain that more such campaigns would finally pay off.

There have been a variety of other long-term campaigns in recent years. The newspapers of Washington, D.C., crusaded for many years for the right of the citizens of the District of Columbia to vote in presidential elections and finally succeeded. The Miami *Herald*, soon after Fidel Castro's terrorists stimulated a mass flight from Cuba, inaugurated Operation Amigo, a friendly effort to help refugee Cubans in the United States. *Newsday*, of Garden City, New York, successfully campaigned for a new charter for populous Suffolk County on the eastern end of Long Island and helped in the process to throw out a Republican machine that had dominated the county for decades. The Louisville *Courier-Journal* devoted a major effort to the cleanup of the crime-ridden gambling center, Newport, Kentucky. Necessarily, the role of the newspapers in the long and agonizing effort to attain civil rights in the South, particularly those Southern newspapers that had the courage to stand for progress, was of enormous importance to the movement as a whole.

The long-term activity of the newspapers in the public interest, significant though it was, scarcely reflected the depth of national interest in public service journalism and the ever-widening scope of the press's efforts. Very little of the work was calculated to pile on circulation through old-fashioned garlands of headlines. If it did happen, it was usually an accident. For there was precious little sensation to be found in urban renewal, science in industry, health problems, conservation of parklands, problems of minorities other than Negroes, traffic safety, water conservation, and the vicissitudes of labor unions, to mention only a few campaign themes.

Such worth-while understakings could rarely be considered a good short-term investment for a newspaper. The drain on the staff was too heavy. The cost was too great. And, unhappily, there could never be any guarantee of success for even the best-planned campaign. Many of them were bound to end in failure and a consequent blow to the prestige of the paper, but that was the risk any editor had to take unless he wanted to publish a shopping throwaway or the kind of a paper that reported a prominent citizen "died suddenly" when everybody knew he had jumped out a window.

As was the case with the sustained campaigns, those of shorter duration also were heavily involved in the cause of good government—accompanied by exposés of bad government, misgovernment, and nongovernment. In 1964, for instance, the New York *Herald Tribune* exposed the outside business interests of some members of the state legislature and may even have helped to defeat some of them. The San Jose *News* delved into a pattern of influence that had been exerted in California's state government. The Boston *Globe* did a series on "Reform in Massachusetts," certainly long overdue, and the Charleston *Mail* exposed "mystery companies" that were doing business with West Virginia's state government. Perhaps the most difficult feat in this area was the *Wall Street Journal*'s carefully documented account of the outside business interest of some federal judges, a forbidding but important subject.

There were other picturesque public service projects. The Cleveland *Plain Dealer* played a major part in the investigation and subsequent conviction of the Cuyahoga County Recorder. The Dallas *Morning News* conducted a detailed inquiry into a railroad commissioner's outside oil interests. The Nashville *Tennessean* exposed workhouse conditions in Nashville through the efforts of John W. Hemphill Jr., who became a voluntary prisoner to do the job. Another reporter, Rodney E. Wenz, finding employment as a psychiatric aid, helped the Rockford *Register-Republic* achieve reforms in an Illinois institution for the mentally retarded.

Some newspapers tackled even more complicated subjects. *Newsday,* of Garden City, New York, ran a long-distance investigation of land sales and was able to spring a trap on some Florida and Arizona land-by-mail promoters, forcing many of them out of business. The Miami *News* investigated alleged irregularities in Florida auto insurance. The Flint *Journal* attacked alleged fraud in a Michigan water supply project. The Oakland *Tribune* and other papers in the San Francisco Bay area campaigned to halt the filling of San Francisco Bay. One of the most complex of all subjects, the national wheat referendum, was explained for city folk by Richard Orr, farm editor of the Chicago *Tribune*.

Some newspapers were content to achieve relatively small victories which were, nevertheless, of benefit to their communities. Thus, the Clinton *Herald* raised funds to remodel and save the only hospital in Clinton, Iowa. The Duluth *Herald and News-Tribune* led a successful drive for a new auditorium. The Gainesville (Fla.) *Sun* fought and won a campaign for better housing. The High Point (N.C.) *Enterprise* successfully campaigned for a school lunch program. The Kansas City *Star* learned that some psychiatric patients had been put in jail for lack of rooms in hospitals and succeeded in halting the practice. The New York *Journal-American*, in two days, persuaded the New York City authorities to rename Idlewild Airport in honor of John F. Kennedy. The Ogdensburg *Journal* battled for and restored regular airline service for its area in New York. The Orlando (Fla.) *Sentinel* put on a successful drive for a theater-convention hall.

These were some of the things newspapers conceived to be in the public interest, aside from the long-term campaigning in which so many others were involved. It did not mean, of course, that all newspapers in the United States were activated by such ideals or, even if they professed to believe in them, that they practiced them. But there was an impressive volume of evidence to establish, without question, that American editors and publishers were placing a very high value on the good will of those who bought more than 60,000,000 newspapers a day in the United States.

And if any reader wanted to know what an editor meant by public service, this was it. In the section that follows, both newspapers and their reporters show in some detail how it was accomplished.

## 19. FOUR YEARS AFTER REFORM

When Jack Nelson returned to Milledgeville State Hospital in Georgia four years after winning a Pulitzer Prize for helping achieve substantial reforms, he was disheartened at first by what he saw. He wrote in the Atlanta *Constitution:*

"You think of the 4,800 deaths and 23,759 admissions at Milledgeville State Hospital since you first visited there five years ago.

"You get lost in a deluge of figures saying there are 12,055 patients in the hospital, 6,000 more on furlough, 3,000 seniles, 2,000 mentally retarded, etc. And you begin to think of mental illness only in cold statistical terms: One in every ten will require treatment in a mental hospital. Half the nation's hospital beds are occupied by mental patients.

"It all seems so impersonal."

It wasn't so impersonal to those who had known the enormous toll of mental illness, who had been close to its victims, who had experienced its manifold and spreading tragedy. Nelson found out about that quickly enough. He learned, too, that Georgia's story was not unique; wherever such gigantic facilities for the mentally ill existed in the United States, the faults of Milledgeville were present in greater or lesser degree.

On April 5, 1964, the Atlanta *Constitution* began publishing a new series on Georgia's problem, and this was the essence of the first article.

## MILLEDGEVILLE REVISITED

### By Jack Nelson

Five years after reform Milledgeville State Hospital has:

Old women sleeping on mattresses on a concrete floor.

Beds jammed together so closely that patients have to climb over the ends when they get up.

Hundreds of patients on back wards getting little or no attention, only custodial care, because of a serious shortage of personnel.

Almost 400 Negro patients doing farm work under conditions described as "slavery" by a farm supervisor and "peonage" by the hospital superintendent.

Literally thousands of patients, seniles, and mentally retarded (officially estimated at almost 5,000), who do not really belong in a mental hospital.

But Milledgeville Hospital is as schizophrenic as many of its patients. It has another personality characterized by an improved treatment program that has shortened the stay of the average patient from a year and 19 days to 82 days. For the first time in its 121-year history the hospital has an education program for child patients.

The institution now operates an outpatient clinic where an average of 400 patients on furlough report every month for checkups and free drugs. Less than 1 percent of the outpatients fail to keep their appointments.

Many other changes, some considered almost miraculous by observers who have seen patients of more than fifteen years rehabilitated and released, have put Milledgeville on the road to an adequate treatment program. But it is a long road, made even longer by the lack of local psychiatric treatment facilities in Georgia. Most Georgia communities, particularly in metropolitan Atlanta, have refused to recognize an obligation to provide such facilities.

Meanwhile the program initiated at Milledgeville in 1959 by Dr. Irville H. MacKinnon, superintendent, has been so successful that the admission rate has doubled during the past five years. In 1958 admissions totaled 3,740; last year, they totaled 6,057. This year they are averaging 600 a month—or 7,200 a year.

In other words, while the hospital has been turning out patients faster, it has been admitting them faster. Thus, the population has remained about 12,000. In 1958 the hospital had an average of 2,500 patients on furlough; now the figure is about 6,000.

Although the readmission rate has dropped from 37 to 27 percent, the number of new patients committed to—or seeking help at—the state's only mental hospital has put an overwhelming burden on the institution.

As State Health Department Director Dr. John H. Venable says: "Every time a new patient is admitted, one has to be discharged to make room."

The hospital is more than 30 percent overcrowded. It has adequate space for only about 8,000 patients. That's why a hundred or more patients generally sleep on mattresses on the floor. Even though beds are jammed together on the wards, there are not enough beds to go around.

———

Things began to happen all over again.

Governor Sanders, like his predecessor, appointed a commission to investigate the *Constitution*'s charges. The commission, duplicating the performance of its parent group five years before, upheld the newspaper's findings and even went beyond them. It denounced overcrowding, housing of patients in firetraps, "grossly inadequate" medical and surgical facilities, a "glaring shortage" of registered nurses and inadequate sanitation.

At the end of 1964, Governor Sanders again was promising a "reasonably substantial increase" in mental health funds.[2] The Medical Association of Georgia again praised the *Constitution* and gave Nelson another award for keeping the public's attention focused on the problems of mental illness.

The *Constitution* did not make the mistake of concluding that the story was over this time. The new awards marked only the end of

[2] Jack Nelson, "Vital Mental Reforms Urged in 2 Reports," and Reg Murphy, "Sanders Raising Mental Budget," Atlanta *Constitution*, Dec. 3, 1964, p. 1.

another chapter in the continuing inquiry, not the end of the case. Even though Jack Nelson moved on to the Los Angeles *Times,* there were other reporters who took his place. The *Constitution* carried on its search for a better approach to the treatment of mental illness.


## 20. "COME UP FROM UNDERGROUND!"

Thomas More Storke hated intolerance. In his more than sixty years as an editor in Santa Barbara, California, he had come to recognize its bloodstained mask wherever he saw it. And in 1960, when he watched a sinister pattern of undercover attacks developing in his part of the world against teachers, churchmen, and government officials alike, he knew that some new senseless hate group was intent on tearing his community apart.

Before long, he learned that the campaign was being waged by the then little-known John Birch Society, which borrowed its morals from the Nazis, its tactics from the Communists, and its unholy purposes from the Ku Klux Klan. An eminent citizen, Attorney General Stanley Mosk of California, made fun of the Birchers, dismissing a section of their membership as a lot of "little old ladies in tennis shoes." But Storke remembered that Adolf Hitler once had been laughed at as a funny little man with a Charlie Chaplin moustache. The John Birch Society could not be shrugged off so lightly.

And so, in his eighty-fifth year, Thomas More Storke prepared to take on this new conspiracy against everything he respected in American life. He had often said, "I believe that the greatest sin of the American press is the sin of omission rather than the sin of commission, the sin of refusing to take a stand on issues that might become too 'hot' to handle." [3]

Storke had always been deeply concerned about anything that affected Santa Barbara. He had been born there November 23, 1876, and re- turned there after his graduation from Stanford in 1898 to begin publishing the Santa Barbara *News,* later to become the Santa Barbara *News-Press.* He had been married twice in Santa Barbara, his first wife having died, and his four children had been reared there. He didn't

[3] He said it again in his Lovejoy convocation speech at Colby College, Nov. 8, 1962, reprinted in *Nieman Reports,* December, 1962, pp. 12–13.

like what was happening now in his city and he said so with telling effect. Although the Santa Barbara *News-Press* had only about 35,000 circulation, the words of its editor on February 26, 1961 burst upon the nation with the clarity of a bugle call. This is the essential text of his first article on the John Birch Society.

## AN ATTACK ON HATRED

### By Thomas More Storke

The editor and publisher of the *News-Press* is in his eighty-fifth year. His entire life has been spent in this community. His memory takes him back many years and his reading even further. He lived when conditions were rugged. When West was West and men were men. He lived during periods when if a man or a group of men openly by word of mouth, or the printed word, called our President, our Vice-President, our Secretary of State, the President's brother, members of the Supreme Court, and others at the head of our government, traitors, they were made to answer. Such slanders often called for a visit from a courageous and irate group which brought with them a barrel of tar and a few feathers. And such instances were particularly likely to occur if the slanderer came from New England. He lived when men were considered cowards when they hid behind their women's skirts and clothed their identity through anonymity.

It is in the light of this background that the *News-Press* tells where it stands on the John Birch Society.

#### AN EDITORIAL

During recent weeks the *News-Press* has sought to enlighten its readers about a semisecret organization called the John Birch Society.

We believe that the *News-Press* has performed a public service by bringing the activities of the society to the attention of the community. Hundreds of our readers have agreed. But a newspaper would be derelict in its duty if it did not express the opinion of the way the society is organized and the tactics it employs.

First, let there be no mistake about this: Communism must be opposed vigorously. Its gains throughout vast areas of the world are shocking. Every American must be alert for Red infiltration. But that does not lead logically to the conclusion that to fight Communism at

home we must throw democratic principles and methods into the ash-
can and adopt the techniques of the Communists themselves, as the
John Birch leaders would have us do.

The *News-Press* condemns the destructive campaign of hate and
vilification that the John Birch Society is waging against national
leaders who deserve our respect and confidence.

How can anyone follow a leader absurd enough to call former President Eisenhower "a dedicated, conscious agent of the Communist conspiracy"? Those are the words of the national leader of the John Birch
Society, Robert Welch, in a manuscript entitled, "The Politician," of
which photostatic copies are available.

The *News-Press* condemns the dictatorial, undemocratic structure of
the society.

The *News-Press* condemns the tactics that have brought anonymous
telephone calls of denunciation to Santa Barbarans in recent weeks
from members of the John Birch Society or their sympathizers. Among
victims of such cowardly diatribes have been educational leaders, including faculty members of the University of California at Santa Barbara, and even ministers of the Gospel.

The *News-Press* condemns the pressures on wealthy residents, who
fear and abhor Communism, to contribute money to an organization
whose leader has said that "for reasons you will understand, there can
be no accounting of funds."

In the Blue Book, the Society's "bible," leader Welch said that the
organization needed one million members. He also said that the dues
are "whatever the member wants to make them, with a minimum of
$24 per year for men and $12 for women."

One million members, divided equally between men and women,
would bring him $18 million a year. Quite a sum to play with without
accountability!

The *News-Press* challenges members of the society to come into the
open and admit membership. A local enrollment "in the hundreds" is
claimed, but so far only a few of those who have joined the organization have been unashamed enough to admit it.

The *News-Press* challenges the responsible local leaders of the society to make themselves known.

The *News-Press* challenges them to tell their fellow citizens exactly what they are up to and specifically what program they have in mind for Santa Barbara.

The John Birch Society already has done a grave disservice to Santa Barbara by arousing suspicions and mutual distrust among men of good will. The organization's adherents, sincere in their opposition to Communism, do not seem to understand the dangers of the totalitarian dynamite with which they are tampering.

The *News-Press* challenges them: Come up from underground!

And if they believe that in being challenged they have grounds for suit—let them sue. The *News-Press* would welcome a suit as a means of shedding more light on the John Birch Society.

---

Storke's attack on the John Birch Society drew an immediate response from his city, and the state and nation as well. Many a fearful community leader gained the courage to fight back. Within a few weeks, more than 20,000 reprints of the *News-Press*'s editorials had been requested by distressed readers who told how Birchers were raising the black standard of suspicion and hate in their communities.

The Los Angeles *Times,* one of the nation's great conservative newspapers, came out with its own attack on the John Birch Society in a series by Gene Blake, beginning March 5, 1961. And on March 12, 1961, Otis Chandler, the *Times*'s youthful and energetic publisher, signed his own editorial warning, "Peril to Conservatives." In Chicago, New York, and elsewhere, other newspapers took up the battle although there were not as many as Storke would have wanted. But he was not alone.

For his newspaper's service in the public interest, Thomas More Storke was awarded the Pulitzer Prize for editorial writing in 1961. In a small community and at an advanced age, he had given leadership to a divided people and courage to the fainthearted at a time when such qualities were desperately needed. Within less than a year he was writing in the New York *Times* on December 10, 1961: "A year ago, Santa Barbara was sizzling with John Birch fever. Today the temperature of the body politic is back to normal."

There is an epilogue to the story. On March 15, 1964, in his eighty-eighth year, Storke sold his cherished *News-Press,* which he founded

with a $2,000 investment in 1900, to Robert McLean, the publisher of
the Philadelphia *Bulletin*, for nearly $10,000,000. But under the terms
of the contract, he said, "I'm staying on for life."

## 21. A CRUSADE IN KANSAS

The Hutchinson *News* undertook a difficult and unpopular campaign
in Kansas in 1961.

It found that only 27 percent of the people in the state elected a
majority of the members of its senate, that only 18 percent elected a
majority of the members of its house of representatives.

The constitutional guarantees of equal representation were being
grossly violated. In the *News*'s home county, Reno, to give only a
single instance, one house district consisted of 49,398 people, the
other 9,718 people.

Power resided, for the most part, in the state's rural areas. The cities,
in Kansas as elsewhere, were grievously underrepresented in the legislature. Consequently, many things in which the *News* believed—better
schools, more efficient local government, improved health and welfare
facilities, and the other pressing needs of an urban society—were either
being blocked or unreasonably delayed.

The men who ran the *News*—John P. Harris, board chairman, Peter
Macdonald, publisher, and John McCormally, editor—knew that they
would have to fight their own people if they made an issue of the back-
wardness of Kansas. They also realized that they would have to do
more than to run angry editorials. Therefore, the future of their paper
was at stake.

They decided to fight. What they did was in the finest traditions of
journalism in Kansas, where William Allen White is still a hallowed
name. For long in advance of the landmark Baker vs. Carr reapportionment decision of the United States Supreme Court, the Hutchinson
*News* appealed to the courts of Kansas for relief and redress.

Why did it fall to a newspaper with 52,500 circulation and modest
revenues to take on so heavy a burden? Quite simply, as Editor Mc-
Cormally put it, "No one else appeared willing or able to assume the
expense or risk the political dangers of seeking such a remedy. The

*News* concluded that it was its responsibility as a community leader to do so."

The reaction was violent. The *News* is published in a city of only 38,000 and it circulates in the surrounding rural area of Reno County that has been the most overrepresented in the legislature. The area's congressmen and other political leaders, most of the other newspapers, and a majority of the *News*'s own readers attacked its efforts.

If the Kansas newspaper's crusade was a lonely effort at the outset, its example proved to be compelling. It was joined as the years went on by other bold ones elsewhere in the land. Many a newspaper in other states, and a few pioneering radio stations, also entered the national battle for reapportionment. The United States Supreme Court decision was one of the major results.

By the end of 1964, despite all the powerful opposition that was ranged against it, the Hutchinson *News* saw victory in sight. Reasonably equal reapportionment of the state senate was won, and improvement in house reapportionment was assured through decisions in the state courts that were upheld on appeal.

But by and large, the campaign was fought out primarily in the *News*'s own columns. Here is the kind of editorial attack that Editor McCormally led, a column that was published in his newspaper on June 29, 1964.

### "IT IS A FEARSOME THING . . ."

#### *By John McCormally*

What, exactly, do the foes of reapportionment of the state legislature fear?

The Supreme Court has ruled that seats in both houses of the legislature should be based on population—that each representative should represent as nearly as practical the same number of people, so that each citizen's vote will count for as much as any other citizen's.

You'd think, from the outcries, that the court had ordered everyone to join the Democratic party, or had banned prayer in church as well as in school.

What are they afraid of—those who now frantically are crying states' rights, imploring the Founding Fathers, and castigating the court?

Why, the people, that's what they're afraid of. Ever since the first kings started toppling and the first revolutionary thoughts began to find their way into print, they've been afraid that if the people ever really got control of their own governments, all hell would break loose.

The Communists are afraid of this, just as the American colonial merchants and landlords were, and just as today's defenders of the status quo in Kansas are.

We play a little game about it. We talk about democracy. We quote Lincoln about government of, by, and for the people. We talk about the will of the people. The will of the majority.

But we don't meant it. We employ all sorts of ploys, of which legislative malapportionment is the favorite, to frustrate the majority—to make sure the people never really get in charge. We've been doing it since the revolution. (Then, ironically, it was the seaboard merchants who wanted to make sure the back country, rabble-rousing farmers didn't get control of the legislatures. Now it is the back country conservatives who are trying to keep the city folks from getting control.)

In Kansas, what are we afraid of? What would the legislature do, if city folks had more representation in it, that we don't want done?

Well, like most grave, philosophical, and patriotic questions, it comes down to money. The worry is that the representatives of the city dwellers—of laborers and slum dwellers and people with lots of kids—would want to spend a lot more money. Naturally, this would raise taxes and take more money away from those who don't live in the cities, but who have a lot of property to be taxed.

This citified legislature would want more money for schools, more for welfare, more for combating juvenile delinquency, improving law enforcement and public health. It would probably give labor a more friendly hearing and be more concerned about the victims of loan sharks. It would be interested in getting more industry into the state and providing more recreation facilities.

How successful it would be is questionable because, even with equal representation, the big cities still would control a minority of the house.

It is also not clear how costly all this would be to rural landowners. The fear seems to be that these demands of the city folks would be paid by increasing taxes on the land of the country folks. But property taxes in Kansas have been used traditionally to finance local, not state, government. The state burdens are carried increasingly by sales, income, and excise taxes. Interestingly enough, the prime movers to get even the local school burden off local real estate, and on to state-collected indirect taxes, have been the city folks—the leaders of the city schools which cannot operate on real estate levies.

It is a fearsome thing, all right, this prospect that the people might one day control their own legislatures.

---

McCormally's eloquence, and the willingness of the Hutchinson *News* to fight for an unpopular cause in its own area, went a long way toward giving Kansans a more equitably apportioned legislature. For its devotion to the public interest, the Hutchinson *News* won the Pulitzer Prize gold medal for public service for 1965. And in a typically journalistic anticlimax, McCormally moved on to another Harris newspaper, the Burlington (Iowa) *Hawkeye*.

## 22. THE FIGHT ON NARCOTICS

Most experienced newspapermen, at one time or another, have written articles on narcotics. It is usually an exercise in utter frustration. Because it is an illicit enterprise based on a disgusting habit that shocks the sensitive and outrages the moralists, very little reliable information is generally available. Even the federal and local authorities, understandably, fear to give leads that may undo months, even years, of patient investigation.

The average newspaper and magazine story about the narcotics traffic, therefore, is usually based on tales gathered from individual users, familiar descriptions from health authorities of the habit-forming properties of various drugs and, occasionally, a story about the breakup of a smuggling ring. Now and then, something slightly different will crop up—an advance in the treatment of addicts, a new twist in legislation, or a tightening of enforcement.

But for two decades or more the only basic news of the narcotics traffic has been that it is increasing in the United States, particularly among younger and less sophisticated groups. As a result, there was widespread interest in an effort that was begun by the Los Angeles

*Times* in 1959 to try to choke off at least a few of the sources of supply for narcotics users in the United States.

The *Times's* campaign was modest. Primarily, it was based on the work of one reporter, Gene Sherman, who was given seven months to conduct as thorough an investigation as was possible under the circumstances. Once he had established to the satisfaction of the editors that 50 to 75 percent of the heroin illegally used in Southern California originates in Mexico and 99 percent of the marijuana comes from the same source, The *Times* decided to try to do something about it.

In Sherman, the *Times* had a talented and experienced investigative reporter, a newspaperman since his sixteenth year and a member of the staff since 1936. He had been born in Oak Park, Illinois, in 1915, brought to Los Angeles by his parents when he was four years old, and educated in the schools there. After attending the University of Southern California, he had edited a number of weeklies. His first assignment at the *Times* had been police reporting, but he had gone on from that to cover the nation and the world, as well. He had written most of the big news of his generation for the *Times*.

When the Sherman series began, consequently, it was not limited to the usual pathetic tales about addicts that most reporters have heard for years. The *Times* put the full authority of its editorial page and all its other manifold resources behind a campaign to win greater cooperation from the Mexican government to halt the smuggling of narcotics into the United States. The attorney general of California demanded a congressional inquiry. Subcommittees of the House and Senate began conducting a new series of studies of the problem. The State Department arranged for an unprecedented meeting between members of Congress and officials of Mexico. A House resolution demanded a White House conference on narcotics.

All this was just a beginning, however. A single newspaper, no matter how powerful, could not hope to fight the whole narcotics traffic when it was plain that the resources of the government of the United States were insufficient to do the job. But the *Times* did break through the fleecy curtain of official apathy. For its efforts, the newspaper won the Pulitzer Prize gold medal for public service for 1960. This was the first article of the series that began in the Los Angeles *Times*, July 12, 1959.

## "NO FUSS, NO BOTHER . . . JUST KICKS"

### *By Gene Sherman*

It's a fourth- or fifth-class hotel on a scale that pegs a flophouse as sixth- or seventh-class—an antiquated, dingy, but curiously successful place in the southeast section of Los Angeles.

The owner is a man in his late years who enjoys a reputation as a shrewd business head. He dresses conservatively, speaks quietly, and associates socially with average people who could be your neighbors.

You may have passed the hotel without giving it a glance. By remote but not impossible coincidence, you may know the owner. His acquaintanceship includes folks like you. For years, he has been one of the city's biggest wholesale narcotics dealers. . . .

She's 17, blonde, cute. She has a winsome smile, an appealing way of tossing her pony tail hairdo, and her clear, blue eyes dance with freshness. She laughs nervously as she talks with wistful pride about her sweetheart. She tries to hide her nervousness with compulsive gaiety in her chatter, but the twisting of her fragile fingers betrays it.

The men listening to her are sympathetic. They have heard the story before. Many times.

She's telling them how her high-school friends gather at one another's house or in parked cars to smoke marijuana they buy from a man in his 20s who can be reached near the school. . . .

A plant grows in a pot in a narcotics enforcement squad room. Its leaves fan into seven long, slender, serrated segments. A healthy, rather attractive specimen of marijuana seized a few hours ago in a back yard from a boy with a long record of "growing pot."

The officer in charge looks at it glumly. Only one lousy plant. This year, due primarily to favorable climatic conditions, the marijuana crop in Mexico is excellent. The shipments into Los Angeles are so conveniently packaged. Manicured, cleaned, pressed into bricks, and wrapped in cellophane.

No fuss, no bother . . . just kicks. . . .

In a plush office in Washington, a high State Department official, flanked by two aides, talks guardedly about the narcotics traffic from Mexico. He has torn time from a schedule crowded with matters of high international significance to entertain a few academic questions about the accessibility of Mexican narcotics to Southern California.

It is a touchy subject. He does not wish to be quoted. U.S. relations· with Mexico are friendly; can we afford to jeopardize them for a purely local interest? Isn't the narcotics problem really our own, to be solved by enforcement?

Privately and off the record, the official speaks strongly about the situation. He would like to see sellers of illegal narcotics—especially to minors—sentenced to death. . . .

A man who has spent most of his federal enforcement career battling narcotics twists a glass of water idly on the luncheon table. He knows as much about the subject as anyone who has spent years in close contact with it.

But he is the kind of a man whose wisdom springs from the realization of how much he doesn't know. As do most men who deal personally with illicit narcotics on a working level, he waves aside the label of "expert."

His job, in concert with other officers from five agencies (federal, state, city police, sheriff's office, district attorney's office) is to stop dope traffic. What he and his brother officers do makes the administrators experts.

"You're confused and floundering?" he repeats. "Let me tell you something—everyone in this business, including the heads of all agencies, is just as confused. They're all floundering."

The truth of that statement becomes increasingly evident the longer one delves into the problem and the more he talks with persons concerned with it. Eventually he becomes absolutely positive of only one fact:

There is a serious illicit narcotics problem.

Even attempting to prove the problem, let alone finding its root, is an indefinite undertaking. Statistics, in the opinion of informed officials, are at best indications irritatingly inconclusive. This is patent in their confusing variance, according to the source. Ask any agent how many addicts there are in Los Angeles and he'll confess to only a guess. Ask how many dope peddlers ply their infamous trade and the answer is also a guess.

Only the most naïve interrogator would ask how much heroin or marijuana comes into the city, state, or country. No one knows. They can only add up the amounts seized from time to time.

The Federal Bureau of Narcotics estimates there are 6,214 addicts in California, or 13 percent of the total in the country. That's the official figure for congressional assimilation and it's ludicrously precise.

But local enforcement agencies laugh at the estimate. The number of addicts in Southern California alone is estimated by different sources at from 10,000 to 40,000—but how can you really tell?

Millions of words have been written on the dope peril by both irresponsible and conscientious pens. The problem has been magnified and dramatized beyond all reason and—even more surprising—has been minimized to trivia.

Because it is a shadowy business and the filthiest, most reprehensible of rackets, it is a subject with which writers of fact and fiction can command attention and politicians can decry with great, passive righteousness.

This is not to belittle the serious attempts to attack the problem which have resulted in medical treatment and legislation to reduce addiction and illicit peddling. It simply is to point out that the subject of narcotics is so foreign, mysterious, and far removed from the average, normal person, so cloaked in mystery and lacking clear definition, that it readily can be adopted as an issue by those who wish to shock, sensationalize, or promote without too much fear of contradiction.

In a way, it's like the automobile traffic problem. Everybody is against it and views it with horror, but nobody agrees what to do about it. Except eliminate it, some way. . . .

Like the cancer it is, the illicit narcotics problem spreads with deadly, insidious certainty from its origin. Nationally the origin may be Communist China, Europe, or the Middle East. In Los Angeles, it primarily is Mexico.

---

The *Times*'s campaign produced results over a period of years. In 1961, the California Legislature tightened penalties for narcotics violators and Governor Brown created a federal-state-local task force with instructions to act on both sides of the Mexican border, if they found it possible. President Kennedy, who had campaigned in California with a promise to call a White House conference on narcotics, did so on September 27-28, 1962. Thus, the President's Advisory Commission on Narcotics and Drugs Abuse was created. In the following year, the advisory group urged establishment of a United States–Mexico Commission, a proposal which was put before Congress for endorsement. By 1965, the bi-national commission was a step closer to reality.

Following the Los Angeles *Times*'s campaign, a number of other major newspapers published long individual articles or series on the problem of enforcement to cut down the narcotics traffic. The New York *Times* early in 1965 reported that the New York Police Department had called the use of and traffic in narcotics its No. 1 problem. Although New York was without doubt the center for most addicts in the nation, it was difficult to estimate even the approximate number of users in the city with any degree of reliability. The New York *Times* on January 4, 1965, for instance, said the number ranged from "an avowedly conservative 23,000 persons to a possibly exaggerated 100,000 persons." This total, however, did not include marijuana users.

The most any newspaper could do, in this extremity, was to focus public attention on the problem and prod the government at all levels into more effective action both against smugglers and for remedial treatment of addicts. The Los Angeles *Times* made a good beginning.


## 23. *THE MEANEST KIND OF GRAFT*

When Samuel A. Stafford paid $6 for a month's supply of government surplus food, he uncovered a scandal that affected thousands of families in the nation's capital who were unable to protect themselves. It was, as the Washington *Daily News* pointed out, the meanest kind of graft. The *News* had put Stafford to work on an inquiry into the Department of Agriculture's surplus food program and he had done the investigation over a period of several months, much of it on his own time.

Stafford was well qualified for such a job of digging. He was then 39, born in Pittsburgh, educated at Oberlin and Stanford, with fifteen years of newspaper experience and service as a combat infantryman in World War II behind him. He had been on the Washington *Daily News* for four years.

The tip for the story had come from another reporter, Martha Strayer, since retired, who had told him that food deliveries were being made to families on public welfare by a gang of "hustlers" who were gouging them. Stafford informed his city desk and was told to go ahead with the investigation. Posing as a private social worker, he went to the food center and saw for himself how the process worked. Then, he confirmed the way the "hustlers" operated. He saw how the poor, many of them Negroes, were actively discouraged from coming to the food center to pick up their supplies so that more business could be thrown to the "hustlers." He obtained his food card with ease, a key bit of evidence that helped expose the racketeers. Next, he questioned the welfare officials closely, and also piled up a number of affidavits from the victims of the "hustlers."

When the Washington *Daily News* began printing his stories, the whole system was shaken so severely that a number of key officials were replaced. The "hustlers" were put out of business. With the editorial support of his newspaper, a member of the Scripps-Howard chain, he was able to force a number of reforms in the surplus food program, not only in the District of Columbia but in Baltimore and other cities as well. It wasn't done easily; reforms in government, on the whole, come slowly. Follow-up articles had to be researched and printed during the ensuing year. The whole thing was a demonstration of public service journalism on the part of the newspaper and the reporter that brought the greatest of all rewards—the heartfelt thanks of needy families.

This was one of the key articles in the 1963 campaign in the Washington *Daily News*, January 31, 1963.

## THE HUSTLERS

### By Samuel Stafford

Although I am a well-fed newspaperman with a steady income, I have just been issued a month's ration of free government groceries by the District of Columbia Department's surplus-food-for-the-needy program. I accomplished this obvious swindle by arranging to have a small bribe ($6) placed in the right hands. Exactly whose hands, I don't know.

I did it to demonstrate what weeks of close, undercover investigation had convinced me was true:

—That something very rotten was going on at the Welfare Department's surplus food division.

—That food intended for hungry Washington citizens—the poor, the aged, the infirm, and the helpless—was being siphoned off by money-hungry bums.

I needed help and got it from an intermediary I'll refer to only as Lefty because he is afraid of being hurt for cooperating with the Washington *Daily News*'s investigation. Lefty knows the "hustlers"—the men who deliver this free food to the needy for a fee—and he knows Welfare employees in the department's surplus food division.

He said he would buy me an official surplus food card from an inside connection who would put any name and address on the card without checking my eligibility.

The official card I bought bears my own name. The address is that of the Washington *Daily News*, 1013 13th Street N.W., Washington, D.C. I was even assigned a phony case number.

Our swindle was perpetrated on January 21. Lefty, I and another man were sitting in a Southeast district home and I asked Lefty, "Can anybody get a surplus food card by paying for it as you've said you and others have done?"

"It's easy," he said.

He called the surplus office and asked for a Welfare employee whose name I knew. The conversation was guarded. Lefty asked if the man was free to talk. The figures "5" and "2" were mentioned. Lefty kept assuring the person at the other end that the "buy" was for himself. Then Lefty carefully spelled out my name and gave the newspaper's address. He hung up and said, "It'll be ready at 1 o'clock." It was then a little after 11 a.m.

Lefty and I drove to the Welfare Department surplus office, now in Southwest Washington, but then at 469 C-Street N.W. We parked in the lot next door. Lefty, with this newspaper's $6 in his pocket, entered the office as I went across the street to observe. He came out in a minute and walked to the parking lot. I recrossed the street and stood behind a car.

Then Lefty muttered and ran toward the surplus office entrance. I followed, crossing the street. A man I recognized as a Welfare surplus employee was running down C-Street in the opposite direction, coat flapping. He looked back over his shoulder every few steps. Lefty didn't catch him for half a block.

I returned to the parking lot, got the car, and drove around the block.

After the Welfare employee had returned to the office, I picked up Lefty on Pennsylvania Avenue. He gave me my brand new food card.

He told me that he had paid the man $5 and that the man had told him he could handle more such business.

I took a cab to the distribution center at 357 Virginia Avenue S.W., entered and went to the counter, was given my supplies, and took them to my newspaper office. There, I checked what I had received. A 10-pound bag of flour had been broken, possibly when it was slammed on the counter. Otherwise everything was in good shape—4½ pounds of dry milk, nearly 4 pounds of chopped meat in two cans, 2 pounds of peanut butter, 3 pounds of vegetable shortening, a pound of butter, and 5 pounds of cheese.

---

Just for the record, Stafford didn't use the food. Instead, the Washington *Daily News* returned it in good condition to District surplus food officials for distribution to those who needed it. The sale of ration cards stopped. The campaign accomplished its purpose.

## 24. A REPORTER GOES TO JAIL

A major reform in Kentucky's archaic prison system was undertaken in the mid-1960s because a reporter went to prison. The reporter, Dick Berger of the Louisville *Times*, was quite willing to be locked up in La Grange State Reformatory. It was part of his job.

The Louisville *Times* had been attempting for some months to arouse public interest in prison reform, never a very exciting or glamorous subject. But until the eager and enthusiastic Berger volunteered for his unusual assignment, nobody seemed to care outside the newspaper itself.

The manner of Berger's approach to his assignment was far different from that of the old-line sensational reporters whose principal business was to create headlines. There had been a number of cases over the years in which reporters had themselves smuggled into prison, or even sentenced for small offenses, in order to emerge with a blood-curdling story of their wrongs at the hands of the authorities, whether real or imagined. One poor wretch had even been caught buying marijuana cigarettes behind the bars, which resulted in an investigation of an investigator.

This wasn't Berger's style. He went directly to David L. Davis, warden of the La Grange State Reformatory, and with the assent of the state authorities was locked up to see for himself the atrocious conditions that prevailed behind the bars. When he emerged, he was able to underline all that prison authorities had been saying privately for years.

Here is a part of his series in the Louisville *Times*, April 8-9, 1963.

### JUST ABOVE THE ANIMAL LEVEL

#### By Dick Berger

Every nerve in my body tingled as Warden David L. Davis marched me up the concrete stairs and into prison.

It was 10:30 p.m. and the main lobby of the La Grange State Reformatory was quiet. Three guards on duty hardly seemed to notice as the warden escorted me into his office.

My hands were handcuffed in front of my body. A thick leather belt had been run through the large center link that held the handcuffs together. The belt was buckled over my spine.

Davis removed the handcuffs. An elderly, white-haired guard watched. Then he searched me. Warden Davis told the guard the story that he and I had concocted: that I was a county prisoner, R. Burns, who was at the reformatory for safekeeping—on a temporary basis.

The guard marched me away, down a series of corridors, through barred doors and gates, until at last I found myself in a passageway onto which four cells opened. The door to No. 1 was opened and I was ordered to go in. I did. The door swung shut, locked.

Eight locked doors now stood between me and the outside world. I was alone.

I had entered the cellblock with three quarters of a pack of cigarettes. I had imposed self-rationing and was smoking the last one next day when they came for me.

A guard took me to the identification room in the basement. My photograph was taken and I was assigned a prison number. The number —57992—was stenciled on the back of my denim jacket, shirt, and pants. I was given an empty pillow ticking to hold personal belongings.

Then I left the cell that had been my home for a day and a half and was marched to the fishtank.

All new convicts sent to La Grange spend their first month in quarantine. They are kept in a room 40 feet wide and 100 feet long, called the fishtank. I shared it with 114 other prisoners. It was built to hold 50.

Life in the fishtank is just above the animal level. Some of the convicts do not bathe. Some have neither underwear nor socks. The state does not issue these items.

New prisoners are given two pairs of denim pants, two shirts, a towel, a bar of laundry soap, and a bar of face soap. You can get work shoes if you want them. Some men prefer to wear their own. The state does not supply razors, or blades, or cigarettes, or tobacco.

Most of the time—day and night—is consumed either by sleeping or talking. A few men read pocket books, trashy magazines, newspapers, the Bible.

Use of a radio is not permitted. Musical instruments are forbidden, but one man had a harmonica. There was always a crowd around him when he played country music.

There are no cabinets or lockers in which convicts can keep their personal belongings. They sleep on their possessions—to keep them from being stolen.

The chief topics of conversation in the fishtank are crime, sex, and parole. Some prisoners will tell others about their cases. Some will not. Most of the prisoners say their trouble stems from women or whisky. Some are addicted to narcotics.

The check forger sleeps next to the murderer. The 16-year-old boy serving his first sentence—for car theft—may bunk next to a 57-year-old dope fiend who has spent most of his adult life in prison.

Supervision by guards is practically nonexistent in the fishtank. Except for the midnight bed check, I saw a guard come through the fishtank only twice in a four-day period.

Bedded down across the aisle from me was a young prisoner of about 30. It was his first conviction, he said. He was married and had two children. There was no food in the house and no money. He said he had written a bad check to feed his family.

He had two years to serve, but with good conduct in prison he would be eligible for parole after serving eight months. He was a quiet fellow, and not given to using filthy language.

He told me: "All I want to do is make my time in this place and get out and never come back. I don't want to bother nobody's business and I don't want nobody to bother my business. I pray to God every night for the rest of them to leave me alone—so that I can make my good time and get out of here."

Mentally I echoed his thoughts. I didn't want trouble, either.

———————

After such a beginning, the Louisville *Times* redoubled its efforts to campaign for prison reform. Its reward, and the reward of all Kentuckians as well, was the development of a four-year program to create a model correctional plan in the prisons of the state.

The Parole Board was enlarged and strengthened by adding qualified members. The probation and parole services were upgraded. Salaries were improved and total jobs were increased. The state's rehabilitation program was greatly expanded. Some of the older buildings were renovated.

Most important of all, the basic philosophy of the state was changed. Instead of pursuing the fixed notion that severe punishment alone is the answer to crime, Kentucky began trying to help adult offenders—particularly the younger ones—with a new program of treatment and education. It was a heartening yield for a brief period of voluntary servitude.

# V. THE FOREIGN
## CORRESPONDENTS

In the violence and uncertainty of an evolving era, the foreign correspondent sought no new worlds to conquer. He was preoccupied with the disarray of large parts of his own. Wherever he went, and whatever he did, the story he told was one of change. More often than not in the less developed areas of the world, the change was drastic.

All the neat and orderly values of the Victorian world had long since been dissolved. The last faded dreams of empire had been laid to rest with the greatest man of the age, Winston Churchill. The whole concept of an imperial power structure was as dead as the tragic adventure of Maximilian in Mexico in another century.

No correspondent in this day could carry the banner of Manifest Destiny, as had George Wilkins Kendall of the New Orleans *Picayune*. Nor was there a place for the soaring romance of Richard Harding Davis or the swashbuckling adventures of Floyd Gibbons. Somehow, they didn't belong any more.

The new correspondents were, on the whole, a sober-minded lot who seemed to agonize over their tasks far more than they reveled in them. The successful ones showed, in addition to their dispatches, a modicum of conscience and a great deal of courage. They worked hard, long hours in the field and out; when they could, which wasn't often, they played as hard as they worked.

While their tribe increased, it still remained comparatively small. What really mattered was that they were reporting to a slowly broadening American audience of some sophistication and influence—an audience that was not so much concerned with the waving of the Stars and Stripes as it was with an honest, independent report on foreign affairs.

Of course, there were the inevitable public opinion surveys that showed, to no one's surprise, a substantial minority of uninformed and indifferent people who didn't know that Berlin was 110 miles inside Communist East Germany, that there was a Labor government in Britain in 1964, that the Communists ruled mainland China. Functional illiteracy was not by any means confined to the United States. For that matter, despite American pride in educational progress, it was also true that of persons 25 years old and over in the United States, only 28.3 percent had completed high school in 1962 and only 9 percent had attended colleges or universities for four or more years.[1] Another block to wider knowledge of foreign affairs was the relative thinness with which foreign news was distributed outside major centers of population. Taken together, these factors made it surprising that so many people did want to know more about international events and that the body of informed opinion in this area was growing.

In any event, London, Paris, Rome, Berlin, and Hong Kong no longer were the ends of the foreign correspondent's world, as they had been a half-century before. It would have stunned the first Pulitzer and Ochs to have learned from their wire services in the mid-1960s, had they been around, that Saigon was the most-used foreign dateline in the American press generally and that Black Africa was in a state of political and social upheaval. This was the measure of change that had come to the art of foreign correspondence.

It was seldom in this new dispensation that a foreign correspondent in Southeast Asia and Black Africa had to go looking for a war. More often than not, it came to him. For where there were guerrillas, Communist-supported and Communist-trained, there were no front lines. The fighting could break out anywhere. And so the action became, as General Earle G. Wheeler said distastefully during an early phase of South Viet Nam's conflict, a "dirty little war." [2]

A correspondent never knew when he would be trapped in the middle of an action. And if it affected the men, it was doubly hard for the few gallant young women who stayed on the assignment despite every danger and occasional bouts of ill health.

Despite a daily expenditure of $1,500,000 in American aid and the presence of more than 100,000 U.S. Army troops and Marines, who

[1] *Statistical Abstract of the U.S.*, 1964–65, table 147, p. 113.
[2] Neil Sheehan, UPI file, Saigon, Jan. 20, 1963.

were involved in the fighting, the Viet Nam story was difficult to tell. To those who did the fighting and the reporting of it, the American public at an earlier stage seemed interested in almost everything else. As an American captain told a correspondent once while they watched Vietnamese troops plunging through flooded rice paddies in search of an elusive foe:

"Sometimes I think people back home don't know there is a war on in Viet Nam. My wife's neighbors don't even know where Viet Nam is." [3]

It was a despairing echo of the plaint of the fighting men in the Korean War a decade before. The American public learned its geography with terrifying lassitude until, in 1965, American bombers roared over North Viet Nam and American Marines landed at Danang. But neither soldiers nor correspondents could take comfort in the sudden clamor to know what was going on in Southeast Asia.

"It is," wrote Neil Sheehan of United Press International, "a new kind of war. American officers, trained to move tanks and armored battalions in sweeping formation, have never before experienced this kind of hit-and-run war. It is a type of warfare waged on terrain which nature seems to have designed especially for guerrilla fighting." [4]

Malcolm Browne of the Associated Press pointed out an additional difficulty—that most regimes in Southeast Asia took a dim view of truthful reporting that gave aid and comfort to the enemy. The same could be said for some elements among the American command in Saigon.[5]

After the downfall of the Diem regime in 1963, there was a change but only in degree. As the military, civilian, and Buddhist factions in South Viet Nam fought for control, the correspondents sometimes were on the verge of despair. Here was no familiar, Western-type war situation but a rather typical conflict in Asian terms. No Herbert Bayard Swope could come striding into this theater of war, analyze it in terms familiar to an audience back home, and take himself off to the comforts of London or Paris.

In one of the worst of the Saigon riots, toward the end of August, 1964, a mob with hatchets chased Malcolm Browne, who was barely

[3] *Ibid.*, Feb. 2, 1963.
[4] *Ibid.*
[5] Malcolm W. Browne, "Viet Nam Reporting: Three Years of Crisis," *Columbia Journalism Review*, Fall, 1964, p. 5.

able to escape in a miserable alley hideaway.[6] Somewhat later, François Sully of *Newsweek* was caught in a mob and reported:

"The scene was frightening. Some 500 student vigilantes with red and yellow armbands were directing an immense crowd of 70,000 marchers. . . . In front of General Nguyen Khanh's headquarters, 5,000 demonstrators milled ominously, kept in line by the vigilantes." [7] It had seldom been the lot of Western correspondents to chronicle such utter chaos. And the end was not yet, for the battle in the Tonkin Gulf in August, 1964, and the American air strikes against North Viet Nam in 1965 showed that the United States was not going to pull out of Southeast Asia on Communist terms. President Johnson made that increasingly clear in his April 17 speech at Johns Hopkins.

Saigon was the focus of the war. Elsewhere in Southeast Asia, there were relatively few correspondents for American newsgathering organizations at that particular time. And as for Red China, the only Westerners in Peking were Reuters, Agence France-Presse, and an occasional British, French, or Canadian newspaper correspondent. Otherwise, Red China was covered from Hong Kong, Tokyo, and elsewhere on the periphery.

In the succession of crises that shook Black Africa in the violent 1960s, the correspondents' story was much the same as in the trouble areas of Asia. They could never be sure in the Congo, for instance, when they would be caught in the middle of a savage and barbaric war. Inevitably, there were casualties and one correspondent, George Clay, a veteran of the National Broadcasting Company service, was killed.

Elsewhere in Africa, it became more or less routine for a revolutionary regime to show how tough it was by detaining American correspondents when it could catch them. Such moves were a part of the creaking propaganda machinery imported from behind the Iron or Bamboo Curtains, along with paid street demonstrators and occasional book-burnings at United States Information Service libraries. Yet, for all their transparency, they never failed to draw a flurry of American headlines.

In the Zanzibar takeover in early 1964 by a strange character who seemed to have emerged from Eugene O'Neill's *Emperor Jones*, four correspondents were arrested and expelled—Robert Conley of the New York *Times*, Peter Rand of the New York *Herald Tribune*, William

[6] *AP Log*, Aug. 27–Sept. 2, 1964.
[7] *Newsweek*, Sept. 7, 1964, pp. 32, 45.

E. Smith of *Time* and John Nugent of *Newsweek*. One of them confessed that he had been "terrified" and gave out an exciting story, but to the rest it was just a part of the job.

At about the same time, Lloyd Garrison of the New York *Times* was detained temporarily in Ghana while police examined his files and belongings.[8] But he, like his fellows, merely reported the incident and went on about his business. There was so much of this attempted intimidation of correspondents by boastful new rulers that it gradually began to lose its value even as a propaganda device.

However, it was clear that neither the traditions nor the practice of independent journalism in the United States were known or respected in many a newly emerged African or Asian nation. At best, a long and painful job of education in American practices could be anticipated; at worst, a prohibition against the sending of news unfavorable to whatever regime was in power.

American correspondents, whether new to the art or not, very quickly learned to distinguish between real danger and propaganda. And one of the most dangerous spots of all was Cyprus in the mid-1960s. In the war between Greek and Turkish Cypriots that cast a pall over the eastern Mediterranean in the summer of 1964, Alvin Rosenfeld of NBC was shot in the face while covering a Greek Cypriot attack near Mansoura. Rosenfeld, no youngster, was a seasoned correspondent of good judgment and excellent reputation who had all the proper noncombatant markings and knew all the right signals. But, as the saying goes, he ran out of luck on a distant battlefield. While riding in a car with a fellow correspondent, Jay Miller, he was hit. The car overturned off the road. For hours, Rosenfeld lay in a ditch, pinned down by Greek fire, until he was eventually rescued and taken to Nicosia in grave condition.[9] Miller had more luck. He was unhurt.

Elsewhere the art of foreign correspondence was practiced in a safer and considerably more conventional manner. Even in the Soviet Union after the downfall of Nikita S. Khrushchev, there was no immediate effort to return to the deep freeze on foreign correspondents that had been practiced in the Stalin era. If the seventeen American correspondents in Moscow had to watch their copy and their movements, it was no more than they expected. The crude censorship of Stalin's day had

[8] *Overseas Press Club Bulletin*, Jan. 25, 1964.
[9] *Ibid.*, Aug. 15, 1964.

been dropped in favor of an implicit self-censorship by every correspondent who wanted to stay in the Soviet Union.

After all, life in Moscow for the foreign correspondent had never been ideal, but conditions seemed to be improving. Because of the strained relations with Communist China, the Soviet Union, before the step-up in the Viet Nam war, appeared not to view the United States with quite as much hostility as it had in the more immediate past. In fact, a popular joke among more sophisticated members of the Soviet hierarchy in 1964 had it that a wise Soviet official would make a trip to the United States now and then to allay suspicion that he might be pro-Peking. In more sober terms, the real policies of the Soviet Union had not always approximated its declared policies, and this was now more true than ever.

This tenuous relationship between the two greatest powers in the world was bound to have its effect on public opinion in the United States, although the antipathy to Communism still was voiced in and out of government almost every day as an article of faith. Yet, when the Labor party came to power in Britain, most leading American newspapers subordinated the news to the overthrow of Khrushchev which occurred the same day. The Khrushchev story was by far the most dramatic and significant. Moreover, while the great centers of Europe retained their traditional hold on the attention of the American news media in ordinary times, it was clear that some of the old appeal had gone. The British had trouble selling some of their goods in the United States. And American tourists were going out of their way, in a surprising number of cases, to avoid France on the ground of high cost and inhospitability. Despite the world-wide appeal of the Ecumenical Council, at least two newspapers, the New York *Herald Tribune* and the Los Angeles *Times*, closed their Rome bureaus. Bonn became a secondary news source and Berlin, home of the world's No. 1 crisis, became important only when the Cold War quickened.

True, two-thirds of the correspondents attached to American news media remained in Western Europe. But increasingly, it was being viewed by many as a base, administrative center, or transmission point. The Algerian war was covered largely by reporters assigned from European centers, as was the fighting in Cyprus. And in several instances, the wealthier newsgathering organizations thought nothing of detaching a correspondent from his permanent European assignment to send him to the Far East for temporary crisis duty. Even Latin America, long neglected by most American news media, was beginning to draw some of the corespondents who would normally have been assigned to a European center in other days; not that this made Latin American coverage significantly better than it had been, however. Except for revolutions and tensions generated by the Castro regime in Cuba, there just wasn't enough interest north of the Rio Grande, with a few key exceptions.

How many American foreign corespondents were working abroad on permanent assignment in the mid-1960s? At an educated guess by the *Columbia Journalism Review*, there were 350 to 450. To this would have to be added a minimum of 100 non-Americans working for American newsgathering media as permanent correspondents and several hundred stringers whose work was regularly used by these organizations. In fact, upon examination, the distinction between a permanent correspondent and a stringer whose work was regularly used generally consisted of the difference in the amount of money each was paid.

A survey of 140 of the Americans permanently stationed abroad turned up this estimate of the adequacy of world coverage by American news media:

|  | Adequate (in percent) | Inadequate (in percent) |
|---|---|---|
| Asia | 47 | 53 |
| Africa | 17 | 83 |
| Western Europe | 74 | 26 |
| Eastern Europe | 20 | 80 |
| Soviet Union | — | 100 |
| Latin America | 35 | 65 |
| Canada | — | 100 |

Yet, in response to a question as to whether American news media have covered the world adequately, 53 percent of the respondents said yes, 14 percent with qualifications, and 46 percent said no, 25 percent with qualifications. Of course, few correspondents outside Western Europe believe their areas are ever well covered and a healthy minority (25 percent in the case of the survey) stationed elsewhere always want to be sent to Western Europe. Nevertheless, the dominance of Western Europe in foreign news no longer can be taken for granted.

If it is borne in mind that youthful and lower paid foreign correspondents are less likely to answer a searching questionnaire than their older and more settled associates, the survey gave an interesting profile of the 140 Americans who responded to it.[10] They were, on the average, in their late 30s or early 40s, college graduates, ten years in the foreign field, either Democrats or independents, deficient in foreign languages except for French and some couldn't speak that language, paid between $12,000 and $15,000 a year, married, and half of them had one or two children. Of the group, only 5 percent had received no college training and only 6 percent were Republicans. The average age was 41, only eight being under 30 and only four being over 60.

Was it a typical group? Undoubtedly it was, except in areas of combat and extreme hardship. There, without question, the younger correspondents generally would be found in the majority. As for the non-American correspondent for American news media, who was not covered in the survey, the most casual examination of the news centers of the world would show that his numbers had increased. After World War II, the wire services began staffing many of their foreign bureaus in part with "locals," citizens of the country in which the bureau was located. Fewer were engaged by newspapers; in some cases, they were brought to the United States first for special training in American methods, while others were attracted to American schools of journalism.

Thus, some of those who began as "locals" developed into full-fledged American correspondents in their own right and were found to be useful in areas other than their own countries. The same was true of others who attended American schools of journalism. Some retained their original citizenship, others became naturalized American citizens. In any event, the result was a broadening of the American correspondence corps and an upgrading of the efficiency of the group as a whole. One of the priceless ingredients of excellence in journalism was a serious competition among correspondents to achieve it. The "melting pot" helped.

Looking over the field from his post as diplomatic correspondent of the AP in Washington, John Hightower had this to say: "The foreign correspondent at this stage of history has come a long way from his prototype. He is more serious, more mature, and probably better informed on the problems of the day. He handles a vital job in com-

[10] Frederick T. C. Yu and John Luter, "The Foreign Correspondent and His Work," *Columbia Journalism Review,* Spring, 1964, pp. 5, 6, 7.

munications, so vital that it is impossible to conceive a working democracy without him." [11]

In the selections that follow, the foreign correspondent is shown at work. Some of the pieces are done by Pulitzer Prize winners, some are not. But all bear the trademark of the professional working under pressure at the most dangerous time of our violent era.

## 25. ROSENTHAL AT AUSCHWITZ

On a dull midsummer's day in 1958, an editor at the New York *Times* picked up a mailer from Poland. He didn't expect much, even though the mailer came from one of the few stylists among the *Times*'s imposing staff of foreign of foreign correspondents, A. M. Rosenthal. Anything Rosenthal wrote for the paper was worth reading, of course; but if he'd thought anything at all of the piece, wouldn't he have cabled it? At the *Times*, almost everything that's fit to print is sent by cable or radio from abroad; the mailer is a nonstatus symbol.

The editor smoothed out the crinkled Rosenthal copy, bearing a dateline somewhat akin to a muffled sneeze, Brzezinka. It was just a short piece about a visit to Auschwitz. Now that the place had been turned into a kind of chamber of horrors, most correspondents assigned to Poland had gone there to record their impressions. So Rosenthal had done nothing new. Nor had he turned up any remarkable discoveries. What could anyone find that was new about Auschwitz?

The editor began reading. And as he read, the humble mailer turned before his eyes into one of those rare and memorable stories that appear in newspapers on one day and are imbedded in the literature of the nation on the next. For Rosenthal, in a mere 700 words, had caught the meaning of Auschwitz.

Abraham Michael Rosenthal had been with the New York *Times* since 1944 upon his graduation from the College of the City of New York where he had been a campus correspondent. He had been born May 2, 1922 in Sault Ste. Marie, Ontario, Canada, and had become an American citizen in 1951. At the United Nations, he had been a

[11] John Hightower, "Goodbye to the Scoop Artist in a Trench Coat," *Dateline*, Spring, 1964, pp. 13–15.

familiar and welcome figure as a correspondent from 1946 until 1954. Then, he had been the *Times*'s correspondent in India until early 1958.

The Auschwitz piece was written at the beginning of his relatively brief term as a correspondent in Poland. He did many, many others, some of them magnificent in concept and depth of reporting. He won many prizes, including a Pulitzer Prize in 1960 following his expulsion from Poland because a Communist regime feared that he was probing too deeply into its affairs. He became a correspondent in other key places in Europe, in Africa, and Japan, and in 1963 he was made the metropolitan editor of the *Times*, a kind of super city-editor.

But if he had done nothing beyond the mailer from Auschwitz, his place in journalism would be secure. After reading it that midsummer's day in 1958, the editor sent it to Lester Markel, the Sunday editor of the New York *Times*. On August 31, 1958, it led the *New York Times Magazine* and became a classic. Here it is, as Rosenthal wrote it.

## "THERE IS NO NEWS FROM AUSCHWITZ"
### By A. M. Rosenthal

BRZEZINKA, POLAND—The most terrible thing of all, somehow, was that at Brzezinka the sun was bright and warm, the rows of graceful poplars were lovely to look upon, and on the grass near the gates children played.

It all seemed frighteningly wrong, as in a nightmare, that at Brzezinka the sun should ever shine or that there should be light and greenness and the sound of young laughter. It would be fitting if at Brzezinka the sun never shone and the grass withered, because this is a place of unutterable terror.

And yet, every day, from all over the world, people come to Brzezinka, quite possibly the most grisly tourist center on earth. They come for a variety of reasons—to see if it could really have been true, to remind themselves not to forget, to pay homage to the dead by the simple act of looking upon their place of suffering.

Brzezinka is a couple of miles from the better-known southern town of Oswiecim. Oswiecim has about 12,000 inhabitants, is situated about 171 miles from Warsaw, and lies in a damp, marshy area at the eastern end of the pass called the Moravian Gate.

Brzezinka and Oswiecim together formed part of that minutely organized factory of torture and death that the Nazis called Konzentrationslager Auschwitz.

By now, fourteen years after the last batch of prisoners was herded naked into the gas chambers by dogs and guards, the story of Auschwitz has been told a great many times. Some of the inmates have written of those memories of which sane men cannot conceive. Rudolf Franz Ferdinand Hoss, the superintendent of the camp, before he was executed wrote his detailed memoirs of mass exterminations and the experiments on living bodies. Four million people died here, the Poles say.

And so there is no news to report about Auschwitz. There is merely the compulsion to write something about it, a compulsion that grows out of a restless feeling that to have visited Auschwitz and then turned away without having said or written anything would somehow be a most grievous act of discourtesy to those who died here.

Brzezinka and Oswiecim are very quiet places now; the screams can no longer be heard. The tourist walks silently, quickly at first to get it over with and then, as his mind peoples the barracks and the chambers and the dungeons and flogging posts, he walks draggingly. The guide does not say much either, because there is nothing much for him to say after he has pointed.

For every visitor, there is one particular bit of horror that he knows he will never forget. For some it is seeing the rebuilt gas chamber at Oswiecim and being told that this is the "small one." For others it is the fact that at Brzezinka, in the ruins of the gas chambers, and the crematoria the Germans blew up when they retreated, there are daisies growing.

There are visitors who gaze blankly at the gas chambers and the furnaces because their minds simply cannot encompass them, but stand shivering before the great mounds of human hair behind the plate glass window or the piles of babies' shoes or the brick cells where men sentenced to death by suffocation were walled up.

One visitor opened his mouth in a silent scream simply at the sight of boxes—great stretches of three-tiered wooden boxes in the women's barracks. They were about six feet wide, about three feet high, and into them from five to ten prisoners were shoved for the night. The guide walks quickly through the barracks. Nothing more to see here.

A brick building where sterilization experiments were carried out on women prisoners. The guide tries the door—it's locked. The visitor is grateful that he does not have to go in, and then flushes with shame.

A long corridor where rows of faces stare from the walls. Thousands of pictures, the photographs of prisoners. They are all dead now, the men and women who stood before the cameras, and they all knew they were to die.

They all stare blank-faced, but one picture, in the middle of a row, seizes the eye and wrenches the mind. A girl, 22 years old, plumply pretty, blonde. She is smiling gently, as at a sweet, treasured thought. What was the thought that passed through her young mind and is now her memorial on the wall of the dead at Auschwitz?

Into the suffocation dungeons the visitor is taken for a moment and feels himself strangling. Another visitor goes in, stumbles out, and crosses herself. There is no place to pray at Auschwitz.

The visitors look pleadingly at each other and say to the guide, "Enough."

There is nothing new to report about Auschwitz. It was a sunny day and the trees were green and at the gates the children played.

## 26. *BIGART COVERS EICHMANN*

If any man has had his fill of the horrors of our age, it is Homer Bigart. Wherever war and civil strife have shattered the hope of the world, there he has been. At 35, he was on the Anzio beachhead for the New York *Herald Tribune*; three years later, for the same newspaper, he was in a bomber making the last raid over beaten Japan, and within a few weeks was picking his way through atom-shattered Hiroshima. At 44, he was in the foxholes of Korea; ten years later, he saw jungle warfare in Viet Nam while reporting for the New York *Times*. And at 57, the *Times* sent him to the heart of embattled Mississippi to record the murderous struggle of the segregationists in a town made notorious by a triple assassination, Philadelphia.

On the morning of December 11, 1961, Bigart was in a hushed Jerusalem courtroom awaiting the fate of Adolf Eichmann, who for four months had been on trial for crimes against humanity. The Nazi who had been charged with the organization of the slaughter of 6,000,-000 Jews had been captured by Israeli agents in Argentina on May 22,

1960. Now, with many other reporters, the New York *Times*'s veteran looked forward to the reading of a 200-page document before Eichmann's fate was pronounced. Yet, for all that, Bigart had made suitable arrangements for getting the verdict out of the court and into his paper in the event that it was announced ahead of time. That was one of his virtues as a reporter. He always kept his lines of communication unblocked when he could.

Where had he learned? Certainly, he was not destined to be a journalist by birth at Hawley, Pennsylvania, on October 25, 1907, nor during his time at Carnegie Tech and New York University. His real experience had begun as a copy boy at the New York *Herald Tribune*; from then on, whether he was interviewing a cop on a street corner or a general after a battle, he was guided by the intuitive good sense of the first-rate reporter and he acquired the training that enabled him to write with both restraint and perception for a mass audience. He won two Pulitzer Prizes, one for his Pacific war correspondence in 1946 and the other he shared with five fellow correspondents in 1951 during the Korean War.

The Eichmann verdict came suddenly and without warning. But just as quickly, Bigart moved. In the terms of the trade, he "topped" a story he had previously sent with the bare news of the court's judgment. In the following account, written for the New York *Times*, December 11, 1961, under deadline pressure and 6,000 miles from his newsroom, Bigart's technique as well as his reporting may be observed.

## THE JUDGMENT

### By Homer Bigart

JERUSALEM (Israeli Sector), Monday, December 11—Adolf Eichmann was convicted this morning of crimes against the Jewish people, crimes against humanity, war crimes, and membership in hostile Nazi organizations.

The former Nazi colonel faces death by hanging.

The verdict came with startling suddenness a few minutes after court opened. Instead of launching into a preamble defending the court's sovereignty, as had been expected, Presiding Judge Moshe Landau coldly ordered Eichmann to stand.

"The court finds you guilty!" Judge Landau said, and he enumerated the crimes. He then ordered the prisoner to be seated while he began reading the massive 200-page judgment.

Eichmann sat stiffly in his chair, showing no flicker of emotion. The shock possibly had come too quickly. Judge Landau read the judgment in Hebrew, which was translated simultaneously into German for the defendant. Sitting with Judge Landau on the tribunal were Judge Itzhak Raveh and Judge Benjamin Halevy.

Eichmann looked cadaverous, but was seemingly less pallid than during the final weeks of the hearings in his trial, which began last April 11 and ran to August 14. The nervous tic that had frequently contorted his face during the hearing was not immediately apparent. He was wearing the same dark suit an Israeli tailor had made for him last spring.

The police said Eichmann had picked up a few pounds since August. His suit still fit him badly. Large bony wrists protruded from his flappy sleeves. His scrawny neck and bald head with beak nose emerged like a turkey buzzard's from a jacket that hung loosely.

From his skeletal frame Eichmann smiled and nodded to his German lawyer, Dr. Robert Servatius. The prisoner ignored the crowded gallery. All through the long trial, he had made his glass cubicle a tiny island of fussy bureaucracy, placing his papers in neat stacks on the desk in front of him. But today he carried only one sheaf of papers. He put his hands on his lap and waited.

A court aide, Joseph Shamech, said, "Beit Hamishpat," which means, "The court." Everyone rose as the judges entered. The youngest of the three, Judge Halevy, entered first in his flowing black robe. Then came Presiding Judge Landau, whose relaxed, tolerant handling of the courtroom drew wide admiration last summer; then, Judge Raveh, who had discoursed with the prisoner on Kantian philosophy.

Eichmann stood rigidly at attention, heels together, head thrown back, hands stiffly at trouser seams, staring at the judges until they were seated.

The law sounds explicit enough. It applies the strong Hebrew term "dino-mitah"—literally translated "shall be sentenced to death"—to persons guilty of crimes committed with "intent to destroy the Jewish people in whole or in part."

When Judge Landau finishes reading the judgment he will call upon Attorney General Gideon Hausner to discuss it. Almost certainly Mr. Hausner will tell the court that it has no alternative but to impose the death sentence.

Eichmann was sentenced to death on December 15, 1961, at the conclusion of the reading of the judgment against him. He was executed on May 31, 1962. It was a mere echo of the doom of the 6,000,000 innocents.

## 27. A WARNING FROM CUBA

"I do ask every publisher, every editor, and every newsman in the nation to reexamine his own standards and to recognize the nature of our country's peril," said President John F. Kennedy in the spring of 1961.

"In time of war, the government and the press have customarily joined in an effort based largely on self-discipline to prevent unauthorized disclosures to the enemy. In time of 'clear and present danger,' the courts have held that even the privileged rights of the First Amendment must yield to the public's need for national security. . . . If the press is awaiting a declaration of war before it imposes the self-discipline of combat conditions, then I can only say that no war ever posed a greater threat to our security." [12]

The President was understandably upset. He lectured the press on its duties to the government just ten days after the disaster of the Bay of Pigs invasion of Cuba on April 17, 1961 by ill-armed, poorly prepared, and unsupported Cuban exiles. For months they had been talking to everybody who would listen about the big news; it had been in the press, on the radio, and on TV. Anybody in Florida who had the slightest interest in the affair knew that it was being masterminded by the Central Intelligence Agency. Consequently, when the whole thing blew up like the overinflated balloon that it was, there should scarcely have been any surprise that the press had the whole story.[13]

After President Kennedy's complaint, leading editors and publishers met with him at the White House to determine what he had in mind.

---

[12] John F. Kennedy, before the Bureau of Advertising, American Newspaper Publishers' Association, New York, Apr. 27, 1961.

[13] "Press Independence and the Cuban Crisis," *Columbia Journalism Review*, Winter, 1963, p. 5.

There was more talk about security violations, but nothing specific; in the end, the following conclusion was reached by the journalists:

"It was the unanimous opinion of the news group that although the national position is critical, to a degree, only the declaration of a national emergency by the President of the United States would make imperative the imposition of news censorship. Further, it was argued that if the situation is critical enough to warrant press control, other wartime measures should immediately be put into effect.[14]

There the matter rested until the following fall, when rumors among Cuban exiles in Florida once more indicated a growing crisis was at hand. There was talk that Russian troops were in Cuba, that Russians were building missile bases, that Fidel Castro soon would have it in his power to become a genuine threat to the United States rather than a somewhat symbolic nuisance. As the press and the electronic media reflected the rumors, anxiety grew in Washington.

At first, the administration kept saying that it had no objection to purely defensive measures on the part of the Cuban dictatorship. For awhile, the tension relaxed. But more and more questions were raised over the nature of the missile installations. Were they, the administration was asked, really defensive? And if so, how did the United States know? The White House and the Pentagon gave more muted assurances. It was clear they had no evidence of a conclusive nature that the missile bases were offensive and therefore directed against the security of the United States.

Among the many journalists who delved into the story was Hal Hendrix of the Miami *News*, who was then 40 years old and had been covering Latin America for his paper for fifteen years. He had excellent sources and he knew how to work with them. Originally he had come from the Midwest, having been born February 14, 1922 in Ray County, Missouri, attended Rockhurst College, and broken in on the Kansas City *Star* in 1944 as a reporter. Three years later, he turned up in Miami on the *News* and in 1957 he became Latin American editor for the newspaper.

Early in October, Hendrix picked up what he thought was conclusive evidence from his sources that the Russian missile bases in Cuba were offensive in nature. He queried the Pentagon and received a brusque brush-off for his pains. The problem for him and for the *News*, a mem-

---

[14] *ASNE Bulletin*, June 1, 1961.

## SERIOUS STEPS

Paul Vathis's 1962 Pulitzer Prize picture showing President Kennedy and former President Eisenhower deliberating during the Cuban crisis.

ber of the Cox group, was whether to publish the story in the national interest or hold back and await a signal from either the Pentagon or the White House.

The *News* decided to publish. Hendrix' story appeared across the top of Page 1 on October 7, 1962, fifteen days before President Kennedy went before the nation with the proofs he needed to force a showdown with the Russians. This is the piece as it appeared in the *News*.

## THE CUBA STORY

### By Hal Hendrix

Construction has begun in Communist Cuba on at least a half dozen launching sites for intermediate range tactical missiles, U.S. intelligence authorities have advised the White House.

Although official U.S. spokesmen have declined to disclose the intelligence reports, the Miami *News* has learned that experts have advised President Kennedy that the ground-to-ground missiles can be operated from inland Cuba within six months.

From the type of construction under way it has been determined that the launching pads will have the capability of hurling rockets that could penetrate deeply into the United States in one direction and reach the Panama Canal Zone in the opposite direction.

Official observers do not believe that the Soviet Union has yet delivered the intermediate range-type missiles to Cuba. But neither do they now doubt that delivery plans have been made.

"The United States has a 'grace period' of about six months in so far as these new missiles are concerned," an official observer commented yesterday. "After that, once the installations are complete and the missiles emplaced, any time there is a flareup in tensions anywhere in the world between this country and the Soviet Union, the Communists in Cuba can rattle the offensive rockets in the Caribbean."

Officials have reported that U.S. plans for a crackdown on free world shipping to Communist Cuba could slow down the launching site construction, but there is no guarantee that the Soviets will not divert their own vessels to this high priority project.

Washington also has been alerted to the fact that Communist Cuba's north coast now is solidly banked with 'defensive' short-range missiles, capable of downing an aircraft in a 25-mile range.

Officially, the State Department has announced that at least fifteen of these SAM bases have been completed, adding that the total may reach twenty-five or more.

Behind the coastal missile emplacements, now manned jointly by Cuban military and Soviet "technicians," are an undisclosed number of ground-to-ground missile bases already operational. These are reported to have a range of about 35 miles, designed for firing on ships at sea and strategic ground installations.

According to reports from Cuba, some of these short-range "defensive" missiles now are installed within easy range of the U.S. Naval base at Guantanamo Bay.

Meanwhile, reports from Moscow and Havana point out that shipments of military materials and personnel still are continuing to pour unchecked into Communist Cuba. The State Department has acknowledged that there are now about 4,500 Soviet "military specialists" in Communist Cuba. Outside the department, observers believe the number is closer to 10,000.

Since July, according to State Department announcements, more than eighty-five Soviet shiploads have arrived in Cuban ports. *Red Star*, the Soviet military publication, notes that ships "are on the seas daily bound for Cuba with support for our Cuban friends."

———

The reports that Hendrix used as the basis for his story were, of course, known to the American government. But in retrospect, it is clear that these reports in themselves could not have been the final basis for the "eyeball to eyeball" confrontation between the United States and the Soviet Union over Cuba. Once President Kennedy had the air reconnaissance photographs that established the offensive nature of the Russian missile bases without any doubt, and had moved the necessary troops and planes and ships, he was ready.

For his part in alerting the nation to its danger, Hal Hendrix was awarded the Pulitzer Prize for foreign correspondence in 1963.

## 28. PORTRAIT OF FIDEL

Fidel Castro, the bearded eccentric who seized power from his lethargic enemies in Cuba, has cast his image in a many-colored reflection through the press.

Herbert L. Matthews of the New York *Times*, who first discovered that he was alive and fighting against Dictator Fulgencio Batista in the Sierra Maestra in 1957, saw him as a heroic figure in the early days. Jules Dubois of the Chicago *Tribune*, who was favorably impressed at first, soon changed and decided that he was a villain. Joseph Martin and Philip Santora of the New York *Daily News*, who shared a Pulitzer Prize for predicting his rise to power, pointed out that he was surrounded by Communists. And the American Society of Newspaper Editors, which invited him to Washington to address its convention after his takeover, nevertheless was deeply troubled by him.[15]

Nobody called him a hero for very long in the American press. His dependence on the Soviet Union became all too apparent. In the aftermath of the Cuban crises of 1961 and 1962, he was nominated by virtual acclamation on the editorial pages north of the Rio Grande as the No. 1 enemy of the United States in the Western world. This was, in a sense, an overblown distinction for a wild-talking fanatic who had been used by far more powerful forces for their own ends.

It took time and a calmer view for a more realistic evaluation of Fidel Castro. Among the journalists who went to Cuba once the dust had settled was Sanche de Gramont of the New York *Herald Tribune*, who at the age of 29 had won a Pulitzer Prize for local reporting. De Gramont was a big, tough, American-educated French citizen, born in Geneva on May 30, 1932 and graduated from Yale in 1954 with an A.B., magna cum laude. His first lessons in journalism were learned at the Columbia Graduate School of Journalism, from which he received his M.S. in 1955. Thereafter, by way of the Worcester (Mass.) *Gazette*, Agence France-Presse, and the AP, he found his way to the New York *Herald Tribune*. In 1956–58, he had to take time out for service as a lieutenant in the French Army in the Algerian War, where he was

[15] John Hohenberg, *Foreign Correspondence: The Great Reporters and Their Times* (New York, Columbia University Press, 1964) pp. 418–22.

decorated with the cross for military valor. On the night of March 4, 1960, he hurried from his office to the Metropolitan Opera, covered the sudden collapse and death of the baritone, Leonard Warren, during the performance of *La Forza del Destino*, and wrote the story back at his office within one hour. It was such a virtuoso performance of journalism under pressure that he won a Pulitzer award in 1961.

That was only the beginning. In Paris, Rome, in the Congo, and in South Viet Nam, at the Ecumenical Council and in the chancelleries of Europe, he became a familiar and even a distinguished figure—tall, broad-shouldered, black-browed and black-haired, a veritable dynamo of energy. In the Congo, caught in a crossfire, he was shot by United Nations troops and nearly lost his life, but made a slow and almost complete recovery.

Here is de Gramont's view of Castro, written September 13 as part of a series for the New York *Herald Tribune* in the fall of 1963.

## "A HARD MAN TO FIND"

### By Sanche de Gramont

HAVANA—It is said that if Fidel Castro lost his voice, the Cuban revolution would crumble. Cuba increasingly represents the Western hemisphere's doomed castaway and Dr. Castro's eloquence is one of the buoys that keep the body afloat.

The leader Maximo likes to call his government a "direct democracy." He claims it is the best government since Athenian democracy, with the added advantage that, unlike Athens, there are no slaves.

But direct democracy is a one-way thoroughfare in which Fidel uses his orator's gifts to keep his hold on the people. When he unhooks his gunbelt, removes the Romeo and Juliet cigar from between his teeth, and prances up to the microphone like a horse at the starting gate, the Cubans know they are in for a series of proclamations which tomorrow will be the law of the land.

The voice is hoarse and throaty, with the intonations of a flamenco dancer, and the performance makes one regret that he had not chosen the stage for a profession. Turn by turn, he explains, praises, cajoles, exhorts, condemns, forgives, demands, pleads, and dictates. He whispers and he bellows, he shakes his beard and bangs his fist. And at the end of the four- or five-hour marathon, he has solved the country's problems.

A word from Fidel is enough. This summer he warned that the price of gasoline might rise and within the hour no gas station would sell any. They waited until the price had risen—from 30 to 60 cents a gallon —the next day.

No one in the regime is safe from Fidel's rhetoric. In March, 1962, he denounced the veteran Communist Annibal Escalante for "putting a straitjacket" on the budding party organization, the ORI (Integrated Revolutionary Organization). "If a cat gave birth to kittens," Fidel roared, "it was necessary to refer the matter to the ORI." Mr. Escalante was not on hand to reply to the charges. Tipped off that the speech concerned him, he had prudently left for Prague the day before.

There is no appeal from Fidel's judgment. Once, denouncing "burocratismo," he used as an example "a petty chief in the Foreign Ministry, who, so they say, is a bit of a soak." The man never dared go back to his job. On another occasion, a privately owned cafeteria which had closed on a weekday attracted the Premier's ire. After that, it had to close for good.

Fidel's likes and dislikes are religiously obeyed. They are building a multimillion-dollar art center in Havana, ambitiously conceived and boldly designed. Why are so much money and time being devoted to art when in the rest of Cuba people are still living in earth huts?

"It's just that Fidel likes art," a Foreign Ministry official explained with a shrug.

Fidel's whims make diplomats tremble. On July 23, he called in the Swiss Chargé d'Affaires and told him to clear out of the U.S. Embassy building because Cuba was nationalizing it. The Chargé told the Premier this would be an unprecedented violation of international law and refused. Fidel threw one of his celebrated tantrums, saying at one point, "The Swiss can go to hell."

In the early days of the revolution, Dr. Castro promised elections within eighteen months. But he apparently found that direct democracy was enough and he now holds that elections are useless. Elections in Cuba, he says, are discredited because in the past they were always fixed.

When the Cuban leader is not issuing proclamations, he is a hard man to find. As press spokesman Paul Lazo said in broken but colorful English, "Fidel has no exactly place." He wanders about the country, paying surprise visits to farms and factories like an inspector general under the tsar. No detail is too puerile for his attention. He recently

THE FIRING SQUAD

Andrew Lopez's 1960 Pulitzer Prize picture in Castro's Cuba.

visited the kitchens of the Havana Libre (formerly the Havana Hilton) to see how a new recipe for pizzas was coming out.

Like Mussolini bare-chested in the rice fields of southern Italy plugging economic autarchy, Dr. Castro likes to support worthy causes through personal example. He cuts cane and picks coffee like a true *campesino*.

Recently he has been accepting invitations to Western embassies in what has been interpreted as a move for better relations with non-Communist countries. He told Dutch Ambassador Gideon Boissevain that "I admire the Russian people because they are willing to make sacrifices for socialism."

The Ambassador replied that "there are other countries where this type of sacrifice is not necessary, and where a person can even write a letter to the editor, or to his congressman, or vote in an election, and where people are reasonably content."

Dr. Castro nodded in silence.

## 29. WAR, FATE, AND THE CONGO

Lynn Louis Heinzerling is a big, quiet man with greying hair and a look of peace and stability on his pleasant, unlined face. He is the kind of man who might be a company president, bank director, or church deacon, if he were so minded, but he hasn't had much time to think about it.

For in the mid-1960s, as he was approaching his sixtieth year, Lynn Heinzerling had seen more of war than many a soldier and the end was not yet. Having survived the worst of World War II in Europe, he was the principal AP correspondent in Black Africa and the winner of a Pulitzer Prize for foreign correspondence in 1961. His main concern was the brutal, inhuman war that was being fought in the Congo.

Just as it is given to some men to lead peaceful lives, never hearing a shot fired in anger, it is the fate of others to live under the bleak shadow of battle. That has been Lynn Heinzerling's lot and he has accepted it uncomplainingly.

Like the great Januarius Aloysius MacGahan, who left his birthplace of New Lexington, Ohio, to cover the Turkish atrocities in Bulgaria and find fame as a foreign correspondent, Heinzerling's beginnings were in a small Ohio town, Birmingham, where he was born on October 23,

1906. He attended Akron University and Ohio Wesleyan in the 1920s, worked for five years as a reporter on the Cleveland *Plain Dealer* and four for the AP in Cleveland and New York, then went to Europe for his first foreign assignment.

He was in Danzig when the first Nazi bombs began to fall on September 1, 1939, and sent the bulletin that meant the war was on in earnest. From then until the end in 1945, there was no peace for Lynn Heinzerling. He was with the British Eighth Army in Africa, the American Fifth Army in Italy, and he followed one campaign after another until the Axis war machine was shattered.

Some might have looked forward after that to a more quiet career, but Heinzerling's assignment was postwar Vienna, the center of European spying and intrigue. Next, he was sent to Berlin and caught the opening of the Soviet blockade of the German capital. At length, in 1948, he was shifted to Geneva and there for nine years he enjoyed the pleasure and contentment that comes with a peaceful life with his wife and growing son.

But in 1957, when he drew his next duty station, it was Johannesburg, South Africa, the window for a continent in turmoil. It was his fate once more to be involved in conflict, for just as he was about to be shifted in 1960 to Vienna, Prime Minister Hendrick F. Verwoerd was shot, and shortly afterward the tinderbox of the Congo burst into flame. The Viennese assignment went to another AP man. As for Heinzerling, he plunged into the Congo.

Here are two examples of his Congo coverage, four years apart, with the following excerpted from his AP file, August 1 and 7, 1960.

## BIRTH OF THE CONGO REPUBLIC

### *By Lynn Heinzerling*

LEOPOLDVILLE—The United Nations has the sickest nation it has ever nursed on its hands today. Only a month old, the Congo Republic is facing a crisis which, without prompt action, could cripple it permanently or even snuff out the remaining signs of life.

Born without proper prenatal care and abandoned by its sponsors after great provocation, it can only survive and prosper through a massive effort by the United Nations or individual countries.

The Congo was a Belgian colony which lived on cheap African labor,

Belgian brains and money, vast mineral resources and great coffee, palm oil, and rubber plantations. The Belgian know-how has largely disappeared because of the panic that followed the crude attempts of the Congolese to assert their new authority.

The Congo has in fact come perilously close to exchanging a thin veneer of civilization for a return to the tom-tom and the tribal life of the nineteenth century. It is a state on which the Belgians tried for eighty years to fit Western civilization from the top. It penetrated only one thin layer, and this only imperfectly.

More than 80 percent of the Congolese still live as their ancestors did in the bush, respecting the ancient superstitions and hating the neighboring tribe.

Independence had barely dawned when the Bakongo and the Bayaka tribesmen in the proudly modern city of Leopoldville were cracking each others' skulls and burning each others' shacks. There was hardly a pause in the warfare between the Lulua and Baluba tribesmen in Kasai Province to note the independence ceremonies.

What went wrong with the birth of this new African nation, so rich in natural resources, so poor in wisdom and statesmanship?

In the first place Belgium, apparently intent on long and profitable exploitation of the Congo, made no effort to develop leaders among the Congolese. There are only a handful of Congolese university graduates— no doctors, no engineers, no lawyers, no accountants. There was no attempt to develop a national consciousness.

When the day of freedom came and the more aggressive of the long-repressed Congolese felt the urge to turn the stick on the white man, there was no authority they respected, no single black man they would follow. Ministers who toured the city trying to restore order were booed and derided.

The ministers had little standing with the army and the masses. They were former clerks in the Belgian administration, salesmen, minor officials in African communities. Premier Patrice Lumumba was a former postal clerk and more recently a beer salesman. It is to his credit, and that of President Joseph Kasavubu, that they saw the danger and called for United Nations intervention.

But before the United Nations could act, the new nation lost many priceless assets—teachers, missionaries, technicians, businessmen, doctors, lawyers, and engineers.

And on the deeply human side, virtually all its white women and children.

There were 10,000 Europeans in the government service in 1959. Even with the Africanization of the service, it was believed that 5,000 would be required to keep the government wheels rolling. Now, it is estimated that only 1,500 remain and many of them are thinking of leaving.

The Congolese simply do not have the educated, experienced men to handle the administration of such a huge operation.

---

Four years later, writing from Cairo, Heinzerling found the Congo in even deeper trouble. The following is adapted from an interpretive article in his AP file, dated October 10, 1964.

## MURDER FOR A SMALL FEE

### By Lynn Heinzerling

CAIRO—Subversion in the Congo has now reached a point where a "People's Republic" has been proclaimed in Stanleyville by the rebels. The "government" is headed by Christophe Gbenya, once a follower of Patrice Lumumba, the first Congolese prime minister who was murdered in Katanga.

Western diplomats do not give the "People's Republic" of Stanleyville much chance of surviving. African nations which might have supported the rebel government have become wary. The Organization of African Unity, a loose organization of delegates of the new African nations, has at last seen the threat which Red China's revolutionary methods poses to unity.

The Sino-Soviet split undoubtedly is one reason for the increased activity of Peking in Africa.

The long campaign to install a Communist government in the Congo by any means is brazen and open. The Soviet Union first tried to insinuate its way into the Lumumba government only a few weeks after independence in 1960. It failed.

A rival government established by Lumumba's follower, Antoine Gizenga, was set up in Stanleyville. It was supported and financed by the Communist bloc and a few African nations. That, too, was unsuccessful.

For the past six months, Peking has been trying to bring down the Congolese government by more direct and bloodier methods. The Red Chinese have supported rebellions at various points in the Congo, supplying funds, advice, and blueprints for sowing subversion and terror.

It is a comparatively easy maneuver to slip across the Congo River into the Republic of the Congo (Brazzaville) and recruit tribesmen for campaigns of arson, pillage, and murder. Tribal animosities in the Congo are so bitter and long-standing that tribesmen will cheerfully annihilate each other for a small fee.

The Congolese government has gathered impressive evidence of the part played by the Soviet Union and, particularly, Communist China in these rebellions, working from Bujumbura, Burundi, and Brazzaville. The Organization of African Unity, meeting at Cairo in July, refused at first to hear Congolese complaints of outside interference. The African leaders, headed by President Kwame Nkrumeh of Ghana, would not accept the new Congo prime Minister, Moise Tshombe, as a delegate.

In August, however, African foreign ministers meeting at Addis Ababa heard Tshombe state his case and efforts are now being made by African nations to end the rebellion in the Congo.

---

The horror of the Congo has left its mark on the civilized world. The shamelessness of those who tried to stop the United States and Beligum from rescuing the pitiful survivors of white massacres will not soon be forgotten. But after it was all over, and the troops were withdrawn, the terror went on.

At 12:30 p.m. on November 23, 1964, a bearded young South African correspondent for NBC, George Clay, arrived by helicopter at a place called Lubutu. He requested permission of Major Michael Hoare, the commander of a column of mercenaries supporting the Tshombe regime, to join the group in the fighting for Stanleyville.

"Mr. Clay asked to be placed as far forward in the column as possible," Major Hoare said. "We departed Lubutu at 4:30 p.m. for Stanleyville. Shortly after dark, our convoy was ambushed by rebels. Later that night once again we ran into heavy fire.

"At approximately 1 a.m. on November 24, a burst of machine-gun fire ripped into the vehicle in which Mr. Clay was traveling. He slumped over dead." When he was found, he had a tape recorder in his hands.

Thus, a correspondent was killed in action. Like Heinzerling and all the rest who were covering the Congo, he had taken the risks that are necessary in the work of a correspondent. There was no coffin, so George Clay's name was scribbled on a sheet and it was wound around his body when he was buried on the battlefield beside the Congo River on November 27, 1964. It was his forty-first birthday.[16]

## 30. *REPORTING THE VIET NAM WAR*

Malcolm Wilde Browne of the AP and David Halberstam of the New York *Times* were newcomers to the hard and dangerous business of war correspondence when they landed in Saigon in the early 1960s. They were pitched headlong into conflict and had to learn to dodge enemy fire, go without food and sleep, write under combat pressure, and still get into New York ahead of the opposition. They couldn't be called front-line correspondents because there was no front line in Viet Nam. It was in the Mekong Delta one day, around Danang in the north on the next, at Long An Province just outside Saigon on the third, and inside the hard-pressed capital city itself on the fourth. The Viet Cong weren't obliging enough to line up so they could be shot at or bombed in those days; nor did they waste their breath in empty proclamations.

It didn't take Browne and Halberstam very long to see that, regardless of the claims of Ngo Dinh Diem and his regime, the war was being lost. They were not alone. Among the small, hard-pressed band of reporters who agreed with them were Neil Sheehan of UPI, Charles Mohr of *Time* magazine, François Sully of *Newsweek* and Beverly Deepe, who replaced him during the period of his expulsion, and Jim Robinson of NBC, another who was expelled. There were others of less prominence, but Browne and Halberstam were the center of attention. Curiously, they were the keenest of competitors and gave each other no help when it could be avoided.

Browne had come to South Viet Nam on November 7, 1961. He was then 30 years old, having been born April 17, 1931, in New York City. While at Swarthmore and New York University, he had majored in chemistry, but he found it dull. While he was in the Army for two

[16] Russ Tornabene, manager, NBC news operations, *The Quill*, January, 1965, p. 42.

years of service, he was assigned in the Army's own inscrutable way to a tour of duty as a reporter for Pacific *Stars and Stripes*. When he was discharged, he began looking for a job as a newspaperman instead of returning to chemistry, and found one on the Middletown (N.Y.) *Record*, where he worked from 1958 to 1960. Then, he joined the AP in Baltimore, hoping for a chance to return to Asia; primarily because he spoke French, he was shipped to Saigon in the following year and proceeded to distinguish himself.

Halberstam, another New Yorker, born April 10, 1934, made a somewhat more deliberate beginning. He had been attracted to journalism while at Harvard and was managing editor of the *Crimson*. After his graduation in 1955, he became a reporter for the Nashville *Tennessean* for four years, then shifted to the Washington bureau of the New York *Times* in 1960. In the following year, he was assigned to the Congo; in September, 1962, at the age of 28, he came to South Viet Nam.

The journalistic battle that Browne, Halberstam, and their colleagues fought against their critics was a violent issue at the time, but with the coming of a new phase of the conflict it was overshadowed by events. Browne and Halberstam were proved right when the Diem regime was overthrown on November 1–2, 1963. They shared the Pulitzer Prize for international reporting for 1964. While Peter Grose came to Saigon for the New York *Times* and Halberstam in 1965 was reporting from Poland, Browne was still on the job in Saigon when the United States carried the war to North Viet Nam with a prolonged series of air assaults. It was at Browne's own request that he remained in the thick of the action.

The following pieces are typical of the work of these younger war correspondents of the age of atomic weapons, space rockets, and Communist guerrillas who defied both. The first is the climactic portion of Halberstam's long dispatch to the New York *Times* on November 2, 1963, reporting the downfall of the Diem regime.

## THE END OF DIEM

### By David Halberstam

SAIGON, South Viet Nam—The coup in Saigon began shortly before noon on Friday, November 1, when the navy commander, Capt. Ho

Tan Quyen, was assassinated while he was driving along the Bien Hoa Highway.

At 1:30 marines began occupying the central police headquarters, the radio station, and the post office. Shortly afterward, the central police called President Ngo Dinh Diem and told him the marines were there and they were not friendly.

Ngo Dinh Diem immediately ordered his military aide to call the headquarters of Gen. Ton That Dinh, commander of the Third Corps. An aide answered and the president said that the marines were at the police station and asked Ton That Dinh to send troops immediately. The aide said Ton That Dinh was not in.

In the meantime a group of high-ranking military men were having luncheon at the Officers' Club of the general staff. At 1:30, General Tran Van Don, acting chief of the joint general staff, announced that a coup was on and arrested all of those at the luncheon.

Fighting was developing between some of the presidential guard units and marines near the post office. Insurgent troops were also moving up on the presidential guard's barracks and firing. At this point the president and his brother, Ngo Dinh Nhu, began broadcasting on a palace transmitter.

The first broadcast called on all division commanders and province chiefs to send troops to protect the president. The message asked for acknowledgment. There was none. Instead, as time passed, the palace receiver got messages from division headquarters pledging loyalty to the military leaders.

The presidential palace became lonelier and lonelier. Ngo Dinh Nhu began calling the provincial chiefs to send irregular units to protect the president. The last of these messages, at 4 o'clock next morning, called on the Republican Youth and paramilitary women's units to move into Saigon and save the government.

The attack on the palace had been scheduled to start at 3:15 a.m. with a heavy artillery barrage. In the early morning, civilians watching the struggle from roofs noted the flashes of double flares that can be used in gauging artillery fire. At 4 a.m., the president's military aide called General Ton That Dinh for the last time and asked for troops to save the palace. This time, Ton That Dinh came on the phone "and cursed, using insulting phrases to describe the family." He told the brothers, "You are finished. It is all over."

He said after the conversation, "I saved them on Aug. 21 but they are finished now."

Most of the real fighting was done around the palace by opposing armored units. One observer described the maneuvering as "two boxers fighting in a closet." Atop the U.S. Embassy a cluster of staff members watched. Early in the morning one decided to go downstairs and tell Thich Tri Quang, the Buddhist protest leader who had taken refuge there.

"Reverend," the American said, "a coup d'état is taking place."

The priest replied, "Do you think I am deaf?"

When the rebels brought in flamethrowers, the issue was decided. For the rest of the morning, the tanks blasted at the palace. At 6 a.m., the firing ceased and then marines stormed and took the palace. But Ngo Dinh Diem and Ngo Dinh Nhu were gone.

There are said to be three main tunnels leading from the palace but the rebels knew and guarded the exit of only one. According to one report, Ngo Dinh Diem and Ngo Dinh Nhu escaped through a tunnel leading to a park north of the palace where they were picked up by a vehicle.

The vehicle took the brothers to a church in suburban Cholon where they apparently hoped to wait for rescue. Armored vehicles were sent to the church and the brothers were arrested. They were placed in an armored personnel carrier.

When the news was telephoned that they were dead, General Ton That Dinh grabbed the phone and made the officer repeat what he had said. Then Ton That Dinh slowly let his arms fall.

Then, all was over. Lieutenant General Duong Van Minh, who had headed the coup, became chairman of the revolutionary committee. General Tran Van Don became minister of defense and General Ton That Dinh became the interior minister.

The government had fallen, the Ngos were dead, and the military leaders had won all they had sought. The war with the Viet Cong, the questions of subversion, loyalty, poverty, and religious conflict at this point became theirs to deal with.

---

Malcolm Browne distinguished himself repeatedly for his ability to think fast under pressure during the ensuing period of crisis. While most of his principal competitors moved on to new assignments, he remained on the job, covering the rise and fall of nine governments in Saigon, the cliff-hanging military career of General Nguyen Khanh, the U.S. naval action in Tonkin Gulf in August, 1964, and the air raids on the Communists' once-privileged sanctuary in North Viet Nam in 1965. That was action enough for any war correspondent—and too much for most.

It was Browne who photographed the Venerable Thich Quang Duc, the first bonze (Buddhist monk) to burn himself to death in the middle of a busy Saigon street on June 11, 1963. He also moved into danger spots all over South Viet Nam with such capable staff men as Peter Arnett and John Wheeler backstopping him and the talented Horst Faas taking pictures. More often then not, he carried a carbine as the best kind of insurance against a Viet Cong surprise.

Changes of assignment brought talented new correspondents into Saigon—Peter Grose of the New York *Times,* who served for a year and went on to Moscow; Takashi Oka of the *Christian Science Monitor,* the durable Keyes Beech of the Chicago *Daily News,* Ray Herndon and Mike Malloy of UPI, Arthur Dommen of the Los Angeles *Times* and others. After François Sully returned to *Newsweek,* the prettiest correspondent in Saigon, Beverly Deepe, who also was one of the ablest, began working for the New York *Herald Tribune.*

Browne, therefore, had no end of competition. Yet, despite censorship and temporary suspension of communications, he often managed to get news into the AP in New York by various ruses. Once he wrapped his dispatch in an old newspaper and persuaded a passenger at Saigon airport to take it out for him. On another occasion, he talked a GI into taking $50 for a place in line to telephone New York on a Sunday morning; in that manner, the AP learned of one of the many coups in Saigon. When the Vietnamese armed forces took over from the nation's civilian council on December 19, 1964, Browne simply slapped a bulletin across the face of a picture that was being radioed to Tokyo at that moment. In 1965, he moved on to ABC Television.

The following pieces from his AP file of September 13, 1963, and December 10, 1964, show how he covered the action in South Viet Nam.

## A VILLAGE DIES

### By Malcolm W. Browne

DAM DOI, Viet Nam (AP)—This jungle town went through a blood bath Tuesday and the generals called it a victory. Perhaps it was. But it is not the kind of victory this shattered town can endure very often.

Vietnamese marines landed by helicopter and chased out 500 Viet Cong guerrillas who seized Dam Doi in the night. In the jungles and paddies the Communists may have lost more than 100 killed, plus machine guns and rifles.

Dam Doi reeks of death. The bodies of women and children lie rotting on corrugated iron litters, waiting for burial. The few buildings still standing are morgues.

More than 100 government soldiers and civilians died at Dam Doi. Probably another 100 were carried off along with four government mortars and more than 75 smaller weapons.

This jungle settlement of 2,000, about 70 miles south of Saigon, has lived with death and the Viet Cong for years. In February, 1962, this correspondent watched another of its agonies. Then, with no troop-carrying helicopters, it took three days to relieve this town.

The district chief led sixty-five troops in a desperate counterattack against the enemy in the jungle outside the fortifications. No one returned. The Viet Cong cut off the head of the district chief.

But the few defenders left inside the earthwork stockade held out until help came.

This time the survivors want to leave Dam Doi and let the jungle claim it. Two months ago an American adviser in Ca Mau, Xuyen province capital twenty-five miles to the north, predicted something like this. "We just don't have the strength to occupy an enemy zone, and this whole province is an enemy zone," he said.

There have been two huge operations in Xuyen province last year and this. Both were billed as victories, but the Viet Cong came back as strong as ever.

In the mountains of Central Viet Nam, government forces and their American advisers are systematically building strongholds to halt enemy movements and to cut Viet Cong supply lines. But it is a different war in these jungles, where the Communists are in force and move fast.

"If and when we win this war," a weary, mud-spattered American said, "the last place we're going to win is down here."

---

Late in 1964, at a low ebb in the fortunes of war for the South Vietnamese, Browne wrote as follows.

## WAR IS LIKE THAT

### By Malcolm W. Browne

SAIGON—The sun was beating down on a grimy yellow stucco building about thirty miles south of Saigon. The concrete supports under the building left a space of about three feet between the floor beams and the ground and about forty troops were camped in this space. It afforded protection from the sun and rain if not from the rats.

The building had been taken over as a headquarters for one of the units involved in pacifying the Mekong River delta. It was siesta time and hammocks were strung under the building, in the building and from trees all around.

In a cubicle in the building, a young Vietnamese artillery officer was dozing on a cot, a cloud of mosquitoes droning over his head. A U.S. adviser strode in, his face hard with irritation.

"I realize you need your beauty sleep, lieutenant," the American said, "but we have some fire missions coming up this afternoon and those guns need to be moved. Let's go, huh?"

The Vietnamese stirred. "Oh, I'm sorry but I go My Tho this afternoon. Captain Thanh said OK, I go."

"I know many pretty girls in My Tho but we gotta war to fight. Can't you go tomorrow?" the American asked.

The lieutenant smiled and shrugged and the American knew he would have to find someone else to take care of the guns.

War in South Viet Nam is like that. War is also a mob of soldiers with fire in their eyes storming a line of Viet Cong bunkers, fighting and dying with courage that would be a credit to any army. But it is a long war and the times for courage are rare. The main thing is just to last it out, somehow, without getting killed.

It is hard to measure the morale of the South Vietnamese fighting forces and the fighting spirit of the people who support them. Morale never seems to be so low that soldiers just stop fighting. But morale never seems to be high enough to satisfy the American standards of what is necessary to win.

Since General Nguyen Khanh seized power as premier last January 30, a lot of things have been done to boost the welfare of the fighting men under his command. The draft was stepped up to get replacements for exhausted line veterans. Last year the draft practically stopped. Last month 12,000 new recruits were hauled into induction centers.

Salaries were increased for all ranks of all services. Now, a private with two children earns the equivalent salary of nearly $30 a month and a major general around $250. Promotion and decoration policies were liberalized.

Life was also made a little easier for the quarter-million men in the "paramilitary forces"—the regional militiamen who have been carrying the brunt of the war (and the casualties) against the Viet Cong for the past four years.

Vietnamese soldiers are not issued food and they must buy or steal and prepare everything they eat. The money issued for buying food became a little freer this year. But despite these benefits, the war has not been going any better. The armed forces wreck one Viet Cong unit after another but the enemy keeps growing in strength and continues to sap the blood and energy of the troops.

And in a continuous undertone the enemy keeps preaching peace to the soldiers. For example, a group of weeping old women walk into a Saigon hospital to talk to wounded soldiers, telling them how the National Liberation Front (Viet Cong) only seeks peace for the nation and an end of twenty years of bloodshed. Some of the men listen before the old women are arrested.

Such things seep into the Vietnamese army, undermining fighting morale. It is a hard and frustrating life. Desertions from the regular army average about 6 per 1,000 men per month. Police currently are looking for about 8,000 deserters but punishment for desertion is only a few months in jail, then reinstatement in the army.

Viet Cong forces of all types, whose numerical strength has been rocketing during the past four years despite heavy battle losses, now number up to 114,000. This gives the government a 6-to-1 numerical edge, but experts on guerrilla warfare from Malaya and elsewhere maintain the government must have an edge of ten or fifteen regular troops for every enemy guerrilla to start winning.

## THE NEW FACE OF WAR

From Horst Faas's 1965 Pulitzer Prize-winning collection of Viet Nam combat photography.

American officials who accept these figures hold that the Vietnamese armed forces would have to be at least double to start holding the line and winning. Prospects of such an increase in armed forces strength are very small. For one thing, much of the nation's draftable youth lives in Viet Cong controlled areas. For another, the fighting spirit of the nation does not seem high enough to tolerate a mobilization going much beyond what it is already.

There are a thousand theories as to why the war is going badly. But for the soldier of the line none of the theories matter much. "In a war you just try to keep going and survive," one soldier said. "I gave up thinking of the future years ago."

## 31. KEYES BEECH AND THE PRINCE

When the new trans-Pacific telephone cable was completed between Honolulu and Tokyo in the summer of 1964, Keyes Beech of the Chicago *Daily News* was in the dark and crowded little office he shares with Robert P. (Pepper) Martin of *U.S. News and World Report* in Tokyo. The *Daily News'* telephone rang. Beech picked it up and heard his editor's cheery voice giving him instructions from Chicago just as if he'd been around the corner, available to cover the nearest mugging, riot, or four-alarm fire.

"That," said the gnomelike Beech heavily as he hung up, "is the end of the foreign correspondent."

Perhaps it might be true, if foreign correspondents sat around like beat men at police headquarters or city hall, waiting for a telephone to ring. But Beech's own career was the best indication that there was little to fear on that score. He was then 51 years old and had been a newspaperman since leaving the eighth grade to become a copy boy on the St. Petersburg *Evening Independent* in Florida.

There wasn't much of the world Keyes Beech hadn't seen, for he had been traveling since a few years after his birth in Pulaski, Tennessee, on August 12, 1913. From St. Petersburg, he moved along and in 1937 turned up on the Akron *Beacon Journal* as a reporter in 1937. Then, in 1942, he became a Marine combat correspondent and saw the worst of the war on Iwo Jima, among other spots in the Pacific. He decided, if he survived, that he would tell the story of this part of the world. Beginning in 1947, he did so as the Far Eastern correspondent of the Chicago *Daily News*. In 1951, with five other correspondents, he won a Pulitzer Prize for his reporting of the Korean War. And in 1952, the lad who never had a chance to go to high school became a Nieman Fellow at Harvard.

Beech traveled all over the Far East for more than a decade thereafter as a roving correspondent from his base in Japan. Wherever he went, he had sources that told him what to expect, where to go, whom to see if he had been away from the area for some time. In a number of spots, he didn't have to be told. And one of them was Cambodia, a place where most American correspondents were unwelcome.

On November 18, 1964, Beech sent this carefully drawn word picture of the enigmatic Prince Sihanouk to the Chicago *Daily News*, one of the few Americans who didn't try to make a joke out of the leader of a small but important emerging country:

## "MADMAN . . . BUT A GENIUS"

### By Keyes Beech

PHNOM PENH—Not long ago, a French general remarked of Prince Norodom Sihanouk, Cambodia's tempestuous but undisputed young ruler: "He's a madman but he's a genius."

As most things do in this capital, the remark got back to Sihanouk. The prince was delighted. As he tells the story today, "I don't mind being a madman as long as I am a genius."

The 42-year-old prince, who can be as charming to his friends as he is nasty to his foes—chief among which he classifies the United States —may not be a genius. But he is an exceptionally able and dynamic leader, who has done an excellent job of looking after his 87,000-square-mile kingdom and its nearly 6,000,000 largely illiterate inhabitants.

"He may not be good for us but he's good for Cambodia," confessed an American who has no love for Sihanouk.

For the last decade, Sihanouk has steered a tricky neutralist course through the Cold War maze of Southeast Asia's Balkan-like politics, cheerfully accepting aid from Communists, anti-Communists, and even neutralists like himself. Mainly because of Sihanouk, with an able assist from the United States he now so cordially despises, Cambodia is everything most of Southeast Asia is not.

It is peaceful and prosperous. It is free of subversion. Its people are united. It covets nobody's territory, if only because it is weak. Its leadership is enlightened and progressive. Its government is less corrupt than most in these parts. Instead of making war, its army is busy building roads, bridges, and schools and opening up virgin lands for aging soldiers.

In short, Cambodia is everything that the West in general and the United States in particular should want in a newly emerging nation.

Why is it, then, that relations between Cambodia and the United States have gone from bad to worse until today Sihanouk is threatening to leap into the arms of the Chinese Communists?

The answer is that the United States is closely allied in a war against Communism with two of Cambodia's most hated enemies, Thailand and South Viet Nam. All differences between Cambodia and the United States stem from this basic fact, plus the complex personality of Sihanouk himself. Says Sihanouk in effect, "You cannot be my friend and the friend of my enemies."

China, he believes, will be the dominant power in Southeast Asia as it was once before. Therefore it makes sense to Sihanouk to get on the bandwagon while there is time. He distrusts all Vietnamese, Communist or anti-Communist. And he is relying on Peking to take a fatherly interest in persuading the Vietnamese to let his country go its way.

## 32. CHANGES IN ROME

The years of the 21st Ecumenical Council of the Roman Catholic Church have had a profound effect on Christendom. Two popes, John XXIII and Paul VI, have led cardinals, patriarchs, and other ecclesiastical dignitaries in a searching examination of some of the basic premises of Catholic thought. The changes that have come about in the scant two years since the first session of the Council in 1962 are symbolic of what is yet to come. For while Christian unity is still a far-off goal, the growth of a deeper understanding between peoples within and without Christianity is surely within reach.

The theme of ecumenism and its attendant theological nuances were not easy to interpret to a mass audience. Yet, this is what the foreign correspondents had to attempt in their coverage of the first three sessions of the council. In writing of the doctrine, De Ecclesia, they were obliged to absorb the meaning of a 30,000-word document on deadline and show how it provided for a sharing of power by the pope and the bishops. This was the doctrine of collegiality, a massive reform in Catholic practice. In the decree on Ecumenism, which calls for eventual Christian unity, the correspondents had to deal with a spiritual rather than an immediately practical concept. And in a third doctrine, the relative autonomy of the Eastern Rite Catholic Churches, they had to weigh the possible effect on both believers and nonbelievers behind the Iron Curtain.

There was still another act of the Council that could scarcely be reported in the old "quote and run" manner. This was the Council's declaration against anti-Semitism and its position against the ancient belief of inherent Jewish guilt for the crucifixion of Christ, which was drafted for later final action. Such concepts as these required the widest understanding and interpretation, a challenge to the skill of the new breed of foreign correspondent.

There were many among the correspondents who met the test, including Protestants and Jews as well as Catholics. Some were specialists in religious journalism, a development that went far beyond the old "church page" of thirty years ago, the extent of religious news then published by many newspapers.

Among these specialists was Harold Schachern of the Detroit *News*, who for nearly a decade had done nothing but religious journalism. He was born in Pontiac, Michigan, and came to his specialty through general assignment work. After his graduation from the University of Windsor (then Assumption College) in 1938, he reported for the Pontiac Press and the Detroit *Times*. Then came three years in the Marines during World War II and varied pursuits, including public relations, for five years thereafter. In 1951, he came back to newspaper work and in 1956 was made the Detroit *News*'s specialist on religion. In this capacity he covered the Ecumenical Council, the deaths of Popes Pius XII and John XXIII, and the conclaves for the election of their successors. His work was broadly representative of the kind of correspondence in American newspapers with a special interest in news of religion.

Here is his evaluation of Pope John XXIII, written on deadline for the Detroit *News*, June 3, 1963.

## JOHN XXIII: A GREAT POPE

### By Harold Schachern

ROME—The throbbing bells of St. Peter's tolled not for a man today but for the world that had lost him.

Historians of the future will have difficulty properly identifying the man whose body soon will lie in state under the Basilica's dome, for to know him it was almost essential to have lived in his time and to have breathed his spirit.

Until he arrived in a world setting, his way was known only to a few, but this priestly way set the pattern for a papacy in which a divided world shared.

As cardinals of the church gathered in this stricken city today to prepare their pope for his burial and to elect his successor, other followers of Calvin, Moses, and Mohammed will mourn his passing as a loss to mankind.

For on the brow of Angelo Giuseppe Roncalli, the son of a Bergamo farmhand, the tiara of the papacy had shone forth not as the crown of a religious empire but as a soft light of understanding shining on all men.

When it is required to sum up Pope John XXIII's unique contribution to history, and it has been considerable, it must rest on this heroic simplicity and honesty that confounds fear.

He undoubtedly is the only pope in the almost four and one-half century history of Protestantism to be regarded by Protestants as saintly and wise. To Moslem, Jew, and nonbeliever he represented goodness.

Pope John will be recalled as the pontiff who summoned the Second Ecumenical Council of the Vatican, a historic move in itself, but it was this new spirit that he fused into it that gave it its revolutionary potential.

He will be remembered throughout the world as the author of two great encyclicals, "Christianity and Social Progress" (*Mater et Magistra*, 1961) and "Peace on Earth" (*Pacem in Terris*, 1963), but other popes had paved the way for them with great writings that served as a natural progression to his conclusions.

But whereas the encyclicals of Leo XIII, Pius XI, and Pius XII caused excitement in Catholic circles and only gradually intruded on the minds of others, the world's ear was tuned to Pope John and his pastoral words came like bursting stars to men seeking a redefinition of values.

In calling Vatican Council II, Pope John imposed none of his own authority on the council fathers. Observers have revealed, moreover, that he attended only two plenary sessions and injected himself only once to avoid a stalemate.

Besides the decisive impulse to summon the council in the first place, what Pope John did take into its sessions was a great and creative will and a drive toward new things. He was the author of a new Catholic style that caught fire in St. Peter's Basilica and spread to the nations. Other councils had sought to introduce new laws and restrictions to the point that may fortify the Catholic faith.

Pope John saw no reasons to fear for Catholic doctrine in the modern world, but only the need for a new style of Catholicism, open and ready to cope with the problems of the twentieth century and under-standable in twentieth-century language.

Pope John will go down in history as one of the great popes. His name will also be proposed for canonization, and for the first time in history, Protestants, Jews, Moslems and even nonbelievers of good will will wish they could vote on the outcome.

## 33. NEHRU IN RETROSPECT

An Indian cabinet minister rose in the Lok Sabha, the Indian parliament in New Delhi on May 27, 1964 and said, "The light is out." It was the formal announcement of the death of Jawaharlal Nehru, India's prime minister throughout nearly seventeen years of independence. The words that were used by the Steel Minister, Coimbator Subramaniam, were the same as those Nehru had spoken in 1948 to tell the world of the assassination of Mohandas K. Gandhi, the Mahatma.

In the offices of the *Christian Science Monitor* in Boston, the editors looked forward to a memorable account by their experienced Indian correspondent, Sharokh Sabavala. He was then 46 years old and had been a much-traveled correspondent for well-nigh two decades, half of that time for the *Monitor*. The hours passed, and there was no Sabavala file and no explanation.

Just as the *Monitor* was about to give up, the story came through. With a correspondent for *Time* magazine and one other man, Sabavala had been penned inside Nehru's home and was unable to get out because of the grief of the uncontrollable crowds. And anybody who has ever seen an Indian crowd could sympathize with Sabavala's plight. But at last he was able to leave and he wrote, in deference to *Monitor* style:

"Jawaharlal Nehru, prime minister since India became independent in 1947, and one of the great figures of the postwar era, passed on Wednesday leaving the political succession unclear and confused. As the news of his passing was given to the Indian parliament, many legislators wept. Soon a crowd of 50,000 men, women and children had gathered outside the prime minister's house, with thousands more streaming out of the streets of New Delhi to join them." [17]

Sabavala was representative of a new trend in foreign correspondents —the national who reported on his own country, or the region with which he was familiar, for a foreign newspaper or news agency. True, there had always been "locals," employees or stringers of foreign news organizations, but not many had become correspondents in their own right. Sabavala was one of a talented group of Asians who were able to interpret their own countries, and surrounding areas, to the United States.

His background was impressive. Born in Bombay in 1918 as a member of a distinguished Parsee family, he had been educated in his native city, in Montreaux, Switzerland, and at Oxford where, in his third year in 1939, he broke off his studies to join a British cavalry regiment. Later, he was seconded to the Indian army as an officer; in 1944, when the Indian freedom movement was rising, he was permitted to resign his commission for political reasons.

Thereafter, he became a journalist. As the correspondent of the Bombay *Eveninger*, he was in San Francisco to cover the founding of the United Nations. Later, he rose to editor of a lively Bombay newspaper, the *Free Press Journal*. In 1953, he began filing for the *Christian Science Monitor* and later visited the home office for on-the-spot train-

[17] Sharokh Sabavala, *Christian Science Monitor*, May 27, 1964.

ing. Three years later, he became the *Monitor's* correspondent in New Delhi, a post he filled with distinction.

Sabavala, a thin and intense man with a monumental impatience for procrastination and stupidity wherever he found it, could be harsher than any of his foreign colleagues in his assessment of India's faults. But as an Indian, he also had a strong conviction of what was right about his country. In the following assessment of Nehru for the *Christian Science Monitor* on May 27, 1964, Sabavala wrote of his own beliefs and his hopes for his country. The piece is slightly condensed.

## FAREWELL TO A LEADER

### By Sharokh Sabavala

NEW DELHI—In a country still using the implements of the Stone Age, and in the short span of half a lifetime, Nehru sought to introduce the Reformation of Germany, the Renaissance of Italy, and the Revolution of France. To top it off, he also introduced the industrial revolution.

It is said that Mohandas Karamchand Gandhi found his people on their knees and he taught them how to stand erect. Nehru taught them how to walk, to march, to run faster and faster without a backward look. The people, his people, although soon exhausted by all this activity, after generations of supine apathy and despair, reacted with boundless devotion.

In his last will (dated June 21, 1954), just released, Nehru says: "I have received so much love and affection from the Indian people that nothing I can do can repay even a small fraction of it and indeed there can be no repayment of so precious a thing as affection. Many have been admired, a few have been revered, but the affection of all classes of the Indian people has come to me in such abundant measure that I have been overwhelmed by it. It can only hope that in the remaining years I may live, I shall not be unworthy of my people and their affection."

History will almost certainly record, despite many flaws and failures, that he was not unworthy.

When Nehru became prime minister of an interim Indian government in 1946, the country still was helplessly dependent on external charity, producing very little in raw materials. The economy was based purely on agriculture. But the methods used to produce food and cash crops were archaic, scientific irrigation was conspicuously absent, and one monsoon failure brought disaster and widespread famine.

Today a considerable part of the landscape has declared its independence from the annual rainfall. Almost every state of the union has its giant dams and multipurpose power and irrigation projects. Many of them are working, and by 1970, when the whole program is to be completed, it will be the world's largest and most comprehensive.

Moreover, India is producing machine tools, automobiles, locomotives, and aircraft. It is producing fertilizers, chemicals, pharmaceuticals, light and heavy engineering goods, power—hydro-electric and thermal. It has begun work on the first of a chain of atomic power reactors. It is making electronics equipment and synthetic diamonds and emeralds. It is making plutonium and radio isotopes as well as plows and bicycles.

None of this is enough, and India is still heavily dependent. But a start has been made, the industrial base has been laid, the Industrial revolution fully introduced.

Nehru brought about a revolution in people's thinking. He shook and disrupted the established customs and mores. He respected age but laid emphasis on youth. He brought to a shut-in, introspective, dreaming society the drive and vigor of the West. But at no time did he deride his own Indian heritage, his inheritance.

In his last years, Indians did not spare Nehru, nor did the outside world. There was resentment at the tremendous pace he was setting. There was and is dissatisfaction with the progress, particularly economic, that has been achieved. There was and is anger at the state of defense unpreparedness under his tutelage. There was by no means universal support for his foreign policy or for his vaguely defined ideas of socialism.

At times this correspondent has seen him come near making a public exhibition of himself as he reacted violently to all this opposition. But never once, through seventeen years of untrammeled power, did he even hint that he disapproved of the democratic way of life and all its slow-moving institutions bristling with checks and balances.

In his last years, Nehru had become almost a monument, which people, Indians and foreigners, approached with awe. But not children. Instinctively, they seemed to realize that here was a new and worthwhile playmate. And during the days of national mourning, when

India brought its tributes, what was so perfect was the children's natural approach—no dread, no aversion, no apprehension, almost a gleeful joy that at last they had caught "Chacha"—Uncle Nehru—resting.

As his ashes reposed under a beautiful laburnum tree in his garden, a little girl approached with a handful of rose petals. She stood before the urn quietly and let them fall one by one, a golden rain. Then turning to her mother, she said: "If he does not get up before I go, tell him I picked them myself, as he taught me to do, from our own garden." The mother wept. And the little girl said, "What's the matter with you? Don't you know Chacha does not like tears? He has told me always to laugh so that I can grow quick and strong like these roses."

---

Sabavala was not always so restrained when he wrote of his India. But against the easy talk of other correspondents that India was breaking up, that no one could hold so disparate and untrained a mass of people together, he could and did match his faith. For in a wild and beautiful land in which everything except hunger, misery, and death were deemed impossible at one time or another, it took an enormous will to look beyond the dismal present into the hope of the future.

## 34. THE FALL OF KHRUSHCHEV

*Izvestia,* the government newspaper, failed to come out at its usual time on the night of October 15, 1964. It was the signal that big news was being made in the Kremlin.

Rumors swept Moscow that Nikita S. Khrushchev, the premier, might be in trouble. The round and forceful Russian boss had been vacationing in the Crimean resort of Sochi.

UPI quickly put out a speculative account that reached New York in early afternoon:

MOSCOW, Oct. 15 (UPI)—Unconfirmed reports swept Moscow tonight of major changes in the Kremlin leadership, possibly affecting Premier Nikita S. Khrushchev.

One wholly unconfirmed report said Khrushchev had been retired and his posts as party leader and premier taken by two aides.

The story was important because it had been sent with the authority of the UPI bureau manager in Moscow, Henry Shapiro, who had been reporting from inside the Soviet Union for thirty years. The Byzantine intrigues in the Kremlin were scarcely a new story to the keen-eyed, 58-year-old dean of American correspondents in Moscow. He had been through it all before.

He had been born in Rumania in 1906, had come to the United States with his family in 1920 and been naturalized eight years later. He made the most of his educational opportunities, earning his A.B. from the College of the City of New York and a law degree from Harvard Law School in 1932. In the following year, he turned up in Moscow to study law but became a journalist instead. He joined UPI in 1937, becoming manager of the Moscow bureau two years later. In the Stalin era and the years of Khrushchev that followed he learned how to cover big news in the Soviet Union.

Before 3 p.m., New York received the following from him:

MOSCOW, Oct. 15 (UPI)—Premier and Communist Party leader Nikita S. Khrushchev has been retired because of age and his posts taken by two aides, reliable sources said today.

Two hours later came the flash:

MOSCOW—OFFICIALLY KHRUSHCHEV OUT AS PREMIER

Then the whole story came tumbling over the wires on the authority of Tass, the official news agency of the Soviet Union:

MOSCOW, Oct. 15 (UPI)—Nikita S. Khrushchev has been retired as Soviet Premier and leader of the Russian Communist Party.

The announcement was made tonight by the official Soviet news agency, Tass.

Tass said that First Deputy Premier Leonid Brezhnev has been elected First Secretary of the Soviet Communist Party Central Committee. It added that Alexei Kosygin has been appointed chairman of the Council of Ministers, or premier.

Tens of thousands of words were filed from Moscow that night by correspondents of all nations represented there. The narrow victory of the Labor Party in Britain, in itself a historic event, had to take second place and the American presidential campaign, in spite of the Walter Jenkins sensation, was a distant third in the play of the news, even in the United States.

But what had happened to the 70-year-old Khrushchev? What did it all mean? How was the West to judge whether the new Russian leadership would try to patch up its quarrel with Red China, or open a new phase of the Cold War against the United States? No one knew. There could be only speculation; meanwhile, queerest of all portents, the stock market fell on New York's Wall Street in a nervous reaction to the overthrow of the latest of the Kremlin's rulers.

As quickly as the Iron Curtain had risen to provide a lightning glance at the Soviet power structure in turmoil, it closed. The new masters of the Kremlin kept their own counsel and let out little, at first, that was meaningful. The old Kremlinologists among the diplomatic corps and the press were called on to assess the prospects, but with admirable restraint they unanimously reserved judgment. Yet, a few—although far removed from the scene—were able to put the fall of Khrushchev in perspective, among them Harrison Salisbury of the New York *Times*.

Salisbury was 56 years old then and he had become an assistant managing editor of the *Times*. He had retired as Moscow correspondent of the *Times* in 1954 and won a Pulitzer Prize for his work the following year, along with many other honors. He had gone back several times, but not to stay, and had even written a novel about Russia, *The Northern Palmyra Affair*. Certainly, he had not lost touch and, more important, he had not lost interest.

Ten days after Khrushchev's overthrow, he published an account of it in the *New York Times Magazine*, October 25, 1964. It follows, in essential part.

## A PICTURE COMES DOWN

### By Harrison E. Salisbury

Late on the afternoon of Thursday, October 15, 1964, passers-by in Moscow's Manezhny Square saw half a dozen burly workmen taking down a great 40-foot portrait of Nikita S. Khrushchev that had been put up a couple of days earlier on the façade of the Moskva Hotel.

No Soviet citizen needed a bulletin from Tass to understand the significance of that action. Nikita Sergeyevich had fallen! The rumors that had coursed through the city for twenty-four hours were correct. A change in the Soviet government once more had occurred without the advice, participation, consultation, or prior knowledge of the 230,-000,000 citizens of the Union of Soviet Socialist Republics.

The taking down of Mr. Khrushchev's portrait was a symbol of the fact that despite the revolution that has occurred since the death of Stalin on March 5, 1953, the central mechanism of rule is still a tight, self-contained oligarchy, arriving at decisions in secret or even by stealth and presenting them to the nation as a *fait accompli*.

The fall of Mr. Khrushchev, like the fall of Vyacheslav M. Molotov, the venerable Foreign Minister and Old Bolshevik; like that of Georgi M. Malenkov, the one-time Premier and anointed heir of Stalin; and of Lavrenti P. Beria, the dread chief of the secret police, was accomplished in a manner more reminiscent of a Florentine court than of a state that prides itself on being the equal of any in the world in technology, in science, in education, in culture.

Mr. Khrushchev never established himself as a full dictator. He never invoked terror against his political opponents. He ruled by a balance of power that was constantly shifting. Sometimes he had the support of the military. Sometimes the military was divided. It was a demanding task, and he himself described a politician's life as the "most difficult thing in the world."

The newspapers began to take public opinion polls. Not on the popularity of Mr. Khrushchev, it is true, but on many live issues. Soviet officials were becoming more conscious of public opinion. The phrase, "The public doesn't want that," or, "People won't stand for it," entered their vocabulary.

They began to feel that the problem of the succession, the problem that is the fatal weakness of the Soviet system, was beginning to be solved.

For there were few intelligent Russians who were not aware of the peril for their country inherent in the kind of power struggle that brought Stalin to the top over Trotsky, Kamenev, and Zinoviev, or Khrushchev over Malenkov, Molotov, and Kaganovich. They well knew that they had no history of constitutionalism.

They knew that no method was provided in the rules of the party for an easy, natural transition. They knew there was no tradition that would ameliorate the cruel and costly struggle for power within the oligarchy.

But in the glow of change after Stalin, in the empiric experimentalism of Khrushchev, many members of the Russian establishment had come to feel that when change came again (and few expected it before Khrushchev's death), it would partake of something more in the spirit of the times, something less conspiratorial, less precipitate, less obviously in the ancient style of Kremlin politics.

Those hopes proved vain. Mr. Khrushchev was displaced in the traditional manner. It was an act agreed upon by a handful of men in the Soviet Presidium. They acted with the aid and support of the army, the chief repository of power in the country. The police, as far as is known, played no major role. But obviously they did not oppose the move.

The Russian public again was confronted with a *fait accompli*. They got the news—as they would have in Stalin's day—by a look at whose picture was being taken down from public display. It was a profoundly disturbing, profoundly discouraging event for most of Russia's post-Stalin technicians, scientists, and writers. Not that they invariably agreed with Mr. Khrushchev. But they had hoped their country had evolved past the point, as one said, "of going through that routine all over again."

And, by their very actions, the new rulers of the Soviet state inevitably set into motion that dangerous process which places the fate of their country in jeopardy as long as it continues—the struggle for power by which the succession is confirmed.

When will the terrible, self-destructive, perilous process end? There is no ready answer to the question. But not a few Russians have said in recent years that the world has become far too complex, technology is far too advanced, society too interrelated, and the world too closely knit to permit the Kremlin to go on indulging in primitive power struggles reminiscent of the days of Ivan the Terrible.

If enough of Russia's technical, scientific, and intellectual elite make clear this viewpoint, the deadly game of Russian roulette may finally be brought to an end.

## 35. "THE LAST OF THE HEROES"

On a gray and dour winter's day in 1965, the old war correspondents came together in London for perhaps their last big group assignment to pay tribute to the greatest of them all, Winston Churchill. They did it in the only way they knew how—the reporting of his funeral—and they did it superbly. All they saw and heard that January 30—and all they felt, as well—went into their stories to be spread out before the millions in the United States who saw it all on television and yet waited on the written word.

They merged with all of London in that memorable processional, dutifully referring to him as Sir Winston when all the time they wanted to call him "the old man," or something still more familiar. For if there was one war leader whom these tough survivors of a hundred battles respected to a man, it was Winston Churchill. He represented an epoch to them, a triumphant and soaring resistance to everything they utterly despised. And so they wrote of him, some with their names across Page 1 and others with his name in their hearts.

Eddy Gilmore, who had reported the war from Moscow for the AP and won a Pulitzer Prize, was writing the AP's day lead. It was fitting that his opposition for UPI should be the equally talented veteran, Robert Musel, who had seen the worst of the war in London. William H. Stoneman, the lean and grim-faced European chief of the Chicago *Daily News* foreign service, wandered the streets that day; so did Drew Middleton of the New York *Times*. Then came Joseph C. Harsch of the *Christian Science Monitor* and many another, some of them veterans of the Pacific like Gene Sherman of the Los Angeles *Times*, and others so young they barely remembered World War II as a personal experience.

Spread out across the United States were all the rest who survive and are still at work. There was a whole section at the New York *Times* that had the very essence of Churchill in it because so large a part of it had been written—unsigned—by Raymond Daniell, the chief of the New York *Times* bureau in London throughout the war. Walter Cronkite, who had flown bomber missions over France and Germany as a UP combat reporter, was the anchor man in the Columbia Broadcasting System's day-long television report. And elsewhere, watching and listening, was another of the great ones whose gravelly voice of doom had begun every broadcast with, "This . . . is London." It was Edward R. Murrow.[18]

The burden, as always, was on the men who had to run for the wire that day. And yet, somehow, they found time to say the things they wanted so much to say about the growling Englishman who had done more than anyone else to save Western civilization.

[18] Murrow died of cancer on April 27, 1965.

There was Drew Middleton: "Hundreds of thousands who watched Sir Winston Churchill's funeral today said farewell to their own bright and desperate yesterdays. For them, Britain buried more than her greatest son. She buried, too, the strongest link with their youth, with the great dangers shared and great odds overcome. They seemed to think there would never be anyone like him again." [19]

There was Bob Musel: "The nation he served so long and so well yesterday gave Sir Winston the most majestic state funeral ever accorded an Englishman. The free world sent its kings and queens and its presidents and premiers in gratitude for a debt it can never fully repay." [20]

And Eddy Gilmore: "To the strains of the 'Battle Hymn of the Republic,' Sir Winston Churchill passed into history today with one of the most memorable funerals in British annals. . . . The muse of history and the angel of death seemed close by on this historic day." [21]

And Graham Hovey of the Minneapolis *Tribune*: "And so the world said hail and farewell to the greatest Englishman of his time—with color and splendor in London, with stark simplicity on a windy Oxfordshire hillside, above all with pride and dignity." [22]

And Art Veysey of the Chicago *Tribune*, who had covered the Pacific war: "It was more than a funeral for a man that London gave Sir Winston Churchill today. It was a city and nation paying homage to an age of trial as terrible and threatening as any England has ever known, which through blood, toil, tears, and sweat—and quite a bit of ingenuity and good humor—was turned into a glittering triumph." [23]

They wrote of the funeral and the sorrowing people of London, of the magnificent scenes in St. Paul's Cathedral and the lusty singing of the "Battle Hymn of the Republic," of the symbolic movement of the flag-draped coffin along the Thames and the final journey by train to the country graveyard. Bill Stoneman saw all this, too, but he wrote of Churchill, the man.

Stoneman was in his sixty-first year then, with a lifetime of the waging of war and the groping for peace behind him. His had been an extraor-

---

[19] New York *Times*, Jan. 31, 1965.
[20] UPI file, Jan. 30, 1965.
[21] AP file, Jan. 30, 1965.
[22] Minneapolis *Tribune*, Jan. 31, 1965.
[23] Chicago *Tribune*, Jan. 31, 1965.

dinary career—born in Grand Rapids, Michigan, on March 15, 1904; graduated from the University of Michigan in 1925, a reporter for three years for the Chicago *Daily News*, then the paper's correspondent from 1928 on successively in Scandinavia, Rome, Moscow, Ethiopia, and London. He had gone through the worst of World War II—with the British in France through heartbreaking defeat, through the London blitz, with the American troops in North Africa, then Italy, across the Channel to Normandy, through the breakout in France, and on into Germany in 1945. For three years he had served as special assistant to Secretary General Trygve Lie at the United Nations, one of the most trying times of his life, and then had gone back to the Chicago *Daily News* and London.

It was out of a full heart that he wrote of Churchill in death that day of January 30, 1965, in the *Daily News*, as he would never have dreamed of saluting him in life.

## FUNERAL FOR AN AGE
### By *William H. Stoneman*

LONDON—History often goes unrecognized, even when it stares you in the face or you become swept up in violent and dramatic events that affect the future of the whole world.

It was that way back in 1940 when Sir Winston Churchill had his greatest moment. Most people were so busy just trying to stay alive that they had no time or energy for long-term reflection on the importance of what was happening around them.

But the few who watched the funeral parade for the grand old man as it moved from Westminster to St. Paul's Cathedral this winter morning could fail to understand its significance.

The very fact that this was a martial display, with thousands of men from the guards, the fancy cavalry regiments, the RAF, the royal navy and the marines, punctuated by the periodic firing of ninety guns, all to stirring military music, served to bring home the truth that this was in fact a funeral service for the age of military heroes.

There will be many more great funeral parades, with even more soldiers and sailors and airmen than marched in Churchill's memory. They probably will go on as long as mankind. But from this day on it will all be little more than ceremonial display. Nobody can imagine that there will ever be another Churchill—a world-honored leader whose reputation came first and foremost from victory in armed conflict.

In the Hydrogen Age there would probably be no more world wars. And if there were, there would be no heroes left.

Although his own martial exploits had been minor and trivial, if dangerous and dramatic, Churchill's personal courage and character, his mastery of the written and spoken word, and the historic accident that brought him to leadership of the free world at its most critical hour, had given him the status of an incomparable military hero.

The fact that he confronted Adolf Hitler—one of the most despicable monsters of all time—gave him far more importance than the other great Englishmen who fought and defeated Philip of Spain, Louis XIV, and Napoleon.

The millions of words that have poured forth in praise of Churchill during the week since his death, the endless television shows and newsreels and displays of excellent photographs covering ninety years of an active life, have also emphasized the happy fact that the "last of the heroes" was also the only one of them to benefit by modern mass media.

Many of today's British leaders, who witnessed the panoply marking the funeral services for Churchill, who heard massed pipers playing their lament, and the sailors piping his body aboard the barge that took it on a last journey up the Thames toward Waterloo Bridge, must have pondered on the contrast between his problems and their own.

Also on the fact that no such honors could be expected, in life or after death, by the heroes of Britain's modern struggle for existence.

In their more candid moments, many of Britain's more intelligent wartime leaders used to reflect on the relative simplicity of the problem that faced them compared to what Britain might have faced if the Germans had had the common sense to attempt the purely peaceful conquest of Europe.

They recognized the difficulty of doing successful battle with the brave, tough, skillful German people. But blowing them up with bombs and holding them at bay on the seas was, they felt, simplicity itself compared to competing with them for markets of the world.

This is the battle that modern British leaders now face on many fronts with no clearcut victory at the end, no medals, no band music, and no thanks.

From the time of Alexander the Great, three centuries before the

Christian era, there had been a succession of men of mighty stature. But not one of the good ones was able to talk to several hundred million people at once, to show his face to the whole world, whenever the occasion required.

———————

Thus, the journalist's farewell to Sir Winston Churchill: born November 30, 1874; died, January 24, 1965.

# VI. SPECIALISTS
## IN THE SPACE AGE

A man clapped his hands for attention at a vodka party at the Soviet Embassy in Washington on the night of October 4, 1957. Somewhat to the surprise of the guests who had attended a panel discussion of satellites and rockets to mark the International Geophysical Year, the interruption came from an American scientist, Lloyd Berkner, the panel chairman. He announced that Sputnik I, a 184-pound instrument satellite, had been shot into orbit by the Russians and at that moment was sending signals back to earth. There was a burst of handclapping, but it could not conceal the Americans' dismay. The Russians had scored a world triumph.

In this unceremonious manner, stunned and unprepared, the United States was pitched into the space age. After the first nationwide howl of anguish, in the familiar tradition of American self-recrimination, scientists, educators, and the military became the principal targets of public indignation. Every self-appointed critic, from the presidents of chambers of commerce to editorial writers, demanded an explanation. But there were so few who were qualified to discuss the space age, let alone write about it for the newspapers, that the portent of Sputnik I became a mindless discussion, based more on emotion than reason.

To make matters worse, the first slim rocket in the American Vanguard program blew up on its launching pad on December 6, 1957, at Cape Canaveral, Florida. Three weeks later, a visitor to that vast stretch of sand and palmetto heard indignant young Air Force officers blaming reporters for this latest blow to American pride and threatening to shoot them if they entered the reservation.[1] It was all a part of the national hysteria.

[1] Personal observation as an Air Force consultant, December, 1957, at Cape Canaveral, Fla., now Cape Kennedy.

Ordinarily sensible government officials talked privately of clapping a form of censorship over the whole space program to prevent the press from revealing more failures. Thus, the newspapers and the electronic media joined the schools, the laboratories, and the Pentagon as the scapegoats for a program that hadn't really failed because it hadn't ever begun. Yet, even Walter Lippmann wailed:

"The fact that we have lost the race to launch the satellite means that we are losing the race to produce ballistic missiles. This in turn means that the United States and the Western world may be falling behind in the progress of science and technology. . . .

"Our people have been led to believe in the enormous fallacy that the highest purpose of the American social order is to multiply the enjoyment of consumer goods. As a result, our public institutions, particularly those having to do with education and research, have been, as compared with the growth of our population, scandalously starved." [2]

The agonizing mood passed slowly. As more than a hundred satellites shot into space in the next few years and Russians and Americans followed them in rocket-propelled capsules that circled the earth for hours and then days, a more sensible attitude developed in the United States. Eight years after those first despairing days of the space age, it was clear that the United States held an overwhelming lead in nuclear warheads that could be delivered by intercontinental ballistic missiles, that the Russians had rockets which could lift larger payloads in the form of spacecraft, and that they were still ahead in their experiments with a device to put a man on the moon. However, even they couldn't be sure that they would stay ahead. The United States, after a disastrous early decision to do its pioneering space work with miniatures, was developing ever larger and ever more costly rockets to enter in the race to the moon.

The national outcry had had its effect. In addition to bolstering the space program, a new and vigorous effort was undertaken to improve American scientific training and general education and to reexamine national goals. As an important side effect, newspapers and news magazines that had always counted on specialized reporting now redoubled their efforts. New programs were offered by both foundations and uni-

[2] Walter Lippmann, "The Portent of the Moon," New York *Herald Tribune*, Oct. 10, 1957.

versities to train specialists in aerospace, science, medicine, education, and other fields.

The wire services, too, increased their interest in specialized fields, as did the television networks. Columnists or commentators with a special interest in science were proving their value in the space age. Thus, the bulk of the press was left with the choice of printing inadequate summaries of space shots or other events that had been brilliantly portrayed on television, or acquiring young reporters with specialized training to provide broader and more meaningful coverage. It was inevitable, therefore, that the trend toward specialization would continue.

The difference between the specialists of the 1960s and their honored forebears in journalism was twofold. Now there were many more of them and they knew a great deal more than their predecessors. Alva Johnston, writing his first Pulitzer Prize-winning science stories for the New York *Times* in 1922, merely raised a corner of the curtain of nuclear physics on the problem of splitting the atom. Two years later, Magner White's account of an eclipse of the sun for the San Diego *Sun* was awarded a Pulitzer Prize as an example of distinguished writing rather than scientific expertise. Nor was there much broader knowledge of nuclear physics at the Harvard Tercentenary meetings, for which five reporters won Pulitzer Prizes for their science coverage in 1937—William L. Laurence of the New York *Times*, John J. O'Neill of the New York *Herald Tribune*, Howard W. Blakeslee of the Associated Press, Gobind Behari Lal of Universal Service, and David Dietz of the Scripps-Howard Newspapers.

As for aviation, Russell Owen of the New York *Times* carried off the first Pulitzer Prize for such reporting in 1930 as a reward for his coverage of the Byrd Antarctic expedition. In the age of space, when a man can orbit the earth in little more than an hour, it is curious to look back to November 28, 1929, when Commander Richard Evelyn Byrd took off from Little America for the first flight to the South Pole with stolid, dependable Bernt Balchen at the controls of a three-engine Ford plane. Owen celebrated the occasion by radioing the New York *Times*:

LITTLE AMERICA, Antarctica, Nov. 28—A huge grey plane slipped over the dappled Barrier at 3:29 o'clock this afternoon (10:29 p.m., New York time), the sun gleaming on its sides reflected in bright flashes from its metal wings and whirling propellers. . . .

With its three motors roaring their deep song, it turned southward and was gone into the wilderness of space over a land of white desolation.

The 1,600-mile round trip took 17 hours, 59 minutes of elapsed flying time and was not duplicated for almost twenty years thereafter. It required aircraft of vastly advanced design and infinitely more powerful engines to make polar flights practical.

Until the intrepid William L. Laurence flew over Nagasaki on August 9, 1945, and saw the second atomic bomb dropped from the lead plane, the *Great Artiste*, no reporter had ever experienced aloft the basic forces that brought the space age into being. Yet, in the years that followed World War II, the explosion of scientific knowledge and the advances of medicine were so great that few of the older journalists could keep abreast of them. Most of them threw up their hands in despair.

Laurence, fortunately, was one of the exceptions. With a serene and matchless optimism, he saw man "on the eve of the greatest industrial, social and economic revolution in the million years of his evolution on earth." He continued in the same vein: "From a civilization limited and controlled by scarcity, he is about to emerge into the green pastures of a civilization built on plenty. From a world torn by strife and war, he is about to enter a new world based on peace, a world built to order with no limit on the realization of his vast potentialities, physically, intellectually, and spiritually." [3]

Nor could the old New York *Times* science editor be shaken by the events at Baikonur, the Soviet missile complex, or its American counterparts. Instead, these merely stimulated his appetite for more experiences in the new advances of science. As matters turned out, this was precisely the effect the space age had on all the specialists in journalism. For at the "Atoms-for-Peace" conference at Geneva in 1958, the largest international science meeting ever held up to that time, 475 journalists swarmed in from all parts of the world, including the representatives of fifty-six major American newsgathering organizations. Over a two-week period, there were ninety-one separate meetings, five sessions running concurrently every day. On the grounds of the United Nations Palais des Nations, there were displays of the peaceful uses of atomic energy by twenty nations. Commercial and industrial exhibits, marathon

[3] William L. Laurence, *Men and Atoms* (New York, Simon and Schuster, 1959), p. 243.

press conferences held by the sixty-seven delegations, and morning and afternoon briefings by United Nations specialists all developed an outpouring of news.

The New York *Times* and the New York *Herald Tribune* both ran the conference news on Page 1 for the first three days. The AP, with a four-man staff, filed 1,500 words every morning and 2,000 words every night. United Press International carried 1,000 words daily and Reuters sent 800 words. The verdict from a technical consultant who watched the journalists in action was a surprised tribute: "The reporters really knew what was going on!" [4]

The specialists expanded. Old organizations were reborn and new ones were kindled by the enthusiasm of young men and women. The National Association of Science Writers, founded in 1934, grew to 655 members and obtained a $110,000 grant from the Rockefeller Foundation to determine public attitudes toward science. They found awareness of science, but only fragmentary knowledge. As a result, in 1958, the Association set up the Council for the Advancement of Science Writing, which soon had 60 members and kept up interest with a $60,000 grant from the Alfred P. Sloan Foundation. A Nuclear Energy Writers Association also sprang up.

The old Aviation Writers Association, founded in 1938, became a giant 1,300-member Aviation and Space Writers Association. The American Medical Writers Association, founded in 1940, attracted 1,750 members. Three new specialist groups followed in the postwar years— the Education Writers Association, in 1947, with 73 members; the Religious Newswriters Association, in 1949, with 100 members, and the Newspaper Farm Editors Association, in 1953, with 100 members.[5]

It was the space age, however, that touched off the renewed interest in the specialist, and the dynamics of space as a result remained the focal point of his interest. At the heart of the $20 billion American space program in the latter part of the 1960s was the picturesque "Gateway to the Moon," Launch Complex No. 39 on Merritt Island, adjacent to Cape Kennedy (as Cape Canaveral was renamed). Here, a billion dollars worth of buildings was being put together to assemble

[4] Stuart H. Loory, "Scientists Meet the Press," *Editor & Publisher*, Sept. 20, 1958, p. 14.
[5] Paul S. Swensson, "Wanted: 30,000 More Journalists By 1970," *The Quill*, November, 1964, p. 20; Earl Ubell, "Knowledge Gap," *ASNE Bulletin*, May 1, 1962, pp. 13–14.

the 520-foot Saturn V "Moon Rockets." By 1970 or before, these fantastic giants were counted upon to hurl three-man Apollo spacecraft into orbit on the first stage of the race to the moon.

That was only the first stage of the grand American design. A second spacecraft, the Lunar Excursion Module (LEM), was also to be shot into orbit, docking with the Apollo. The plan called for two astronauts to leave the Apollo, get into the LEM and journey to the moon and back, again find the Apollo and dock with it, then return to the earth with the Apollo.

All who saw these magnificent preparations were awed by them. Now there was no longer anger and self-examination, but an entirely different attitude in the United States. A visiting editorial writer expressed it best after examining the vast moon project. He asked in wonderment:

"Why this enormous effort and expense? . . . All the obvious reasons about scientific advancement, business and technological benefits, prestige . . . these failed to satisfy.

"For here we are in the same realm as when we ask: Why a great symphony? Or big game hunting? Or climbing Mount Everest? When man pits himself against the stuff of the universe, including himself, to overcome and to mold, we glimpse something that defies reason . . . or editorial explanation." [6]

It is against this background of striving and achievement that the specialists have operated in the early years of the space age. A selective accounting of the variety, scope, and effectiveness of their work is presented herewith.

## 36. THE SECRET OF PROJECT ARGUS

On August 27, August 30, and September 6, 1958, the United States exploded three atomic bombs 300 miles above the earth's surface over the South Atlantic area. The triple blast was called Project Argus. It was a closely held military secret, for which the Department of Defense was responsible.

However, even before the firing, the plan became known to Hanson W. Baldwin, the military editor of the New York *Times*. He turned to

[6] Clarke M. Thomas, "At the Gateway to the Moon," *The Masthead*, Winter, 1964–65, pp. 2–4.

Walter Sullivan, then a science writer for the *Times*, for advice on how to handle the atomic secret; both, from the outset, agreed that the story should not be published prior to the tests. They took no one into their confidence and sat on the story, awaiting developments.

If there was one journalist in the United States who did not have to be told the importance of security on matters affecting the vital interests of the nation, it was Hanson Baldwin. His whole career had been spent in training for and writing on military affairs. He was born in Baltimore, March 22, 1903, graduated in 1924 from the United States Naval Academy at Annapolis, served for three years in the Navy as a junior officer, then resigned and turned to journalism. After two years on general assignment for the Baltimore *Sun*, he came to the New York *Times* in 1929 for a career that would extend across the better part of four decades.

From the outset he was the *Times*'s military and naval correspondent and in 1942 he became military editor. In the following year he won a Pulitzer Prize for his reporting of the conflict in the Pacific—Ernie Pyle's "war of magnificent distances." He had access to the nation's top military leaders and planners and was read by all the services with great care, although the Army and Air Force sometimes groused that he was from Annapolis and tended to favor the Navy's interests. It was a typical Pentagon quibble, based probably on the occasional sentimentality of an old Navy man. But no one had ever accused Baldwin openly of overt security violations for the excellent reason that he knew a good deal more about it than most of the officers who shuttled in and out of the security sections on three-year hitches.

Sullivan, too, had had a measure of indoctrination. He was younger, born January 12, 1918 in New York City and graduated from Yale in 1940. He, too, had spent most of his career on the New York *Times* from then on, nearly a decade of it as a foreign correspondent; in 1960 he was to succeed the fabulous William L. (Atomic Bill) Laurence as the *Times*'s science editor.

Once the triple blast was set off above the earth's atmosphere, it soon became known to those associated with Project Argus that Baldwin and Sullivan had the story. Some were in favor of letting them publish it, for news of the results of the atomic experiment was leaking out in scientific literature. There were strong suspicions that the Russians, who were scarcely tyros in the field, had all the information they needed. If the Russians didn't, it soon became obvious to Baldwin and Sullivan that a *Newsweek* correspondent, Henry T. Simmons, was very close to the truth; *Newsweek* was asking pointed questions about Project Argus.

What to do? Should the appearance of national security be preserved or should the New York *Times* be beaten by *Newsweek*? This, perhaps, was not precisely the way the *Times* reporters put the problem to themselves, but certainly *Newsweek*'s aggressive drive for the news was a factor in their thinking.

On December 28, 1958, Sullivan wrote to the Pentagon and asked permission to publish. However, he and Baldwin were told that even if the Russians knew of Argus, there were still some benefits to be gained from secrecy. The reporters kept trying. From some of the scientists deeply involved in government work, they learned that permission to publish was being withheld for purely political reasons; the government didn't want to be embarrassed. They asked Dr. James R. Killian Jr., President Eisenhower's scientific adviser, to help, warning that they couldn't withhold publication much longer.

Finally, in mid-March, Baldwin learned that the Pentagon was planning to permit a general release of the story. That did it. On March 17, 1959, he and Sullivan recommended publication to Turner Catledge, then the *Times*'s managing editor and later its executive editor. Orvil Dryfoos, who was then the publisher, asked many questions, saying, "I do not want to do anything that is going to harm the country."

On March 18, Baldwin notified the Pentagon that the *Times* at last was to break the story of Project Argus and Sullivan called Dr. Killian at the White House.

"From then until the presses rolled four and a half hours later," Sullivan wrote, "Hanson and I waited in fear that some reaction from Washington would forestall publication: an urgent phone call to the publisher or some prior announcement to take the edge off our story. When I phoned the White House, I had been warned to expect a return call almost immediately. To our great relief, none came." [7]

The Project Argus story led the *Times* for March 19, 1959. *Time* magazine promptly labeled it "the year's biggest news beat." Today, with an agreement against atomic atmospheric tests still in effect be-

[7] Walter Sullivan, "Year's Biggest Beat Long a Secret of *Times* Reporters," *Times Talk*, March–April, 1959.

tween the United States and Russia, Baldwin's beat is a scientific curiosity. The essential part of it follows.

## THE GREAT EXPERIMENT

### By Hanson W. Baldwin

Secret nuclear test detonations at more than 300 miles above the earth were conducted by the United States early last September. The tests, which have not previously been revealed and are believed to have been undetected by other countries, resulted in data of great military and scientific importance.

These data, though incomplete and controversial, indicate possible widespread interference with radar and radio by high altitude nuclear detonations. In a military sense the findings have great potential significance to the development of an antiballistic missile system and to the security of the nation's early warning and global communications system.

From the scientific point of view the data reveal much new knowledge about the earth's magnetic field and the behavior of radiation in the upper atmosphere and in space.

The nuclear detonations at the high altitudes were known under the code name of Project Argus. They have been described to this newspaper as "the greatest scientific experiments ever conducted." They were conducted by the Navy under the supervision of the Defense Department and the Atomic Energy Commission.

Project Argus involved three nuclear explosions in the South Atlantic. Two earlier ones over Johnston Island in the Pacific, which were not part of the project, also contributed to the scientific findings.

The secrets of the Project Argus tests which, paradoxically, produced global effects, were known in general or specific terms to hundreds of officers, enlisted men, and scientists, but were well kept for more than six months.

This newspaper withheld publication until a growing accumulation of technical and scientific papers and reports, including a paper by a Russian scientist, made it clear that the Soviet Union knew of the theoretical effects to be expected from high-altitude nuclear tests. It was also learned last week that a high official of the Defense Department had recommended announcement of the tests together with release of some of the scientific measurements taken.

This recommendation followed a long, behind-the-scenes debate among scientists and military personnel about the desirability of announcing Project Argus and some of its results. The majority of scientific opinion apparently favored publication.

The three Project Argus detonations involved relatively small yield nuclear devices in a virtual vacuum more than 300 miles high. The force of the explosions is believed to have been in the kiloton range (1,000 tons of TNT) rather than in the megaton range (1,000,000 tons).

The nuclear test devices were boosted into space by special multistage liquid and solid fueled rockets—described variously as five- or six-stage devices. They were launched with precision and remarkable reliability from the pitching deck of the *Norton Sound,* a 15,000-ton former naval seaplane tender, converted some years ago into an experimental guided-missile launching ship.

The results of the detonations were originally to have been monitored by two United States satellites.

One, Explorer IV, was successfully launched by the Army from Cape Canaveral last July 26 into an orbit that carried it as close as 178 miles to the earth and as far as 1,358 miles away. A second satellite, launched from Cape Canaveral on August 24, failed to get into orbit.

The high-altitude Argus explosions resulted in the creation of artificial auroras—one deep over the South Atlantic, another in the North Atlantic. Apparently both were unseen by foreign observers.

The September tests, and the earlier ones at lower altitudes over Johnston Island in the Pacific, stemmed from a military-scientific need to know what would happen when a nuclear detonation occurred in thin air and in a virtual vacuum high above the earth.

The theoretical postulates had been provided by a series of secret papers, which grew out of a basic study by Nicholas C. Christofilos, a self-taught physicist of Greek-American extraction. He is employed at the Atomic Energy Commission's Livermore (Calif.) Radiation Laboratory, operated by the University of California.

Project Argus—and the earlier tests at Johnston Island—provided the first practical, experimental confirmation of the so-called "Christofilos effect."

Oversimplified, what the Pentagon was anxious to establish, as one official put it, was whether the electronic radiations released in the upper altitudes by a nuclear detonation represented, in effect, a "teaspoonful of radiation in the sea of radiation around the earth" or the reverse.

The Johnston Island tests, which were publicly announced at the time, were conducted last August 1 and 12. The Army, under the auspices of the AEC, launched modified Redstone missiles with nuclear warheads of a very large yield.

The scientific results of the Argus tests were described in guarded superlatives as contributing major knowledge to the little we know about the region 300 miles above the earth. Particularly significant was the knowledge gained about the characteristics of electronic emissions in space and the behavior and intensity of the radiation bands that surround the earth.

---

While both Baldwin and his co-worker, Walter Sullivan, were well aware of what this knowledge was, they repeatedly stressed in their articles on the day the story broke that the results were still secret. However, Sullivan reported quite bluntly that Dr. James A. Van Allen of the State University of Iowa, who had been in charge of the experiment, correctly surmised that there were belts of radiation about the earth that were so intense that they "swamped" the radiation counters on the Explorer IV satellite.

"Was the volume of the Van Allen radiation so massive that the added amount from a nuclear blast would be insignificant?" Sullivan asked. There was little doubt from the context of the Baldwin-Sullivan articles that the answer was yes.

Sullivan, in fact, showed a lively acquaintance with the Van Allen radiation belts when he wrote: "From the scientific point of view, further tests along the lines of Argus would be invaluable in mapping the magnetic field and determining the boundaries of the 'cones of escape' over the two poles. These cones constitute the circumpolar regions in which the lines of magnetic force vanish into space instead of arching back to earth. It is in the 'cones of escape' that trapped electrons are thought to be absent, providing a safe departure route for space travelers." [8]

[8] Walter Sullivan, New York *Times*, April 30, 1959.

Thus, the Argus tests were disclosed. And the republic did not rock on its foundations. The public calmly accepted the outcome as history.


## 37. *OUR EYE IN THE SKY*

Chalmers Roberts pioneered in one of the most important functions of the journalist in the space age. He sought to explain new and difficult concepts in politics, diplomacy, and even science through the columns of the daily newspaper.

In doing so, he had to solve many a puzzle. But then, he liked puzzles and enjoyed working at them. As a result, he produced lucid and readable analyses that could be understood by the layman. He unraveled the Quemoy-Matsu crisis, the Suez war, and the U-2 incident for the readers of the Washington *Post*, among others. His U-2 report was so complete, in fact, that it was used by the Senate Committee on Foreign Relations as a part of its documentation.

This kind of journalism was the product of a lifetime of study and experience, plus the persuasiveness that was needed to convince hard-headed editors that readers would respond to such material. Roberts was born in Pittsburgh on November 18, 1910, graduated from Amherst in 1933, and in the same year began working for the Washington *Post*. He roamed the country and the world in the ten years that followed, holding a variety of jobs in journalism and government, including service on the Japan *Times* in Tokyo and with the Office of War Information in London. After three years with the Army Air Force during World War II, he resumed his journalistic career and in 1949 came back to the Washington *Post*. He was, successively, a reporter, foreign affairs specialist, and, beginning in 1959, the chief of the *Post*'s national news bureau.

One of his most fascinating explorations was the story behind the Samos satellite—"our eye in the sky." He undertook the study with the help of Howard Simons, the *Post*'s science writer, who was then 34 years old, a graduate of Union College and of the Columbia University Graduate School of Journalism. The essential part of their description of the Samos project, published in the Washington *Post*, December 8, 1963, follows.

## SAMOS

### *By Chalmers Roberts and Howard Simons*

On Thursday afternoon, July 21, 1955, at Geneva, Switzerland, President Eisenhower startled the world by proposing his "open skies" plan to break the East-West deadlock on disarmament. But before the day was over, Nikita S. Khrushchev had told the President that his idea was nothing more than a bald espionage plot against the USSR.

Today, nearly eight and a half years later, the Eisenhower "open skies" plan is still in a diplomatic pigeonhole. But the miracle of science is providing a substitute far superior to what Mr. Eisenhower had in mind. It is an instrument so effective that it promises to break down the long cherished Russian ability to keep the Soviet Union a closed society.

This instrument is an orbiting satellite named Samos. In fact, it is a series of such satellites circling the globe together or in sequence. Every twenty-four hours, by unofficial calculation, one of these satellites, an incredible camera in its innards, passes over the Soviet Union between eight and twelve times and over Red China two to four times. The spacecraft orbit the globe at 17,000 miles per hour every ninety minutes.

At selected times, on command from the ground, a precious photographic capsule is ejected. It comes down through the atmosphere and is caught in the Pacific Ocean by aircraft of the 6593d Test Squadron operating from Hickam Air Force Base, Hawaii.

The effectiveness of the product of this multimillion-dollar U.S. government reconnaissance satellite enterprise is a matter of deepest secrecy. Nonetheless, a good deal has been printed in technical journals in the U.S. and in publications in the USSR. For example, Ralph E. Lapp, a nuclear physicist, said in an Ann Arbor, Michigan, speech recently:

"Development of orbital intelligence techniques may be expected to advance to the point where film will show automobiles on the streets of Moscow."

Samos is, indeed, the successor to the fantastically successful U-2 which flew unhindered across the Soviet Union for four years before the world-shaking flight of Francis Gary Powers on May 1, 1960.

Samos travels in a north-south path around the world at 17,000 miles an hour. The world meanwhile is traveling west to east at better than 1,000 miles an hour. One writer has likened Samos' task to that of "trying to photograph a horse race from a moving elevator."

Moreover, Samos shoots pictures, presumably on continuous strip film, from about 150 miles above the earth. To get a picture of a missile from this height would be like trying to photograph an object in Washington half the size of the Washington Monument from the top of City Hall in Philadelphia.

There is the problem of clouds and darkness. Robert S. Rochlin, a Disarmament Agency staff member, has estimated that on the average the earth is 60 percent covered by clouds "so that the satellite will see the sunlit surface of the earth only about 20 percent of the time." For example, he says, "there is statistically only about one chance in twenty that the noon skies over Moscow will be less than 75 percent covered with clouds."

But it is now apparent that U.S. engineers and scientists have overcome most of these hurdles. They appear to have developed an orbiting stabilized platform carrying a massive camera capable of returning pictures from 150 miles' altitude that are as good as those returned from the U-2 at 70,000 feet.

To achieve this success, American experts apparently have employed a mixed bag of photographic tricks. They have stabilized the Samos so that one camera always points toward the earth and another points toward the stars. Presumably, every time a picture is taken of the earth, a picture is also taken of the stars. In this way, photo analysts can get a precise "fix" on an area photographed.

But the key to the success, apparently, has been the development of cameras with enormous focal length. Technically, focal length is the distance from the lens to the film.

During World War II the Air Force used massive 1,500-pound aerial cameras with a 48-inch focal length. By 1960, according to Amrom H. Katz of the Rand Corp., in an unclassified article, "camera lenses of at least 100-inch and 240-inch focal length" had been developed by the USAF.

Obviously these cameras would be such huge monsters that lofting them into space would be a problem. Again, scientific ingenuity seems to have overcome this challenge through a technique called "folded optics." What this means, essentially, is that light is folded back and forth between mirrors before it reaches the film. This accordion approach permits long focal-length cameras that can be comfortably carried in a Samos satellite.

As good as today's Samos appears to be from available clues, there are better things to come. Not only better photographic satellites but better cameras, better film, and better ways to interrogate satellites, process the information, and analyze it.

Take for example the proposed Samos television system that would make it possible for ground stations to ask a Samos what it has learned each time it passes overhead. An adequate though still relatively crude system has been used successfully in the well-publicized U.S. weather satellites. Now a far more sophisticated system has been perfected for America's next series of weather satellites.

## 38. JOHN GLENN DOES IT!

The usually unemotional "A" wire of the AP punched out these burnished words on February 20, 1962, under the byline of Saul Pett from Cape Canaveral, Florida:

"We pushed with our bodies and we pushed with our minds and we wanted in the worst way for John Glenn to go in the best way. Go, go, go, go up, John Glenn, go straight, go true, go safe."

All over America people watched the fiery liftoff on television at 9:47 A.M. and the thin white trail of vapor that marked the flight of John Glenn's rocket into orbit—the first American to make it. And among the 50,000 spectators along Cocoa Beach who saw the Atlas vanish into space, an elderly woman murmured, "He's in the hand of the Lord now." [9]

No American then alive will ever forget the suspense of the next five hours as Glenn orbited the earth three times, sending back cheerful messages all the while. For this was the nation's answer to the cosmonauts of the Soviet Union, who already had done it twice—Major Yuri Gagarin on April 12, 1961, and Major Gherman S. Titov on August 6, 1961.

While Glenn was aloft, it was television's story and the new journal-

[9] Gay Talese, New York *Times*, Feb. 21, 1962.

ists of the electronic media met the test with magnificent nonchalance. For five hours they poured out descriptive material to accompany whatever pictures they were able to get, but they could not top the drama of the liftoff of the Atlas rocket. When Glenn came down, television couldn't get close to him at once for obvious technical reasons, and the wire services and the radio and the newspapers took up the brilliant narrative.

It was, all in all, one of the greatest days in the long and spangled history of American journalism. For if television turned its cameras on the sky that day, abandoning thought of all else, many a newspaper did the same with its pages. In New York, seven newspapers used 41 pages and 94 pictures. In Tokyo, six newspapers used 61 pictures, and in the Communist world, in Belgrade, there were five columns of detail in the small, managed press.[10]

Of the many who were at Cape Canaveral that day, covering for the press and for television, a handful had been wartime pilots and therefore had a special feeling for one of their own. Among them was Richard Witkin of the New York *Times*, who was then 44 years old and had been one of the pioneers in aerospace reporting. He was a thin, lively, fast-talking, swift-moving New Yorker, born August 8, 1918, a graduate of Harvard, Class of 1936, and of the Columbia Graduate School of Journalism, Class of 1940.

During World War II, he had spent four years in the military service. Having spent seven months with the Coast Artillery at Camp Davis, North Carolina, he switched to the Army Air Corps as an aviation cadet. When he was honorably discharged in 1945, it was as a captain holding the Distinguished Flying Cross, the Air Medal with five clusters, and a record of having flown thirty-three combat missions over Germany, Austria, and the Balkans as a B-24 pilot. When peace came, it was his fate to report the proceedings of the United Nations for the UP for nine years, including a Paris session and the Geneva conference of 1954. In the latter year, he shifted to the New York *Times* and became a journalistic Buck Rogers for a decade before he settled down to a career as a political expert.

This is the beginning of his fine story about Glenn's flight as it appeared in the New York *Times*, February 21, 1962.

[10] *AP Log*, Feb. 15–21, 1962.

## "A REAL FIREBALL OF A RIDE!"

### By Richard Witkin

CAPE CANAVERAL, Fla., Feb. 20—John H. Glenn Jr. orbited three times around the earth today and landed safely to become the first American to make such a flight.

The 40-year-old Marine Corps lieutenant colonel traveled about 81,000 miles in 4 hours 56 minutes before splashing into the Atlantic at 2:43 p.m., Eastern Standard Time. He had been launched from here at 9:47 a.m.

The astronaut's safe return was no less a relief than a thrill to the Project Mercury team because there had been real concern that the Friendship 7 capsule might disintegrate as it rammed back into the atmosphere.

There had also been a serious question whether Colonel Glenn could complete three orbits as planned. But despite persistent control problems, he managed to complete the entire flight plan.

The astronaut's landing place was near Grand Turk Island in the Bahamas, about 700 miles southeast of here. Still in his capsule, he was plucked from the water at 3:01 p.m. with a boom and tackle by the destroyer *Noa*. The capsule was deposited on deck at 3:04 p.m.

Colonel Glenn's first words as he stepped out onto the *Noa*'s deck were: "It was hot in there." He quickly obtained a glass of iced tea.

He was in fine condition except for two skinned knuckles hurt in the process of blowing out the side hatch of the capsule.

The colonel was transferred by helicopter to the carrier *Randolph*, whose recovery helicopters had raced the *Noa* for the honor of making the pickup. After a meal and extensive "debriefing" aboard the carrier, he was flown to Grand Turk by submarine patrol plane for two days of rest and interviews on technical, medical, and other aspects of his flight.

The *Noa*, nearest ship to the capsule as it parachuted into the ocean, took just twenty-one minutes to close the six-mile gap, lift the capsule aboard with a bomb block-and-tackle rig, and place it gently on the deck.

Colonel Glenn first was set to wriggle out of the narrow top. But when difficulty was encountered in getting one of the bulkheads loose, the explosive side hatch was blown off and the man from space stepped out on deck, apparently in excellent shape.

The whole continent watched on television as Colonel Glenn's capsule was launched. The world listened by radio. And 50,000 persons had a direct view from here and the beaches around as the Atlas rocket booster bore Project Mercury's capsule upward with a thrust of 360,000 pounds.

The Friendship 7 was lofted into a trajectory that varied between a low point, or perigee, of about 99 miles and a high point, or apogee, of 162 miles. It traveled at a speed of about 17,530 miles an hour and went from day to night three times before whirling east across the Pacific on the final leg of the flight.

Some 300 miles west of the California coast, three retro, or braking, rockets slowed the capsule enough to bring it out of orbit. The elated astronaut on board radioed, "Boy, that was a real fireball of a ride!" as the capsule rammed back into the atmosphere.

Besides generating heat that gave him a spectacular moment of fireworks outside his capsule window, the reentry ended Colonel Glenn's long hours of weightlessness and shoved him forcefully back against his contoured couch. At 2:43 p.m., a 63-foot red-and-white parachute deposited the Friendship 7 on gentle Caribbean waters. Once the capsule had been picked up by the *Noa* and safely placed on deck, Colonel Glenn emerged triumphant in his gleaming silver space suit.

---

There were other flights, longer in duration and more spectacular, in the years that followed. For the United States, Commander Walter M. Schirra Jr. flew six orbits on October 3, 1962, and Major Leroy Gordon Cooper made twenty-two orbits on May 15–16, 1963. For the Soviet Union, the length of the space voyages steadily increased until their fifth man in orbit, Lieutenant Colonel Valery F. Bykovsky, completed eighty-one orbits on June 14–19, 1963. Then, the Russians put the first multipassenger space craft, the Voshkod (Sunrise), into orbit on October 12, 1964 with three men and on March 18, 1965, Lieutenant Colonel Aleksei Leonov left the orbiting Voshkod II and ventured alone into space for ten minutes.

The United States, not to be outdone, sent Major Virgil I. Grissom and Lieutenant Commander John W. Young into a three-orbit voyage

## AMERICA'S FIRST ASTRONAUT

John Glenn before his tracking antenna.

in the multipassenger Gemini capsule on March 24, 1965. Then, a little more than two months later, up went the Gemini 4 spacecraft for a four-day flight with Major James A. McDivitt and Major Edward H. White 2d, during which White floated in space for twenty minutes on June 4 and landed triumphantly with his partner on June 8. At last, the Russians had been bested.

However, none of these American flights stirred up the fervor and exaltation of that first orbit by John Glenn. It was his misfortune that an accident—an injury to his inner ear when he slipped on a bathroom rug on February 26, 1964—ended both his career as an astronaut and his first effort as a politician. But that could not cancel out the thrill of his greatest day.


## 39. *THE DRUG THAT CRIPPLED BABIES*

What does it take to make news in an age when science and medicine have stunned the public imagination with their achievements? A 40-year-old reporter for the Washington *Post*, Morton Mintz, may well have wondered in the summer of 1962 as he began research on a drug called thalidomide. Another *Post* reporter had urged him to look into it, having heard just a little from a Senate committee that was investigating profiteering in the pharmaceutical industry.

Mintz, a thorough professional, was born January 26, 1922, in Ann Arbor, Michigan, graduated from the University of Michigan in 1943, and, following three years in the Navy, became a reporter on the St. Louis *Star-Times and Globe-Democrat* and the Washington *Post*. He had come to the *Post* in 1958. As he quickly discovered, there was quite a lot about thalidomide in the record already, but no newspaper had paid very much attention to it. It was the name of a new sedative which since 1957 had been marketed in West Germany under the trade name of Contergan to relieve morning sickness in pregnancy. As early as 1961, British, German, and Austrian investigators had become suspicious of it.

On April 11, 1962, Dr. Helen Taussig of Johns Hopkins University, a respected pediatrician, told the American College of Physicians and Surgeons in Philadelphia about thalidomide. In her report, based on her own researches in Europe, she said that an estimated 7,000 babies had been or would soon be born in West Germany with marked deformities. She also attacked existing laws affecting such drugs in the United States, warning that American babies also were in danger. The New York *Times* and the AP reported the speech, but few others paid much attention to it.

Dr. Taussig kept fighting. She showed color slides of deformed infants to a House subcommittee headed by Rep. Emmanuel Celler (D-N.Y.) and declared that doctors in the United States were issuing some of the suspected thalidomide pills. In an issue of *Science* magazine, dated the following day, there was an editorial by Dr. Taussig which credited Dr. Frances Oldham Kelsey of the U.S. Food and Drug Administration with blocking the public sale of the sedative in this country. There was another reference to Dr. Kelsey's work in a piece by Dr. Taussig in the *Journal of the American Medical Association* for June 30.

Mintz went to Dr. Kelsey and interviewed her. He was slightly astonished to find that he had not been the first reporter to talk with her; however, nobody else had told her story. On July 15, 1962, he did so in a long, dramatic article for the Washington *Post*. The impact of the reporter's work and the prestige of his newspaper finally broke through the thick wall of public indifference and, what was worse, journalistic apathy.

Overnight, Dr. Kelsey was famous. Her story was published by newspapers and magazines throughout the land. It echoed from radio and television. Thalidomide suddenly was recognized for what it was. And despite Dr. Kelsey's courageous and stubborn act, it was found that more than 1,000 doctors had been passing it out to their patients under a legal loophole that permitted "clinical investigation." To cap the climax, Mrs. Sherri Finkbine, an expectant mother who had used thalidomide, had to leave the United States in search of an abortion to prevent the birth of what could have been a deformed baby.

In the furor, the pharmaceutical lobby for once was thrown for a loss. President Kennedy demanded a stiff new bill to give the FDA stronger powers to keep suspected drugs off the market and the Congress quickly gave it to him. It was signed into law on October 10, 1962.

Morton Mintz won national recognition for his work, for with a single story he and the Washington *Post* had shocked the nation and made possible a sweeping reform that might otherwise not have been achieved. Yet, considering all that had happened, he could not have been blamed if he had meditated at odd times in his city room on the meaning of the first question of journalism: "What is news?" [11]

Here is the main part of his celebrated article in the Washington *Post*, July 15, 1962.

## DR. KELSEY'S STORY
### By Morton Mintz

This is the story of how the skepticism and stubbornness of a government physician prevented what could have been an appalling American tragedy—the birth of hundreds or indeed thousands of armless and legless children.

The story of Dr. Frances Oldham Kelsey, a Food and Drug Administration medical officer, is not one of inspired prophesies nor of dramatic research breakthroughs.

She saw her duty in sternly simple terms, and she carried it out, living the while with insinuations that she was a bureaucratic nit-picker, unreasonable—even, she said, stupid. That such attributes could have been ascribed to her is, by her own acknowledgment, not surprising, considering all of the circumstances.

What she did was to refuse to be hurried into approving an application for marketing a new drug, thalidomide, the chemical name for a new sedative. She regarded its safety as unproved, despite considerable data arguing that it was ultra safe. It was not until last April, nineteen months after the last application was filed with the FDA, that the terrible effects of the drug abroad were widely reported in this country. What remains to be told is how and why Dr. Kelsey blocked the introduction of the drug before these effects were suspected by anyone.

The application for marketing the drug had come to Dr. Kelsey simply because it was her turn to take the next one in September, 1960. The European data on the drug left her "very unimpressed." In an interview, she said she had "lived through cycles before" in which a drug was acclaimed for a year or two—until harmful side effects became known. And, she said, she could not help regarding thalidomide as "a peculiar drug." It troubled her that its effects on animals were not the same as on humans—it did not make them sleepy.

[11] Arthur E. Rowse, "The Thalidomide Story," *Nieman Reports*, December, 1962, p. 10.

Could there be danger in those few people whose systems might absorb it? Could there be a harmful effect on an unborn child whose mother took it? (In other countries, obstetricians were innocently prescribing it as an anti-emetic for pregnant women.)

Dr. Kelsey regarded the manufacturer's evidence of thalidomide's safety as "incomplete in many respects." The drug was not, after all, intended for grave diseases or for the relief of intolerable suffering, but primarily for sleeplessness, for which many drugs of known safety were already on the market.

All of this being so, she saw no need either to hurry or to be satisfied with the approach that, nine chances out of ten, it's safe. She was determined to be certain that thalidomide was safe ten times out of ten and she was prepared to wait forever for proof that it was. When the sixty-day deadline for action on the application came around, Dr. Kelsey wrote the manufacturer that the proof of safety was inadequate. Perhaps with the understandable feeling of frustration, the manufacturer produced new research data, new reasons for action. Each time a new sixty-day deadline drew near, out went another letter: insufficient proof of safety.

Dr. Kelsey's tenacity—or unreasonableness, depending on one's viewpoint—was upheld by her superiors all the way. In February, 1961, she chanced to read, in a British medical journal, a letter from a British doctor questioning whether certain instances of peripheral neuritis—a tingling and numbness in the feet and the fingers that is sometimes irreversible—might not be due to the intake of thalidomide. To her this was a danger signal.

But neither she nor the applicant yet had the slightest inkling that the drug could be responsible for the birth of malformed babies. That awful circumstantial evidence became known to the applicant in a cablegram from Europe on November 29, 1961. He reported it to Dr. Kelsey early the next day. Although this was followed by a formal withdrawal of the application, as late as last month the applicant described the birth abnormalities as "alleged effects" of thalidomide.

"The American public," said Assistant FDA Commissioner Winton B. Rankin, "owes Dr. Kelsey a vote of thanks."

The 47-year-old Dr. Kelsey lives at 5811 Brookside Drive, Chevy Chase, with her husband, F. Ellis Kelsey, a pharmacologist, and their daughters, Susan, 15, and Christine, 12. She is grateful for the praise but recognizes that, had thalidomide proved to be as safe as the applicant believed, "I would have been considered unreasonable."

She intends to go on "playing for that tenth chance in ten" to assure safety in new drugs "to the best of my ability." For twenty years she taught pharmacology. She knows the dangers and she has not the slightest intention of forgetting them.


## 40. SCIENCE FOR THE MILLIONS

All over the world in this age of exploding knowledge, there are scientists and physicians—and even science-minded editors—who despair of ever attaining even a small measure of public understanding for their work. Science and medicine, they argue, can only be for the elite; the public must accept their august pronouncements on trust and pay a large share of the cost in terms of government-sponsored research. Such pessimism might be justified if it were not for an expanding and ever more knowledgeable corps of science writers who serve the press and the electronic media. It is their job to narrate the latest in science and medicine, to explain it, even to teach it when necessary.

Among the foremost practitioners of this difficult and demanding art is Alton Lauren Blakeslee, who writes on science and medicine for the AP. If anyone can be said to explain science for the millions, it is he. Like his long-time competitor, Delos Smith, the science editor of UPI, he must sometimes explain the seemingly inexplicable. Together, they cover more newspapers and newspaper audiences daily with the latest in science than any other two reporters on earth.

Blakeslee and Smith take their jobs seriously, but they refuse to be solemn about the nature of their work. "You don't have to be stuffy in writing about science and scientists," Smith once said. "Science is a human pursuit followed by human beings and the latter have no objection whatever to its being so recognized. You may take any approach you wish—provided it is accurate. Scientists concentrate so hard on accuracy they're keenly aware when it is achieved and when it isn't. On the other hand, most of them are or have been professional teachers. It's easier—much easier—to get facts straightened out with a scientist than with a politician, a policeman, or a football coach."

Blakeslee would have subscribed to this. After all, he had been brought up in a science writer's home. He was born June 27, 1913, in Dallas, the son of the AP's pioneering science writer and Pulitzer Prize winner, Howard W. Blakeslee, and Marguerite Blakeslee. He attended Duke and received his A.B. from Columbia in 1935. In the tradition of thorough training for journalism, he served his first four years on a smaller newspaper, the Wilmington *Journal* in Delaware, before joining the AP in 1939.

During World War II, he was up to his neck in military affairs on the AP's foreign desk. But thereafter, he turned to science writing, spending four months in 1946–47 in Antarctica with the Byrd expedition. Following the death of his father in 1952, he stepped into the science and medicine vacancy and practiced his art with such distinction that he won the awards of the American Association for the Advancement of Science, two Lasker awards, the James T. Grady medal of the American Chemical Society, and the Howard W. Blakeslee award of the American Heart Association.

Alton Blakeslee does not pretend to write for the understanding of a small child or an addle-pated adult. He proceeds on the assumption that his readers have a basic interest in science and medicine and the intelligence to absorb new information, if it is presented to them in a comprehensive manner. Not all his stories are easy to read, nor does he contend that this is always desirable. The old-time editors could always handle easy-to-read stories by running the first four paragraphs and cutting the rest without reading. That can't be done with a Blakeslee story. It has to be run as written, in the main, always allowing for normal editing practices or it shouldn't be run at all.

Here, from his AP file, dated December 19, 1962, is an example of his work, a part of a series on mental health that won him his second Lasker award.

## NEW HOPE IN MENTAL HEALTH

### By Alton L. Blakeslee

NEW YORK (AP)—"The devil still talks to me," she said, "but I don't bother to holler back."

Thus did a tranquilizer drug bring one woman a ticket back toward mental health. From then on, she could cooperate with psychiatrists to work out an understanding of her emotional illness.

The "mood drugs," such as tranquilizers to calm excited minds and psychic stimulants to combat depression, are part of an exciting chemical era in mental illness. There are two great objectives.

One is to develop far more effective drugs for various types of mental illness. The other is increasing, if controversial, evidence that much mental illness may stem from faulty body chemistry.

If specific chemical errors could be pinpointed, they probably could be corrected to prevent or cure mental ills, much as Vitamin C scurvy. Psychiatrists are divided over the prospects of such chemical controls.

Tranquilizers, coming on the scene about eight years ago, and antidepressants, are having tremendous impact. Men and women sick for months or years have described the mental effects as the lifting of a curtain or cloud, or brightening of a dark room.

Drugs have provided a bridge to home for many thousands of men and women. Many continue taking them. With early, prompt use of drugs, through clinics or private physicians, many persons would never have to go to mental hospitals in the first place, declares Dr. Nathan S. Kline, director of research at Rockland State Hospital, New York.

Other psychiatrists are less convinced of the value of drugs—some thirty different tranquilizers and more than a dozen antidepressants are available now. Some say equally good or better results are obtained with intensive psychiatric treatment of patients, but admit to the shortage of psychiatrists.

The National Institute of Mental Health has set up the Psychopharmacology Service Center to speed the screening and testing of new compounds. To many researchers, a great, encouraging fact is that mood drugs do affect the brain, even though the mechanisms are not fully understood.

And certain other drugs, such as mescaline and LSD, actually produce hallucinations or other symptoms of severe mental illness in healthy persons—more reason to suspect that faulty body chemistry could be the reason for at least some types of mental illness.

In another sign, scientists have found abnormal chemicals, or abnormal amounts of regular body chemicals, in the blood and urine of schizophrenic patients. Whether these are the result or, possibly the cause of mental illness is not yet known.

A few conditions now are known in which an inherited chemical defect or dietary deficiency causes mental retardation in children. Damage is avoided if the trouble is detected in time. And studies of twins indicate some people may inherit a vulnerability to schizophrenia, the flight from reality which constitutes the major type of serious mental illness.

In the traditional view, mental illness is born from breakdown in human relationships or from extreme emotional stress. The wounded mind may withdraw, or turn to behavior relieving its stress and pain. Some scientists believe mental illness is a result of both environmental reactions and faulty chemistry.

Psychotherapy presents puzzles. It is a method of listening to patients and helping them discover reasons for their behavior, and new insights. There are many approaches.

But psychiatrists do not understand how it works, or why one method helps some patients, but not others. It is difficult to prove conclusively that psychotherapy works at all. Yet, thousands of persons obviously are relieved of their distress, and manage to resume useful lives. Psychotherapy itself is a target of research to determine which methods are best for what types of patients, and when.

Researchers are exploring other questions:

What goes wrong in our ways of rearing children that so many become emotionally ill? What special stresses do adolescents undergo, and how can they be handled? What are the full causes of juvenile delinquency? Can a predisposition to schizophrenia be detected and preventive measures started?

Research dollars are increasing. This year about $75 million is being spent in research by the institute, the National Association for Mental Health, state governments, universities, and other organizations. In ten years, says the institute's Dr. Robert H. Felix, we can expect to have the basic knowledge for far more effective action against mental illness.


## 41. THE CANCER DETECTIVES

Some of the most practical instruction in science and medicine in the Midwest is carried on from one day to the next in the pages of the Minneapolis *Tribune*. Here is no catchall doctor's column offering free advice about a host of illnesses, from hangnails to cancer, but a careful

and detailed study of new information and new methods that should
be of vital interest to the public. The *Tribune*'s science pages are not
sugar-coated for popular consumption. Neither do they have the didactic
quality of a textbook intended for specialists. They use the devices of
good journalism to attract and hold the interest of the reader.

News, therefore, has a very broad definition on the *Tribune*. It may
deal with the latest in the field of atomic particles—"the beasts in the
nuclear zoo," as Alton L. Blakeslee has called them—or with some new
discovery in the life sciences. Often, there will be discussions of the
public service aspects of medicine in the newspaper's general area, such
as an analysis of medical costs, the expansion of health services, or an
evaluation of hospital care. But whatever is attempted, the *Tribune*
usually documents its science and medicine reports with the same care
that it gives to any other news. The basic factual information still
comes first, the necessary interpretation follows.

Much of the hard work that has gone into developing the *Tribune*'s
science service was done by Victor Edward Cohn, who since 1947 has
reported on science and medicine for the newspaper. He was born in
Minneapolis, August 4, 1919, and managed to edit his college newspaper
and be elected to Phi Beta Kappa as well at the University of Minnesota, from which he was graduated in 1941.

Cohn's first chores on the Minneapolis *Star*, and later the *Tribune*,
were on the copy desk, from which he escaped in 1947, never to return.
He won many honors for his writing, including the awards of the American Association for the Advancement of Science, the Lasker award, and
the Howard Blakeslee award of the American Heart Association. But
none gave him more satisfaction than a signal recognition of his work
by the most difficult of all audiences for a newspaperman, his doctors;
in Cohn's case, the Minnesota Medical Association.

The following is adapted from a series on science which the Minneapolis *Tribune* published in 1964 to cover the latest advances in scientific knowledge. In it, Cohn and the *Tribune* buried the myth that a
good newspaper could be influenced by its advertisers against the best
interests of the public. Throughout the nation, the responsible press
was the first to print the news prominently that there was a link between
cigarette smoking and cancer. This is how Cohn summarized the situation in the Minneapolis *Tribune*, March 30, 1964.

## THE CASE AGAINST CIGARETTES
### By Victor Cohn

Doctors in the 1930s began seeing more and more lung cancer, which until then was uncommon. A few began saying the change might be associated with a profound change in men's tobacco habits that had started in the 20s.

Until then, most tobacco had been used in snuff, pipes, chewing tobacco, and cigars. The handy cigarette had become popular only in World War I and its popularity and the pleasures of deep inhalation of its smoke had been increasing yearly.

Two young New Orleans doctors, Alton Achsner and Michael De-Bakey, today noted surgeons, began asking their patients whether or not they smoked. Nearly all, Ochsner and DeBakey reported in 1936, smoked cigarettes. This won some medical notice, but critics scoffed. Just a few surgeons' unreliable observations, they said.

In 1938, Dr. Raymond Pearl of Johns Hopkins made the first notable statistical study, reporting that smokers had a far shorter life expectancy than nonsmokers. Other studies followed, but the subject still was mainly ignored.

By the late 1940s, however, there existed an important new force against cancer: the American Cancer Society, a fund-raising organization. In 1949 Dr. E. Cuyler Hammond, a Yale statistician and the society's statistical research director, told it that "some factor or factors" seemed to be causing a "tremendous" increase in lung cancer.

One of the society's first responses was a small grant to Washington University, St. Louis, for another surgeon, Dr. Evarts Graham, and his young assistant, Dr. Ernest L. Wynder. Graham was one of the country's most distinguished surgeons and the first to remove an entire human lung.

Graham and Wynder in 1950 studied the cases of 605 men with lung cancer. They found that 588 were heavy cigarette smokers. Graham himself stopped smoking the following year at age 67. He died in 1957 of lung cancer.

Graham and Wynder had created a medical furore. Their study and all studies before theirs, however, were what statisticians called "retrospective"—they examined life histories, which can be inaccurate. In 1951, therefore, the Cancer Society and Statistician Hammond began one of history's largest health studies: a "prospective" or forward-looking study that trained 22,000 volunteers to interview 187,783 men aged 50 to 70 and to follow them for an average of forty-four months.

In October, 1953, Hammond's associate, Dr. Daniel Horn, took his first look at the clicking IBM cards, coding results. He was so startled that he dropped his cigarette to the floor and never smoked again.

On June 12, 1954, Dr. Hammond—who had switched to a pipe— read the first results to the American Medical Association in a jammed San Francisco high-school auditorium. Hammond and Horn found that regular cigarette smokers had an annual lung cancer death rate ten times higher than nonsmokers and that lung cancer was a rare disease among men who had never smoked.

Other studies, American and British, produced like results. Most doctors now asked for clinching evidence.

In 1953 the earnest Dr. Wynder—now moved to Memorial Sloan-Kettering Cancer Center, New York—painted mice with cigarette tars: smoke residues containing many tobacco and smoke chemicals. The mice got cancer.

No one, however, was able to produce lung cancer in mice even with machines that forced them to inhale cigarette smoke throughout their lives. Mice and men, of course, often are susceptible to different diseases. Someone had to look more closely at man.

The doctor who did it was Dr. Oscar Auerbach, pathologist at the East Orange, New Jersey, Veterans' Hospital. Beginning in 1955, he and his associates studied thousands of slices of tissue from human lungs.

Ultimately, in a completely "blind" study, Auerbach was handed unlabeled slices from nonsmokers, light smokers, and heavy smokers. He had no idea which was which. He merely classified them as cancerous or normal or someplace in between, showing pathological changes or pre-cancerous conditions. On this basis he was able to identify the slides with high accuracy as coming from heavy smokers, light smokers, or nonsmokers. The heavy cigarette users had the cancers or serious changes.

Auerbach's most striking results were announced in 1959. A recent medical article called them "monumental."

By this time Dr. Anderson C. Hilding, a keen Duluth, Minnesota, pathologist, had shown how cigarette smoking might affect our lungs. Working alone, partly in his basement at home, he had found that smoke affects the cilia, fine hairlike structures in the lungs and air passages that ordinarily sweep out soot and dirt and keep the lungs clean.

By this time, too, it had been shown that cigarette smoke contains small quantities of many poisons and irritants, including a number of known cancer-causing agents, like 3-4 benzpyrene and arsenic. Things like this—and increasing debate—prompted four health organizations to ask President Kennedy to appoint an expert commission to weigh the mounting evidence.

Surgeon General Luther Terry named a ten-man group that worked for fourteen months. Then, on January 18, 1964, it called cigarette smoking 1) a leading cause of lung cancer; 2) a significant cause of chronic bronchitis and cancer of the larynx; 3) a strongly possible factor in pulmonary emphysema (another serious lung disease) and heart disease, though cause-and-effect proof here is still incomplete; 4) a major "health hazard" in all.

Few medical scientists have disagreed.


## 42. THE EXPLORERS

After a five-year cruise on the *Beagle*, during which he lingered in the Galapagos Islands in the eastern Pacific, Charles Darwin published his epochal *Origin of Species* in 1859. A little more than a century later, an American expedition of fifty scientists retraced part of the route along which Darwin traveled on his investigation. Like him, they based much of their studies on the Galapagos. But unlike him, they took a reporter along who often managed to send daily pieces on their work. He was David Perlman, science correspondent of the San Francisco *Chronicle*.

Perlman operated in a glamorous journalistic tradition. He made the work of the scientific explorers exciting and readable, just as his journalistic forebears had in many another venture to conquer mountains, deserts, uncharted seas, and polar ice. If anything, he was more enthusiastic than the scientists themselves. Often, he wrote his articles in the Galapagos at night by lantern or flashlight and got them out by a variety of ingenious methods. Sometimes, he used helicopters, or Navy

tenders; on other occasions, he would raise a radio "ham"—an amateur
radio operator—in the San Francisco area and transmit his piece by
radio telephone. The *Chronicle* printed everything he wrote.

Perlman was then 46 and had been a newspaperman for two decades.
He had been born in Baltimore and taken two degrees from Columbia
University, his A.B. from Columbia College in 1939 and his M.S. from
the Graduate School of Journalism the following year. He worked
briefly on the San Francisco *Chronicle* in 1940. In the following year,
he enlisted in the Army Air Corps and four years later was discharged
as a captain after seeing service in Europe. Until 1951, he worked in
Europe for the Paris edition of the New York *Herald Tribune* and for
*Collier's* as a roving correspondent before returning to the *Chronicle*.
It was then that he began exploiting his bent for scientific journalism,
of which the following, the essential part of the concluding Galapagos
article, from the San Francisco *Chronicle*, March 15, 1964, is an example.

## IN DARWIN'S STEPS

### By David Perlman

Aboard the *Golden Bear* at Guayaquil, Ecuador—Our expedition to the
Galapagos ended in a flaming sunset that burnished the black coats of
Santa Cruz Island's sea lions and colored the lava reefs of Academy
Bay.

Fifty scientists are on their way home now after one of the most
massive scientific assaults ever made in any part of the world. In every
island of the archipelago they followed the footsteps of Charles Darwin,
deepening his insights into the laboratory of evolution that makes the
Galapagos so remarkable, and adding a wealth of scientific knowledge.

It was a complex, expensive experiment: the National Science
Foundation spent $120,000 to support it. The University of California
Extension dedicated a staff and a year's work to sponsor it. The navies
of two countries—the United States and Ecuador—provided helicopters, a seaplane tender, and a patrol boat to cruise the 23,000 square
miles of sea where the islands lie.

A dozen tax-supported university campuses and as many other government and private research institutions contributed the time of senior
scientists, graduate students, and undergraduates to the two-month

project. The Shell Oil Company, solving a major logistical crisis that threatened the very launching of the expedition, donated 8,000 barrels of fuel oil to send the scientists off aboard the *Golden Bear*.

Was it worth all this to mount an expedition for five weeks of research in a remote set of Pacific islands?

We won't know the final answer until all the research results are analyzed and published, and that will take many months. But an interim report can only answer yes.

This expedition seems to have been an immense success. It added significantly to human knowledge of a particular oceanic island area. It provided a fund of new facts to apply to the broader questions of human evolution, ecology, and the physical processes of weather, Vulcanism, and the endless actions of the sea.

It filled many gaps in knowledge about the eastern Pacific Ocean, an area so incompletely examined up to now that scientific understanding of the entire Pacific basin suffered as a result. This expedition's collectors—botanists, entomologists, and ichthyologists—gathered hundreds of specimens for detailed study later. They found many species never seen before in the Galapagos, and many that had never before been recorded anywhere.

When these new plant, animal, and insect species are carefully examined, and their family relationships with other life forms determined, the infinitely complex picture of evolutionary linkages will become clearer.

Students of animal behavior had exotic material to work on: spine-crested marine and land iguanas that slither in thousands like colonies of ancient dragons; lively lava lizards that skitter around every Galapagos rock; the varied races of giant tortoises, one of the most ancient animals on earth, that are now almost extinct on many islands after two centuries of unbridled hunting by men, and the depredations of feral pigs and dogs.

The ornithologists on the expedition had a satisfying variety of bird forms to work with. The flightless cormorant, abandoned down a strange side alley of evolution where the great auk and the dodo once hid, sat for a behavior portrait. Darwin's finches, thirteen different species of them, varying from island to island in a vivid display of evolutionary adaptation, had their voices recorded for a study of genetics and learning in vocal behavior. Flamingos and boobies and swallow-tailed gulls were observed nesting. Hawks and owls were observed feeding, penguins swimming.

The geologists gathered sack after sack of lava samples and piled up evidence persuasively indicating that the Galapagos islands, a cluster of huge, active submarine volcanoes whose tips alone stand above the sea, have been isolated from the American continent throughout history. Another pioneering area of research was meteorology. Detailed studies were made of the atmosphere above the Galapagos by daily balloon flights that carried radiosondes to measure temperature and pressure. The archipelago seems to boast an exceptionally varied climate. This may act to speed adaptation and the evolution of new species.

Now the expedition is over. During the coming months scientific journals in a dozen disciplines will be carrying research reports on the Galapagos work. Some will be detailed lists of species found. Some will be accounts of experiments. But all will help clarify the question of how life evolves and varies under the evolutionary spur of natural selection—the concept with which Charles Darwin first revolutionized all human thought.

## 43. THE NATURE OF LIFE

The newspaper is often the only scientific textbook available to a mass audience today. Consequently, science writers become teachers as well as reporters, particularly when they must explain the newest developments in a time of rapidly expanding knowledge. Ian Menzies did considerable writing of this kind as the science editor of the Boston *Globe*, one of his most widely read series being "The Nature of Life."

At the time he wrote these articles, Menzies was 43 years old. The Scottish-born journalist worked only briefly in his native land as a reporter on the Glasgow *Herald* before being called up in 1939 for service in the British navy during World War II. During his six and one-half years of duty, he participated in the Norwegian, North African, Sicilian, and Normandy landings and won the Distinguished Service Cross. In 1947 he came to the Boston *Globe* as a reporter and nine years later was put in charge of a five-man staff that covered science, medicine, and education. He was a Nieman Fellow at Harvard in 1962.

The following, published April 14, 1963, is a part of his series in the Boston *Globe* on the nature of life.

## WHAT IS LIFE?

### *By Ian Menzies*

Man is on the threshold of understanding the nature of life. What seemed an unresolved mystery only twenty years ago is now being pieced together like a giant jigsaw puzzle.

With brilliance and almost frenetic haste the missing pieces are being sought by biologists, biochemists, physicians, physicists, working in scores of laboratories throughout the world. It is said that we are living in an age of discovery in the life sciences which at least parallels the great scientific achievements of a Newton, or the physicists Maxwell and Rutherford.

The goal is the understanding of the master plan of life.

Somewhere, possibly soon, some research scientists will put together seemingly lifeless chemicals which will interact to create life. Somewhere else, with the brilliant intuition which already has marked research in this area, someone will resolve the key to that code.

Even today, much is known. If the tempo of this pace is maintained the year 2000 may see the beginning of a new era in the medical–life sciences more dramatic than that of either the nuclear or the space age.

A new world of understanding is already flowering in the life sciences. Not only is the story of life unraveling here on earth but broader vistas are opening—that life also exists elsewhere in the universe. Some form of life probably exists within our own solar system, apart from the earth, most likely on Mars, but even more sophisticated life may exist in galaxies hundreds of light years away.

The life referred to—either created in a test tube or existing on Mars—may be extremely small, a tiny bacterium, but it is life if it can reproduce itself. However, the most exciting thing today is that science knows the template or die on which the master plan for life is handed down.

It is deoxyribonucleic acid, or DNA, a tenuous thread present in every one of the trillions of cells in the human body and in all living cells. DNA carries the code when one male sperm cell and one female egg fuse together to form the single fertilized cell.

It is DNA (half from the father; half from the mother) in this single combined fertilized cell which carries the instructions to form a child, a dog, a mouse, a whale, and nothing else. It is this specific DNA which carries the instructions for variety within a single species; which determines whether a child will be white, black, yellow, brown, have long or short arms, curly or straight hair.

DNA is the heredity baton passed down within a species from generation. to generation. This compound was only identified as the heredity factor in 1944 by three scientists at the Rockefeller Institute in New York—Oswald T. Avery, Colin M. MacLeod, and Maclyn McCarthy.

But even in the short time since 1944, so many rapid advances have been made that for those outside the immediate field the entire subject is a bewildering puzzle. Adults, even those with a college education, including science courses, are mystified, though school-age youngsters accept and have an overall understanding of the subject.

Communication on DNA between parent and child has become difficult, even ironical, since without DNA the relationship wouldn't exist in the first place. Yet the subject, dealing as it does with ourselves, has a compelling interest and is basically simple. Not only are we now able to postulate more intelligently how the world might have begun, how life and man evolved, but how in the future we may be able to influence evolution and use more fundamental means to correct disease.

The Brave New World of Aldous Huxley may be closer than we think, but also may be the solution of cancer, the understanding of aging, and in the more distant future the ability to engineer the growth of new limbs. It is possible to visualize the chemical factories which could supply the vital compounds man needs to live without his present dependence on meats and plants.

This would make man less of a parasite while preserving food supplies despite a growing population.

Many will fear the results of this new knowledge. Others will reply that man always has feared new knowledge. Still others believe that man, realizing nature in himself, will become more humble, more tolerant, more aware of his privileged position and act accordingly.

## 44. AN ITEM FOR THE PAPER

A young businessman stopped in at the Charlotte *Observer* in the spring
of 1960. He had an item for the paper—a meeting at which a North
Carolina chapter of the National Organization for Mentally Ill Children
had been founded. One of the editors talked to him in the newsroom
and took enough for a small story; all the young men wanted, in
reality, was a notice calling attention to the next meeting.

The editor was interested in much more than a mere meeting notice.
For his visitor told him, quite casually, that there were beds in all of
North Carolina's state institutions for only ten mentally ill children.
The *Observer's* top management decided almost as soon as they learned
of the story that something would have to be done about it. They
assigned their reporter for science and medicine, Donald MacDonald
Seaver, to do the job.

Don Seaver was then 31 years old and had been with the *Observer*
for three years. He had been born March 16, 1929, in Johnson City,
Tennessee, but he was a Tar Heel by adoption, having received his A.B.
in journalism from the University of North Carolina in 1957 and won
election to Phi Beta Kappa.

Soon after he set out on his investigation, he learned that the
*Observer's* visitor had been right. Although there were places for only
ten mentally ill children in the state's institutions, literally thousands
needed treatment. What it meant was that the state was neglecting those
children and their families whose problems were the most urgent.

All such inquiries are necessarily slow-moving and even tedious.
Physicians and psychiatrists are not the kind of people who can be
hurried and hospitals, as a rule, have somewhat more urgent problems
than providing information for inquiring reporters. It took tact, knowledge, and extraordinary patience on Seaver's part to get to the heart
of the story—the institution at Butner where the few fortunate children
were being sheltered and to learn what was being done for them. He
also talked at length with private agencies, with psychologists and psychiatrists, hospital authorities, and parents of children who were in urgent need of care.[12]

[12] Letter from Tom Fesperman, written as managing editor of the *Observer*.

On July 3, 1960, Seaver was ready to report on his "item for the paper" in the *Observer*. It was the first article of a series, the main part of which appears here, that shocked North Carolina into action after too long a period of neglect.

## "THE CHILDREN NEED HELP"

### By Don Seaver

Thousands of North Carolina's children are in serious trouble—with no place to go for help. They are mentally ill.

Their difficulties range from deep-seated psychoses to learning problems in the public school. Estimates of the number of children who are psychotic—a severe form of mental illness—in North Carolina range as high as 12,000.

Many of them need 24-hour-a-day care and treatment if they are to recover. They cannot be adequately treated in the adult wards of the state mental hospitals.

North Carolina today has exactly ten beds for the treatment of all its thousands of psychotic children. They are located in the special children's unit at Umstead State Hospital in Butner, near Durham. The children range in age from 5 to 12.

There is nothing for psychotic teen-agers.

The Butner unit has a long waiting list even though it has not advertised its services and takes only those it believes can be helped. Dr. S. A. Ginn, consultant in child psychiatry at the Charlotte Mental Health Clinic, estimates that he has seen twenty such children here in the past three years.

"That is the most frustrating thing here," he said. "Most of these children can't talk. They must be watched. Butner took none under six for a while. We tried treating some here for a time, but we couldn't provide the day-to-day care they needed. They actually needed residential care. One family just built a fence in their back yard and turned their little boy loose."

A young Charlotte couple struggled for three years with their only son, knowing something was wrong, before they learned the terrible truth. Their son was psychotic and needed intensive care immediately. It took them weeks to get used to the idea that their child would have to be kept in a hospital—perhaps for years.

But they were one of the lucky couples—an opening appeared at Butner and their son is there today. They were given an alternate choice—a child psychiatric center in Kansas, which would have forced the family to pull up stakes and move to the Midwest.

The family must participate in the treatment program on a regular basis.

The Mecklenburg County Public Welfare Department presently is helping to support a psychotic boy in a Pennsylvania private hospital at a cost of $150 a month. This has gone on for six years. The boy is now 12 and it will be another four years before he will be taken into the state hospital system.

Public money will have contributed $18,000 to a hospital in another state for his care. He is but one who has been helped in this way. Yet, the number of psychotic children is only a small part of all the North Carolina children who are mentally ill.

In fiscal year 1959, of 4,318 persons treated in the state's 11 mental health clinics, 59 percent were under 18 years old. More than a third of these were under 10. Those being treated are nowhere near all who need the clinic's help.

According to Dr. Robert M. Fink, mental health consultant for the State Board of Health: "Our clinics now are actually serving nine one-hundredths of 1 percent of our population." Two surveys in states with comparable populations have shown that on any given day between 6 and 7 percent of the population is suffering from some type of mental illness.

Clinic service across North Carolina is spotty. All eleven labor under long waiting lists. In the month of June, approximately 640 persons were waiting.

Personnel and the money to hire them are in short supply. Outside the Chapel Hill Child Psychiatry Center, there are only four child psychiatrists in the state of North Carolina.

Dr. W. C. Rippy, director of the Butner children's unit, estimates that 80 percent of the psychotic children will become hopeless cases if their treatment is delayed until they are old enough to enter the adult wards of the state hospital system. Delay may keep them in those wards until they die.

He believes that 60 to 75 percent can be successfully treated if the treatment begins early enough.

The state of North Carolina sponsors a special education program that provides for the physically handicapped child. It provides for the mentally retarded. It does not provide for the emotionally disturbed child.

---

The *Observer*'s series produced action. In four years, North Carolina steadily expanded its funds and its services for the treatment of both emotionally disturbed and mentally retarded children. In June, 1964, the new Western North Carolina Training School at Morganton was dedicated, with a capacity for 1,500 children. It was designed to help both the disturbed and the retarded children, with the realization that the two conditions are often combined. The school, however, emphasized treatment and training rather than custodial care. At Murdoch, at Butner, and elsewhere, further facilities were made available for psychotic children. Such was the immediate result of the "item for the paper." [13]

[13] Letter from Don Seaver, Duke University, Jan. 19, 1965.

# VII. THE PERSONAL
# TOUCH

There have been many forms of personal journalism in American life, but they have never been neatly divided into eras. Some of the worst kinds of personal journalism, and some of the most exalted, have existed side by side; moreover, sad to relate, it has happened at times that the bad has driven out the good.

Consider, for example, the soggy prose of an uninhibited Irvin S. Cobb, who was a contemporary of the muckrakers of more than a half-century ago. At the murder trial of Harry Thaw, Cobb wrote as follows for the New York *Evening World*:

"Evelyn Nesbit held nothing back; she told it all. . . . How, with all the wiles of the serpent, her elderly seducer had brought hideous shame to her; how, when the chance of honorable wedlock came to her, she bared her secrets to the young lover; how the dreadful news had maddened him; how finally she had seen Stanford White, the seducer, slain by Harry Thaw, the husband." [1]

The copy desk passed it in cold blood, which was enough to make a man want to turn humorist in his later years to forget it all. But at the time, curiously, and for more than a generation thereafter, the bravura style of writing that Cobb affected was much admired in many a city room throughout the land. It was the forerunner of the early tabloid school. There was one editor who caused his rewrite men to shudder by announcing that no one henceforth could begin a story for his paper with an article, a common noun, or even a proper noun. No writing system quite came up to that until Rudolph Flesch arrived and, whether or not he intended it, the word-counting began.

[1] New York *Evening World*, Feb. 17, 1907.

There were other devices to trap the unwary reader into perusing a newspaper that would do almost anything for circulation. The assumption was, in the phrase of one editor of the day, that the reader might not buy the sheet again unless he came across something that made him say, "Gee Whiz!" The standards of the day sank steadily toward the lowest common denominator. One of the most famous features in New York newspapers was the sob-story interview as it was practiced by Frank Ward O'Malley, a reporter for the New York *Sun*. His fame rested in part on the following, which he ascribed to the mother of a murdered patrolman: "God comfort the poor wretch that killed the boy because he is more unhappy tonight than we are here. Maybe he was weak-minded through drink." [2]

The stimulus to emulate O'Malley lasted for many years in city rooms where the more sensational arts of journalism were practiced. After the gangland execution of Dutch Schultz, as a hoodlum named Arthur Flegenheimer was called, a rewrite man on a New York paper was told to telephone the Dutchman's widow for an interview. For some minutes, the rewrite man did his best while the city editor hung over his desk. "Well, Bump," the city editor demanded, "what did she say?" The crestfallen Bump replied, "Nothing much." "Good!" cried the city editor. "Give me a column of quotes!"

Meyer Berger, the great New York *Times* reporter, had a somewhat different experience with the Dutch Schultz story. While the gangster was still alive and on trial for income tax evasion, Berger described him at one point in an otherwise sober account as a "pushover for a blonde." The next day, the angry Dutchman collared the reporter and demanded whether he had written the offending phrase. When Mike uneasily admitted his guilt, the hoodlum asked plaintively, "What kind of language is that to use in the New York *Times*?" [3]

Berger's was a far different but even more personal form of journalism. Unlike a Cobb or an O'Malley, he never set up a loud caterwauling when he sought to touch the emotions. In 1947, he wrote quietly and with restraint in the *Times*:

"The first war dead from Europe came home yesterday. The harbor was steeped in Sabbath stillness as they came in on the morning tide in 6,248 coffins in the hold of the transport *Joseph V. Connolly*."

[2] New York *Sun*, Oct. 23, 1907.
[3] New York *Times*, Feb. 9, 1959.

He told of the procession headed by a coffin bearing the body of an unknown soldier, and went on: "Then came the long march up Fifth Avenue's pavement. The crowds at the curb were moved. Some let tears run freely. Some wiped them away. Some made the sign of the cross as the caisson rolled past them. In the Metropolitan Tower, bells tolled and the pealing echoes hung over the marchers. In Fifth Avenue's canyons, muted brass played 'Onward, Christian Soldiers.'"

Approaching Central Park, Berger recorded this incident:

"A little street sweeper held his broom stiffly with his left hand while his right hand rose in salute as the caisson rolled past him. No one smiled. Men and women stared at the street sweeper with grave understanding, and bowed their heads to their chests in a silent salute." [4]

Irvin S. Cobb and Meyer Berger were separated by something more than time. They lived in different worlds—the difference between the florid pretensions of the world before the first great war and the realities that brought the monumental changes after the second war. True, not all journalists in 1912 were Cobbs any more than all the journalists after World War II were Bergers, but they fairly represented the standards of the kinds of journalism they practiced. While the bravura manner survives here and there, as a debased form of personal journalism, in the main its day is done.

The change came primarily during the great depression, when the romantic pretensions of the journalist went out of style. Serious newspapers had never been greatly impressed by the uninhibited manner of reporting news and the posturing of the sensational sheets. Now, with the coming of a change in public taste, even the sensational editors began to see that their writers no longer had the broad appeal that once had been so important in newspaper sales. An effort to find a more agreeable style began to grow in many of the newsrooms of the land, and with it came more tolerance for the personal touch.

My own experience was fairly typical. Late one afternoon in the early 1930s, when I was working for a newspaper with a very large circulation, a reporter at police headquarters telephoned an account of a cheap, inconsequential murder. A gangster in Brooklyn had been rubbed out by a rival mob, in the phrasing of the time, and his body was found in a Brooklyn gutter. The way to handle such a murder in those days, in the New York afternoon field, was to make it sound as

[4] New York *Times,* Oct. 27, 1947.

if Edward G. Robinson had been the executioner and write a lead that fairly screeched. But, looking at my notes, the whole thing somehow sickened me and I could no longer do it.

The city editor told me it was late, to keep it short, and do it in a hurry because the last edition was ready to go to press with the late racing news. I wrote only the sordid and unspectacular truth in a few paragraphs: a small-time thug had been killed and nobody, not even the police, seemed to care about it. The story barely made the final edition on Page 1 under a small headline and no byline, certainly a depressing and unexciting account. I would have forgotten about it, except that it drew favorable letters from readers, an unheard of reaction for a news short, and nods of approval from my colleagues. It was a very small thing, looking back on it, but it helped change my point of view. After all, in addition to reporting the news, was it not also the business of the journalist to try to give a truthful reflection of his times?

I could equate such an attitude only with personal journalism, for it ran contrary to every canon of so-called objective journalism as it was practiced at the time. But looking around me, I saw that almost everything in journalism that had any meaning involved a personal commitment. Even though we pretended that there was a sharp separation between editorials on the editorial page and news in the news columns, it simply wasn't so. The complicated new measures of the Roosevelt administration had to be explained and interpreted to readers; the reasons why Tammany Hall was rotten had to be demonstrated, not merely listed with the objectivity of a grocery bill; the horrors of the systems that Hitler, Mussolini, and Stalin were practicing had to be brought home to readers. All these things couldn't be reported with the basic techniques that go into the writing of a weather report or an automobile accident.

It was true, of course, that this was a different form of personal journalism. A less-than-discerning public had always associated the phrase with James Gordon Bennett of the New York *Herald* and Horace Greeley of the New York *Tribune*, the first Joseph Pulitzer, and Marse Henry Watterson of the Louisville *Courier-Journal*—the beginning, middle, and end of a phase of journalism. To them, personal journalism meant the domination of a newspaper by a single powerful editorial voice. But with the passage of time, the newspaper had come to act more like an orchestra than a soloist, and on occasion the shrill sound of its editorial trumpet was drowned out by the bigger brass on all sides of it.

Thus, in the evolution of a new form of personal journalism, there were many voices, not one. Everything on the editorial page was signed except for the editorials themselves, and there were some who wanted to rip aside even the cherished anonymity of the editorialist.[5] As for the columnists, there was no doubt that they were becoming increasingly personal. Page 1, which had seldom featured the names of writers in an older era, was now studded with them, and the rawest cub reporter was likely to sulk if he wrote a half-column story that appeared without his name on it. The reporter of consequence, whatever his specialty, enjoyed more liberty of expression and was given greater latitude for critical comment than in any other era of American journalism.

Truly, as Arthur Krock wrote, many a funeral had been held for personal journalism, but it had never been obliging enough to die.[6] No one who picked up a daily newspaper could doubt that it existed in a livelier reincarnation than ever before.

In such an encouraging atmosphere for the journalist, a foreign correspondent of the stature of A. M. Rosenthal could write about India for the New York *Times* as follows:

" 'Oh, be careful, you know Indians are terribly, terribly sensitive.' I heard that before we went to India, heard it countless times during almost four years in India, hear it now from Indians and from foreigners. It is a piece of non-insight, meaning nothing. . . .

"Indians are sensitive; so are Russians, Poles, Afghans, Americans, and Rumanians, and I am quite sure that Bolivians are as sensitive as a cherry blossom in a sudden cold wind. This is the age of sensitivity.

"But for me this was the delight of India: once you had established your credentials as a fairly decent sort who basically wishes the country well, has some affection for it and does not regard its inhabitants as strange or exotic little brown men, then almost always the credentials remain open-dated and do not have to be renewed." [7]

Mary McGrory, writing for the Washington *Star*, was able to produce this highly personal view of a visiting dignitary:

[5] Ralph Coghlan, "Strip Away the Veil of Anonymity," *The Masthead*, Winter, 1964–65.
[6] Arthur Krock, in *Walter Lippmann and His Times*, Marquis Childs and James Reston, eds. (New York, Harcourt, 1959), p. 83.
[7] *New York Times Magazine*, May 21, 1961.

"Toward the end of her debut appearance in her campaign for love and understanding in the United States, Viet Nam's Mme. Ngo Dinh Nhu protested prettily that she is not a magician. It was the politest and shallowest of disclaimers. She may not carry a card in the union, but she can mesmerize an audience. She opened with a claque at the Waldorf-Astoria ballroom—the conservative National Review led the tepid initial applause. She closed with a cult.

"Mme. Nhu's looks alone would guarantee her a welcome. She is black-eyed, ivory-skinned, lissome. She was poured into a peacock blue sheath with white pants underneath. Her famed double-whammy glance flashed hardly at all during her hour and a half appearance. And Mme. Nhu possesses a formidable intelligence. She has obviously read her press notices and learned that her searing statements about 'barbecued monks' were not winning her friends. Yesterday she was the soul of discretion. She said some of her best friends were Buddhists." [8]

Finally, this was a bow by Walter Wellesley Smith, the good grey deacon of the New York *Herald Tribune*'s sports pages, to the city of Louisville after the sacred running of the Kentucky Derby:

"It is now Sunday afternoon in a city so strangely quiet it makes a guy think he has suddenly gone deaf. The sun is trying without much success to push through clouds that have been lashing Louisville with rain and wind and thunder and lightning since the last polluted paupers were being eased out of Churchill Downs.

"It poured all Friday and Friday night, too, but Derby Day itself was one of the loveliest in years, the golden filling in a soggy sandwich. How lucky can a gambling hell get?" [9]

This, I submit, is the most personal kind of journalism. It is not the dreary thing that is known to professors of English as journalistic writing (although, if they refer to the works of Irvin S. Cobb at the Thaw trial, they have something). Realistically, a journalist must use different techniques when he is writing a book, or doing pieces for the monthly magazines, news magazines, newspapers, the electronic media, or the wire services. But as to the substance of what he writes, he either is worth reading or he is not; he either has something to say or he has not. In this sense, the journalist cannot be separated from other writers,

[8] Washington *Star*, Oct. 10, 1963.
[9] New York *Herald Tribune*, May 8, 1961.

as so many have tried to do, by pleading that he operates under special conditions.

Every writer operates under special conditions, whether or not he is a journalist. Dean Jacques Barzun of Columbia, probably the most admired intellectual of our time, goes to his desk between 11 and midnight when he is writing a book and works until 2 or 3 in the morning. Is the effort in his case really so different from the heart-stopping routine of Brooks Atkinson during his twenty-five years as the New York *Times*'s drama critic? Normally, Atkinson came in from an opening night at about 10:30 p.m., set down his thoughts in less than an hour, and wound up by 12:05 a.m., with his own proofreading, so the edition could go to press. Barzun and Atkinson are both stylists. The non-journalist puts himself under pressure and the journalist has pressure thrust upon him.

The point cannot be disputed. For too many decades, the muddle-headed journalist has raised the specious plea of pressure and deadlines to excuse work that is frequently sloppy, wooden, and sometimes meaningless, as well. He has taken refuge in the contemptuous labels that litterateurs have coined for his work, such as Matthew Arnold's "Journalism is history in a hurry." More often than not, to justify a slipshod effort, he has said with piteous breast-beating, as did the journalist H. G. Wells:

"I am a journalist. I refuse to play the artist. If sometimes I am an artist it is a freak of the gods. I am a journalist all the time and what I write goes now—and presently will die."

How sentimental and how absurd! If journalists have excused poor writing too often because of lack of time, because what they did was written on the wind, who is to say that this is because the journalist often did not try hard enough to live up to his responsibility as a writer?

Charles P. Cooper, the brusque old New York *Sun* managing editor who taught my generation of journalists at Columbia, used to scowl at us fiercely and say: "Good journalism not only approaches literature. It *is* literature."

The evidence is respectfully submitted herewith.

## 45. *MERRIMAN SMITH IN DALLAS*

None except those who lived through four appalling days in November, 1963, will be able to comprehend the bewilderment, pity, and cold anger that transfixed the United States when President John Fitzgerald Kennedy was assassinated in Dallas and his slayer was shot to death before 50,000,000 television witnesses.

This was a tragedy of our time. No voices chanting slowly of the death of kings, no stately heralds or noble messengers could have told this frightening tale without arousing utter disbelief, terror, and perhaps panic as well. It was remarkable that none of these things happened, and that the United States once more was able to accomplish a transfer of presidential power swiftly and surely in a time of crisis.

Without doubt this was wrought in large part by Lyndon Baines Johnson as he succeeded to the Presidency and immediately flew back to Washington. But the reporters played a role, too. Those who had been tested in a lifetime of competition to be first with the news performed a hard and melancholy task that unbelievably sunny November 22 and thereby served the nation.

If there was one who stood out from his colleagues that day in the performance of his duty, it was a stocky, 50-year-old Georgian with the poise of a matador and the noisy energy of a piledriver. He was no unheralded, untried reporter, this sallow-faced, moustached Merriman Smith. For more than a generation, twenty-two years, to be exact, he had covered the White House for United Press and its merged successor, United Press International.

Like so many others, Smith had begun as a sports writer. Savannah-born and educated in part at Oglethorpe but more successfully in a dreary cavalcade of small newsrooms, he had gone on to UP in 1936 and become its White House correspondent in 1941. To the unknowing, he usually had to be identified as the reporter who broke up a presidential news conference by calling out, "Thank you, Mr. President." It had been the title of one of his books. To the ceremonious, he was dignified as the dean of White House correspondents. To those who worked against him in a strange and nerve-racking profession, he was a good reporter, the highest accolade they could give.

Smith was in the fourth car of the presidential motorcade that day as it rolled slowly from Dallas' Love Field to the Trade Mart, eleven miles away, where President Kennedy was to speak. The President and Mrs. Kennedy had flown in that morning from Fort Worth in Air Force One, the presidential jet. At 11:50 a.m., waving to welcoming Texans from the back seat of the open presidential limousine, with Governor and Mrs. John B. Connally of Texas in the jump seats, the Kennedys seemed supremely happy. It was a perfect day, 76 degrees and shining bright with sunlight. Applause burst from the crowds along the route. The visit had begun in triumph.

The ride was uneventful until the presidential limousine rolled past the old court house and turned right around an open-faced triangle called Dealey Plaza. Directly ahead was an ugly, red-orange brick building, the Texas School Book Depository. In front of it, the motorcade swung sharply left along Elm Street on its way to the modern new Stemmons Freeway and the final stage in the 45-minute trip. The Kennedy car was loafing along at eleven miles an hour. It was just 12:30 p.m.

"You can't say that Dallas isn't friendly to you today," said Mrs. Connally, turning to the President with a smile.

Mrs. Kennedy, sitting to the left of the President, was waving to the crowds. She heard a loud "pop," like a sound from a motorcycle exhaust, then a cry from Governor Connally. When she turned, she saw the President's left hand at his throat. Then, another "pop," and the President's skull was ripped open by a bullet. "Oh, my God, they have shot my husband—I love you, Jack!" she exclaimed.

Roy H. Kellerman, a Secret Service agent in the front seat, glanced back, saw Governor Connally in his wife's lap and the President collapsing in his wife's arms. Another agent, Clinton J. Hill, was climbing on the trunk. "Let's get out of here, we are hit," Kellerman ordered the driver. He radioed ahead to the lead car, "We are hit. Get us to the hospital immediately."

In a few moments William Greer, the driver, gunned the engine and the limousine roared past the frightened crowds toward the Stemmons Freeway.[10] No one knew then what had happened or how it had happened. But in the presidential limousine the mortally wounded Kennedy

[10] The Warren Commission report is the source for this account of the Kennedy assassination.

was unconscious and his blood was staining his wife's gay pink suit.

Back in the fourth car, all Smith knew was that somebody had been shooting. What he did that day and how he did it became a classic of journalism, the basis for the Pulitzer Prize in national reporting that was awarded to him in 1964. Here is the essence of his story of the events of that day, as it appears in the UPI file of November 23, 1963.

## DALLAS: NOVEMBER 22, 1963

### By Merriman Smith

It was a balmy, sunny noon as we motored through downtown Dallas behind President Kennedy. The procession cleared the center of the business district and turned into a handsome highway that wound through what appeared to be a park.

I was riding in the so-called White House press "pool" car, a telephone company vehicle equipped with a mobile radio-telephone. I was in the front seat between a driver from the telephone company and Malcolm Kilduff, acting White House press secretary for the President's Texas tour. Three other pool reporters were wedged in the back seat.

Suddenly we heard three loud, almost painfully loud, cracks. The first sounded as if it might have been a large firecracker. But the second and third were unmistakable. Gunfire.

The President's car, possibly as much as 150 or 200 yards ahead, seemed to falter briefly. We saw a flurry of activity in the Secret Service follow-up car behind the Chief Executive's bubble-top limousine. Next in line was the car bearing Vice-President Lyndon B. Johnson. Behind that, another follow-up car bearing agents assigned to the Vice-President's protection. We were behind that car.

Our car stood still for probably only a few seconds, but it seemed like a lifetime. One sees history explode before one's eyes and for even the most trained observer there is a limit to what one can comprehend.

I looked ahead at the President's car but could not see him or his companion, Governor John B. Connally of Texas. Both men had been riding on the right side of the bubble-top limousine from Washington. I thought I saw a flash of pink which would have been Mrs. Jacqueline Kennedy.

Everybody in our car began shouting at the driver to pull up closer to the President's car. But at this moment we saw the big bubble-top and a motorcycle escort roar away at high speed.

We screamed at our driver, "Get going! Get going!"

We careened around the Johnson car and its escort and set out down the highway, barely able to keep in sight of the President's car and the accompanying Secret Service follow-up car.

They vanished around a curve. When we cleared the same curve, we could see where we were heading—Parkland Hospital, a large brick structure to the left of the arterial highway. We skidded around a sharp left turn and spilled out of the pool car as it entered the hospital driveway.

I ran to the side of the bubble-top.

The President was face down on the back seat. Mrs. Kennedy made a cradle of her arms around the President's head and bent over him as if she were whispering to him.

Governor Connally was on his back on the floor of the car, his head and shoulders resting in the arms of his wife, Nellie, who kept shaking her head and shaking with dry sobs. Blood oozed from the front of the Governor's suit.

I could not see the President's wound. But I could see blood spattered around the interior of the rear seat and a dark stain spreading down the right side of the President's dark suit.

From the telephone car, I had radioed the Dallas bureau of UPI that three shots had been fired at the Kennedy motorcade. Seeing the bloody scene in the rear of the car at the hospital entrance, I knew I had to get to a telephone immediately.

Clint Hill, the Secret Service agent in charge of the detail assigned to Mrs. Kennedy, was leaning over into the rear of the car.

"How badly was he hit, Clint?" I asked.

"He's dead," Hill replied curtly.

I have no further clear memory of the scene in the driveway. I recall a babble of anxious voices, tense voices—"Where in hell are the stretchers . . . get a doctor out here . . . he's on the way . . . come on, easy there." And from somewhere nervous sobbing.

I raced down a short stretch of sidewalk into a hospital corridor. The first thing I spotted was a small clerical office, more of a booth than an office. Inside a bespectacled man stood shuffling what appeared to be hospital forms. At a wicket much like a bank teller's cage, I spotted a telephone on the shelf.

"How do you get outside?" I gasped. "The President has been hurt and this is an emergency call."

"Dial 9," he said, shoving the phone toward me.

It took two tries before I successfully dialed the Dallas UPI number. Quickly I dictated a bulletin saying the President had been seriously, perhaps fatally, injured by an assassin's bullets while driving through the streets of Dallas.

Litters bearing the President and the Governor rolled by me as I dictated but my back was to the hallway and I didn't see them until they were at the emergency room entrance 75 or 100 feet away.

Telephones were at a premium in the hospital and I clung to mine for dear life. I was afraid to stray from the wicket lest I lose contact with the outside world.

My decision was made for me, however, when Kilduff and Wayne Hawks of the White House staff ran by me, shouting that Kilduff would make a statement shortly in the so-called nurses' room a floor above and at the far end of the hospital.

I threw down the phone and sped after them. We reached the door of the conference room and there were loud cries of "Quiet!" Fighting to keep his emotions under control, Kilduff said,

"President John Fitzgerald Kennedy died at approximately one o'clock."

I raced to a nearby office. The telephone switchboard at the hospital was hopelessly jammed. I spotted Virginia Payette, wife of UPI's southwestern division manager and a veteran reporter in her own right. I told her to try getting through on pay telephones on the floor above.

Frustrated by the inability to get through the hospital switchboard, I appealed to a nurse. She led me through a maze of corridors and back stairways to another floor and a lone pay booth. I got the Dallas office. Virginia had gotten through before me.

Whereupon I ran back through the hospital to the conference room. There Jiggs Fauver of the White House transportation staff grabbed me and said Kilduff wanted a pool of three men immediately to fly back to Washington on Air Force One, the presidential aircraft.

"He wants you downstairs and he wants you right now," Fauver said.

Down the stairs I ran and into the driveway, only to discover Kilduff had just pulled out in our telephone car.

Charles Roberts of *Newsweek*, Sid Davis of Westinghouse Broadcasting, and I implored a police officer to take us to the airport in his squad car. The Secret Service had requested that no sirens be used in the vicinity of the airport, but the Dallas officer did a masterful job of getting us through some of the worst traffic I have ever seen.

As we piled out of the car on the edge of the runway about 200 yards from the presidential aircraft, Kilduff spotted us and motioned for us to hurry. We trotted to him and he said the plane could take two pool men to Washington, that Johnson was about to take the oath of office aboard the plane and would take off immediately thereafter.

I called the New York bureau of UPI and told them about the impending installation of a new President aboard the airplane. Aboard Air Force One, all of the shades of the larger main cabin were drawn and the interior was hot and dimly lighted.

Kilduff propelled us to the President's suite two-thirds of the way back in the plane. There were twenty-seven people in this compartment. Johnson stood in the center with his wife, Lady Bird. U.S. District Judge Sarah T. Hughes, 67, a kindly-faced woman, stood with a small black Bible in her hands, waiting to give the oath.

The compartment became hotter and hotter. Johnson was worried that some of the Kennedy staff might not be able to get inside. He urged people to press forward but a Signal Corps photographer, Capt. Cecil Stoughton, standing in a corner on a chair, said if Johnson moved any closer it would be virtually impossible to make a truly historic photograph.

It developed that Johnson was waiting for Mrs. Kennedy, who was composing herself in a small bedroom in the rear of the plane. She appeared alone, dressed in the same pink wool suit she had worn in the morning when she appeared so happy shaking hands with airport crowds at the side of her husband.

She was white-faced but dry-eyed. Friendly hands stretched toward her as she stumbled slightly. Johnson took both of her hands in his and motioned her to his left side. Lady Bird stood on his right, a fixed half-smile showing the tension.

Johnson nodded to Judge Hughes, an old friend of his family and a Kennedy appointee.

"Hold up your right hand and repeat after me," the woman jurist said to Johnson.

Outside a jet could be heard droning in to a landing.

Judge Hughes held out the Bible and Johnson covered it with his large left hand. His right arm went slowly into the air and the jurist began to intone the Constitutional oath: "I do solemnly swear that I will faithfully execute the office of President of the United States."

The brief ceremony ended when Johnson, in a deep, firm voice, repeated after the judge ". . . and so help me God."

Johnson turned first to his wife, hugged her about the shoulders and kissed her on the cheek. Then he turned to Kennedy's widow, put his left arm around her and kissed her cheek. As others in the group—some Texas Democratic House members, members of the Johnson and Kennedy staffs—moved toward the new President, he seemed to back away from any expression of felicitation.

The two-minute ceremony concluded at 3:38 P.M. EST and seconds later, the President said firmly, "Now, let's get airborne."

------

Lee Harvey Oswald, the thin, hateful, 24-year-old leftist who was to be convicted by the Warren Commission of the crime long after his death, already was in custody at that moment. He had been seen leaving the Texas School Book Depository, from which witnesses had spotted a man shooting at the President from a sixth-floor window. He had been traced to a bus, a taxi, to his miserable room, and to the corner of Tenth Street and Patton Avenue, where he had shot and killed Patrolman J. D. Tippett at 1:10 p.m. rather than submit to questioning. A few minutes after that, he had been dragged fighting and yelling from a movie house, the Texas Theatre, by police who had gone in to get him.

Aboard Air Force One, at the airport, Lyndon Baines Johnson was being sworn in as the thirty-sixth president of the United States while the police were just beginning to question Oswald at headquarters. And while the interrogation proceeded, the presidential jet was bearing the party—and the coffin of the assassinated Kennedy—back to Washington. That night, Smith wrote as much of the story as he could remember for the UPI, but it wasn't the end. At 11:20 a.m. on Sunday, November 24, Oswald was shot and killed by Jack Ruby, a 52-year-old strip tease impresario, in the basement of the Dallas city jail. And on Monday, November 25, while the world wondered, John Fitzgerald Kennedy was laid to rest at Arlington.[11]

All the tremendous work of the reporters and the wire services and the newspapers, all the seventy hours of telecasts and radio programs, all the reassurances of the new President and the quickness with which the machinery of government picked up once more in Washington helped the American people to pass safely through a period of trial during the transfer of power. But neither this, nor the 300,000 word accounting of the Warren Commission ten months later, could ever dispel the intense emotion that engulfed all who lived through those four days.

Some of that feeling was distilled into words by Mary McGrory in a brief editorial for the Washington *Star* on November 23, 1963:

"He brought gaiety, glamor, and grace to the American political scene in a measure never known before. That lightsome tread, that debonair touch, that shock of chestnut hair, that beguiling grin, that shattering understatement—these are what we shall remember.

"He walked like a prince and he talked like a scholar. His humor brightened the life of the Republic. While striving for his great office, he had often concealed his amusement at the incongruities of life, lest he be thought not only youthful but frivolous as well. When safely ensconced, he saw no reason to hide his wit. It glinted at every press conference. It informed his private utterance. Shown his latest nephew in August, he commented, 'He looks like a fine baby—we'll know more later.'

"One day he strolled onto the porch outside his office and found an old friend admiring the garden. The lawn was a source of unreasoning pride and constant concern to him; the flowers, while he was uncertain of their names, pleased him. He indicated the tangle of petunias and ageratum and said dryly, 'This may go down as the real achievement of this administration.'

"His public statements were always temperate, always measured. He

[11] Main sources for these experiences: the Warren Commission Report; *Four Days: The Historical Record of the Death of President Kennedy*, compiled by UPI and the *American Heritage* magazine (New York, 1964); *The Torch Is Passed*, the AP story of the death of a President (New York, 1964); *Times Talk*, Vol. 16, No. 11 (December, 1963), published by the New York *Times*; the AP *World* magazine, Winter, 1963–64, pp. 5–6; *Columbia Journalism Review*, Winter, 1964; *The Quill*, January, 1964, an assessment by John Tebbel.

derided his enemies—he teased his friends. He could be grave, but not for long. When the ugliness of yesterday has been forgotten, we shall remember him smiling."

## 46. JIMMY BRESLIN IN NEW YORK

Jimmy Breslin, a round and thick-chested Irishman who looks like a stevedore and writes like a poet, came to the New York *Herald Tribune* as a columnist on May 31, 1963. For credentials, he was able to offer three books and more than a hundred magazine articles, but there wasn't much of the columnist about him except for the way in which he was featured. He was all reporter—and all New York reporter, at that, which is a way of saying that he belonged.

Breslin was then 32 years old, married, and the father of four children. Nobody had to say for him that he had been born and brought up in New York City, that he had learned his newspapering in a hard school, and that he knew how to make a typewriter sing some fascinating tunes. As soon as he started moving around, all these things became self-evident.

Within a few weeks, he was the talk of newspapermen all over town. Some were saying that he wrote like Damon Runyon, which would have pleased Damon a lot. Others, of a more literary type, allowed that he derived from Hemingway. Some of the legmen, who didn't like his tough kind of competition, had harsher things to say. One of them— without seeing him—was rash enough to threaten by telephone to punch him in the nose. This was a tactical error. Anyone who had heard the awesome Breslin roar, noted the bearish Breslin build, and seen the ominous Breslin waddle, straight out of a Japanese *sumo* ring, knew it scarcely paid to pick a fight with him.

Breslin's talent actually was developed on the sports pages. Like many another honor graduate of the wonderful world of win, lose, or draw, he adjusted easily to his broadened assignment. When President Kennedy was assassinated, he flew to Dallas and wrote a story the *Trib* bannered as "A Death in Emergency Room One"—an account of those last desperate moments at Parkland Memorial Hospital when doctors tried in vain to save the President. A little more than two weeks later, he was in New York during a brief visit by President Johnson and was struck by the contrast in police methods.

This is the essence of Jimmy Breslin's story in the New York *Herald Tribune* on December 9, 1963 about the New York police—the Finest— and the way they protected a President. If it reflects a bias toward New York City, it is only natural. Many a New Yorker would live nowhere else, even if they gave it to him, and Breslin is one of them. His is personal journalism in the New York manner.

## THE FINEST PROTECT A PRESIDENT

### By Jimmy Breslin

Up to the left, maybe half a mile up, this light-red brick factory building stood six stories high against the winter sky, and the black limousine carrying Lyndon Baines Johnson, the thirty-sixth President of the United States, was going to pass right under its windows. This was yesterday afternoon, coming into Manhattan on the Long Island Expressway, and for a little moment everything became strange and a bad feeling came into your stomach. The same kind of a feeling you had when you first looked up at the light-red bricks of the six-story Texas School Book Depository building in Dallas. But now, as the cars moved closer to the building, there was something else. At first, it looked like a flagpole on the roof of the building.

Then it moved, and you could see what the object was. It was a patrolman of the Police Department of the City of New York and he was standing on the roof of this light-red brick building, and the wind blowing the bottom of his overcoat and his hands on his hips, the right hand directly over his gun, and now the bad feeling went away and you knew everything was going to be all right yesterday.

Which it was.

The President of the United States flew into town at 12:40 p.m. yesterday. He flew back to Washington at 2:32 p.m. In the one hour and 52 minutes in which he was in this city, the cops of our town, in one of the most tremendous performances they ever have given, threw a navy-blue blanket over Lyndon B. Johnson. They were everywhere.

Look straight up and there were two helicopters circling Johnson's car. Look at any rooftop, and there was a blue uniform, with the wind blowing at the overcoat. Look at the rows of windows in an office building, any office building, and there was somebody with binoculars, scanning the building across the street from him. They were out in Jamaica Bay, off the Idlewild runways, patroling in boats, and they arrested hunters out there. They were on the streets and up on the overpasses, and none of them looked at the President. The police had their backs to the motorcade and their heads moved back and forth as they checked on crowds and buildings and anybody who was going to try and take a shot at Lyndon Johnson yesterday was going to run into trouble.

President Johnson came to New York to attend funeral services for Herbert H. Lehman, New York's former governor and senator. The services were held at Temple Emanu-El, 65th Street and Fifth Avenue.

Forget all those books and stories about the F.B.I. and the Secret Service. Yesterday, the New York cops, the finest law enforcement body the nation has known, stepped out and showed everybody how things are done here in the Big Town.

"We are very serious about this," Police Commissioner Michael Murphy was saying just before he went to church in the morning. Mr. Murphy makes understatements. He had everything but field artillery on the streets yesterday.

At the end, at 2:27 p.m., Air Force One, its jets whining and throwing a wave of fumes across the landing apron, started to move out and take President Johnson back to Washington. And Michael Murphy, his fingers in his ears to shut out the roar, ducked down behind a green communications car, and stayed clear of the wave of kerosene exhaust which would have flattened him if he had been standing up.

At 2:34 p.m., Inspector John Kinsella of the Department's Bureau of Special Services, the undercover group, came trotting over from a parked Port Authority radio car.

"Both planes airborne," he said.

Murphy nodded. "The credit is out there," he said. He pointed to a group of patrolmen. Now usually, this type of statement is the essence of corn. But yesterday it seemed the natural thing to say. For after yesterday, when you hear somebody say "New York's Finest," please regard it as something more than a cliché. These fellows who are paid with your money went out yesterday and did the kind of job people write stories about.

"What you don't seem to understand," Murphy said as he went to his car, "is that we guard Presidents all the time. And we guard them like that all the time, too. So I would have to say that today was nothing more than a routine matter. We just took a job and handled it right."

He got in the car and was driven home. He was in plenty of time for dinner.

"How was it?" his wife said when he came into the house.

"All right," he said. "The important thing is how did you do?"

"Roast beef," Kate Murphy said. "Give me a few minutes and it'll be ready."

## 47. AFTER THIRTY YEARS IN RUSSIA

To some Western correspondents, an assignment to Moscow is an unpleasant duty akin to drudgery. They know that they are not welcome. They realize that they are considered to be in more or less the same category as spies. They find that even the slightest contact with the higher echelons of the Soviet government often takes considerable time and patience before it can be suitably arranged. Many of them complain, in addition, of the dreariness of living, the suffocation of personal freedom under a police state, the unending flow of propaganda boasts, and the lack of many of the amenities of an open society.

It takes an extraordinary correspondent to put up with all this and remain on the job for any length of time. Walter Duranty of the New York *Times* was such a man. During his long tour of duty in Moscow before World War II, Duranty used to say that Russia fascinated him and that he enjoyed the "novelty, variety, and fantasy" of life there.[12] Henry Shapiro of UPI is another who has thrived on hardship behind the Iron Curtain. After thirty years in Russia, he could still be philosophical about his lot, even in the face of "spontaneous" demonstrations of agitators who attacked the American Embassy while police indulgently looked on.

At a time of relative calm in Soviet-American relations, Shapiro wrote these personal observations for UPI, August 10, 1963.

[12] Walter Duranty, *I Write As I Please* (New York, Simon and Schuster, 1935), p. 329.

## MY LIFE IN MOSCOW

*By Henry Shapiro*

MOSCOW—It does not take much to change the attitude of the Russian man-in-the-street from hostility to friendliness for Americans.

Although as an American, I am a citizen of the Soviet Union's No. 1 antagonist and as a journalist a member of a much suspected profession here, my life in this country has been in serious danger only once in the past thirty years. Then, it was not because of hatred but quite the reverse.

It happened on May 9, 1945, when Dictator Stalin's voice suddenly boomed from a thousand loudspeakers on Moscow's principal thoroughfares announcing the victorious end of the war. Within minutes hundreds of thousands of Russians appeared on the streets and began to surge toward Red Square, the traditional Russian center for popular demonstrations.

When I appeared on the square dressed in an American war correspondent's uniform, somebody in the crowd shouted, "Vot Amerikanets" (There goes an American). A dozen arms seized me and tossed me into the air three times while others shouted, "Long live Soviet-American friendship," and "Long live peace."

I was pressed, squeezed, and manhandled as I joined the throng which suddenly changed course and marched toward the American Embassy on Makhovaya Square, five minutes from Lenin's Tomb. I was grateful to be back on my own feet, and in one piece.

At the Embassy a one-armed soldier shouted, "We want the American ambassador," and echoes came from hundreds of men, women, and children. In the absence of Ambassador W. Averell Harriman, the chargé d'affaires, George Kennan, appeared on the Embassy balcony and, addressing the crowd in flawless Russian, hailed the victory. "Now," he urged, "let us work for peace."

It looked then as if the successful wartime coalition, contrary to all the lessons of history, might become a permanent alliance for peace and progress. But only two years later, after the breakdown of the Moscow conference of foreign ministers in 1947, the Cold War was on full blast.

In 1952 the gentle and scholarly Kennan, who had returned to

Moscow as ambassador, was declared persona non grata and not allowed to remain in the Soviet Union. During the bitter anti-American propaganda campaign that followed, Harriman became one of the principal targets of ridicule and hate, a favored subject for cartoonists' caricatures of a "warmongering American imperialist."

In the succeeding years there were at least four angrily hostile demonstrations outside the American Embassy. The worst was on the occasion of the landing of U.S. Marines in Lebanon and the time of the Bay of Pigs invasion in Cuba.

During these riots thousands of Russians massed in front of the American Embassy, breaking windows, disfiguring the walls with ink bottles, and shouting such slogans as, "Down with American imperialism," and "Shame to the American warmongers." In the angriest clashes only last-minute intervention by regular Red Army troops protected the Embassy from mob invasion and bodily injury to diplomatic personnel.

Yet, as I mingled with the street crowds during the Lebanon demonstration, I overheard a middle-aged woman say, "You cannot blame the American ambassador (Llewellyn Thompson) who loves his children as much as we do and he believes in peace."

The truth is that during the worst years of the long Stalin era nightmare, few individual American residents were subjected to personal indignities. I live in a large apartment house inhabited entirely by Russians. During the Stalinist period many of my neighbors stopped talking to me, except to greet me politely but coldly when we came face to face. But no children threw stones at my car or apartment windows and no one bothered me in the streets.

The enormous reservoir of good will for foreigners generally and particularly for Americans was never drained here even by cold war bitterness. It was more than poetic justice, therefore, for Ambassador Harriman to return to Moscow as President Kennedy's special envoy and help successfully negotiate the first major East-West accord since the Austrian treaty of 1955.

Nevertheless, the wartime comradeship and cordiality cannot easily be restored unless the nuclear treaty results in substantial East-West agreements on wider fronts. There is every indication that both sides hope this is the real beginning.

Shapiro was lucky. During increasing anti-American demonstrations in 1964 and early 1965, a New York *Times* correspondent's automobile was destroyed, a correspondent of Agence France-Presse was attacked, and Adam Clymer of the Baltimore *Sun* was struck in the face and later was expelled from Russia.[13] It took a lot of faith and considerable personal courage to remain on the job and roam the streets of Moscow during a time when nobody really knew what the Kremlin would do next.

## 48. BILL MAULDIN AT PLEIKU

Bill Mauldin arrived in South Viet Nam early in 1965 to record his impressions of his third war. As a mature burgher of 43 who had survived World War II and Korea and collected two Pulitzer Prizes for his exemplary cartooning, he scarcely expected to become a part of the hostilities in Southeast Asia. But when Communist guerrillas opened up on American installations before dawn on February 7 at an air base called Pleiku, he didn't have to be told that he was caught in a mortar attack. All he could think of at first was that the correspondents in Saigon would feel "it was a hell of a note with all this happening and only a cartoonist there."

For all his modesty, Mauldin did a first-rate job that night. He helped the wounded, then covered, sketched, and photographed the battle scenes with the seasoned skill of a great professional. After he got everything off to his newspaper, the Chicago *Sun Times*, he had the added satisfaction of knowing that his son, Warrant Officer Bruce Mauldin, had shown courage and skill under fire.

There wasn't much about war that Bill Mauldin didn't know. He had been born October 29, 1921 at Mountain Park, New Mexico, and at 19 had broken off his studies at the Chicago Academy of Fine Arts to become a soldier. He was one of the earliest to be called up, for he was in uniform a year before Pearl Harbor. In the 45th Division newspaper, he began publishing irreverent little cartoons about two bedraggled soldiers, Willie and Joe, and their reflections on war, officers, and their fellow dogfaces.

When it became known that some generals were shocked and offi-

---

[13] "Embassy of U.S. Stoned in Soviet," New York *Times*, Feb. 10, 1965.

cers of lower rank were horrified, the young cartoonist took on a new importance in the eyes of his readers. Soon, Willie and Joe were picked up by *Stars and Stripes*, the Army newspaper, and Sergeant Bill Mauldin and his cartoon, "Up Front," became famous. Just as Ernie Pyle celebrated his "God-damned Infantry" in the best-read prose of World War II, Mauldin made the foot-slogging GIs immortal on his sketching pad. He nearly had his head blown off in combat for his pains, and was given a Purple Heart for his honorable wounds; a Legion of Merit followed later. In 1945, he was awarded his first Pulitzer Prize and Willie and Joe became VIPs.

It was to be expected that Mauldin would go in for cartooning in civilian life, but the transition was hard to make. Like Sergeant George Baker and his wonderfully expressive "Sad Sack," Willie and Joe found out that they didn't have too much to say to the people of the United States once World War II had ended. Their creator had to carve out a whole new career for himself as an editorial cartoonist. Even during the Korean War, it wasn't particularly feasible to revive Willie and Joe. Finally, on the St. Louis *Post-Dispatch*, Mauldin hit his stride and in 1959 was awarded his second Pulitzer Prize for his cartooning.

Like Herblock of the Washington *Post*, he became an institution and his cartoons were widely reproduced. When he shifted to the Chicago *Sun-Times*, he kept up the pace. His "Weeping Lincoln"— dashed off on impulse after President Kennedy's assassination—touched the heart of the nation.

The *Sun-Times* also sent him to Viet Nam. If Pleiku is at all remembered in years to come, it will scarcely be because of any feat of American arms but because Bill Mauldin was there. Like William Howard Russell, who recorded the defeat of the Light Brigade at Balaclava for the *Times* of London on October 25, 1854, and Bennet Burleigh of the London *Daily Telegraph*, who saw Fuzzy Wuzzy break the British square at Tamai on March 13, 1884, Mauldin wrote of a small but calamitous loss at Pleiku with the touch of a master. Here is his story as it was published in the Chicago *Sun-Times* on February 9, 1965.

UP FRONT IN VIET NAM

*By Bill Mauldin*

PLEIKU, South Viet Nam—The mortar barrage on Camp Holloway and the 52d Aviation Battalion began at exactly 2 a.m. Sunday, February 7. It was intense and murderous, some eighty rounds in five minutes saturating a bivouac area, perhaps two blocks square.

The enemy was using captured 81 mm. weapons of our own manufacture. I was sleeping in the east half of a hut house, or "hooch," of Lt. Col. John C. Hughes, of Herrin, Illinois, the battalion commander, on a cot belonging to Maj. Glenn Parmeter, who is on leave in Hong Kong.

My son, Bruce, a warrant officer and helicopter pilot in the battalion, whom I had come to visit, is billeted in the town of Pleiku, near 2d Corps headquarters which was also hit. I had just spent the evening in Pleiku having a reunion celebration with Bruce and had left him in his billet.

My first awakening thought at the roar of the mortar barrage was that Chinese New Year was still being celebrated. When a round hit nearby, I realized what was going on and began to worry about Bruce, assuming (correctly) that he would try to get back to his outfit, and worrying that the attack might be general in scope, in which case the road to camp would be a bad place for him.

Any further speculation on my part was cut off by Col. Hughes, who roared at me to get myself into the bunker out back, as he tore out the front door to take charge of his battalion. So emphatic was my response that I found myself arriving at the bunker barefoot and in my underwear.

The barrage was at its height as I started down the earthen steps to the sandbagged shelter. By the light of the drumming explosions I could see the barbed wire of the southern edge of camp a few feet away, and I fully expected to see hostile faces on the other side moving up under cover of the mortars. It turned out that the only infantry penetration was to the east, where the parked aircraft were attacked.

A young soldier from headquarters company came up to me at the bunker entrance. He was also in his underwear, but mine was white and his was red. He was holding both hands over a large wound in his right side and was covered with blood from several lesser cuts. Mortar shells are designed to cut people up and apparently we make good ones.

"Help me," he said, "I've got to lie down."

I tried to help him into the bunker but he refused to come down those dark steps. He said he had decided he was going to die and he wanted to lie down on something comfortable.

From the looks of the wound I felt in no position to question his prognosis, so I helped him into the hut and put him on my cot, where I found a small light and took a closer look at his side. I couldn't tell whether the large fragment had gone into his guts or had simply cut him open in passing, but hoped for the latter.

At this time, the mortar barrage had been going on for about four minutes, interspersed with grenades and some recoilless rifle fire. Again I asked my friend to let me take him into the bunker but he was adamant about staying above ground.

"I'm pretty sure I'm going to die in a minute," he said in a real tone of apology, "and I would appreciate it if you would let me hold onto your hand and say my prayers."

What can you do? I let him hold my hand and he recited the Lord's Prayer. As he finished, the mortars let up and Col. Hughes came in, mad as a hornet. He had seen our light and wanted to know what the blank I was doing upstairs.

"Oh," he said, looking at the cot, "I'll send some litter bearers back."

He went back to his command post. Shortly, four soldiers with carbines came in on the colonel's orders to help move the wounded man. Lacking a stretcher, we carried him on my mattress for the two-block walk to the dispensary. For some reason I had stupidly assumed that my boy, who had made his peace with his Maker and was now uncomplainingly enduring the rather bumpy ride we were giving him, was the only casualty in the area.

Now, as we made our way among the riddled "hooches," we found ourselves part of a regular gory procession with hurt men stumbling out of practically every tent, each leaving his special trail of splatters, so that next morning there were scores of little red trails converging into one big one leading to the medical hut.

Most of the wounded were being supported or carried. Few had only one cut and some had dozens. Of the initial five-dozen casualties treated, only eighteen were walking wounded. Although the mortars had stopped, the war was still on, with a fire fight at the airstrip, where the Viet Cong were going after the parked helicopters and twin-engine Caribou troop carriers. There was the thump of TNT as some of the attackers managed to get charges under the machines.

The dispensary was at the edge of the strip, and when we got there we could see several aircraft burning. At no time did I see any sign of panic, even though there was every excuse for panic. An enclosed garrison in a hostile environment had been hit suddenly and hard, and there was no way of knowing if we were going to be overrun. But our new Army seems to be a bunch of pros.

Those who weren't hit had their weapons in hand and were going quickly but calmly about their business, and it is worth noting that later in the morning a number of these were surprised to find blood had run down into their shoes from punctures they didn't know they had. The first casualty count was seven dead in the battalion and 43 wounded. A later count showed eight killed and 108 wounded.

Inside the dispensary looked like a Technicolor scene out of *Gone With The Wind*. Badly wounded men were sprawled over every bit of floor and huddled on every piece of furniture. Blood was pooled and splattered everywhere and I kept slipping in it as I made my way through barefooted.

Our boy had to give up his mattress because there wasn't room for it. He didn't mind. I believe, at this point, he had begun to believe he was going to make it after all, and this turned out to be right. I told him good-by, he smiled a trifle wanly, and I headed back for the colonel's hut to get my pants.

I believe this was my worst time in the whole affair, because it suddenly occurred to me that in my state of undress I resembled a Montagnard, local Vietnamese hillbilly, who runs around in shirttails and not much else. This could lead to a misunderstanding in the dark with an armed soldier on the alert for infiltrators. So every time I passed a soldier, I made a point of pretending to stumble, then uttering a four-letter word in unmistakable English.

Back at the hut, I got dressed, found my camera and sketchbook, and went out to cover the war like a gentleman correspondent. At 2:35 a.m., the firing had stopped. At 2:45 a.m., I heard a loud commotion at the front gate, angry voices, and a shot. I never did learn what the shot was about, but the ruckus was created by my son, Bruce, who had come to save his beloved helicopters and was having trouble getting past the sentries.

Later I watched him help direct operations as the wounded were evacuated by air and told him he was doing a fair job for a man who couldn't even get to his own war on time. He told me to go to hell.

---

Warrant Officer Bruce Mauldin was Bill's oldest son, and at the time of the Pleiku battle had been in the Army for three years. At home at Porterville, California, he had a wife, Judith, and two children, Michelle, 18 months, and Bruce Jr., 6 months. While the old man went back to work at his drawing board in Chicago, the younger Mauldin carried on in Viet Nam. Helicopter pilots were in particular demand in that war.

## 49. THE BUCHWALD POLL

Satire, George S. Kaufman once said, is what closes on Saturday night. But he never knew Art Buchwald. In his fortieth year, the chunky, cigar-smoking columnist was playing to capacity in almost 200 newspapers after turning out a daily column of humor for more than fifteen years. The remarkable part of his performance was that he did it all himself and he did not limit himself to a few jokes. In this sense, he was no Franklin P. Adams, who took in contributors by the yard even in his affluent years, and he certainly was no Bugs Baer, who was required to write only a few gags. Buchwald's humor, much of it gently satiric, was based on ideas—and he had a lot of them.

He became a humorist—and a journalist—by accident. He was born October 20, 1925 in Mount Vernon, a suburb of New York City, and never finished high school, running off to the Marines when he was 17 and getting into World War II. Despite his lack of a high-school degree, he managed to enter the University of Southern California and remained there three years, as he tells it, before the authorities found out above his dark educational past and disqualified him for a college degree. Having nothing better to do, he went to Paris and stumbled into the precarious business of writing for the New York *Herald Tribune*'s Paris edition, never a very lucrative occupation.

Buchwald made it pay. In hard and difficult times, he made people laugh—a rare and wondrous gift in any journalist. When he saw that he couldn't keep on writing indefinitely about American tourists, French girls, and the well-advertised glories of Paris, he came home.

In Washington, he found an inexhaustible mine of material for humorous comment and became almost as much of a fixture, in his own way, at Walter Lippmann, James Reston, Edward T. Folliard, or the Washington Monument. In the following piece, which appeared in the Washington *Post*, June 8, 1954, and other newspapers (copyright Publishers Newspaper Syndicate), he showed what could happen if pollsters are taken with grim seriousness.

### POLITICAL POLL—1776

#### By Art Buchwald

The political pollster has become such an important part of the American scene that it is hard to imagine how this country was ever able to function without him.

What would have happened, for example, if there had been political pollsters in the early days of this country? This is how the results might have turned out:

When asked if they thought the British were doing a good job in administering the colonies, this is how a cross-section of the people responded:

| | |
|---|---|
| British doing good job | 63% |
| Not doing good job | 22% |
| Don't know | 15% |

The next question, "Do you think the dumping of tea in the Boston Harbor by militants helped or hurt the taxation laws in the New World?

| | |
|---|---|
| Hurt cause of taxation | 79% |
| Helped cause | 12% |
| Didn't think it would make any difference | 9% |

"What do you think our image is in England after the Minute Men attacked the British at Lexington?"

Minute Men hurt our image in England              83%
Gave British new respect for colonies              10%
Undecided              9%

"Which of these two Georges can do more for the colonies—George III or George Washington?"

George III              76%
George Washington              14%
Others              10%

It is interesting to note that 80 percent of the people questioned had never heard of George Washington before.

The next question was, "Do you think the Declaration of Independence as it is written is a good document or a bad one?"

Good document              12%
Bad document              14%
No opinion              74%

A group of those polled felt that the Declaration of Independence had been written by a bunch of radicals and the publishing of it at this time would only bring harsher measures from the British.

When asked whether the best way to bring about reforms was through terrorism or redress to the Crown, an overwhelming proportion of colonists felt appeals should be made to the King.

Reforms through petition              24%
Reforms through acts of terrorism              8%
Don't know              68%

The pollsters then asked what the public thought was the most crucial issue of the time.

Trade with foreign nations              65%
War with Indians              20%
The independence issue              15%

The survey also went into the question of Patrick Henry. "Do you think Patrick Henry did the right thing in demanding liberty or death?"

Did a foolhardy thing and was a trouble-maker              53%
Did a brave thing and made his point              23%

Should have gone through the courts                                    16%
Don't know                                                             8%

On the basis of the results of the poll, the militant colonials decided they did not have enough popular support to foment a revolution and gave up the idea of creating a United States of America.

———————

Buchwald was something more than a humorist. He was a social critic with a keen sense of public responsibility. For while many a politician or academic fell all over themselves to support the pretensions of the pollsters, Buchwald saw the polls for exactly what they were and did not forget that the human spirit was considerably more important. Walter Lippmann once put it this way: "It is more necessary than ever in these days that a candidate for the highest office should convince the nation that they are in the presence of someone who is able to lead them, not merely to wait for the Gallup poll and follow." [14]

## 50. NEW GIANT OF MANHATTAN

The average California editor who comes to New York City generally goes into a tantrum, splutters with indignation, fusses or gives up, and falls in love with the place. Fortunately for New York and for San Francisco, Richard E. Pearce was not an average editor. As the chief editorial writer of the San Francisco *Examiner,* he was doing a study of urban planning for the people of his city and he didn't let any preconceived notions get in his way. He didn't intend to be a Chamber of Commerce cheerleader for San Francisco; nor, for that matter, was he inclined to fall all over himself because of the new marvels of construction that he saw in New York.

Pearce went ahead with his work, conscious that he was facing a considerable challenge. He had been a newspaperman for more than thirty years—born in Springer, Oklahoma, on September 21, 1909, graduated from the University of Oklahoma in 1931, a reporter in Oklahoma City and San Francisco until 1954, and the *Examiner's*

[14] Clinton Rossiter and James Lare, eds., *The Essential Lippmann* (New York, Random House, 1963), p. 491.

editorial page director since that time. What he wrote about New York had the stamp of personal journalism on it—and also some reflections on the penalties that continued growth brings to great cities. The following selection is from the San Francisco *Examiner* of July 1, 1963.

## A CALIFORNIAN LOOKS UP

### By Richard E. Pearce

The new Pan Am Building in New York City is truly enormous. It stands astride midtown Manhattan like some towering barrel-chested giant among a lesser race of giants. It is just breathtaking. It is also a question mark of major importance to all other large cities. That particularly includes San Francisco.

The great, octagonal building, the world's largest commercial structure, has risen at precisely the most congested pinpoint in the most congested sector of the nation's most congested city.

That pinpoint is Grand Central Station in midtown Manhattan, the major center of Manhattan's underground transportation network, the heart of an area where street traffic is so impossible that for many years walking has been quicker.

There, utilizing air rights above the tracks where Grand Central's trains come to rest, this $100 million structure has been planted on stilts to thrust for 69 stories into the sky, and to overpower with its bulk the scores of other great commercial towers and slabs hard by it.

It is so vast that it houses 25,000 workers. It is so big that the telephone company had to give it an exchange all its own, then lease two floors just to hold the telephone equipment. It is so immense that its battery of escalators emptying into Grand Central Station had to be made reversible for the rush hours.

The giants of Greek mythology picked up Mount Pelion and piled it on top of Mount Ossa to reach lofty Olympus. That feat was hardly more incredible than this piling of supercongestion upon supercongestion. And the process goes on and on. Today six more big buildings are under construction within three blocks of the Pan Am Building, one of them 50 stories high and another 41.

Why?

What forces are at work to bring about this superconcentration of the crush of downtown humanity? And, most pertinently, is this a preview for other large American cities of the shape of their downtowns when the national population has doubled and trebled?

These were the questions I put to professional planners and public leaders in New York and the half dozen other cities I studied. Their opinions were far from unanimous. Some called the Pan Am Building an isolated phenomenon and a mistake from a planning standpoint.

Most planners expressed the view that New York was not typical of American cities—there can only be one New York, as there can be only one Washington—and that our other big city downtowns will not develop in this superconcentrated fashion.

A handful of planners and others regard the Pan Am Building as the most striking current evidence that a profound centripetal force continues to work on our metropolitan downtowns, causing them to swirl inward and upward in an ever-increasing, ever more compact concentration of skyscrapers.

This is the view I share, for I saw evidences of the force at work in every other large city I examined except Washington. That city has a 13-story height limitation and so its downtown is growing horizontally, much to the dismay of some of its leaders.

The centripetal force is clearly visible in San Francisco. Surely downtown Montgomery Street is our most congested area. And it is there, at Montgomery-Market-Post that the Dillingham interests are preparing to put up the city's tallest structure, the 42-story Wells Fargo Bank Building. Note, moreover, that most of San Francisco's postwar construction of high-rise commercial buildings has been concentrated within a short walk of this point—the Equitable Life, the Crown-Zellerbachm, the John Hancock, the International, the Bethlehem Steel, the Hartford, and the projected Standard Oil and many others of lesser size.

Again, what is the nature of this force that swirls inward and upward in defiance of congestion? Most answers given me were prosaic but plausible. Usually this point of business concentration is also the focal point of mass transportation. Too, the world of business likes to operate cheek-by-jowl, where it's only an elevator ride or a short walk to the other fellow's office, and where plenty of good restaurants are close by for luncheon conferences.

The whole subject posed by the Pan Am Building is important not only because our planners and politicians need to know the shape and

## THE NEW METROPOLIS

Scene from a helicopter approaching New York's Pan Am building.

nature of our future downtowns, but also because this determines, too, the kind of citizens the city will require.

If as the evidence suggests, downtown is destined to become ever more a headquarters place for management, finance, etc., it will require more and more skilled and educated people in all kinds of pursuits. It will have less and less need for the uneducated and the unskilled in the bottom economic strata. Yet, paradoxically, at this very time the cities find themselves with an immense supply of the uneducated and the unskilled because of the rural Negro migration from the South.

Mass migrations of the unskilled into our big cities is an old story. These people were badly needed by the cities in those early times when the assembly line was still a vague notion and automation was not yet dreamed of. The immigrant Irish, the Italians, the Poles, and others were the brawn—the cheap labor, to put it plainly—that built our cities while fighting their way up into a higher economic class. What is there for the hands of the unskilled Negro to do in this era of Pan Am buildings?

While the big city downtowns swirl inward and upward, an opposite or centrifugal force continues at work spinning people and some kinds of businesses farther and farther outward in vast, mushy chunks of urban sprawl.

———————

Thus, a San Francisco editor was able to raise questions for New York. But he couldn't answer them. That was the unenviable job of his colleagues in New York.


## 51. THE SILENT THIRTY-EIGHT

When A. M. Rosenthal came home from Tokyo to take charge of the local coverage of the New York *Times* as its new metropolitan editor, he decided to visit as many city officials as he could to become more familiar with their problems—and his own. While he was a New Yorker by adoption if not by birth and knew the ways of the big city as few do, he had been away for nearly a decade as a foreign correspondent. He realized that change was the big story in New York and he went at it without preconceived notions.

One of his earliest visits was to Police Commissioner Michael J. Murphy. During their talk, the commissioner expressed his concern over the apathy of the New Yorker and his unwillingness to help the police for fear of becoming involved—a familiar phenomenon, as Rosenthal knew, in every big city he had ever seen. But Murphy had something different—the story of a murder in which thirty-eight witnesses had actually seen or heard the slayer at work and had done nothing to alert the police until after the crime was committed.

If it troubled the commissioner, it shocked Rosenthal. When he returned to his office, he asked one of his most experienced reporters, Martin Gansberg, to go to the neighborhood where the murder had been committed and get the real story. Until then, the slaying had been just another item in the news and nobody had bothered to go behind it.

Marty Gansberg was then 44, having been born in Brooklyn on May 6, 1920. He was graduated from St. John's University in 1941 and in the following year became a copy boy on the *Times*. He did everything in the next twenty years—reporter, copy editor, assistant makeup editor, editor of the international edition, Paris news editor of the edition and, in 1963, a reporter on the metropolitan staff who worked on special assignments from time to time.

The story of the silent witnesses was one of the big ones. He wrote it, Rosenthal edited it, and together they shocked the city—and the opposition—when the article was published on Page 1 of the *Times*. Two weeks later, Rosenthal did a piece for the *Times Magazine*, examining the wider implications of the story of the silent witnesses. He wrote a book, *Thirty-Eight Witnesses*, sponsored by the *Times* book division, which was translated into a number of foreign languages and became the basis of a motion picture script.

There was a reason for the enormous reaction to the story of the silent witnesses, just as there had been to Meyer Berger's studied reconstruction for the *Times* of the mass murders in East Camden, New Jersey, by a crazed slayer, Howard Unruh. These things touched the hearts and the minds of people and turned a community to look inward on the darkness where it buried its problems.

Here, in abridged form, are the two stories—Gansberg's report of what happened in the New York *Times* of March 27, 1964, and Rosenthal's commentary on it from the *New York Times Magazine* of May 4, 1964.

## THE "GOOD PEOPLE"

### By Martin Gansberg

For more than half an hour thirty-eight respectable, law-abiding citizens in Queens watched a killer stalk and stab a woman in three separate attacks in Kew Gardens.

Twice the sound of their voices and the sudden glow of their bedroom lights interrupted him and frightened him off. Each time he returned, sought her out, and stabbed her again. Not one person telephoned the police during the assault; one witness called after the woman was dead.

That was two weeks ago today. But Assistant Chief Inspector Frederick M. Lussen, in charge of the borough's detectives and a veteran of twenty-five years of homicide investigations, is still shocked.

He can give a matter-of-fact recitation of many murders. But the Kew Gardens slaying baffles him—not because it is a murder but because the "good people" failed to call the police.

"As we have reconstructed the crime," he said, "the assailant had three chances to kill this woman during a 35-minute period. He returned twice to complete the job. If we had been called when he first attacked, the woman might not be dead now."

This is what the police say happened beginning at 3:20 a.m. in the staid, middle-class, tree-lined Austin Street area.

Twenty-eight-year-old Catherine Genovese, who was called Kitty by almost everyone in the neighborhood, was returning home from her job as manager of a bar in Hollis. She parked her red Fiat in a lot adjacent to the Kew Gardens Long Island Railroad Station, facing Mowbray Place. Like many residents of the neighborhood, she had parked there day after day since her arrival from Connecticut a year ago, although the railroad frowns on the practice.

She turned off the lights of her car, locked the door, and started to walk the 100 feet to the entrance of her apartment at 82–70 Austin Street, which is a Tudor building, with stores on the first floor and apartments on the second.

The entrance to the apartment is in the rear of the building because the front is rented to retail stores. At night the quiet neighborhood is shrouded in the slumbering darkness that marks most residential areas.

Miss Genovese noticed a man at the far end of the lot, near a 7-story apartment house at 82–40 Austin Street. She halted. Then, nervously, she headed up Austin Street toward Lefferts Boulevard, where there is a call box to the 102d Police Precinct in nearby Richmond Hill.

She got as far as a street light in front of a bookstore before the man grabbed her. She screamed. Lights went on in the 10-story apartment house at 82–67 Austin Street, which faces the bookstore. Windows slid open and voices punctured the early-morning stillness.

Miss Genovese screamed: "Oh, my God, he stabbed me! Please help me! Please help me!"

From one of the upper windows in the apartment house, a man called down: "Let that girl alone!"

The assailant looked up at him, shrugged, and walked down Austin Street toward a white sedan parked a short distance away. Miss Genovese struggled to her feet.

Lights went out. The killer returned to Miss Genovese, now trying to make her way around the side of the building by the parking lot to get to her apartment. The assailant stabbed her again.

"I'm dying!" she shrieked. "I'm dying!"

Windows were opened again and lights went on in many apartments. The assailant got into his car and drove away. Miss Genovese staggered to her feet. A city bus, Q-10, the Lefferts Boulevard line to Kennedy International Airport, passed. It was 3:35 a.m.

The assailant returned. By then, Miss Genovese had crawled to the back of the building, where the freshly painted brown doors to the apartment house held out hope of safety. The killer tried the first door; she wasn't there. At the second door, 82–62 Austin Street, he saw her slumped on the floor at the foot of the stairs. He stabbed her a third time—fatally.

It was 3:50 by the time the police received their first call from a man who was a neighbor of Miss Genovese. In two minutes they were at the scene. The neighbor, a 70-year-old woman and another woman were the only persons on the street. Nobody else came forward.

The man explained that he had called the police after much deliberation. He had phoned a friend in Nassau County for advice and then he had crossed the roof of the building to the apartment of the elderly woman to get her to make the call.

"I didn't want to get involved," he sheepishly told the police.

Six days later, the police arrested Winston Moseley, a 29-year-old business-machine operator, and charged him with the homicide. Moseley had no previous record. He is married, has two children, and owns a home at 133–19 Sutter Avenue, South Ozone Park, Queens. On Wednesday, a court committed him to Kings County Hospital for psychiatric observation.

The police stressed how simple it would have been to have gotten in touch with them. "A phone call," said one of the detectives, "would have done it."


## THE SICKNESS CALLED APATHY

### By A. M. Rosenthal

It happens from time to time in New York that the life of the city is frozen by an instant of shock. In that instant the people of the city are seized by the paralyzing realization that they are one, that each man is in some way a mirror of every other man. They stare at each other—or, really, into themselves—and a look quite like a flush of embarrassment passes over the face of the city. Then the instant passes and the beat resumes and the people turn away and try to explain what they have seen or try to deny it.

The last 35 minutes of the young life of Miss Catherine Genovese became such a shock in the life of the city. But at the time she died, stabbed again and again by a marauder in her quiet, dark, but entirely respectable, street in Kew Gardens, New York hardly took note.

It was not until two weeks later that Catherine Genovese, known as Kitty, returned in death to cry the city awake. Even then it was not her life or her dying that froze the city, but the witnessing of her murder—the choking fact that thirty-eight of her neighbors had seen her stabbed or heard her cries, and that not one of them, during that hideous half hour, had lifted the telephone from the safety of his own apartment to call the police and try to save her life. When it was over and Miss Genovese was dead and the murderer gone, one man did call —not from his own apartment but from a neighbor's, and only after he had called a friend and asked her what to do.

The day that the story of the witnessing of the death of Miss Geno-vese appeared in this newspaper became that frozen instant. "Thirty-eight!" people said over and over. "Thirty-eight!"

It was as if the number itself had some special meaning and, in a way, of course, it did. One person or two or even three or four witnessing a murder passively would have been the unnoticed symptom of the disease in the city's body and again would have passed unnoticed. But thirty-eight—it was like a man with a running low fever suddenly be-ginning to cough blood; his friends could no longer ignore his illness, nor could he turn away from himself.

At first there was, briefly, the reaction of shared guilt. Even people who were sure that they certainly would have acted differently felt it somehow. "Dear God, what have we come to?" a woman said that day. "We," not "they."

For in that instant of shock, the mirror showed quite clearly what was wrong, that the face of mankind was spotted with the disease of apathy—all mankind. But this was too frightening a thought to live with and soon the beholders began to set boundaries for the illness, to search frantically for causes that were external, and to look for the carrier.

There was a rash of metropolitan masochism. "What the devil do you expect in a town, a jungle, like this?" Sociologists and psychiatrists reached for the warm comfort of jargon—"alienation of the individual from the group," "megalopolitan societies," "the disaster syndrome."

People who came from small towns said it could never happen back home. New Yorkers, ashamed, agreed. Nobody seemed to stop to ask whether there were not perhaps various forms of apathy and that some that exist in villages and towns do not exist in great cities.

Guilt turned into masochism, and masochism, as it often does, be-came a sadistic search for a target. Quite soon, the target became the police.

There is no doubt whatsoever that the police in New York have failed, to put it politely, to instill a feeling of total confidence in the population. There are great areas in this city—fine parks, as well as slums—where no person in his right mind would wander of an evening or an early morning. There is no central emergency point to receive calls for help. And a small river of letters from citizens to this newspaper testifies to the fact that patrols are often late in answering calls and that policemen on desk duty often give the bitter edge of their tongues to citizens calling for succor.

There is no doubt of these things. But to blame the police for apathy is a bit like blaming the sea wall for springing leaks. The police of this city are more efficient, more restrained, and more responsive to public demands than any others the writer has encountered in a decade of traveling the world. Their faults are either mechanical or a reflection of a city where almost every act of police self-protection is assumed to be an act of police brutality, and where a night club comedian can, as one did the other night, stand on a stage for an hour and a half and vilify the police as brutes, thieves, homosexuals, illiterates, and "Gestapo agents," while the audience howls in laughter as it drinks Scotch from bootleg bottles hidden under the tables.

There are two tragedies in the story of Catherine Genovese. One is the fact that her life was taken from her, that she died in pain and horror at the age of 28. The other is that in dying she gave to every human being—not just species New Yorker—an opportunity to examine some truths about the nature of apathy and that this has not been done. . . .

Two weeks later (after the murder), when this newspaper heard of the story, a reporter went knocking, door to door, asking why, why.

Through half-opened doors, they told him. Most of them were neither defiant nor terribly embarrassed nor particularly ashamed. The underlying attitude, or explanation, seemed to be fear of involvement, any kind of involvement.

"I didn't want my husband to get involved," a housewife said.

"We thought it was a lovers' quarrel," said another woman. "I went back to bed."

"I was tired," said a man.

"I don't know," said another man.

"I don't know," said the others.

There are, it seems to me, only two logical ways to look at the story of Cathrine Genovese. One is the way of the neighbor on Austin Street—"Let's forget the whole thing."

The other is to recognize that the bell tolls even on each man's individual island, to recognize that every man must fear the witness in himself who whispers to close the window.

———————

Winston Moseley was found guilty of murder in the first degree in the slaying of Catherine Genovese on June 12, 1964 and sentenced to death in the electric chair four days later. In Queens Supreme Court, just a few minutes' walk from the scene of the crime, an aroused judge said, "I don't believe in capital punishment but I must say I feel this may be improper when I see this monster. I wouldn't hesitate to pull the switch myself."

# VIII. THE INTERPRETERS

John Murmann Hightower, a soft-voiced and unassuming native of Coal Creek, Tennessee, came to Quebec in the August doldrums of 1943 with a fretful group of correspondents. At 34, he was covering his first major foreign assignment for the Associated Press—the Roosevelt-Churchill strategy conference known as Quadrant. He could see, of course, that all the headlines would be made months hence on many a battlefield thousands of miles away. While he was not privy to the decisions that were being taken, and could not have broadcast them to the world if he had known them, he could discern the broad outlines of Allied strategy. As a result, he began putting out a series of careful analyses of the problems that were being studied at Quebec.

It was exactly what the clientele of the AP wanted. Most editors, relieved over being able at last to take well-reasoned interpretive articles about Quebec off the wires instead of bits and pieces of news, gave prominence to Hightower's dispatches. It was the foundation of his career as one of the foremost diplomatic correspondents of his time.

Walter Lippmann and James Reston had greater prestige among the powerful elite groups in government. But as the diplomatic correspondent of the AP in Washington for more than two decades, Hightower has had a larger world mass audience for a longer time than anybody else in the mottled history of foreign correspondence. Where others have helped cause wars and overthrown kings and cabinets, it has been his particular virtue to spread understanding.

Hightower had no unique preparation for his responsibilities. He grew into them. He came up from Coal Creek, where his father worked on the Southern Railway, to the Knoxville *News-Sentinel* by way of the University of Tennessee, which he attended for two years. In 1933, in the pit of the great depression, he moved on to the Nashville AP.

Three years later, while covering the Tennessee delegations at the national conventions, he favorably impressed Byron Price, then the chief of the Washington AP bureau. And in 1936, at the age of 27, he landed in Washington just after Franklin D. Roosevelt's triumphant reelection.[1]

Although the AP's subscribers did not formally recognize that there was such a thing as interpretive reporting until 1954, it was being done throughout the years of the New Deal. When so many new facets of government were developing, reporters could not toss a lot of unassimilated facts at either editors or readers and expect them to understand. These things had to be explained. Very often, the writer had to put himself and his interpretation of events into the story in order to make it jell. But at a time when such matters were considered journalistic treason, they had to be masked under the faded trappings of "objective" journalism. The mysterious but omniscient "impartial observer" came into his own as a source for statements the correspondent knew to be perfectly true. Moreover, when the "impartial observer" became overworked, it was generally possible to find someone in Washington who would say what the correspondent wanted him to say in order to illuminate some obscure corner of the news.

Anonymity had been the hallmark of "objective" journalism, in which the reporter and writer submerged their personalities and spoke only for their organization. The coming of radio in the 1920s, and the mass following of the commentators, breached that wall between the reader and the journalist. The arrival of the editorial columnist, with his personal style and signed articles, was another blow against the anonymous writer. The United Press, which as early as World War I began running an interpretive column by J. W. T. Mason called "Today's War Moves," popularized its specialists by giving them bylines regularly.[2] It took years for the AP to learn the lesson, but once bylines came they helped established the authority of the interpreters.

As long as sources were available, there was no dearth of background material—the interpreters' stock in trade. But with the coming of World War II, few responsible officials cared to talk for publication. The sources dried up. It was at this point that Ernest K. Lindley, an editor of *Newsweek* magazine, a Rhodes scholar, and member of Phi Beta Kappa, revised and brought up to date an old device of the Quai

[1] *AP World* magazine, Autumn, 1964, p. 34.
[2] *UPI Reporter*, May 9, 1963.

d'Orsay—the unattributed source. Under the Lindley rule, as it came
to be known, an official could talk with a correspondent on an informal
basis with assurance that neither he nor his office would be named as
a source. The correspondent agreed, in turn, to attribute his information to some nebulous agency—informed sources, informed officials,
diplomatic circles, and all the rest of the rigmarole that has become
familiar long since.

For semantic purposes, information or views obtained under the
protection of the Lindley rule became known as "background information," which speedily gave rise to such notorious practices as the "background news conference," "background luncheon," and "background
dinner." Naturally, "background" covered a lot of information that
the government wanted to put out, but not on its own responsibility.
As a result, the Lindley rule became popular in government for one
reason and equally popular with correspondents for quite another.[3]

The system had obvious advantages. A correspondent was able to in-
form the public of certain trends in government thinking long before
a new policy took shape, in some cases; in others, he could warn that
a particular policy was being changed or abandoned. In a wartime
situation, it was just about the only way in which even a modicum of
public reaction could be obtained in advance of changes in sensitive
policy areas.

If there was a disadvantage, it was the manner in which a correspondent laid himself open to manipulation by those government officials
who sought to play on public opinion for their own reasons. But efforts
to manage the news were scarcely novel, either then or now. And any
sophisticated journalist knew perfectly well that the only correspondent
who could be managed was one who was willing to let himself be
managed. Whatever the government was selling, the correspondent did
not have to buy.

This somewhat complicated method of communication was perfected
under the strain of wartime necessity. Soon enough, the correspondents
were able to make effective use of it. Had it not been for their aggressive
diplomatic reporting and the steady stream of interpretive articles
which they stimulated, the American public would not have been very
well informed of the rebirth of an international peace-keeping organization during the war and its growth afterward.

[3] James Reston, New York *Times*, April 11, 1963.

As it was, the correspondents helped blaze a trail through the semantic underbrush at the United Nations conference in San Francisco in 1945, the General Assembly sessions in London and New York the following year, the meetings of the Council of Foreign Ministers from 1946 to 1948, the organization of the Marshall Plan, the North Atlantic Treaty Organization and their offshoots, the Japanese Peace Treaty signing in 1951, the Big Four Summit at Geneva in 1955, the disastrous Paris Summit of 1960, and the Kennedy-Khrushchev conference in Vienna in 1961.

In the process, Hightower won a Pulitzer Prize in 1952 and a half-dozen other awards in recognition of his work. By 1965, he was dean of the diplomatic correspondents in Washington and one of the five members of the AP staff who were given the honor of a designation as a Special Correspondent. At 55, he was still slim and active, a striking grey-haired figure just under six feet, with a liking for nine- and ten-hour days and no prejudice against working week-ends when necessary.

There were other distinguished wire service interpreters who left their mark on Washington, Raymond Clapper and Joe Alex Morris of the UP among them. In 1958, after a long career as a war correspondent and foreign correspondent, Stewart Hensley came to the State Department as the chief diplomatic correspondent for United Press International. Hensley was away on extended foreign assignments each year and adapted to a different kind of routine than Hightower's. Yet, wherever they were, both essentially had the same assignment—to explain American foreign policy and to interpret it for both American readers and for the world at large.

The difference between the personal journalism of the powerful editorialists at the turn of the century and the interpreters of the 1960s was illustrated strikingly by a contrast between their approach to world affairs. In 1919, toward the close of a long career as editor of the Louisville *Courier-Journal*, Henry Watterson wrote as follows:

"I claim to be the only son of the seventh daughter of the seventh son in a straight line from Brian Boru, the Scottish prophet—and I know everything that has been, or ever will be, and I tell you—confidentially, of course—that the world is on its last legs; Marconi with his wireless to get in touch with Mars; some fool to explode from the top of Washington Monument a bomb, which will stifle the universe and destroy all living things, including the fantastical profiteers of

Miami and the horsey girls over at Palm Beach. I am not a pessimist. Dear, no, but I am neither blind nor deaf, and I refuse to be dumb. . . . Where shall we look for a ray of hope?" [4]

In that brave new world after the winning of the war to end all wars, when the only visible blight on the land was prohibition, Watterson's readers might have permitted themselves a tolerant smile over the old man's maunderings. Who among them would have dreamed then of a nuclear blast that could kill all living things, the fantasies of rocket travel about the earth, the exploration of outer space by radio?

It all came to pass in the lifetime of the postwar generation, styled by its elders the "lost generation." Once the world had to face up to these awesome realities, it wasn't sufficient to listen to a Watterson crying woe. The interpreter had to walk quietly in the light of reason, however thin it might be, amid the gathering darkness. Thus, at a hard and dangerous time of crisis, Hightower wrote this analysis of his time:

"The Geneva conference (of 1955) produced no diplomatic settlements. It created the impression that Russia and the United States had finally convinced each other that neither wanted an atomic war. In this hopeful atmosphere, the Atlantic alliance lost vigor and force. There was much more concern about how to get along with the Soviet Union than how to keep the Western coalition strong." [5]

This view fluctuated with the ebb and flow of events, but essentially the approach was far more rational than the black despair of Watterson in a world that was still safe from the atom and the earth-girdling missile. Walter Lippmann put it this way in projecting an essentially hopeful view of the position of the United States in world affairs:

"In my view . . . the world balance of forces has, I venture to say, become rather more favorable to the Western community. I know from my newspaper experience how risky it is to be optimistic and I know that the prudent man who wishes to play it safe will always lean to Cassandra, never to Pollyanna. For if Cassandra is right, which I am sorry to say is all too frequently, the man becomes without any trouble at all a true prophet. If, on the other hand, Cassandra is wrong, everybody is too well pleased to remember what he said.

[4] Joseph Frazier Wall, *Henry Watterson: Reconstructed Rebel* (New York, Oxford University Press, 1956), p. 324.
[5] Washington *Star*, Jan. 19, 1958.

"Nevertheless, in the historic confrontation between international communism and the Western society, our position is, I believe, improved." [6]

These are scarcely times when the world is able to depend, as it did 2,500 years ago, on a priestly interpretation of the strange cries of the Delphic oracle, seated on her golden tripod. Both the editorial columnists, as exemplified by Walter Lippmann and James Reston, and the reporter-analysts, as typified by John Hightower and Stewart Hensley, have had a heavy responsibility to discharge in the interpretation of the meaning of their age and the measurement of its leaders. The following selections indicate how well the interpreters have been able to do it.

## 52. *LBJ, AS RESTON SAW HIM*

Most Presidents of the United States have conceived it to be their duty to read what is written about them in the newspapers that come to hand day by day. There is no record extant that any of them consider this to be a pleasurable exercise, except for the day on which the journalists, like the Supreme Court, follow the election returns.

If it has made some Presidents unhappier than others, this is undoubtedly because some Presidents have read more newspapers than others. Thus, in the post World War II period, John Fitzgerald Kennedy never really enjoyed his relatively good press because he read too much of it, and Dwight David Eisenhower never truly believed that he had a tolerant and even an indulgent press because he read too little of it.

While most Presidents have respected the press, and some have assiduously cultivated the more eminent journalists in Washington, even the weakest of them have seldom expressed outright fear of adverse comment. Nor have the leading newspapers often let themselves be intimidated by righteous presidential wrath, although a few here and there have not been above lowering their lances at critical points in a joust with the White House.

The point has been made repeatedly since the founding of the Republic: The Presidents and the press are, on the whole, natural antagonists rather than natural allies. And this was as true of the 36th

[6] Address to American Law Institute, quoted in the New York *Herald Tribune*, May 26, 1962.

President, Lyndon Baines Johnson, as it was of his predecessors. As Walter Lippmann put it only six weeks after a splendid inauguration in 1965:

"No one can say that the relations between the President and the press are happy, and as usual, each is blaming the other. Yet, so far as I know, no one has a formula for making the press relations of the White House happy, or even happier. Even in the simple past, the relations were far from perfect.

"But in our times we have to take into account the radical changes which have taken place in the past twenty-five years. There is the change in the volume and complexity of the news, in the size of the Washington press corps, in the range of the President's powers and responsibilities, and the rise within government as makers of policy of specialized experts and technicians. . . . I do not know the remedy. But the President's relationship with the press is a great matter of state, and should be regarded as such." [7]

President Johnson seemed at first not to be angered as much as he was puzzled by the attitude of the press. He was making news—fairly pouring presidential messages before Congress at a rate unheard of since FDR's 100 days. The criticism nettled him. But if he did not create the image of a President who relished his skirmishes with the press, as did FDR, LBJ seemed at least to stand his ground with firmness and dignity. On occasion, he overcame his resentments and played the part of evangelist in the White House rose garden, exhorting visiting editors to support his dream of a Great Society. He led the suffering correspondents on long forced marches about the White House grounds and, when he flew south, at the LBJ ranch in Texas, thus demonstrating superior physical conditioning and at the same time paying off some of his more voluble critics by leaving them gasping for breath.

While an artful President had the inestimable advantage of television in this era of more or less scientific politics, it was still not possible for him entirely to create his own image. The world, unfortunately, was always too ready to believe ill of the great and near-great; therefore, those who wrote critically about the President from close view at the White House invariably had a large and attentive readership. Not all critics, of course, could make themselves felt when they assessed a

[7] *Newsweek*, March 1, 1965.

President. But certainly, among those whose works were borne first to the presidential office for daily perusal was James Reston.

After twenty-odd years of activity in Washington and abroad, the small and sad-eyed Scot was in imminent danger of becoming an institution before his 60th year. To one who was born at Clydebank November 3, 1909, and brought to the United States by his parents at the age of four, this was perhaps as much of a Horatio Alger story as was that of Johnson himself. Winner of two Pulitzer Prizes in 1945 and 1957, chief of the New York *Times* Washington bureau for eleven years and latterly an associate editor and editorial columnist of the *Times*, Reston had lapsed insensibly into the role of an elder statesman of journalism.

It was, therefore, a matter of some consequence when he undertook to measure the stature of Lyndon Baines Johnson for the *New York Times Magazine* of January 17, 1965, just before the thirty-sixth President took the oath of office for his first elected term of office in 1965. An inaugural, as Reston correctly observed, starts with a prayer and ends with a dance; what he did not say, although he might have, was that it is also a time when there is an undeclared truce between Presidents and press. The following is an excerpt from Reston's piece about LBJ.

## PORTRAIT OF A PRESIDENT

### By James Reston

Lyndon Baines Johnson is to the politics of America what his state of Texas is to the other states. He is a gargantuan figure; he is a whopper. Measuring him for history is like measuring an active volcano with an inch-tape. He barbecues people who try and eats them for breakfast.

When you interview him, he ends up with your life story. He does not want to be analyzed or classified; he wants to be loved. Anything you say he said, he can usually neutralize with something else he said on the other side. If you say he's liberal, he can prove he's conservative, or vice versa. If you suggest he's from the South, he will insist he's from the West, or the other way around. If you don't tell the precise truth about him, which is almost inevitable, he thinks you are dishonest, and if you do, he feels you are disloyal.

This, however, is the caricature of Mr. Johnson and, like all caricatures, it magnifies one feature and minimizes all the rest. It is amusing, but it is unfair. The big, slouching Texas Ranger on the ranch, the master politician on the telephone, the restless, sleepless "arm-twister," trading favors for votes in the smoky back room—all so dear to the cartoonists—are all true, but misleading.

He is more than that—far more. It is too early to say that he is a leader of men in the classic sense of being "quick to know and to do the things that the hour and his nation need," particularly in the foreign field. He has not yet proved that he can get and keep and inspire the best men in the nation to serve him, or even that he has mastered the art of using his staff and his time effectively. But he is a shrewd and knowledgeable man, an elemental force of nature who commands respect and even a certain amount of fear.

"When you come into the presence of a leader of men," Woodrow Wilson observed, "you know you have come into the presence of fire— that it is best not incautiously to touch that man—that there is something that makes it dangerous to cross him."

Johnson conveys this feeling and it is both his strength and weakness. His technique works but it hurts. He can make men do what he wants them to do but he does not make them like it or him in the process. There is a kind of intimidating shamelessness about him that makes men feel that if they don't go along there may be the most frightful and embarrassing row. But he is a highly intelligent man who is not to be dismissed as just another brilliant political operator.

He is far more complex than the boys in the back room. The master politician on Capitol Hill and in the White House is not the same as the "Last Hurrah" types out of Tammany, Boston, or Chicago, though Johnson has been hurt by the popular confusion of the two. The political leader in the capital has to deal not only with the masses of men but with a highly intelligent Cabinet, an expert civil service, and a staggering catalogue of problems and ideas.

This is not, by any fair test, an unintellectual process. It involves a great deal more than physical strength, tactical skill, personal acquaintance, and a telephone. It requires immense concentration on the facts of a great many issues at the same time, a quick knack of identifying and absorbing the essence of complicated and critical questions, and a

## LBJ AT HIS TEXAS RANCH

John Frair takes a classic picture of the President.

limitless memory for those intimate personal and political facts that will move men to compromise.

There is much confusion on this point. Lyndon Johnson is not Dean Acheson, with a clear vision of the world and a carefully worked-out plan of the role America might play in the human story. But he clearly did not get where he is on a bag of tricks alone.

He does not concentrate on thinking programs through but on getting them through. He does not believe in "inevitable conflicts," or think in terms of tidy programs imposed or manipulated from the top. He is one of those old-fashioned, small "d" democrats who think that The People and their representatives, if presented with the facts, will find reasonable solutions. He sees politics as an exercise in adapting oneself to all sorts of people and situations, of discussing and bargaining with legitimate groups in search of a consensus.

His university really has been Capitol Hill, his classroom the committee hearings. He retains the memory of his experiences in Texas and in the Congress, but it would never occur to him to try to organize them into a system. Life to him is full of surprises, more so as the tempo of change increases, and he would no doubt support H. G. Wells's dictum that "to be honest, one must be inconsistent."

This, of course, only adds to the caricature of Johnson the manipulator. But there is another side to it. He is an incorrigible believer. He believes in everything that works. He shares all the popular ideals, assumptions, and illusions of the nation. Kennedy was troubled by what he called the "myths" of the American past. Johnson loves them. Kennedy came to the White House wondering out loud whether a country governed such as ours could endure. Johnson could no more think or say that than he could denounce Lady Bird or the flag. He believes in the American system. He accepts it as he accepts the weather in his hill county of Texas; a little irritating and even cruel at times, but inevitable.

Similarly he accepts the congressional system the way it is, warts and all. Kennedy was in the Congress. Johnson is of it. He struggled to the top through the system and therefore thinks it's all right. He is not a critic of the elders of the Congress but their companion. He has lived with them for thirty years, spoken for them in their elections, stood up with them at their family weddings and christenings and funerals, drunk whisky with them in Mr. Sam Rayburn's "board of education" hideaway in the House.

The pessimism and complexity of the modern world, accordingly, do not bother him. Unlike many of his intellectual critics, he is not paralyzed by excessive contemplation or doubt. He is all for the businessman making a pile, having made one himself. He believes in Horatio Alger's triumphant ragamuffin (who, after all, is Johnson). He believes in the hard doctrines of John Calvin and individual responsibility and now that the planned deficit and tax cut have increased prosperity, he even believes a little in John Maynard Keynes. He is fiercely patriotic. He genuinely believes that God looks out for Uncle Sam. He has no doubt that this nation was set apart to achieve good and noble purposes, that America is indeed the New Arcadia, or will be if he has his way.

---

In the indulgent mood of Inauguration Day, which can affect even the most Calvinistic interpreter, Reston concluded his piece, "So let us pray." It must have made fairly pleasant reading for one who was not the most beloved of American Presidents, for all his skill, and who even at that moment of triumph was annoyed by what he believed to be a too-critical group of White House correspondents.

Tom Wicker, Reston's able successor as chief of the New York *Times*'s Washington bureau, put the problem of the reporters as follows: "The difficulty of the reporter in Washington today—which is to say the difficulty of his readers as well—is not to get the news, even directly from the President. It is rather to know how to evaluate and credit it, to sift the self-serving from the genuine, to find the real accomplishment or the real failure beneath the shimmering surface, to penetrate the avalanche of words and images to whatever may be true or revealing." [8]

Under LBJ, the interpreters had a full-time job.

## 53. A DIFFERENT WASHINGTON

There have been few who have begun farther down the journalistic ladder than Vermont Connecticut Royster and mounted quite as high.

[8] *New York Times Book Review*, Feb. 7, 1965.

In 1936 he was a reporter for the New York City News Association, which meant that he chased all over town for small items that were distributed to the newspapers. A little more than two decades later he was the editor of the *Wall Street Journal* and the winner of a Pulitzer Prize for editorial writing. Even for a journalist with the talent of a Royster, that was traveling.

Royster was a product of the supposedly leisurely Southern tradition. He was born in Raleigh, North Carolina, on April 30, 1914, and graduated in 1935 from the University of North Carolina with an A.B., and membership in Phi Beta Kappa. He was in New York the following year, and proceeded directly from City News to the *Wall Street Journal* as a reporter. Soon he was shifted to Washington and for five years, until war came in 1941, he came to know and to admire the beauty and graciousness of the capital, even if its weather left something to be desired.

During World War II, Royster demonstrated that he could make progress in the Navy, too, which was somewhat of a feat for a sedentary journalist. He went in as an ensign, was on active duty for forty-eight months in the Atlantic, Caribbean, and Pacific, and was mustered out as a lieutenant commander. When he returned to the *Wall Street Journal*, it was as chief Washington correspondent. In 1948, he became associate editor of the newspaper, won his Pulitzer Prize in 1953, and in 1958 assumed the editorship.

Even in the supposedly impersonal editorials that Royster wrote for the *Wall Street Journal* in such abundance, there was a distinctly personal style and, at times, a rather wry humor. It was scarcely a surprise, therefore, when his name turned up at the head of a column in his newspaper. This was Royster's view of Washington in the *Wall Street Journal* on April 24, 1964.

## THE BIG CHANGE

### By Vermont Royster

WASHINGTON—A returning visitor to Paris, London, or Rome can be pretty sure of what he will find when he gets there. A returning visitor to Washington sometimes needs the reassurance of the familiar cherry blossoms to be sure he didn't get off at the wrong airport.

Britain can change prime ministers, or even a Parliament, without disturbing the accustomed air of either Pall Mall or Cheapside. In Paris or Rome they can change the whole form of government—and indeed have done so—without noticeable effect in the salons or sidewalk cafes. Not since 1792 has politics made a Frenchman change his hat.

But in this mercurial city the ladies seem lately to have changed their hats, the men their haberdashery, the cafes their cuisine, the diplomats their demeanor, the journalists their jargon, and the public servants their working hours. The political accents also sound different, and not just because people talk with a drawl instead of a twang.

We don't know whether this is a tribute to President Johnson, a sad commentary on Capital courtiers, or simply a mark of the ephemeral nature of everything in Washington. Whatever .it is, it's impressive.

Just a year ago President Kennedy gave a party for the nation's editors here assembled. The ladies put on their best dresses, the menfolk their best demeanors, and everybody walked sedately through the White House, sipping punch and feeling just a little bit like provincial nobles at Versailles.

The President was extremely gracious; Mr. Kennedy stood for awhile in the rotunda talking with ease, wit, and dignity. After awhile everybody went home with the feeling that it had been a lovely if somewhat staid reception.

Just the other day President Johnson gave a party for the same editors. Again everybody was all dressed up, but everybody found out it would be different before they even got inside the White House.

All the guests were first assembled on the lawn along with a podium, microphone, and TV cameras. Instead of the expected few words of welcome they heard a half hour speech on civil rights, poverty, education, and the Bible, while the ladies' high heels wobbled on the grass and the men grew impatient for the punch.

By Emily Post standards it was probably the wrong speech at the wrong time. Still, most of the guests thought it "just like Lyndon" and seemed to be flattered by all the attention; if nothing else, it let them know this was going to be an unusual affair.

And it was. Inside there was a full buffet, a real bar, two orchestras, and a President who loved to dance. Mr. Johnson was in full swing and so, within a few minutes, was the whole East Room. The orchestra shifted its tempo from Guy Lombardo to Chubby Checker and by the time the appointed departure hour rolled around the party was just getting started. Finally everybody went home with the feeling that while it might not have been exactly a rule-book reception, it was a lovely wingding.

The difference between the two White House parties, we suspect, is more than one of manners; it reflects a difference between the two Presidents in their whole manner of looking at themselves, their jobs, and the world around them.

The Kennedy administration gave Washington an "old worldly" air, as if the President were a sovereign and the White House a court. In manners this meant French cuisine, haute couture, chamber music, and poetry readings. In political manner it meant White Papers to Congress, literary speeches, and diplomacy by State dinners.

The Johnson administration gives Washington the air of a Texas fair, with the President a folksy fellow and the White House a small-town mansion. In manners this means ham and cornbread, flowered dresses, hoe-down music, and tall tales of the prairie. In political manner it means politicking as if Congress were city hall, country preacher speeches, and diplomacy over barbecue.

Andy Jackson has taken over from John Quincy Adams and all Washington shows it. Hats are bigger, clothes more comfortable, conversation louder, and while you may stand in line at a steak house you can find an empty table at any French restaurant.

If it's been months since you brought the high-school seniors to see the Capital, you'd better bring 'em back. They'll hardly recognize the place.

## 54. CHILDS LOOKS AT CONGRESS

The Congress of the United States came under anxious scrutiny in the first half of the 1960s. During a time of increasing demands for action at home and attention to very large interests abroad, both the House and the Senate seemed at times to neglect the essential business of a democratic society. Accordingly, there was a rising volume of criticism in the press, and among the foremost newspapers to examine congressional performance was the St. Louis *Post-Dispatch* on September 8, 1963.

"As the Congress crawls along an obstacle course that stretches into the wintry distance, with much of its business still unfinished, a shadow of doubt falls across the Capitol," Pulitzer's paper said on its front page.

"The questions is no longer whether this President and this Congress can work together under a Constitution of divided powers in a time of great national need; the question is whether the system itself is workable in the face of swift change when America has assumed world responsibility."

Such was the introduction to a critical series of articles, "How Effective Is Congress?" The aging committee chairmen, the sluggish pace, the failure of President John F. Kennedy to prod the legislators, and the mistakes of the White House lobbyists all were examined in detail. The climactic article was written by one of the best of all Washington correspondents, Marquis William Childs, the chief of the *Post-Dispatch*'s bureau in the capital.

It was no simple matter for a correspondent, no matter how authoritative, to enlarge on the faults of the Congress, whether they were temporary or built into the system, whether they were real or merely surface manifestations of the time-consuming processes of self-government. The Senate, for all its infirmities, was the most exclusive club in the world and the House, while it often seemed like a rabble, operated under the political code of self-preservation. While an attack on one was not necessarily considered an attack on all, both Senate and House were likely to take a jaundiced view of persistent critics. However, the critics were not awed; one of them, Vance Trimble, then the news editor of Scripps-Howard Newspaper Alliance, won a Pulitzer Prize in 1960 for exposing congressional nepotism.

Childs had no such headline-catching material. It was not his job to investigate, but to interpret the shortcomings of the congressional system in such a way that it could be understood by the average citizen. He was eminently fitted to do the job, having been at it for many years and risen to the top of his profession. Nearly 200 newspapers published his syndicated Washington column and television audiences were familiar with both his presence and his views as a frequent commentator.

The world of Marquis Childs was Washington, but his roots were in the Midwest. He had been born March 17, 1903, in Clinton, Iowa; graduated at twenty from the University of Wisconsin, and taken his

Master's in 1925 at the University of Iowa. After three years of intermittent work for the UP, he joined the *Post-Dispatch* staff in 1926 and thereafter, for nearly four decades, his work appeared in its pages.

This was his view of Congress in the fall of 1963, condensed from the original article that appeared in the St. Louis *Post-Dispatch* on September 14.

## HOW EFFECTIVE IS CONGRESS?
### By Marquis W. Childs

WASHINGTON—Lazy, indifferent, inefficient, venal, outdated—these are some of the epithets that with increasing frequency over the years are heaped on Congress. So tarnished is the image that Congress itself has begun to notice.

The contempt for Congress and the state legislatures is such that it is regarded here as seeming to reflect a distrust of representative government. The institution, as a few members of Congress realize, is not sacred. The power to nullify and obstruct has in other lands proved to be also the power of self-destruction.

The reforms that critics both in and out of Congress put forward match the abuses these same critics cite. First and foremost are unlimited debate—the filibuster—and the custom of seniority in the selection of committee chairmen.

The first is written into Senate Rule 22 requiring a two-thirds vote to shut off discussion. This means the Southerners with a little help from conservative Republicans can go on talking as long as they can muster enough voices to hold the floor indefinitely.

Seniority is untouchable because this is the means by which a few men go on year after year exercising the power to delay and obstruct. These committee chairmen, whose average age in the Senate is nearly 66, would have to approve any substantial change in the system. They show no signs of voting themselves out of power.

Reforms far more basic than any of those officially put forward are frequently discussed. One is with respect to campaign contributions and the glaring abuses that come to light. There is no effective reporting system covering such contributions. Special interest groups manage to funnel in large sums through one channel or another. And a member of Congress understandably feels beholden to his contributors. Reports circulate after every election of members who take considerable amounts which they report neither as campaign contributions nor as income for tax purposes.

A number of proposals have been advanced for tightening the reporting system and for limiting the size of contributions. The goal is to get small sums from many contributors and eliminate dependence on a few big money types who almost always have an ax to grind. But despite several investigations into these abuses, Congress shows no signs of giving serious consideration to corrective measures.

A related abuse has to do with conflict of interest. Congress is quick to pounce on anyone in the executive branch suspected of using his government office for private gain. But examples abound of members of Congress whose interests are closely related to their official power.

Subjects for academic debate by political scientists and commentators cover even more far-reaching proposals aimed at the division of powers and the deep conflicts that result.

These include: A regular "question period" like that in the House of Commons in London when officials of the executive branch would appear on the floor of Congress to submit to questioning; reconstruction of the Cabinet to include leading members of Congress, thereby approximating the parliamentary system; establishment of a central council chosen by the President to formulate the government's program and direct its execution, the council to be made up of members representing the executive and legislative branches.

Proposals of this type are aimed at abating the guerrilla warfare between executive and legislature which goes on in many areas. For example, the Senate-House Atomic Energy Committee makes all the major decisions for the atomic energy program and with a battery of experts is prepared to veto initiatives taken by the executive.

Many of the complaints by the executive deal with the jealousies between the two houses. Thus, if the Secretary of State or the Secretary of Defense could make a presentation to a joint Senate-House Foreign Relations or Armed Services Committee, hundreds of man-hours would be saved. But each Cabinet officer must go separately to the House and the Senate to tell the same story.

The divisions in the Congress reflect the divisions in the country and this is true particularly over civil rights. The Southern minority occupying most of the important committee chairmanships is out to punish the President for his strong stand. No procedural reform that could conceivably be adopted would end this warfare, but there are changes which with sufficient prodding the Congress might adopt that would quicken the legislative pace.

---

Childs and the *Post-Dispatch* would have been the last to claim that their series had any direct influence on the laggard pace of Congress. Other powerful newspapers, too, were examining the weak spots in congressional procedures. At the time of President Kennedy's assassination, the press criticism of Congress had become rather formidable.

In the changed atmosphere of President Johnson's first weeks in office, the lagging Kennedy legislative program came to life. Under the stimulus of Johnson's legislative skill, the tax cut went through Congress. As for the civil rights bill, the shock of seeing Alabama police dogs tearing at Negroes in pictures widely displayed in the nation's press almost certainly had their effect upon the Senate and House. In any event, the most significant civil rights bill since the Civil War finally did pass through Congress.

Yet, as the eighty-ninth session began in 1965, the problem of producing congressional action on necessary legislative proposals had to be faced all over again. True, some rules were liberalized. True, there were top-heavy Democratic majorities in both houses that actively supported the Johnson program. But despite all the skill of the thirty-sixth President, he had to let the legislators take their own time; in the end, they gave him what he wanted. But there was no doubt that continued criticism by the press remained a vital part of the machinery of self-government in the United States.

## 55. HIGHTOWER SEES A SPLIT

In the early 1960s, it became clear that the Soviet Union and Communist China were having their troubles with each other. At first, they spouted the complicated language of Communist theoreticians to show their mutual displeasure. Next, they used tiny Albania, the only European pawn of Peking, as a symbol of their argument. Then came the fireworks at the XXII Congress of the Communist Party of the Soviet Union from October 17 through October 31, 1961, when Premier Chou En-lai went home after an argument with his Moscow hosts.

Philip E. Mosely, who had been director of Columbia University's Russian Institute and at the time was director of studies for the Council on Foreign Relations, remarked on the "clear if somewhat muffled Sino-Soviet divergences over revolutionary strategy." The argument, he added, "has left a wide-open field for speculation about its implications for the future." [9] But as a prudent and expert Kremlinologist, he kept his predictions within range of what was possible.

Merle Fainsod of Harvard University, another American expert on the Soviet Union, wrote, "The effect of the Congress was to dramatize the rift in the world Communist movement and to set the stage for a continuing struggle for ascendancy between Khrushchev and Mao." But, he went on, "The reverberations of the struggle will probably be contained within the Soviet Union itself." [10]

Neither the scholars nor government experts were ready to conclude, immediately after the XXII Congress, that the Soviet Union and Communist China would take steps against each other that might, at some future time, prove irrevocable. As for the journalists, they were even more cautious, which wasn't precisely in character.

Even after the Cuban crisis, when the American government was able to force Premier Nikita S. Khrushchev's Soviet regime to back down, few who wrote for daily publication would have been willing to gamble on the effect of the defeat on Moscow-Peking relations. That kind of complicated diplomatic sounding seemed to be scarcely within the province of a newspaper reporter, let alone a wire service correspondent with a limit of 600 to 900 words. It was more appropriate for a scholarly paper or, perhaps, a draft of a position paper to be worked up in a quiet State Department planning office by someone who could take advantage of the classification machinery.

Nevertheless, in an AP news analysis, "Winds of Change," carried on PMs budget, AP "A" wire on November 22, 1962, John Hightower raised the strong probability of an open split between the Soviet Union

[9] "Khrushchev's Party Congress," *Foreign Affairs*, January, 1962, p. 183.

[10] "The 22d Party Congress," special supplement in *Problems of Communism*, Vol. X, No. 6, November–December, 1961 (Washington, D.C., U.S. Information Service), page XI.

and Communist China. While he was not the first to do it, that is scarcely material. His piece was addressed to a world audience, which spoke well for the AP's faith in its diplomatic correspondent.

What Hightower did was to write: "There is a sense of great drama in Washington as the last scenes of the Cuban conflict are played out. There is a feeling that something big is about to happen." He pointed out that within the month there had been three crises—the American demand for the removal of Russian offensive missile bases in Cuba, the Chinese Communist attack on India, and the rising tensions between Moscow and Peking. He went on: "In Moscow and Peking, in New Delhi and in other Western capitals as well as Washington, old policies are being reviewed and historic new decisions are in the making."

Then, in the essential part of his article, he posed his thesis.

## THE SINO–SOVIET CRISIS

### By John Hightower

Militarily, the result of the Cuban crisis can hardly be considered decisive for more than a few years. Its immediate effect is to roll Soviet nuclear power back thousands of miles onto Soviet territory. But it will be only a matter of time until Soviet nuclear submarines can threaten American security from points close to shore.

There is a parallel between the Kremlin's power play in the Western hemisphere and the Red Chinese invasion of India. In each case, there was a bald use of force to achieve a political objective. The Russians are believed to have been aiming for a U.S. surrender over Berlin before they were thwarted. The Communist leaders in Peking wanted full control of long-disputed territory on India's northern border; probably, they also were determined to humiliate India by military defeat and thus assert dominance in Asia.

But while they proved their military superiority, their scheme in the long run threatens to backfire.

Among Western diplomats there has been a widely held theory that, in attacking India, the Red Chinese wanted, apart from their more immediate aims, to force Russia's hand in the long power struggle within the Communist bloc. The issue between Peking and Moscow has centered on which of them should lead the bloc, and whether, on the average, methods of force should be preferred to the methods of economic and political pressures and indirect aggression.

It seems unlikely that the Chinese attack on India should not have proved extremely embarrassing to Khrushchev; and the obvious reluctance of the Soviet government to back its ally suggests that this is so.

U.S. officials assume, in fact, that the Chinese-Indian crisis has brought on a hidden crisis between Peking and Moscow, with future effects on both their policies which are, for the moment, incalculable.

An open split between them would change the political map of the world. It would raise the serious possibility of trouble between the two great Communist nations along their extensive Asian borders. It would open up a whole new range of possibilities for the Western powers as the Russians adjusted to unprecedented new conditions."

---

The open split came in the summer of 1963. The central committee of the Chinese Communist Party, championing Stalinism, wrote in its blistering letter of June 14 to Moscow that it was "sheer illusion" to assert, as Khrushchev did, that it is possible to end all war while "the system of imperialism and the exploitation of man by man still exists." Khrushchev, already branded a "coward" for pulling back in the missile crisis, now was accused of a policy that would "help the imperialists in their policies of aggression and war."

In a scarcely less provocative reply on July 14, the Central Committee of the CPSU asked Mao: "If both the exploiters and the exploited are buried under the ruins of the old world, who will build the 'bright future'?" [11] Out of these and other documents, much of the genesis of the Moscow-Peking quarrel now could be reconstructed, some things that had been suspected and others that were totally new to the Western world. One of the unforeseen consequences was Khrushchev's fall from power on October 16, 1964. But whether the new regime could do anything effective to patch up the schism in the Communist world was still open to question in the spring of 1965, although it was clear that the Viet Nam war had outraged both.

No one could say whether a widening conflict in Southeast Asia would

[11] Philip E. Mosely, "The Chinese-Soviet Rift: Origins and Portents," *Foreign Affairs*, October, 1963, pp. 17–18.

pull the two Communist giants together in a more or less temporary common front against the United States. That was one of the risks Washington took in punishing North Viet Nam with air attacks in an effort to force Hanoi to halt its support of the Viet Cong south of the 17th parallel.

The interpreters were quick to recognize the changed situation. "The war in Viet Nam," Hightower wrote on February 14, 1965, "has entered a new phase. It ceased to be a small struggle with only a potential of world-wide danger. It became a hazardous conflict directly involving the interest and prestige of the United States, Russia, and Red China."

If there was one thing on which all Western diplomats and commentators gloomily agreed, it was that the way to a rickety and uncertain peace in Southeast Asia would be both tortuous and difficult.


## 56. THE RUSTING IRON CURTAIN

Joseph Arnold Livingston, financial editor of the Philadelphia *Bulletin*, made a six-week trip behind the Iron Curtain in the summer of 1964. It was his fourth visit since 1956.

Livingston knew, of course, that there had been changes in the Soviet's economic system. Yevsey Liberman, a professor at Kharkov University, had been giving voice to previously unthinkable thoughts—centralized planning wasn't good enough and profit-making was no sin. Naturally, Livingston scarcely expected that the Soviet version of profit would coincide with the profit motive in the Western world. But the very notion that such things could be discussed behind the Iron Curtain was a sensation.

As the *Bulletin*'s financial editor traveled from one Soviet satellite to another in Eastern Europe, he became conscious that other things weren't quite the same. In Sofia, he saw a young Bulgar excitedly buying a new drip-dry shirt and putting it on atop the soiled shirt he was wearing. In Moscow itself, he noted people lining up to buy stretch nylon socks. These and other Western novelties simply were unavailable through Soviet factories and they had begun to slip through the Iron Curtain.

A Polish diplomat, commenting on the changing ways of Communism, remarked to Livingston: "The problem of growth is the growth of problems." And the American found that Moscow was unable to handle them all. The United States and the pull of the dollar were having an unlooked-for effect in Eastern Europe, despite the growing annoyance in Moscow with the Americans' intervention in the war in Southeast Asia.

Livingston was no starry-eyed dreamer. He was a veteran economic journalist with a substantial reputation in the United States—a 60-year-old financial writer, New York-born, educated at the University of Michigan, with a 40-year record of service on some of the outstanding newspapers in America. He was well aware that a bad turn in the Viet Nam war or too great a show of independence among the European satellites could bring Soviet retribution. Nevertheless, late in 1964, he felt sufficiently confident to report what he had seen in Eastern Europe. The main part of his first article, published in the Philadelphia *Bulletin* on November 11, follows.

## "THERE WILL BE PROFITS . . ."

### By J. A. Livingston

The countries of Eastern Europe, all of them, are hungry for dollars.

If they can't get American money, they'll settle for West German marks, French, Belgian, or Swiss francs, British pounds—any hard currency to buy what the Soviet Union can't supply:

The industrial know-how of the West.

Over and over during my trip behind the obviously corroding Iron Curtain, I encountered receptivity to capitalistic ways—sometimes open, sometimes covert, but always present.

The unceremonial ouster of Nikita S. Khrushchev from the Kremlin strengthened this receptivity, this turning away from centralized direction of the Communist world by Moscow autarkists (those favoring autocratic rule).

In Bucharest, an influential official in the Romanian hierarchy said: "Why don't we attract more American tourists? Vacationing here is a bargain. You can't get such accommodations as cheaply in France, Italy, or Germany . . . We've got to build another hotel here. We hope to get Hilton to do it."

"But Hilton will have to make a profit," I said. "It's an American corporation and not in business for love. Does this mean you're willing to pay for Hilton know-how and management?"

"We'd have to."

"You mean, you'd let capitalists own property—invest in Rumania? You'd have to pay interest or a share of profit or both. Doesn't this run counter to government ownership and control of everything?"

He looked directly at me, smiled, and moved his right hand this way and that several times as if to say, "We're flexible."

I remembered that gesture in Yugoslavia when I suddenly decided to fly from Belgrade to attend the opening of the Industrial Fair in Zagreb. The Pan American World Airways representative volunteered to get me a room in the Esplanade, a hotel which I'd been assured had been overbooked. He had an "in."

This is a Pan Am hotel in the sense that Pan Am supervised its renovation and receives a fee for consultation. For the benefit of American know-how, the Yugoslavs pay a fixed percentage, based on volume. Yugoslavia is a socialist society but it has imported capitalistic ways.

In Budapest I thought anew of that expressive Rumanian gesture while talking to Imre Vajda, a prominent economist and former planner in the Hungarian government. Because Hungary's industrial and engineering development is intensive, not extensive, Vajda hopes that some day, British, West German, French, and even American companies will join Hungarian enterprises in the production of complex machinery in Hungary for sale in Eastern and Western Europe.

"But," I said, "there'll be profits and the western firm will want a share of them."

"Of course."

"But wouldn't this be exploiting the Hungarian worker?"

"We have to purchase know-how," Vajda responded. "Joan Robinson, the British economist, once said to me, 'It's terrible to be exploited but it's even more terrible not to be.' We have to pay for the development of our productivity. We'd pay a higher price if we were to avoid capitalist help."

The Communist world is in ferment, if not torment. World communism, as a political creed and a system of rigid economic domination, is in the grip of change beyond the control of the men in the Kremlin.

It wasn't happenstance that in Prague Josef Horn, president of the Chamber of Commerce of Czechoslovakia, questioned me minutely about business methods in the United States. He intends to lead a trade delegation to the United States to explore the possibilities of selling Czech machinery there.

"Isn't that like carrying coals to Newcastle?" I asked. He knew the saying but insisted he had to find out.

Never before has Horn been to the United States. His venture into the capitalist heartland has but one meaning. The United States has what Czechoslovakia wants—engineering and technological capability which the Soviet Union cannot supply. Autarky—self-sufficiency—is enforceable within the Communist bloc as long as the bloc is self-sufficient. Today, it isn't.

All Eastern European countries have been through an economic upheaval. Before World War II, about 60 to 70 percent of their trade was with the West. Today, 60 to 70 percent is with the Soviet Union and other Eastern bloc countries. They're still adjusting to this radical change. And much of their industrial development, by Western standards, is archaic. The result is an intense search for goods marketable in the United States to earn dollars in order to buy advanced industrial equipment.

The planners in these countries have learned that it's unwise to put too many eggs in one basket, the Soviet basket. They seek independence and efficiency. This turning westward is evolution, not revolution.

———

For this and subsequent articles that described the desire of the Soviet's satellites in Europe to end their economic dependence on Moscow, Joseph Arnold Livingston won the Pulitzer Prize for international correspondence in 1965. Nor was he the only financial expert who won signal recognition because of his ability to interpret the dismal science to a mass readership. Louis M. Kohlmeier of the *Wall Street Journal* captured the Pulitzer Prize for national reporting at the same time because of his ability to report the intricate details of how President and Mrs. Lyndon B. Johnson built their family fortune. It was proof, if further proof were needed, that economic journalism at last had come of age.

## 57. THE FADING DREAM

The United Nations was close to paralysis in its twentieth year. With the Security Council tied up by Soviet vetoes on any matter of substance displeasing to the Kremlin, the General Assembly—once heralded as the "Parliament of Man"—fell into a quagmire of inaction from December 1, 1964 until February 18, 1965.

On the surface, the issue was the refusal of the Soviet Union, France, and other nations to pay for the UN's peace-keeping operations in the Congo and elsewhere. The United States threatened to invoke Article 19 of the Charter, denying these nations the right to vote because of their financial delinquency, as soon as any motion was made on the floor.

There was a great outcry by the Afro-Asian nations which by that time had come to dominate the Assembly's proceedings. On the one hand, most of them didn't want to alienate the friendship—and available funds—of the United States. On the other, they didn't want to make the Russians mad at them, either. So they did nothing except for those few necessities on which everybody could agree without a showdown vote.

Beneath the surface, what really was happening was that the United States was slowly turning away from its reliance on the Assembly. In 1950, under the Uniting for Peace resolution, the Americans had made it possible to go directly to the Assembly for action when a veto tied up the Security Council in cases involving threats to the peace. Now, it appeared hopeless to expect anything from an Assembly dominated by powers who feared to take action to support the very basis of the Charter. Only the Security Council was left; there, at least, the United States could still muster a majority against the Communists or even use the veto if it became necessary. Nobody talked about a reversal of American policy. It was, however, clearly a trend.

So, in effect, the United States, France, and the Soviet Union all pursued different policies which in the end produced but one result— impotence for the United Nations. At the near-end of the nineteenth Assembly, the pawn of the Chinese Communists, Albania, tried to force a showdown between the United States and the Soviet Union, but failed. As the faltering world organization began a rather mournful celebration of its twentieth anniversary, the correspondents who had followed its career wrote of its failures rather than its successes.

The last day of the fateful nineteenth Assembly—the fading of a dream—was reported as follows by Paul Ward, a Pulitzer Prize-winning correspondent of the Baltimore *Sun* on February 19, 1965.

## THE UN GOES HOME

### By Paul Ward

NEW YORK—The Soviet Union and the United States collaborated yesterday afternoon in action that defeated Albania, Communist China's only European ally, and put the UN General Assembly out of business until Washington and Moscow reach agreement on its future operations.

They also got forty-five Afro-Asian bloc members and all the Latin American members except Cuba to acknowledge—along with all the Soviet bloc members save Rumania—the UN's dependence on Soviet-American concord.

There was, however, a subsequent clash between United States and Soviet delegates that suggested such concord will not be reached soon or easily in respect to the United Nations.

The acknowledgment of the smaller powers' dependence was registered when the Assembly voted, 97–2, to sustain a ruling by its president, Alex Quaison-Sackey of Ghana, that sidetracked a motion by Halim Budo, Albania's Deputy Foreign Minister. The Budo motion would have brought about what many delegates referred to as a "collision" between the United States and the Soviet Union, since he sought to upset the Assembly agreement to take no votes until its adjournment.

The collision that did result entailed a conditional agreement on the United States' part not to insist, as it has since December 1, that a penalty provision in the UN Charter be enforced against delinquent members and that the Soviet Union, France, and twelve others, including Albania, be denied voting rights when the roll finally was called.

The deal also involved a compensating Soviet agreement not to rub in the fact that Washington had had to yield ground on that point, if only temporarily, as Adlai E. Stevenson, its ambassador here, stressed.

---

Thomas Jefferson Hamilton, one of the most scholarly of correspondents, saw the United Nations in action for almost a generation. As the chief of the New York *Times*'s bureau from 1946 on, he was neither jubilant over the world organization's successes nor downcast over its failures. To him, it always seemed that the greatest single triumph of the United Nations was that it managed, despite all its handicaps, to continue to exist.

Hamilton came to the United Nations with almost every academic honor it was possible for a young man to attain. He was born September 20, 1909, in August, Georgia, and graduated magna cum laude from the University of Georgia in 1928. In the process, he was elected to Phi Beta Kappa. Two years later, he became a Rhodes scholar.

With these credentials, it wasn't too difficult for him to begin newspaper work in his native state. For three years, from 1931 on, he worked at the Atlanta *Journal*, then shifted to the AP for three years in Washington and London. In 1937, he joined the New York *Times*'s London bureau, covered the last of the Spanish Civil War, and then shifted to London until the beginning of American participation in World War II. After three years in the Navy, he came to the United Nations in 1946 and served until shortly before Adlai E. Stevenson's death in 1965. This was Hamilton's view of the United Nations on January 31, 1965.

## THE FUTURE OF THE UN

### By Thomas J. Hamilton

The twentieth anniversary of the United Nations is only a short time off. It is worth recalling, therefore, the premise on which the world organization was founded—that the Great Powers who had won the war against the Axis would use the organization to enforce peace.

Despite their hard-fought arguments at the wartime conferences, Roosevelt, Stalin, and Churchill had usually managed to work out generally acceptable decisions on grand strategy. Although few expected the United Nations to produce the millennium, it was still anticipated

## A COMMENT ON THE COLD WAR

Frank Miller's 1963 Pulitzer Prize cartoon.

in 1946 that Washington, Moscow, and London would work together with equal effectiveness in the successor to the League of Nations.

From the start of its operations the organization's capacity to keep the peace was severely limited by the disunity of the Great Powers.

The Soviet veto prevented the Security Council, which was assigned the primary responsibility for keeping the peace, from taking meaningful action against the Soviet satellites. However, the Soviet Union abstained when the Security Council was confronted with the issues of the Palestine war, the Indonesian war of independence, and the near-war between India and Pakistan over Kashmir. In all these areas, the fighting came to a stop in 1949.

The following year, the Soviet Union walked out of the Security Council and all other UN bodies then meeting, and this was interpreted by the fainthearted as a sign that Stalin intended to leave the United Nations if Communist China was not admitted. The walkout, it is now clear, was intended to keep Communist China out of the United Nations. In any event, it enabled the Security Council to authorize the defense of South Korea, and the Soviet Union promptly resumed its seat.

The mood of exultation that followed the UN successes in Korea was the high point of the organization's prestige. To get around the veto in case of aggression in the future, the United States induced the Assembly to adopt the Uniting for Peace resolution, under which the Assembly claimed the right to take action if the veto prevented the Security Council from acting.

However, Communist China's intervention drove UN forces back into South Korea. The frustrations produced by the ensuing stalemate forced the United States, which was carrying most of the burden, to agree to the peace without victory of Panmunjom.

Since 1950 the Soviet Union has further hampered the work of the Security Council by using the veto to prevent action against Soviet proteges. The original aim of the Uniting for Peace resolution has been defeated by the influx of neutral and neutralist states, particularly the newly independent Asian and African states, which began in 1955. Thereafter, the use of the Assembly to recommend armed action against an aggressor became out of the question.

Beginning with the Suez crisis, the Assembly, with the encouragement of Secretary General Hammarskjold, turned to peace-keeping interventions, confining itself to disputes in which the United States and the Soviet Union were not directly involved. No matter how authorized—

some, including the Congo and Cyprus interventions were voted by the Security Council—these soon became the political *raison d'être* of the United Nations.

In the last year, the Soviet Union and France have exploited the financial crisis resulting from their unpaid assessments to speed the trend back to the Security Council. Regardless of whether the Council is able to wrest control over peace-keeping interventions from the Assembly, the Soviet Union and France have already established the principle that if a Great Power does not like a peace-keeping intervention it cannot be made to pay for it.

Thus another section of the Uniting for Peace resolution has become a dead letter, and the authority of the Assembly has been cut back to the pre-1950 level.

———

Despite the gloomy outlook, a new American ambassador to the United Nations, Arthur Goldberg, began a long struggle to revive the world organization in late 1965. His first move was to adjust the UN's financial problems.

## 58. LIPPMANN VIEWS THE WORLD

Bernard M. Baruch once reflected dourly that although he had often been called the "adviser to Presidents," his advice was never taken when he thought it would have counted. Walter Lippmann, a journalist all his days, could not make the same complaint. One of his columns in 1933 was credited with influencing President Franklin D. Roosevelt to pull the United States off the gold standard.[12] Both before and afterward, no journalist in Washington was read so carefully at the White House as a general rule and at least two Secretaries of State were put out of countenance by his cool analyses of foreign policy.[13]

This is not to say that Lippmann was always profoundly right, or that he pretended to reflect the sentiment of the nation. Quite consciously in his 1922 work, *Public Opinion*, he questioned whether mass man really counted and preferred to put his trust in a hazily defined

---

[12] Arthur M. Schlesinger, Jr., in *Walter Lippmann and His Times*, Marquis Childs and James Reston, eds. (New York, Harcourt, 1959), pp. 211–12.
[13] Marquis Childs, *ibid.*, p. 1.

elite. It was a view that changed with time. In his political choices, he was anything but representative of the majority of America in 1936 when he cast his ballot for that pearl of Republicanism, Alfred M. Landon of Kansas. He was able to live it down, along with millions of others.

The importance of Lippmann was that he was able so often to create a climate of opinion in Washington that had a profound effect on the making of policy. This was not because he was widely read. His public probably was much less than that of George Sokolsky, the standard-bearer for the Hearst Newspapers after Arthur Brisbane's death. The public that did read him was, by and large, the most influential in the land. And not the least important components of that readership were his fellow journalists, on whom his impact was always great.

While he was the editor of Pulitzer's New York *World*, he was the very antithesis of the newspaper crusader. After the end of the *World*, he spoke as follows before the Academy of Political Science:

"It is vain to suppose that our problems can be dealt with by rallying the people to some crusade that can be expressed in a symbol, a phrase, a set of principles, or a program. If that is what progressives are looking for today they will look in vain. For the objectives to which a nation like this could be aroused in something like unanimity are limited to a war or to some kind of futile or destructive fanaticism. Our objectives in time of external peace and of internal sanity are beyond the power of any man or faction or party to formulate or declare. They are too many-sided. They have to be elucidated by continual free discussion. They have to be accepted with at least a modicum of good will. They have to be proved by experiment rather than imposed by authority. They cannot be deduced from a formula and imposed by legislative fiat.

"These are the ways of liberty. They are laborious and often disappointing. But however we may momentarily forget them and seek some shorter road to righteousness, or prosperity, or justice, we are driven back to them sooner or later." [14]

Thus, the man of reason. However irritating his views may have been to some of his associates in these and other matters affecting the press, however often he seemed to be impractical or wrong, those who read him could not help but be impressed with him. He had that sparkling,

[14] Quoted by Allan Nevins, *ibid.*, pp. 70–71.

compelling, intangible quality called style that is worshiped in Washington as the prime quality of the superior man. When it came time to evaluate him for a literary tribute if not for posterity, his friends could not entirely agree on what made him great. For Harry Ashmore remarked that his accomplishments were probably all negative, while James Reston wrote: "I know that he has given my generation of newspapermen a wider vision of our duty. He has shown us how to put the event of the day in its proper relationship to the history of yesterday and the dream of tomorrow." [15]

Lippmann's greatest accomplishment was that he remained his own man, that his cool voice was a summons to reason and reflection in an age when both were in short supply. For more than a half-century he passed judgment on public affairs, surmounting the disparate forces released by two world wars, the cold war, a great depression, the coming of human flight, the explosion of two atomic bombs, and the age of rockets and space flight. His vital statistics need no elaboration at this late date—born in New York City, September 23, 1889, graduated from Harvard in 1910, writer and editor of the *New Republic*, a figure at the Versailles peace conference after World War I, and editor of the *World* thereafter. After the *World* died, his column was distributed for many years by the New York *Herald Tribune* and later by the Washington *Post*. He worked at his home in the former deanery of the Washington Cathedral and sent his columns twice a week to the Washington *Post* by Yellow cab.

Lippmann was no cloistered writer, however. His tall, grave figure and his expressive, deeply lined face were familiar in American government departments and in foreign chancelleries, at the United Nations and in many another place where the great and near-great and the curious hangers-on gathered. In 1957 he was awarded a special Pulitzer Prize citation for his consistent editorial leadership and in 1962, in his seventy-third year, he won a Pulitzer Prize for his exclusive interview with Soviet Premier Nikita S. Khrushchev. This particular form of recognition came to him late in life only because he had consistently held, as editor of the *World*, that he should not be considered for an award because he was in so dominant a position on Pulitzer's paper.

The clarity of Lippmann's style, the keenness of his vision, and the

[15] Harry Ashmore, *ibid.*, p. 166; James Reston, *ibid.*, p. 238.

precision of his thought are illustrated in the following excerpt from one of his columns in the New York *Herald Tribune*, February 2, 1965, written in his seventy-sixth year.

## THE STATE OF THE WORLD
### By Walter Lippmann

The postwar period which has lasted for twenty years has kept us all preoccupied with the unfinished business of the world war. It has not been possible to make a settlement of that war, either in Europe where Germany and the continent are partitioned, or in Eastern Asia where Korea, China, and Indo-China are partitioned and Japan is separated from the Ryukyus. This postwar period is not ending. The period we have entered upon is already plainly visible in Europe and, quite dimly, it is just beginning to appear in East Asia. This postwar period will see a general movement toward the settlement of the second World War.

The hard core of the settlement will be the inevitable return to normal after the convulsions which the world war produced. Thus, in Europe, the collapse of Hitler's Nazi empire brought the Russians to the Elbe River in the middle of Europe. The Soviet tide will have to recede. In fact, it has quite visibly already begun to recede. In East Asia, the collapse of the Japanese empire brought the United States to the Asian mainland and to some of the islands off its shores. This is an extension of our political power beyond its normal and natural limits, and like the Russians in Europe the American tide will have to recede.

It is as abnormal for the United States to be in Seoul, in Okinawa, in Quemoy and Matsu and Formosa, in Saigon and Hue, as it is abnormal for the Russians to be in Berlin, Warsaw, Prague, Budapest, Bucharest, and Sofia. The settlement of the world war, which must come some day, is certain to mean correction of the great displacements of power —of the Russian power into the heart of Europe and of American power onto the mainland of Asia.

The historical reality cannot be understood in terms of battles which are won or lost. The whole historical process is more like a geological phenomenon, like the subsiding of the earth and the return of the waters after a great upheaval. It is a callow kind of jingoism to talk of victory for us and defeat for the Soviet Union as it accommodates itself to the growing intercourse between the two halves of Europe. And it is panic-mongering to flagellate ourselves into paroxysms of anguish and shame at the prospect of negotiating settlements which end our entanglements in Asia.

The role of the United States in the world today is to use its power, its resources, its brains, and its experience to see that this inevitable adjustment in Europe and Asia comes to pass decently and honorably. The time has come to stop imagining ourselves to be the "leader" of Europe. The time has come to stop beating our heads against stone walls under the illusion that we have been appointed policeman to the human race.

Two days later, in the same newspaper, Lippmann reinforced this theme in a column that did not equate Asia so heavily with Europe in the general disengagement policy he proposed. It was a measure of the times that he no longer spoke of a Berlin crisis, although the wall was still up and the disposal of forces was still the same as it had been, but emphasized the greater danger of an Asian confrontation with Red China.

"I count it an event of high policy," he wrote, "that this extravagant concern with European affairs will not work any longer and does in fact act as a boomerang.

"Not many people in this country realize how deeply and intimately we involved ourselves in postwar European affairs. That is why so many Americans do not appreciate the extent of anti-Americanism in Europe. There is a clandestine history which will no doubt some day be written about our interventions in Europe's domestic affairs. It is enough to say now that, though our motives were high and the cause was good, once this meddling was no longer indispensable to the salvation of Europe, it became intolerable to the Europeans. . . .

"As compared with Europe, the situation in Asia is far more threatening and far less promising. Though it should be possible to postpone and then to avoid a mortal confrontation with Red China, there is a possibility of it which we must always reckon with. I do not believe we can avoid a confrontation by precipitating it. And as long as we are entangled on the mainland of Asia, a confrontation with China would take place under the most unfavorable conditions for the United States. For we should have to choose between, on the one hand, a wanton massacre of Chinese by nuclear weapons and, on the other hand, fighting a war on the Asian continent against the Chinese masses.

"In my view, our true power in the Pacific, which is unequaled and unquestioned, is diminished because we have become entrapped in a land war. Our true interest, then, is to negotiate a settlement which releases us from the trap and frees us, as the paramount power on the sea and in the air throughout the Pacific, to work toward a general settlement in Asia."

## 59. *IDEALS AND ERWIN CANHAM*

"It is easy to get into human minds with sensation, with passion, with conflict," Erwin Dain Canham once wrote. In his more than forty years as a journalist, half of them as editor of the *Christian Science Monitor*, he never took the easy way. It was his mission as a journalist to raise the standard of hope in a troubled land. Because he believed in the old-fashioned virtues and in the strength of the American ideal, he made them compelling reading. And to those who had been nourished on the thin gruel of skepticism and despair over the nation's destiny, he brought the challenge of new times and new opportunities.

Canham made the *Christian Science Monitor* the voice of American idealism. Its purpose, as defined in the words of Mary Baker Eddy in its first editorial on November 25, 1908, was "to injure no man, but to bless all mankind." Yet, as far as Canham was concerned, it was a religious newspaper only in a legal sense as the publication of the Christian Science Publishing Society in Boston. He agreed wholeheartedly with its first editor, Archibald McLellan, that it must also be a "real newspaper," to which both he and McLellan contributed immeasurably.

There was another part of the *Monitor*'s appeal that impressed Canham. He once pointed out that it went into at least 4,500 newspaper offices every publishing day. "Thus," he said, "its thinking, whenever acceptable and stimulating, is plowed into the soil of local journalism." [16] The profession returned his interest and his respect, for it elected him the president of the American Society of Newspaper Editors in 1948–49.

Canham's entire career was spent on the *Christian Science Monitor*.

[16] Erwin Canham, *Commitment to Freedom: The Story of the Christian Science Monitor* (Cambridge, Harvard University Press, 1958), pp. xvi–xvii, 423.

He was born in Auburn, Maine, on February 13, 1904, graduated from Bates in 1925 and, in addition to being elected to Phi Beta Kappa, became a Rhodes scholar. While he was at Oxford, he spent his vacation-time at Geneva helping the *Christian Science Monitor's* correspondent, Hugh Spender. From 1926 to 1928, he covered the sessions of the League at Geneva and in 1930 became the *Monitor's* Geneva man. For seven years, from 1932 to 1939, he was the chief of the *Monitor's* Washington bureau and in 1945, after brief terms as news editor and managing editor, he became the editor. In 1963, he was made editor-in-chief.

The *Monitor* was deeply concerned with the problem of morality in American life and devoted considerable space to all its aspects. Canham, in his conclusion to the series, took a long look at the situation of the United States in world affairs. The central part of his article of January 18, 1963 follows.

## MORALITY IN WORLD AFFAIRS

### By Erwin D. Canham

What is morality in international relations? Woodrow Wilson thought he knew and tried to define his terms. He was derided by many Europeans.

"You Americans," they said, "are always talking about morals in international relations. What a smug delusion! Keep morality out of it. National interest is all that matters."

Dwight D. Eisenhower thought he knew. He accepted personal responsibility of U-2 flights over Soviet territory, after his subordinates had lied about them. He, too, was scolded for telling the truth.

Machiavelli thought he knew. And his "realism" of self-interest and deception remains an all-too-pervasive pattern of international diplomacy today.

Marx, Lenin, Stalin, Khrushchev thought they knew. They, too, have preached and practiced treachery as an international way of life when they sought to serve their own zealous Communist goals.

And, it must be agreed, many self-proclaimed moralists and religionists down through the years—blinded by their own self-righteousness—have lived according to the fatal doctrine that their own frequently noble ends justified the most ignoble means. Indeed, to paraphrase, it may well be that more crimes have been committed in the name of morality than any other.

What is the challenge to international morality in our time?

The ultimate awesome challenge is that of total atomic destruction. Humankind was not created for suicide. Therefore we all must strive everlastingly for the conditions which will prevent disaster.

Some people advocate unilateral disarmament by the United States and its allies as a gesture to persuade the USSR and the Chinese Communists to lay down their arms. However appealing the doctrine in an absolute or philosophic sense, human experience does not encourage it. There is every reason to expect that the Communists would proceed to push their aggressions into the defenseless societies.

Of course, nobody should deny the dangers of the present situation nor the fact that armaments races of the past have led to wars. But today's armaments race is of a totally new character and magnitude. For the first time, total disaster is involved. So a deterrent of unprecedented power exists.

Let us strive to prove that the elements also exist for the reduction of armaments. "Overkill" is unnecessary. So surely the first rule of international morality today is to work harder than ever for the ordered and dynamic survival of free society through the curbing of the tools of destruction.

If international morality today requires a decent respect for the good of all, then much more than survival is needed.

The second great challenge (after the destructiveness of nuclear power) is the population explosion. The rise in populations derives not only from a high birth rate but a much lower death rate both in infancy and old age.

The thorny moral question of birth control is only part of the problem. In any case, it is surely a moral duty to help the world's peoples to sustain and nourish themselves. Aid alone cannot do the job. Application of better methods of economic development in agriculture and other technologies can be taught, but must be sustained largely by the needy peoples themselves.

Much remains to be done. It can be tackled not by the United States alone but with the several other nations which have achieved unprecedented prosperity. Some of them have long invested heavily in the underdeveloped world. Their aid is needed now more than ever.

Their own responsibility in the face of population pressures from Asia and Africa is quite as great as America's.

If the first moral imperative of our time is protection against destruction, and the second is protection against starvation, then surely a third, intertwined with the others, lies in the war against ignorance.

At its lowest plane, the war against ignorance begins with illiteracy. To read and write is a great thing, but it is barely the beginning of wisdom. Nothing is more sensational in our time than the vast stockpile of knowledge that has been built. We have learned in a few decades more about our relation to the physical environment than all that was discovered down the long aisles of history. Perhaps 90 percent of the trained natural scientists who have ever lived on this planet are still with us.

The assimilation and dissemination of technical information is valuble. We have fabulous new methods of communication. They can be used. But through it all there is need for much more: for the understanding without which knowledge is dross. So surely one of the great moral challenges of these times, perhaps the greatest, is to add spiritual dimension to our material achievements.

Such dimension is not lacking totally today. It is not even lacking in the field of international relations. A sense of mutuality—awareness of the importance of the good of all—keeps cropping up. It helped motivate American policy in its aid programs. It begins to move among other nations.

Such dimension is not lacking among natural scientists who recognize the limitations of materialism and cry out for parallel search and development of men's hearts and spirits. The poets sing anew and the seekers pray.

---

Thus, the interpreters sought to explain the problems of the nation and of the world to their publics. Whether they were skeptics or pragmatists or idealists, they were joined together in the common tyranny of the deadline and the journalist's obligation to write for today when he knows almost certainly that he might write somewhat differently tomorrow. Yet, they persevered.

# IX. THE PROFESSION

Many a young man drifted into the newsrooms of the nation at the turn of the century either by accident or because he could think of nothing better to do. Ring Lardner's story, at the beginning, was fairly typical. As a 20-year-old gas company employee in 1905, he had made an inconspicuous start in life reading meters at $8 a week in his native Niles, Michigan, and learning the fine art of dodging rats in the cellars he entered. As he phrased it, "When I entered a cellar and saw a rat reading the meter ahead of me, I accepted his reading and went on to the next house."

At about that time, the editor of the South Bend (Ind.) *Times* came to Niles, which was twelve miles away, looking for a cub reporter. He wanted Ring's brother, Rex, a stringer for the rival South Bend *Tribune*. But Rex was away. Ring, seeing a brilliant chance to escape from the rats, suddenly acquired a great interest in newspaper work. He offered his services, slightly stretching the truth by posing as his brother's helper for the South Bend *Tribune*.

Ring won; the rats lost. Without benefit of the Michigan vocabulary test, psychological word games, and interviews with personnel experts, he was taken on the *Times* staff at $12 a week. This wasn't bad business for that era. Since the interurban from Niles cost $2.40 a week, it left him with a net wage of $9.60 and relieved him for the time being of further association with rats.

For these prices, he covered police and courts in the morning, baseball games in the afternoon, and touring circuses and road shows at night. Such industry could not long go unrewarded. The Chicago *Inter-Ocean*, knowing a bargain when it saw one, took him on as a

sports writer at $18.50 a week.[1] The rest is history—Lardner, the base-
ball writer; Lardner, the author of *You Know Me, Al*; Lardner, the
short-story writer and musical comedy dabbler; and finally, by grace of
H. L. Mencken, Lardner, the literary gentleman.

The career of another Midwesterner, Grove Patterson, twice president of the American Society of Newspaper Editors, was different only
in degree. Patterson worked his way through Oberlin and after graduation was hired in 1905 as a reporter by the slightly absent-minded
Frederick A. Rowley, owner and publisher of the Lorain (Ohio) *Times-
Herald*. The wage was $12 a week here, too, but the crafty Patterson,
at the end of his first week, took care of that. "Mr. Rowley," he asked,
"did we agree definitely on salary?"

"Why, yes," said the publisher. "I told you $15 a week, didn't I?"

Patterson was marked for national leadership. He edited papers in
Cleveland, Detroit, and Newark, and eventually settled down as the
editor-in-chief of Paul Block's Toledo *Blade*. He left his epitaph in this
solemn understatement: "Journalism is not an ordinary business." [2]

There is further testimony on this score from Kansas City, where an
assistant city editor in 1917 told an 18-year-old newcomer from Oak
Park, Illinois, "Young man, when a man becomes a member of the staff
of the Kansas City *Star*, we give him his experience. We don't want
men from big papers and we don't want boomers who run around the
country from one paper to another. We train our men, and we train
them well." [3]

The going rate for cub reporters at that time on the *Star* was $60 a
month. The newcomer was Ernest Hemingway. He stayed for all of
seven months, then hustled off with another reporter to join the Red
Cross as an ambulance driver on the Italian front in World War I.
Despite his later success as a novelist and short-story writer, he carried
on a lifelong flirtation with newspaper work, notably in the Spanish
Civil War and World War II, but never depended on it for a living.

One other bit of evidence remains to be considered in this chain of
chronological circumstance. In 1932, over the protests of the New York

[1] Donald Elder, *Ring Lardner* (Garden City, N.Y., Doubleday, 1956), pp. 37–47
passim.
[2] Grove Patterson, *I Like People* (New York, Random House, 1948), pp. 63–65,
270.
[3] Charles A. Fenton, *The Apprenticeship of Ernest Hemingway* (New York, Farrar,
Straus, and Young, 1954), p. 30.

*Herald Tribune*'s managing editor, Grafton Wilcox, and its city editor, Stanley Walker, a new, fat, and nervous reporter joined the staff at $18 a week. He was Joseph Alsop, just out of Harvard. Picturesquely, he related long afterward that his anxious family had feared he might take to alcohol, like a certain relative, and therefore had arranged with the publishers of the *Herald Tribune* to save him from himself by making a newspaperman of him. It was curious reasoning, but it worked. The grateful beneficiary therefore maintained in later years, with pride in his own fortunate experience, that "you can still achieve a fair measure of success as a reporter without any of the long, specialized prior training that is the mark of a professional man. So that fact has got to be faced: newspaper reporting is a craft, or trade, like undertaking, which it sometimes resembles." [4]

The argument, however, is unconvincing. It is perfectly true that when the elder Alsop came from Harvard, journalism had all the earmarks of a trade, and a poorly paid one at that, with little evidence of professionalism. The fact is that under the conditions of newspaper work that were fairly prevalent well into the great depression, one didn't really have to be either an Alsop or from Harvard to be a newspaperman. Some pretty good ones started as mere alcoholics and worked their way up. It may be a measure of the advance of the professional outlook that neither the alcoholics nor the drifters are in evidence today, although the graduates of Harvard, Columbia, and other major universities have a very high visibility, to use a Madison Avenue term, on Page 1.

A more conventional argument against professional training for newspaper people comes from those who point out, with a proper amount of sarcasm, that the Lardners, Pattersons, and Hemingways—indeed, the Damon Runyons and the Meyer Bergers—became journalists without it. In a sentimental moment, Ralph McGill once expressed alarm that the swing toward professional training would tend to rob newspapers of future Lardners, Runyons, and Bergers, none of whom had much formal education of any kind. One might as well argue that had there been no journalism schools, there would never have been an Ernie Pyle (from Indiana), a James Reston (from Illinois), or a Lester Markel (from Columbia).

[4] Joseph and Stewart Alsop, *The Reporter's Trade* (New York, Reynal, 1958), pp. 3–4.

Yet, despite the misgivings of those who bewail, bemoan, or belabor professional preparation for journalism, the hard and not utterly unpleasant truth is that it has been accepted during their lifetime. It exists. It is supported by substantial forces inside and outside newspaper work. It cannot be disregarded merely by pretending that it does not have substance, or—with more reason—insisting that it could be done better. Through the beliefs of those principally concerned, the journalists themselves, what was once a trade or craft is now broadly recognized as a profession. An unregulated profession, by grace of the First Amendment to the Constitution of the United States; an undisciplined profession, even an imperfect profession, but still a recognizable body of knowledge and practice that may be professionally identifiable.

Necessarily, journalism therefore shares all the advantages and drawbacks of the professional estate—the terrifying number of meetings of professional groups, the long reports, the commissions, and, praise be, the magnificent youngsters who believe totally and without apologies that journalism should be, and sometimes now is, a public responsibility. Nor can the issue be confused by calling journalism a business, which it also is, in the same sense as is the work of a physician, a lawyer, or a clergyman. The first law of independence in a democratic society is solvency, and if the books of a profession strike a balance in black ink rather than red, it is neither a crime nor a sin.

The professional movement in journalism has taken more than a century to achieve the necessary strength and maturity. Its groping beginnings were in the middle of the nineteenth century when some seventeen state editorial associations were founded between 1853 and 1880 for the benefit of small dailies and weeklies. Out of this grew the National Editorial Association in 1885, the voice of the small newspaper. In the same year the Washington correspondents came together and decided it was high time for a professional association of their own, the Gridiron Club. Two years later, as a force entirely apart, the American Newspaper Publishers Association was founded, but its first concern was with business and advertising, a historic concern of the publisher rather than the editor.[5]

Schools of journalism came more than two decades afterward—the

[5] Edwin Emery and Henry Ladd Smity, *The Press in America* (New York, Prentice-Hall, 1954), pp. 394–97 passim.

University of Missouri's in 1909, Columbia University's in 1912, and those of other major institutions thereafter. It is a comforting thought that their modern critics are considerably milder than were the New York editors who, in 1912, assigned reporters to follow journalism students from Joseph Pulitzer's School and write gay stories about their appalling ignorance. Why, didn't everybody know that the journalist was born, not made? That he was the very devil of a fellow who could know everything without being taught anything?

Despite that, the resolute students banded together in honor societies—Sigma Delta Chi, Theta Sigma Phi, and others, the forerunners of today's professional groups. In 1917, when the first award of the Pulitzer Prizes was made to stimulate a more professional outlook in journalism, the American Association of Schools and Departments of Journalism was established. Even more important, five years later, was the founding of the American Society of Newspaper Editors. Here, at last, the working press, so-called, joined the movement, for the editors established as their major purpose "the consideration of common problems and the promotion of professional ideals." [6] Thy learned very early that one way to oblivion was the promulgation of codes of conduct that, by the very nature of the journalist, were impossible to enforce. The ASNE code, for all that, is a high-minded statement of principles.

The editors were on more practical operative ground when they began holding seminars to dissect their own work. Moreover, between this group and the journalism schools, there was significant liaison almost from the first, although it wasn't accompanied immediately by a great deal of understanding on either side. Nevertheless, the result was an accreditation process which grew into the Association of Accredited Schools and Departments of Journalism, with forty members, and after World War II, the Association for Education in Journalism. By that time, Columbia had long since abandoned undergraduate instruction in journalism and in 1935 had established the first all-graduate journalism school.[7]

There was a brief time early in 1933 when the newly born American Newspaper Guild teetered between the notion of pure professionalism

[6] *Ibid.*, pp. 732–37 passim.
[7] Richard Terrill Baker, A *History of the Graduate School of Journalism, Columbia University* (New York, Columbia University Press, 1954), pp. 103–12.

and broad unionism. Heywood Broun, the large and unkempt columnist for the New York *World-Telegram*, rather quickly announced the basic decision in New York during his organizational efforts there as the Guild's first president. A few are still around who remember the soft-spoken Heywood, a Northerner who affected a Southern drawl, brushing aside the suggestion that the Guild should be a kind of super Sigma Delta Chi. To one organization meeting, which had developed into a bibulous contest undreamed of by the saintly Samuel Gompers, Broun proclaimed with glass aloft, "Let us not deceive ourselves. We are no mere professional group. We are a labor union, and by God I like it!" [8] For all the Guild's comparative neglect of the advancement of professional standards, it measurably strengthened the underpinning of professional journalism by helping increase minimum wages in the field.

Professionalism, in any case, was now well on the way. In 1946, another major stride was taken with the establishment of the American Press Institute at Columbia. Sevellon Brown, editor and publisher of the Providence (R.I.) *Journal-Bulletin*, was able to persuade thirty-eight fellow publishers to invest $150,000 in the API at the outset, but it was the first director, Floyd Taylor who put it over with the help of his associates, J. Montgomery Curtis and Walter Everett.

When Floyd Taylor died in 1951, the API was so well established that Curtis was able to step in as director, with Walter Everett as his associate, and expand the work. Its charter read:

"The purpose of the American Press Institute is to contribute to the improvement of American newspapers by giving opportunity to experienced newspapermen and women of all categories to study and discuss at Columbia University the techniques of their work and the social, economic, and political problems of the day." [9]

After nearly two decades, the API was able to count more than 600 sponsoring newspapers in early 1965 and an attendance of more than 4,000 newspapermen and women at API seminars at a cost of nearly $2,500,000. [10]

There were other successful movements in the long struggle toward professionalism in journalism. One of the most effective in the academic

---

[8] The author was an interested observer.

[9] Baker, *Graduate School of Journalism*, pp. 118–22.

[10] J. Montgomery Curtis, "What Is the Truth About Newspapers?" speech before the National Retail Merchants Promotion Association, May 11, 1964.

field was the work of the Nieman Foundation at Harvard, created under the terms of an endowment in the name of Lucius W. Nieman, founder of the Milwaukee *Journal*. Since 1937, up to a dozen fellowships each year have been granted to working newspapermen for a year of graduate study. [11] Similar fellowships were set up later at Columbia University under the leadership of Dean Edward W. Barrett of the Graduate School of Journalism, one in advanced science writing endowed by the Sloan-Rockefeller Foundation, and another in advanced international reporting, endowed by the Ford Foundation.[12] The Council on Foreign Relations also granted an annual fellowship of its own for a highly qualified foreign correspondent to enable him to pursue graduate study at an institution of his choice.[13]

The educational movement was pursued at the pre-college level, too. In 1958, out of a basic concern that the best talent was not being attracted to newspaper work, the *Wall Street Journal* set up the Newspaper Fund, Inc. Acting on the theory that some fundamental professional appeal should be made to students in the high schools, where so much career counseling had been adverse to journalism, the Newspaper Fund created a new system of scholarships.

There were summer scholarships for high-school teachers who were registered in summer teaching courses in journalism at a number of major colleges and universities. In the first six years, 2,375 teachers received such training at a cost of more than $1,000,000. The Fund also placed 430 promising college students in summer newspaper jobs, with $500 internships each, at a cost of $215,000 in the first six years.[14]

As in the case of the API, the work was under the supervision of an experienced professional, Paul S. Swensson, former managing editor of the Minneapolis *Tribune* and since then the executive director of the Newspaper Fund. He argued that the appeal of journalism had to be broadened, both in its principles and in its potential rewards. There were, he said, more than 3,000 vacancies each year in daily newspaper work alone, attributable to death, retirement and changes of occupation, and that there weren't enough graduates of journalism schools an-

[11] Emery and Smith, *Press in America*, pp. 739–40.
[12] Columbia Graduate School of Journalism, 50th Anniversary Report of the Dean, p. 8.
[13] Council on Foreign Relations, annual report for year ending June 30, 1964, p. 67.
[14] Curtis, speech before NRMPA.

nually to fill the vacancies. The proponents of professional training for journalism, therefore, still had a long way to go.

Certainly, with the additional needs of the newspapers and wire services, the news magazines and the developing news staffs of a number of radio and television stations, the opportunities in journalism were brighter than they had been a half-century before.[15]

There was no doubt that the journalist had improved his stature in the United States in fifty years—professionally, economically, socially. The changing role of the journalist is reflected in the pages that follow.

## 60. STEINBECK OF THE AMERICAN

John Steinbeck came to New York for the first time in 1925 when he was 23 years old. He arrived by ship from San Francisco with $100 in his pocket and got a job next day wheeling cement for the construction of the Eighth Avenue Madison Square Garden. Although he was big, tough, and strong, it nearly killed him, as he later admitted. When an uncle wangled him a job on the New York *American*, therefore, he was profoundly grateful—at first.

The *American* in the 1920s was William Randolph Hearst's most dignified and least successful newspaper. All it had was the prestige in the Hearst chain that came with the benign favor of "the Chief," as Hearst was called in the telegrams that descended on his editors in an unending stream. It could not compete with the rowdy new tabloids for shock, sexy pictures, and ten-minute sensations. Nor, for that matter, could it match the appeal of the New York *Times, Herald Tribune*, and *World* for the more solid citizenry (although even the *World* was faltering late in the decade).

The *American*, therefore, was supported by its lustier and less inhibited big brother, the New York *Evening Journal*, and went through periodic economy waves. The editors, wise in the ways of Hearstian economics, were able to keep their basically veteran staff without too much trouble by padding it with green youngsters who could be fired in droves whenever a staff reduction was ordered. In all probability, it was on the up-

---

[15] Paul S. Swenson, "Wanted: 30,000 More Journalists by 1970," *The Quill*, November, 1964, pp. 18–24.

swing of one such cycle that Steinbeck came to the newspaper as a reporter.

The newcomer from California already was dreaming of becoming a novelist. He could write. He had had more than a nodding acquaintance with higher education at Stanford, although he hadn't stayed long enough to graduate. Had he been turned loose for more than a brief time to roam around New York and write what he saw, like Mark Hellinger of the *Daily News* or Nunnally Johnson of the *Evening Post*, he might have been a sensation. But he was thrust into a dark, smelly cubbyhole at Federal Court with the district men, who telephoned their stuff to rewrite men and seldom even attempted to write a story. Most of them hadn't written a line for the paper for years.

Steinbeck's end as a journalist on the *American*, therefore, was almost foreordained. However, he didn't seem to care too much. What he saw of the lives of reporters in that period could scarcely have attracted him to journalism as a life's work.

New York was on a prohibition era binge then. Even for reporters who were bored with newspaper work, there was a certain amount of glamor in the speakeasy civilization of the day. Living was cheap and New York had its attractions. For a few months, as a youngster, Steinbeck experienced a bit of it and noted it down in a reminiscent mood years later. The following is a part of a piece he did about his New York experiences for the *New York Times Magazine*, February 1, 1953.

### "THIS GOLDEN ROMANCE"

#### By John Steinbeck

About that time (toward the end of 1925), my rich and successful uncle came to town from Chicago. He was an advertising man with connections everywhere. He was fabulous. He stayed in a suite at the Commodore, ordered drinks or coffee and sandwiches sent up any time he wanted, sent telegrams even if they weren't important. The last still strikes me as Lucullan.

My uncle got me a job on a newspaper—the New York *American* down on William Street. I didn't know the first thing about being a reporter. I think now that the $25 a week that they paid me was a total loss. They gave me stories to cover in Queens and Brooklyn and I would get lost and spend hours trying to find my way back. I couldn't learn to steal a picture from a desk when a family refused to be photographed and I invariably got emotionally involved and tried to kill the whole story to save the subject.

But for my uncle, I think they would have fired me the first week. Instead, they gave me federal courts in the old Park Row Post Office. Why, I will never know. It was a specialist's job. Some of the men there had been on that beat for many years and I know nothing about courts and didn't learn easily.

I wonder if I could ever be as kind to a young punk as those men in the reporters' room at the Park Row Post Office were to me. They pretended that I knew what I was doing, and they did their best to teach me in a roundabout way.

I learned to play bridge and where to look for suits and scandals. They informed me which judges were pushovers for publicity and several times they covered for me when I didn't show up. You can't repay that kind of thing. I never got to know them. Didn't know where they lived, what they did, or how they lived when they left the room.

I had a reason for that, and it was a girl again. I had known her slightly in California and she was most beautiful. I don't think this was only my memory. For she got a job in the Greenwich Village Follies just walking around—and she got it with no trouble whatever. It was lucky because that's about all she could do. She got a hundred dollars a week. I fell hopelessly in love with her.

Now New York changed for me. My girl lived on Gramercy Park and naturally I moved there. My old hotel had some tiny rooms—six walk-up flights above the street. I had nothing to do with New York. It was a stage set in which this golden romance was taking place. The girl was very kind. Since she made four times as much money as I did, she paid for many little dinners. Every night I waited for her outside the stage door.

I can't imagine why she went to the trouble of trying to reform me. We would sit in Italian restaurants—she paid—and drink red wine. I wanted to write fiction—novels. She approved of that in theory, but said I should go into advertising—first, that is. I refused. I was being the poor artist, shielding his integrity. I wonder now what would have happened if anyone had offered me a job in advertising. I was spared that choice.

During all this time, I never once knew or saw one New Yorker as a person. They were all minor characters in this intense personal drama. Then everything hapened at once. And I am glad it happened in the sequence it did. The girl had more sense than I thought.

She married a banker from the Middle West and moved there. And she didn't argue. She simply left a note, and two days later I was fired from the *American*.

And now at last the city moved in on me and scared me to death. I looked for jobs—but good jobs, pleasant jobs. I didn't get them. I wrote short stories and tried to sell them. I applied for work on other papers, which was ridiculous on the face of it. And the city crept in, cold and heartless, I thought. I began to fall behind in my room rent. I always had that one ace in the hole. I could go back to laboring. I had a friend who occasionally loaned me a little money. And finally, I was shocked enough to go for a job as a laborer. But by that time short feeding had taken hold. I could hardly lift a pick. I had trouble climbing the six flights back to my room. My friend loaned me a dollar and I bought two loaves of rye bread and a bag of dried herrings and never left my room for a week. I was afraid to go out on the street—actually afraid of traffic—the noise. Afraid of the landlord and afraid of people. Afraid even of acquaintances.

Then a man who had been in college with me got me a job as a workaway on a ship to San Francisco. And he didn't have to urge me, either. The city had beaten the pants off me. Whatever it required to get ahead, I didn't have. I didn't leave the city in disgust—I left it with the respect plain unadulterated fear gives. And I went back to my little town, worked in the woods, wrote novels and stories and plays, and it was eleven years before I came back.

--------

The man who came back from California was a far different Steinbeck—the author of *Tortilla Flat*, *In Dubious Battle*, and *Of Mice and Men*. In 1940, he won the Pulitzer Prize for his classic, *The Grapes of Wrath*, and at the apex of his career in 1962 he was awarded the Nobel Prize for literature. But he hadn't been good enough for the New York *American*.

## 61. ROMULO LOOKS BACK

On a day of splendor and bright sunshine in Manila in 1963, Carlos Pena Romulo wandered happily through the well-appointed offices of his old newspaper, the *Philippines Herald*. To the Filipinos who crowded about him, he murmured a Tagalog proverb: "He who does not look back to where he has come from will never reach his goal." [16]

That October 28 was a good day to look back. At 62, the redoubtable Romulo was beginning a new career as president of the University of the Philippines. Outside the *Herald*, there was a memorial to one of his most celebrated feats as a journalist—a bronze plaque that had just been dedicated as a reminder of the Pulitzer Prize that had been awarded to him in 1942. Across the wide blue waters of Manila Bay, the first efforts were being made to restore the grandeur of Corregidor, where Romulo had served on General Douglas MacArthur's staff, as a monument to Filipino-American friendship.

Romulo had traveled far since 1923 when he had first become editor of the *Herald*. That was soon after his graduation from the University of the Philippines and the completion of his advanced studies at Columbia University. It was as the editor and publisher of the *Herald* and its associated papers that he had taken his memorable swing through Asia in 1941 on the eve of World War II. In his twenty-eight articles, written during the trip, he had predicted the outbreak of Japanese aggression, its subsequent overthrow, the rising of Asian peoples, and the end of colonialism in the Pacific. It was for this that he had won the Pulitzer Prize.

The war was almost a separate chapter in his life. He had been through it all—from Corregidor south to Australia, and back across the Pacific islands with the American forces to the Philippines, and finally to Japan itself. As mementos he had the Purple Heart, the Silver Star with oak leaf cluster and, from the Congress of the Philippines, he was to receive soon the Congressional Medal of Honor.

As a true child of the twentieth century, he had moved from war to the threshold of world organization as a spokesman for the smaller nations at the founding of the United Nations at San Francisco in

[16] *Philippines Herald*, Oct. 29, 1963.

1945. Thereafter, he had been the president of the fifth United Nations General Assembly, the Philippine ambassador to the United Nations, the foreign minister of the Philippines, and the Philippine ambassador to the United States.

Now, he was back where it had all begun; not, to be sure, in the modern *Herald* building with its polished desks and clean and well-ventilated quarters, but in a musty hole that was scarcely any better or worse than many an American newspaper "office" of the day. Romulo's recollection of the less-than-affluent times of the journalist was published September 8, 1963 in *Galley Proof*, a *Herald* staff magazine; even though he wrote as a Filipino, his description coincided with the experience of Americans who had worked in the 1920s on a variety of newspapers in their own land.

## THE OLD, OLD HERALD

### *By Carlos P. Romulo*

You honored me greatly with the title of "Editor Emeritus," and I am especially glad that the word did not become *emerita* in the composing room; otherwise, that would have tagged me once and for all, in fidelity to the dictionary meaning, a crustacean.

You want to pump out of this aging hull the bubbling bilge of reminiscence; instead, allow me to revive the past with a seething sense of envy. Your working conditions now are beyond compare. We used to have a firetrap. Only during my more charitable moments did I think it was an Eiffel Tower, since indeed my cubicle was in one such elevation, soon to be demolished by Japanese bombs.

I remember the peril to life and limb that always awaited us at the old *Herald* building. If I survived the daily constitutional up the stairs to my office, a worse fate awaited me whenever I ventured into the composing room. For there it was literally hell on earth, the place having become a tremendous improvement over an oven.

Lope K. Santos then was the editor. In my mind's eye now I see the intense, if perhaps truculent, figure of this Tagalista, soon to leave his people with a monumental grammar of the national language, stirring his cup of coffee.

To Mauro Mendez, the sound of a spoon scraping against the sides of a coffee cup was an imperious signal. It told him in so many words to begin writing his editorial for the day. The office Mendez worked in, by the way, had the comforts, to say nothing of the size, of a genuine dovecote—which ought to explain the tenor of some of the best editorials of those days.

You will see from these notes that my envy is not unjustified. You have become so peripatetic and could go at a moment's notice as readily to Sandakan as to Stockholm. In our day, only Escolta [a section of Manila] was within reach and to get to Cebu one needed strings and prayers.

What sort of money you now earn, I do not have a very good idea. But I recall how the pay scale used to be in our day. There was someone on the roster who knew what the situation was and took advantage of it by lending money to his colleagues, a favor and an accommodation which operated quite out of the reach of the usury law. Hence, even if this infamy has now been proscribed, my memory on this score is dulled by a natural reluctance to name names.

But this I distinctly remember also: We had a staff that was alert; we had columnists who did not only steer away from gossip but plunged deep into social and political philosophy. To read S. P. Lopez then was to know for certain that sooner or later he would become Secretary of Foreign Affairs.

And this especially appears to be the crowning feature of all: No one of our roster had a twin whose name could be found on somebody else's payroll. Somehow, we were uniquely constituted in those days; one did not seem to require a double and, certainly, masks were hard to come by.

The foregoing makes up a rather dispersed and random narrative, but I think it will do. I am always glad to see proof that the old galley is still afloat. Three cheers for the men at the oars!

## 62. A FRIEND OF RED SMITH'S

Heywood Broun once observed that there were two schools of sports writing—the "Ah, Wonderful!" school, of which he considered himself a leading exponent, and the rival collegium, headed by Westbrook Pegler, whose motto was, "Ah, Nuts!" There was some truth to this pleasantry until 1945, when a third school, which may be known simply as "Aha!" was founded on the New York *Herald Tribune*. It consisted of one member, Red Smith, and it has retained its exclusivity to this day.

There were two reasons for Red Smith's reputation. The most important of these was his respect and affection for the English language, which he used with precision, grace, skill, and perennial good humor. The other reason was even more obvious to those who read him regularly: he belonged to the sports page and, except for occasional forays in the jungles of general news, liked to remain there. No doubt he could have moved out any time, as did such one-time sports writers as Ring Lardner and Ralph McGill, James Reston and Heywood Broun, Bob Considine and Damon Runyon, but he chose to remain in his spiked and sweaty Camelot.

Few medallions exist for sports writers and there are no summit conferences to cover along the way to the daily deadline, so there are no remarkable feats to chronicle in the life of Walter Wellesley Smith except that he has existed as a sports writer for almost forty years. He was born in Green Bay, Wisconsin, in 1905, and began writing about the muscular champions, their athletic ladies, and the inevitable clowns almost immediately after his graduation from Notre Dame in 1927. He worked on only four newspapers—the Milwaukee *Sentinel* from 1927 to 1928, the St. Louis *Star* from 1928 to 1936, the Philadelphia *Record* from 1936 to 1945, and the New York *Herald Tribune* since then.

It was typical of him that he usually wrote from the point of view of a disembodied spirit in the sports arena. He was seldom present, in person, in his columns or his accounts of victories, defeats, or the manifold reasons therefor. Rather, he was the spectator who wandered by, asking a casual question; the unidentified visitor, lurking on the fringes of the crowd; the nameless person who made an observation to the chief actor of a particular account; sometimes, even, an aggrieved member of the faternity of sports writers who was not otherwise introduced to the reader.

To get at Red Smith himself, therefore, represented a difficult chore, for some men reveal themselves only to their friends. And it was in a piece about one of his friends, Grantland Rice, that this most retiring of sports writers chose to make one of his infrequent public appearances. The selection, in slightly abbreviated form, is given here but it requires a word of explanation.

Fame on the sports pages is a fleeting thing, which means that most sports writers, however famous, are soon forgotten after they retire or die. The remarkable part of Grantland Rice was that he retained his fame to some extent long after his death in 1954. His friends were determined that they would inter only his mortal remains; therefore, they raised funds, created scholarships and fellowships, arranged for seminars and lectureships, and held annual luncheons or dinners, all in the name of Grantland Rice. It was as a part of this devoted movement to keep the memory of Grantland Rice alive that Red Smith wrote of him. The following excerpt is from *Editor & Publisher*, February 7, 1959, a report of the Third Grantland Rice Lecture at the Columbia Graduate School of Journalism.

## THE BEST OF GRANTLAND RICE

### By Red Smith

Grantland Rice's favorite literary hero was the one James Thomas Field celebrated in the line: " 'We are lost!' the captain shouted as he staggered down the stairs," because for Granny it conjured up a vision of a gallant old sea dog, tanked to the ears, and running for cover.

The heroine he loved best was that mettlesome dame, sweet Alice, Ben Bolt, "who wept with delight when you gave her a smile, and trembled with fear at your frown."

And he found one of the loveliest of descriptive lines in a popular song: "Through the sycamores the candle lights are gleaming."

If you can reconcile these ideas you'll begin to have some understanding of what Granny Rice was like. He loved beauty but knew poetry was where you found it. There was laughter in him and a warm sense of the ridiculous. He could jeer gently as well as cheer.

The greatest privilege I have had in my life, and I'm deeply and humbly grateful for it, was the privilege of going around and about with Granny for a few years, as a friend.

We went everywhere together, and it's odd how often, when we think of him now, we remember him at the race track. I think that's because he loved the race track so, and had so much fun there. He was a horse player, not a horse lover. "My interest in the thoroughbred horse," he said, "is four inches of nose at the wire."

So many times we think of him at Sunshine Park, which is a little

Shoeless Joe of a track outside Tampa in Florida. There was one dismal winter in California, with snow and smog and rain and cold—what they call unusual weather out there. A young newspaperman came to interview Granny. "Mr. Rice," he said, "what is your favorite race track? Santa Anita? Hollywood Park?" "Sunshine Park," Granny said, and that shook the young man because he'd never heard of it. Granny identified it for him and the kid tried again. "Mr. Rice," he said, "what is your favorite city? For climate, I mean." "Quebec," Granny said. "When you go there for snow, you get it." End of interview.

Touts would descend on Granny like flies. They'd pluck his program out of his hands and mark it. One day, incidentally, Granny stopped to buy one of those selection cards and when he'd paid his fifty cents the man said, "Want a couple of live ones?" "Aren't they on here?" Granny asked. "No," the man said, and Granny wanted to slug him.

Anyhow, he loved the place. He could stand in the clubhouse just outside the restaurant. Here was the bar at his elbow. The mutuel windows were four steps away. Without moving from there, he could see the horses run. There were chairs, but Granny hated to sit down at a race track. He'd walk us limp all afternoon, then hustle us through dinner in time to catch the first race at the dog track.

Have I mentioned how Granny enjoyed playing the daily double? Frank Graham means to be buried in the infield at Saratoga, and I must say that Mrs. Anne Claire, the track superintendent, has been almost too cooperative about it. Whenever they meet she says, "Anytime you're ready, Frank." Granny and Frank were together in Saratoga and Frank said, "See that big tree out there? I'm going to be buried under it." Granny said, "What for? Why'd you pick that place?"

"It's lovely," Frank said. "I can lie there and hear the horses pounding through the morning workouts and if I behave myself maybe I'll be allowed to sit up about post time for the first race and see what's going on."

"Post time for the first race?" Granny said, and he was truly horrified. "You'll miss the daily double!"

One spring they named the double for Granny at Sunshine Park, calling the first race The Grantland and the second The Rice. He had the winner of the first coupled twice with an outsider in the second. The two tickets would have been worth $1,200 but his outsider lost the second by a nose. Now he had to present a trophy to the jockey who had just beaten him out of $1,200.

"Mr. Rice," the kid told him, "my horse was trying to quit all the way down the stretch. I just barely held him together to the wire." Picture Granny with a $1,200 knife in his heart, presenting the trophy and smiling through his tears for the camera. "Why didn't you let the son of a bitch quit?" he said, smiling.

Please, when I tell these stories, don't let me give the impression that Grantland Rice was some sort of horse-degenerate or slob. This was the greatest talent we have known, and the greatest gentleman. He was a man who walked with the famous, and because he was so kind he accepted them as his equals.

When we went down to Philadelphia to see Rocky Marciano win the heavyweight championship from Jersey Joe Walcott, Granny joined us tardily. On the day of the fight, or maybe the day before, he showed up from Washington where he'd been attending a Celebrities' golf tournament. He had a big white patch over one eye; leaving Jimmy Demaret's hotel room, he had slipped on a rug and cracked his head, opening a cut that required four stitches.

Before going to the fight we visited a friend of Granny's who lived in the hotel and had a few martinis. The fight was a brute that went thirteen rounds. When Marciano won, 2,000 wild men from Brockton, Massachusetts, swarmed through the press rows down to the ring to salute him, because they had bet their lives on the guy. They walked on our typewriters and trampled our ears. I saw Granny across the ring, whacking at the typewriter with people walking right over him. He was the first one finished and away.

There was an Army-Notre Dame football game in New York when his working ticket went astray. Know what he did? This is the man who did more for football than Walter Camp, Pudge Heffelfinger, or the whole Rules Committee. He went down Broadway, bought a ticket from a scalper, sat in the stands with his typewriter on his knees, and apologetically begged room in the pressbox afterwards to write his story. "Why didn't you throw some weight around?" I asked him. "Tell you the truth," he said, "I don't weigh much."

There was a day Frank Graham tells about when they were freezing in the press box in the Yale Bowl. "Would you like a drink?" Granny said between halves. Frank was ready to sell his soul for one. "Come with me," Granny said.

He went prowling down the press box until he saw a young writer with a big jug. "Hello, there!" Granny said. The kid looked up. "Oh, Mr. Rice! Uh, have a drink?"

"Why," Granny said, "don't mind if I do." He knocked one off. "Mind if my friend has one?" Frank polished one off. "Thanks a lot," Granny said. "Great to see you again."

"You're a fiend," Frank told him as they went back to their seats. "Impersonating Grantland Rice."


## 63. *RESTON MAKES A WISH*

The strikes that closed down all newspapers of general circulation in various metropolitan areas were among the least welcome developments of modern times. Such events occurred in New York, Detroit, Cleveland, Minneapolis, and San Jose, Calif. There was scarcely any guarantee that the sickness was curable without the death of at least some of the patients. One of the big ones, the New York *Mirror,* with a circulation of nearly a million, had to give up not long after the 114-day New York strike of 1962–63. It created more excitement by its passing than it ever did while it was alive, which in a way was symbolic. Nobody in journalism wanted to see any newspaper die; yet, nobody seemed able to stop the wave of strikes.

The American Newspaper Guild had more than its share of strikes from the 1930s onward in an effort to force substantial increases in the wages of journalists and improvements in their working conditions. But the Guild was not at the root of the mass movement of the 1960s; in some instances, it became the captive of the mechanical unions which were forcing the issue. Whether or not the fear of automation and a long overdue revolution in newspaper making was actually argued in the negotiations, there was little doubt that it was a principal motivating factor in many cases. The mechanical unions were fighting for their lives, but they didn't seem to be going about it with much tactical skill. Rather, they more often presented the spectacle of people rushing toward mass economic suicide.

Nor did the publishers arouse much enthusiasm for their cause. A. H.

Raskin, in a much-admired account of the New York strike of 1962–63 in the New York *Times*, wrote: "What of the future? In the closing days of the tie-up, the Mayor (Robert F. Wagner) told the publishers that they would have to get over the attitude that everything could be handed down in lordly fashion from on high. He advised them to make labor relations a front-office job, 365 days a year, and not leave it to functionaries at contract time." [17]

After the Detroit strike of 1964, Barbara Stanton of the Detroit *Free Press* reached this equally unhappy conclusion: "It took 134 days to settle the Detroit strike. And neither labor nor management, at any newspaper in the country, has figured out how to solve—or avoid—the next one." [18]

The literature of the strike was uniformly dolorous, with but one exception. That was a pre-Christmas piece written by James Reston while he was still chief of the Washington Bureau of the New York *Times*, published in the Western Edition of that newspaper December 24, 1962, and reprinted in the *National Observer*, December 31. The Western Edition kept on going during the strike, but was suspended thereafter because of its losses. Probably, it was an indirect casualty; had the *Times* maintained its modest profit ratio, the chances might have been better to keep a losing operation in business for awhile longer.

This was what Reston wrote.

## A LETTER TO SANTA CLAUS

### By James Reston

Dear Santa:

All I want for Christmas is the New York *Times*. I don't ask for any of these new fur bed sheets, or electric socks, or automatic spaghetti winders, but a man is entitled to have old friends around at a time like this.

Somebody struck the *Times* in the belief that it's a newspaper, but that is obviously ridiculous. The *Times* is a public institution, like the Yankees or Barney Baruch. When everything else is changing, the *Times* remains the same—typographical errors and all.

Reading the *Times* is a life career, like raising a family, and almost as

[17] A. H. Raskin, New York *Times*, April 1, 1963.
[18] Barbara Stanton, *Columbia Journalism Review*, Winter, 1965, pp. 4–8.

difficult. But I've become accustomed to its peculiar ways and can't break the habit. It is a community service, like plumbing. It will light more fires and line more shelves and cover up more rugs on a snowy day than any other publication in the world, and I need it, Mister, especially at Christmas.

This is the season of peace and somehow—I don't know why—peace seems to have a better chance in the *Times*. Everybody else seems to be shouting at us and giving the human race six weeks to get out. But the *Times* is always saying that there was trouble in the sixteenth century, too.

It never seems to think anything is quite as good or as bad as others make it out to be. It is always saying: "On the one hand," and, "On the other hand," and in the confusion it manages to give the impression that if things are *that* complicated nobody will quite know how to start a war.

One of the great things about a newspaper, especially on Sunday, is that you can split the thing up and let everybody in the family settle into a quiet trance with the section he likes best. This cuts down on the noise. You can throw away what you don't want, and the ads don't sing.

The television makes us all feel a little obsolescent once in a while, but it stuns the mind. It makes you want to listen to all the news you don't want to hear in order to get around to the news you do want to hear. You can't split up Chet Huntley or throw away a part of David Brinkley—not at least without a fight.

This is one of the great advantages of the *Times*: you get so much more to throw away. It is impenetrable but indispensable. Other papers cover the news and the *Times* smothers it, but the reader benefits. People are always dying in the *Times* who don't seem to die in other papers, and they die at greater length and maybe even with a little more grace.

If a good professor is promoted to the head of the English Department at Tufts, or even has the bad luck to be stuck with the presidency of Rutgers, the event is duly recorded—complete with ten-year-old one-column photograph—and is read with pride or sympathy on every campus in the land.

All this, Dear Santa, makes it hard, I know, to get the *Times* down a chimney, but striking the *Times* is like striking an old lady and deprives the community at Christmas of all kinds of essential information.

If some recklessly beautiful girl gets married at the Waldorf this week, the television may let us see her gliding radiantly from the church and tossing her bouquet to some lucky member of the Hasty Pudding Club, but what about all those ugly girls who get married every Sunday in the *Times?* Are they to be ignored just at their unlikely moment of triumph? The pretty girls may marry again, temptation and pretty girls being what they are, but the ugly girl hits the center aisle but once, and the event must be recorded then in the annals of human hope.

Without newspapers the procedures of life change. Tired men, sick of the human race after a long gabby day at the office, cannot escape on the train into the life story of Y. A. Tittle or the political perils of Harold Macmillan, but must go on talking to strangers all the way to Westport. Once home, they are bereft of excuses to avoid fixing that dripping tap or shoveling the walk.

Even history and geography seem different. Yemen was in deep trouble in the *Times* when the strike started, and things weren't very jolly in Afghanistan or Kashmir, but we never discovered how the thing came out.

So please do what you can to get the papers back. It's bad enough on the public, but think of a reporter. I've been fielding the *Times* on the first bounce on my front stoop every morning for twenty-five years, and it's cold and lonely out there now. Besides, how do I know what to think if I can't read what I write?

P.S.—Don't forget the *Herald Tribune*, too.

---

There was no Santa Claus in the New York newspaper strike. It wasn't until April 1, 1963, that publication resumed. If there was a lesson in the wholesale tieup, it was that everybody lost.

The publishers of the nine affected newspapers lost the advertising in the 700,000,000 copies of the papers they did not print. The nearly 18,000 union members directly affected by the closing of the newspapers lost a substantial part of their salaries; despite strike benefits that were paid, these came from union defense funds made up entirely of membership contributions.

The business world in New York City, from department stores to theaters, was severely affected by a slowdown in purchasing due to lack of advertising stimulus. The public, despite the efforts of radio, television, and a peculiar mosquito press that sprang up overnight, suffered a crippling news blackout that slowed down the governmental process in the city.

To quote the Raskin summation in the *Times*: " 'This is a history of failure—the failure of men and machinery, of politics and personalities, of miscalculated maneuvers and misjudged aspirations.' That epitaph for the city's longest and costliest newspaper strike comes from a ranking official of the Publishers Association of New York City. A top unionist makes a virtually identical evaluation, then adds almost prayerfully, 'This should be the strike to end all newspaper strikes.' "

It wasn't. As a result of the newspaper strike in New York in 1965, it was inevitable that the greatest city in the nation would have only four or five daily newspapers at most.

## 64. REQUIEM FOR A POET

Much of Mary McGrory's work in the Washington *Evening Star* is read with appreciation by her fellow journalists. It is a somewhat rare form of recognition in a profession that is not always as generous as it might be with its garlands. Born August 22, 1918, Miss McGory did not begin her career as a journalist after graduating from Emmanuel College in her native Boston; she became, instead, a secretary to a book publisher, the Houghton Mifflin Company. It wasn't until 1942 that she progressed to the Boston *Herald* where she was an editorial assistant, just a step up from the bottom rung in newspaper work.

On August 4, 1947, Mary McGrory came to the Washington *Star* through a journalistic side door. She was, to the newsroom, one of those surpassingly strange people—book reviewers. To the average reporter, it was almost incomprehensible that someone could get up in the morning and have nothing to do all day but to read a book and, if the book happened to be short enough, write a review. Miss McGrory strung along, however, until 1954 when she was transferred to the *Star*'s national reportorial staff and made a name for herself with her features on the Army-McCarthy hearings. Her literary caricatures became celebrated in Washington; so, too, her longer and more sympathetic character studies.

One of the most distinguished of her commentaries was her piece on Robert Frost after his death in 1963. He was so greatly loved by journalists that he seemed almost like one of their own; much more so, in fact, than Walt Whitman, the editor for a brief time of the Brooklyn *Engle,* and William Cullen Bryant, the editor for more than half a century of the New York *Evening Post.* Neither was the journalists' poet in the same sense that Frost was. Mary McGrory reflected it in the following, a part of a longer evaluation of him and his work in the Washington *Star,* January 29, 1963.

## FAME AND ROBERT FROST

### By Mary McGrory

Robert Frost was the rarest of beings, a great lyric poet who was honored in his own time as a sage.

He knew nothing of the isolation that genius can impose. He often cited what happened to Homer in contrast to his own fate:

> Seven cities claimed the Homer dead
> Through which the living Homer begged his bread.

Robert Frost lacked nothing that the world could give him in the way of recognition or attention. His poetry was loved and understood. So was he.

Success and fame came to him when he was 40 years old and in another country. *A Boy's Will,* his first published volume, appeared in England in 1915. Soon afterward he came home to an acclaim that stopped just short of idolatry and lasted for almost half a century.

He was enfolded into the life of his times as are few gifted human beings. He was welcome at the White House and the Kremlin. He was quoted endlessly by John F. Kennedy during his campaign for the Presidency and he became the first poet in American history to play a part in a presidential inauguration.

Generations of students knew his rough white thatch, his piercing blue eyes, and his voice that Padraic Colum compared to "an eagle's bark." Cabinet officers sat worshipfully at his feet and murmured his most famous lines as he spoke them. He won the Pulitzer Prize for poetry four times. Even Congress, traditionally the last bastion of philistinism, capitulated in 1951 and gave him a gold medal.

His views on poetry, politics, love, death, art, and science were eagerly besought and recorded at hundreds of interviews. His press conferences at the Library of Congress, where he zestfully served several terms as consultant in poetry, were major news events, from which reporters emerged overwhelmed by charm and gnomic utterances.

The old bard would lean back, cross his high-laced shoes, and bemoan the fact that high government officials didn't consult him about everything.

He provided the Kennedy inaugural with its most poignant moment. He stood up to read a slightly and specially revised version of "The Gift Outright," which he called "my most national poem." But he was blinded by the glare from the snow and faltered. When he finished he was applauded by thousands and comforted by two Presidents.

Robert Frost relished his celebrity. When Vermont made him its poet laureate in 1951, he wrote a quatrain which summarized his pleasure:

> Breathes there a bard who isn't moved
> To know his verse is understood
> And happily more or less approved
> By his country and his neighborhood?

The fellow poets who envied his popularity never denied his great gift. He was hailed as the finest American poet since Walt Whitman. When he recited his most famous lyrics, "On Stopping by Woods on a Snowy Evening" and "The Road Not Taken," he was, as often as not, accompanied by half the audience.

> The woods are lovely, dark and deep
> But I have promises to keep
> And miles to go before I sleep.

Almost any American who did not hear the poet recite these lines heard them from the candidate for the Presidency, John F. Kennedy. "Something there is that doesn't love a wall" is known the world around. In an age when poetry meant obscurity, his expression was crystal clear. His themes were of his homeland, New England, birches, and cows.

His poetry had the sweetness and the harshness of the Yankee landscape. It has not been imitated. He resisted all attempts to draw him

POET AND PRESIDENT

Robert Frost at the inaugural for President John F. Kennedy.

into the murky and cryptic imagery that was the vogue when he was
young and unknown. His models were Latin lyricists, Theocritus and
Catullus.

In "The Lesson for Today," he wrote his own epitaph:

> And were an epitaph my story
> I would have a short one ready for my own.
> I would have written of me on my stone:
> "He had a lover's quarrel with the world."

Few quarrels were more lyrically or rewardingly conducted.


## 65. CRITICS AND CULTURE

Now that culture has fallen on the land like manna, everybody is looking around for critics to pick it up and see whether it is any good. The
relatively few newspapers that have excelled in the care and feeding of
these troublesome journalists want more. Others are cautiously experimenting with the breed which, however necessary it may be, is
unlikely to increase in popularity as quickly as it has grown in stature.

There is, however, a fundamental difficulty. Discerning critics are in
short supply and always have been. As for new ones, despite all the
supposed wonders of psychological testing and other foxy personnel
methods, they are hard to find. Once discovered, they must live up to a
heritage of independence, toughness, durability, and professionalism
that has been fashioned for them by their peers.

Wherever they begin work throughout the nation, the newcomers
to the difficult and demanding field of daily newspaper criticism will
find distinguished examples of critical wisdom and longevity—and few
morning glories. While science may eventually offer automated criticism
at the flip of a punch card and the twist of a dial (and vestiges of it
have already been noted here and there), it is obviously beyond the
capacity of the computers now in the newsrooms to offer the judgments
that were given daily for so many years by Brooks Atkinson in the New
York *Times* and Lewis Gannett in the New York *Herald Tribune*, to
cite but two distinguished practitioners of the art.

Nor is there much hope at present in electronic criticism. For while
television has taken cognizance of the arts in a limited number of longer
shows, some of them superb, the daily one- or two-minute electronic

capsules of criticism can scarcely be as effective as the full-dress performance of a competent critic in a daily newspaper. It is on the newspapers, therefore, that the mass audience has continued to depend for an adequate daily assessment of what it is reading, seeing, and hearing.

To such an audience, the critic has seldom come into full view except when he is hired, fired, retired—or insulted by the President of the United States. Not many, of course, are likely to share the experience of Paul Hume, the music critic of the Washington *Post*, who was less than flattering in his appraisal of Margaret Truman's high C and was called to account by her angry father. The critic, therefore, is not likely to be pulled from his accustomed place in the back of the paper even though larger audiences are now inquiring into his methods and his values.

Using such respected figures as Atkinson and Gannett as examples, there is nothing very mysterious about either of them. Both were well-educated (at Harvard) to begin with. Both served their time as reporters, learning the basics of journalism before they became critics. Both served as daily critics for a quarter-century before going on to less taxing endeavors. Both infuriated university professors from time to time by insisting that their value systems were highly personal and not particularly complicated. As Atkinson usually phrased it, "I like it—or I don't like it."

Nobody could have made book reviewing for a daily newspaper sound easier than Gannett did, but not many in his time were able to do the job quite as well. Once, after a lecture at an Eastern university, he was asked by a student: "How do you find time to read so many books?"

He answered gravely: "That's how I make my living."

Many a university audience marveled that this affable, friendly, outgoing man, slim and straight as a Maine pine, could perform such prodigious literary tasks and show no sign of strain. Sometimes, he once said, he would read by the Consolidated Edison clock that tolled each quarter-hour over New York's Union Square, where he had a penthouse apartment with a garden. (He lugged in the soil himself in sacks from his farm home on Cream Hill Road, West Cornwall, Connecticut.) If he had a massive tome, such as a now-forgotten double-decker called *Sironia, Texas*, he would set himself a schedule of covering so many pages each quarter-hour and then time himself. If he had a relatively short novel or a book of poetry, he would relax and enjoy himself—if he could. If he had to pick out an unheralded first novel for review, and he conscientiously attempted to cover the field, he would try to be sportsmanlike about his reviewing (he thought of critics as specialists) and confine his attacks to those who were better able to stand them and who really merited them.

The academics were frequently aghast at the swift, professional appraisals with which Gannett would greet a new book or Atkinson a new play, however important they had been considered in advance and no matter how much money had been spent to bring them into being. Atkinson, from his customary aisle seat at the side of the theater, would depart on opening night at about 10:30 p.m., confer briefly with the editor of the page upon reaching the *Times* office, and then write his review quickly in longhand. A boy would whisk ·the copy to the composing room, a paragraph at a time; in forty-five minutes to an hour at most, the thing was done. Then, the critic would go to the composing room, read his own proof for typographical errors, and by 12:05 a.m. the page would go in. Within the hour, the opening nighters would know if they had seen a hit or a bomb.

"But how can you do this?" Atkinson would be asked by despairing theater people or students. "Don't you realize the time and effort that has gone into a production such as this, the enormous amounts of money?"

Atkinson would reply patiently, "How else can I do it for a daily paper?"

He often observed that, even when he had more time to write, as with his pieces for the Sunday paper, his judgments seemed to him to be sharper and more crisply phrased when he set them down at once after seeing the play. His was not a school for second-guessers and it is one that has persisted. Early in 1965, a long-heralded musical named *Kelly* opened on Broadway at a cost to its sponsors of $650,000, withered under a unanimous blast of critical disapproval, and closed after a single night.

With the exception of such unhappy instances as this one, it is about as easy to measure the effectiveness of a critic as it is to calculate the effect of sunlight, spring rain, or catastrophic storm on a flowering meadow. The mood, style, background, and knowledge of the critic all play their part in the final assessment of his work. In the following example, excerpted from his column in the New York *Times* on Septem-

ber 22, 1964, Brooks Atkinson gives a thoroughly professional performance.

## THE JOY OF O'CASEY

### By Brooks Atkinson

Perhaps it can be put this way: I knew that like all men Sean O'Casey
must die some day. But it never occurred to me that he would. In the
thirty years during which I knew him, he surmounted so many disasters
that I was forgetting a basic fact of life.

He did not surmount a heart attack last Friday in a Torquay, England, nursing home, where he had been a patient before. The Irishman
who wrote the most glorious English of his time has dropped his pen.
But this is written in honor of the personal side of O'Casey—a god of
wrath in his public postures but a kindly man with a modest view of
himself in private life.

Both the public and the private personalities were authentic. An
enemy of everything that corrodes the spirit, he was a belligerent writer.
He could be outrageously quarrelsome in print. But at home he was
simple, frank, warm and talkative, and very civil in the pursuit of an
argument. The public fire became a private glow.

When I first met him in New York, when *Within the Gates* was
produced, he was a sharp-faced, thin, animated Irishman with thick
glasses to compensate for weak eyes. When I last visited him in December, 1962, in his cheerful flat on the third floor of a remodeled
house on a hill in Devon, he was still sharp-faced and thin.

The lenses in his spectacles were still thick, but they could no longer
compensate for eyes that had almost lost their vision.

Joyous may not be too radiant a word to describe his inner spirit in
his last years. He was an optimist about the future of mankind. Despite
the many hardships of his life (he once remarked that he regarded
himself as a failure) he always enjoyed the experience of being alive:
"Tired, but joyous, praising God for His brightness and the will to-
wards joy in the breasts of men"—to quote a line he once wrote about
himself as a tenement boy in Dublin. Although O'Casey aged, he
never changed.

How he found time to write so many letters to so many people was
always a mystery because none of the letters were tossed off without

style. In late years, when his sight was dim, a friend typed them for him and his wife, Eileen O'Casey, helped him with everything.

No portrait of Sean would be complete without an expression of admiration for the main talents as well as the devotion of this energetic, good-humored woman. Last March he itemized her household activities as follows: "Eileen is snatching a little time to read the letters coming to me and a snatch of words from a book now and then, shopping and cooking, dealing with problems that at times disturb Shivaun (the O'Casey daughter) today and Breon (the son) and his family tomorrow, and keeping an eye out to save me from bumping into things, or tripping over them so that I don't end my life with a bang."

He didn't end his life with a bang. His heart stopped beating. In eighty-four years of unselfish living it was the first time his heart had failed him.

---

It is ironic that Atkinson won his Pulitzer Prize in 1947, not for his work as a critic, but for his appraisal of the Soviet Union while he was a correspondent in Moscow. He retired from the *Times* in 1965.

## 66. THE FUTURE OF TELEVISION

The coming of network television after World War II changed the face of journalism and measurably increased its stature. From the moment that millions of Americans realized they could watch the proceedings of the national political conventions in 1948, seeing more and probably knowing more than most of the delegates in the hall, the work of the journalist took on a different dimension. Newspapers, however great or small, had to recognize that they were no longer the first source of information for set events. Magazines devoted to synthesizing a week's news in print or pictures realized that they had to enlarge the scope of their work. Thus, almost overnight, television marched to the center of national attention and took up the key role that radio had been filling, with only partial and grudging recognition, for more than twenty years.

This is not to say that the television newsmakers and newsmen proved equal to their heavy responsibilities from the outset or that they developed a format, adequate for their medium, to deal with the news. Television had many faults to overcome in the 1960s. Edward R. Murrow, the first and most important television newsman of his day, was profoundly right when he criticized his fellow professionals for trying to package their news too tightly in too short a time and for relegating it to nonprime viewing hours in too many instances.[19] Nor could there be any honest disagreement with the criticism of Newton Minow, who as Federal Communications Commissioner attacked the cultural "wasteland" of television.[20] These shots hit home.

As for the newspaper criticism of television, which was understandably heavy, too much of it was ineffective because it was so clearly self-serving. There were not many newspaper television critics who had the stature, the professional respect, and the fundamental integrity of such men as Jack Gould of the New York *Times* and John Crosby of the New York *Herald Tribune*. The decision of critics like Crosby to turn to other and pleasanter pursuits was a matter for regret in a newly developing area of journalism where there were few experts and even fewer disinterested and competent critics.

Yet, the efforts of Gould, Murrow, Crosby, and a few other powerful voices of dissent were not in vain. As the pressures for a better break for news reporting mounted on the networks, those in charge of television's destinies began to realize that they had new responsibilities. But it took the New York newspaper strike of 1962–63 to break the pattern of five- and fifteen-minute news programs. However, few could say that the coming of the thirty-minute national news program was a complete answer. Often, the telecasters turned to the amusing and the trivial to find relief from much of the heavy, somber news of the day.

No one of importance in the handling of television news contended, therefore, that it could be a substitute for the newspapers, much less supplant them in its present format. The experience of viewers in five cities, where there had been maximum dependence on television during general newspaper strikes, illustrated the complementary nature of the media. The accommodation between the press and radio now was extended to television. In the 1964 presidential election, the responsibility for coverage was shared between the networks and the wire services, and individual contractual arrangements were made between various newspapers and the networks. Despite some local failures and a

[19] Edward R. Murrow, "Why Should News Come in 5-Minute Packages?" *Nieman Reports*, January, 1959; a condensation of his speech to the Radio and Television News Directors in Chicago, Oct. 15, 1958.

[20] Newton Minow, report of speech in New York *Times*, May 10, 1961.

large bundle of individual gripes from irreconcilable editors, the co-operative system worked. It was a good sign for the future.

There was, of course, one field in which television excelled so clearly that the nation could take pride in the achievements of its electronic journalists. That was the on-the-spot transmission of the great American ventures into space in the 1960s, which contrasted so vividly with the secrecy of the Soviet system. There were other landmarks for American television journalism—the four days and nights following the Kennedy assassination, the presidential inaugurations of the 1960s, the all-day telecast of the funeral of Winston Churchill. These were the events which showed the new journalists at their best; they could not, of course, cover up the many areas in which television was still wanting.

And so, after nearly two decades, television did have some reason to count its gains in the news field. It could face its critics with at least some of the confidence displayed by newspapers that had a heritage of two centuries of publication on the North American continent. One of the most thoughtful discussions of the broad role of television was held by Jack Gould and Harry S. Ashmore, a Pulitzer Prize-winning editor while he was with the *Arkansas Gazette* in Little Rock.[21] In it, Gould looked beyond the news role of the electronic media and sketched some of the basic developments for the future—more responsibility, an enlarged spectrum of broadcast channels, subscription television, and a more realistic program of educational television.

In summing up his discussion with Jack Gould, Ashmore raised some questions for television.

## WHAT PRICE TELEVISION?
### By Harry S. Ashmore

Here is the heart of the matter.

Show business, of a fairly trivial order, can command a massive TV audience and sure-fire advertising sponsorship; programing that rises above the norm is at best a financial risk, since the TV industry has not found—and does not appear to be actively seeking—a way to merchandise a selective audience, even one that runs as high as ten million.

[21] Harry S. Ashmore, comment on interview with Jack Gould, in a booklet, *American Character* (published October, 1961, by the Center for the Study of Democratic Institutions, Santa Barbara, Calif.), pp. 29–32 passim.

To suggest that this is not a tolerable situation is not to trample on the flag, or even condemn the profit motive out of hand. . . . have as much concern as the next man with keeping the economy viable through the rising sales of razor blades and proprietary drugs; I, too, wish everyone used a good deodorant. My intelligence is not unduly insulted by TV's programing, but it is outraged by the pious argument that the public interest is coincident with the existing effective monopoly on the air waves.

Nor am I unsympathetic to the industry's concern over the possible consequences of government intervention. Finally, I am by instinct as well as occupation a First Amendment man, and I would not see the Constitution's immunities denied to any part of the communications media.

But I insist that consideration of what should be done about broadcasting must not be cut off, as the industry obtusely and so far successfully insists, with recognition of the valid limits on government action. This is not the end of the argument, but the beginning.

The government has had a regulatory role in broadcasting ever since it first became practical to transmit sound by radio. If the operating agency, the Federal Communications Commission, has never seemed quite certain as to its duties beyond that of traffic control, the agency's authority and responsibility are nevertheless real.

Only the FCC, for example, can provide the remedies discussed hopefully by Mr. Gould: more broadcast channels in the present spectrum and ultimately a shift of all TV to the UHF band; a legitimate accounting of how the stations and networks are employing their valuable licenses in the "public interest, convenience, and necessity"; development of subscription TV as a means of serving minority viewers at their own expense; support in a variety of ways for the languishing experiment in educational television. Nothing here smacks of censorship, and in the unlikely event of transgression by the bureaucrats we, the people, can safely rely on being alerted by a mighty chorus of electronically amplified watchdogs.

In sum, Mr. Gould is pleading for greater diversity in television. Far from being an assault on the sacred precepts of free enterprise, this could be a blueprint of salvation for private broadcasting; diversity means competition, and competition is the life of trade.

Neither is he seeking to shackle the industry; on the contrary he is seeking ways and means of freeing TV's discouraged creative spirits from the dead hand of the common denominator. He reminds us that censorship is not the exclusive province of government; it occurs in a particularly insidious way when broadcasters conclude that their final obligation is to make everybody happy, or at least to make nobody unhappy.

Mr. Gould cites the generally good record of the networks in the sensitive area of news and public affairs, yet it is a reasonable assumption that for every aired program dealing with a subject in contemporary controversy a dozen are still-born in executive conference.

I do not think we can afford to be complacent about television. This technological marvel is one of the great accomplishments of our time. In a historical moment, broadcasting has hooked up virtually the whole of a sprawling nation in a system that enables all of us to see the same sights and hear the same sounds, and in so doing it has pre-empted the leading role in mass communications.

The potential here is as great as that of the invention of the printing press. Surely we ought to be able to employ this miracle to produce something more than a fast buck—something, say, on the order of a Gutenberg Bible, which, after all, turned out to be quite a best-seller.


## 67. "THE RIGHT TO KNOW"

A campaign to restrict pretrial information to the press began in the 1960s with the publication of the Warren Commission Report and appeared to be gathering headway. The New Jersey Supreme Court issued an order forbidding prosecution and defense lawyers and police officials from making "prejudicial statements" in pending cases. The Philadelphia Bar Association wanted the same thing done in Pennsylvania. Similar efforts were developing elsewhere. Even the Department of Justice itself was taking an active interest on behalf of the federal government.

Once more the press found itself on the defensive; once more, a battle that began more than two centuries ago on the North American continent had to be fought again. At stake was what many leaders of the press had come to call "the people's right to know." However, so many sham battles had been fought under that heady slogan for so

340          *The Profession*

many dubious causes that efforts to interest the public in it were very difficult to sustain. Yet, this time the fight was a real one and the issues went to the very heart of the honest differences over the right of a free press versus the right of a fair trial.

The Los Angeles *Times* was one of the leaders in the effort to prevent bench and bar from choking off information that had been freely given in the past. In 1942, the newspaper had won the gold medal emblematic of the Pulitzer Prize for public service for its campaign to uphold the freedom of the press. It was as a result of a case involving the *Times* that the U.S. Supreme Court had held on December 8, 1941 that "clear and present danger" to the administration of justice must be established before the press can be held in contempt of court.

Gene Blake, the *Times*'s legal specialist, was one of the best-informed journalists to explore the issues. He was then 45 years old, having been born February 16, 1920, in Boise, Idaho. In 1941, upon his graduation from the University of California with a journalism degree, he joined the *Times* as a copy boy. By 1953, allowing for three years in the Coast Guard during World War II, he had worked his way up through the ranks to become a specialist in legal reporting of all kinds. It was his fate to be an eyewitness to the murder of Lee Harvey Oswald by Jack Ruby in Dallas and to cover Ruby's subsequent trial. He knew at first hand, therefore, the reasons why the Warren Commission had recommended better protection for the rights of the accused.

As the recipient of honors from the American Bar Association, the State Bar of California, and the press itself, Blake discussed the background of the controversy in a series of articles in 1964 for the Los Angeles *Times*. The following, setting the case in its historical perspective, is excerpted from the article of May 19.

## A TEST FOR THE PRESS
### By Gene Blake

Gagging the press through contempt of court power has been tried often in this country but so far has been held inimical to basic American rights in a long line of court decisions.

That doesn't necessarily mean the system firmly implanted in England will continue to be shunned here. Recent U.S. Supreme Court decisions have contained dire hints to the contrary. It might be that the proper case by which the court could establish a new precedent just hasn't come before it.

Freedom of the press was established in America in 1735 when Andrew Hamilton won an unheard-of jury verdict for the publisher John Peter Zenger. It was written into the First Amendment of the Bill of Rights. Nevertheless, the power of courts to summarily punish newspapers for contemptuous publication came to America with the colonists. It wasn't until 1809 that some state legislatures, led by Pennsylvania, confined the summary contempt power to a limited number of misbehaviors committed in the immediate presence of the court.

In 1831, the Federal Contempt Act limited punishable contempt to misbehavior in the presence of the court "or so near thereto as to obstruct the administration of justice." A backward step was taken in 1918 when the U.S. Supreme Court, in the case of *Toledo Newspaper Co., vs. United States,* completely ignored the intent of the 1831 statute.

The Toledo *News-Bee* has been convicted of contempt for attributing bias to a judge in a squabble between the city and a transit company. The Supreme Court upheld the conviction, ruling that the newspaper's action constituted a "reasonable tendency" to obstruct justice.

"The reasonable tendency of the acts done to influence or bring about the baleful result is the test," the court held.

Justice Oliver Wendell Holmes strenuously dissented. Shortly afterward, in a freedom of speech case (*Schenck vs. United States*), Holmes spoke for a unanimous court in enunciating a new test. "The question in every case," he said, "is whether the words used are used in such circumstances and are of such a nature as to create a clear and present danger that they will bring about the substantive evils that Congress has a right to prevent."

In 1941, in the case of *Nye vs. United States,* the Supreme Court formally reversed its position in the Toledo case. The words "so near thereto," in the Federal Contempt Act, mean physical proximity, the court ruled. And in the same year, in the cases of the *Times Mirror Co. vs. Superior Court and Bridges vs. California,* the Supreme Court formally applied the "clear and present danger" test to newspaper contempt cases in place of the "reasonable tendency" test.

The Los Angeles *Times* had been held in contempt, particularly for an editorial commenting on the pending sentencing of convicted defendants in a labor assault case. Labor leader Harry Bridges had been held in contempt for sending and publicizing a telegram interpreted as threatening a strike if a court ruling were to stand.

In a 5–4 decision, the contempt convictions were overturned, with both cases decided together on the same principle.

Justice Hugo L. Black wrote the majority opinion. "Free speech and fair trials are two of the most cherished policies of our civilization and it would be a trying task to choose between them," he said, but added: "The substantive evil must be extremely serious and the degree of imminence extremely high before utterances can be punished."

Black conceded that "legal trials are not like elections, to be won through the use of the meeting hall, the radio, and the newspaper." But he said it cannot be assumed that "to preserve judicial impartiality it is necessary for judges to have a contempt power by which they can close all channels of public expression to all matters which touch upon pending cases."

Justice Felix Frankfurter, leader of the court faction that would have imposed more stringent controls on the press, wrote the dissent. "The Bill of Rights is not self-destructive," he said. "Freedom of expression can hardly carry implications that nullify the guarantees of impartial trials."

Nevertheless, the principle enunciated in the *Times* and Bridges cases has been unswervingly followed by the court in all subsequent cases—*Pennekamp vs. Florida* and *Craig vs. Harney* in 1946 and *Wood vs. Georgia* in 1961. "It was expected," wrote Justice Stanley Reed. in the Pennekamp case, "that from a decent self-restraint on the part of the press and from the formula's repeated application by the courts, standards of permissible conduct would emerge which would guarantee the courts against interference and allow fair play to the good influences of open discussion."

But perhaps the court's most significant action was its refusal even to review the 1950 Maryland case of *Baltimore Radio Show vs. State*.

In 1939 the Baltimore Supreme Bench adopted Rule 904 forbidding pretrial publication of material "which may prevent a fair trial, improperly influence the court or jury, or tend in any manner to interfere with the administration of justice." In essence, it was the English system.

Radio stations tested the rule by broadcasting details of the arrest, confession, and prior record of Eugene H. James, a Negro accused of murdering an 11-year-old white girl and raping a white woman. He subsequently was convicted in a nonjury trial and executed. The radio stations then were convicted of contempt and fined, but the Maryland Court of Appeals reversed.

"Knowledge that the public authorities are active may have a tendency to allay public excitement and fears, so often magnified by word of mouth," the court noted. "Trials cannot be held in a vacuum, hermetically sealed against rumor and report. If a mere disclosure of the general nature of the evidence relied on would vitiate a subsequent trial, few verdicts could stand. . . . The broadcasts did not create such a clear and present danger as to meet the constitutional test."

By refusing to hear the case, the U.S. Supreme Court did not indicate that it necessarily agreed—but at least that it did not disagree at that time.

## 68. FREE PRESS AND FAIR TRIAL

Anthony Lewis won two Pulitzer Prizes before he was 40 years old. His reporting of the U.S. Supreme Court was singled out by Harry W. Jones, director of research of the American Bar Foundation, as "the firest news coverage of constitutional and legal affairs that I have ever read." Professor Paul A. Freund of Harvard Law School said his work had "won the admiration of the legal profession" for its clarity and understanding.[23]

The evolution of this lean and slender New Yorker as a rather cheerful expert on the law had not been a particularly painful process, on the whole, but it had meant a lot of hard work. Born in 1926 in New York City and graduated from Columbia College, he had worked briefly for the New York *Times* at the outset of his career and gone on to other opportunities. In 1954, as a reporter for the Washington *Daily News*, he had helped clear an obscure Navy employee, Abraham Chasanow, who had been wrongfully dismissed as a security risk. That had brought him his first Pulitzer Prize in 1955. The second one had come in 1963 for his coverage of the U.S. Supreme Court.

[23] Letter from Professor Paul A. Freund, Jan. 31, 1963, in Anthony Lewis Pulitzer Prize exhibit, Butler Library, Columbia University.

With such credentials and the added prestige of serving as the New York *Times*'s correspondent at the high court, Lewis undertook to analyze the renewed controversy over free press versus fair trial in 1964. He was assured in advance of a respectful hearing by both sides. The following is his summation of the issues, in condensed form, from the *New York Time Magazine*, October 18, 1964.

## THE PUBLIC INTEREST

### By Anthony Lewis

A question that has long nagged at the conscience of Americans concerned about justice is posed most acutely by the report of the Warren Commission on the assassination of President Kennedy: Does this country's practice of unbridled liberty for the press, radio, and television to report on pending criminal cases permit any man charged with a notorious crime to get a fair trial?

Chief Justice Earl Warren and his six colleagues on the commission were highly critical of what happened after the arrest of Lee Harvey Oswald. In the corridors of the Dallas Police Headquarters reporters and cameramen were so numerous and unruly that witnesses could hardly get through. Under the pressures of the press, officials repeatedly disclosed damaging evidence and said Oswald's guilt was certain. A desire to please the press was one reason for the ill-handled transfer that led to Oswald's murder.

If he had lived, the commission said, his "opportunity for a trial by twelve jurors free of preconception as to his guilt or innocence would have been seriously jeopardized by the premature disclosure and weighing of the evidence against him."

What happened in Dallas in November, 1963, was an extreme case. But the American Bar Association was stating the obvious when it observed, in a comment condemning conditions in Dallas, that "excessive and prejudicial publicity with respect to criminal cases is not unusual in America."

There is a *public* interest, as the Warren Commission phrased it, in being kept informed about criminal proceedings. This high interest is often cited by the press, but the desire to provide titillation and entertainment is usually the real motive for lofty demands to get the facts and admit the cameras. The honest argument for press entry in each case is that a useful social function will be served in the particular circumstances, not that the press has some "right."

The constitutional right that is involved here is the one guaranteed by the Sixth Amendment: "In all criminal prosecutions, the accused shall enjoy the right to a speedy and public trial, by an impartial jury."

The public trial, it should be noted, is for the benefit of "the accused," not of the press. Its purpose, in the minds of the Constitution's framers, was to prevent the former English practice—made infamous by the Star Chamber—of trying men *in camera*, without access to friends or to public opinion.

"The public trial exists," Justice William O. Douglas explained a few years ago, "because of the aversion which liberty-loving people had toward secret trials and proceedings. That is the reason our courts are open to the public, not because the framers wanted to provide the public with recreation."

In the absence of direct control over press comment, the courts have been forced to other remedies. These are to delay a trial if a community has been saturated with adverse publicity about the defendant, or move the trial to another city.

Appellate courts are finding more and more often that convicted defendants could not have had a fair trial in the circumstances of publicity and that there should have been a change of venue. When this is decided at the appellate level the result is to require a new trial, often long after the event.

The Supreme Court first reversed a conviction because of newspaper influence on a jury in 1959. In 1961 the Supreme Court found an Indiana conviction unconstitutional because the jury had read numerous articles describing the defendant as a "mad-dog killer." This was followed in 1963 by a decision throwing out a Louisiana trial held after the defendant's alleged confession to the sheriff had been filmed and shown to the community on television three times. Justice Potter Stewart used the term "kangaroo-court proceedings" for that episode.

The lower courts have got the message from the Supreme Court and are bearing down harder on trial by newspaper. In the summer of 1963, a federal district judge in Ohio issued a writ of habeas corpus releasing Dr. Samuel Sheppard after ten years in prison for the murder of his wife on the ground—among others—that newspaper and broadcast in-

## THE MURDER OF LEE HARVEY OSWALD

Robert H. Jackson's 1964 Pulitzer Prize picture showing Jack Ruby firing
the fatal shot in Dallas.

timations of his guilt before trial had fatally infected the proceedings with unfairness.

This technique, the setting aside of past convictions because of the influence of publicity, has obvious and serious deficiencies. If an innocent man really was railroaded to jail by public passion, it is not much cheer to him to have a new trial ten years later. And the public may suffer as well as defendants. Years after a crime, at a new trial, it may be difficult or impossible for prosecutors to reassemble the evidence needed for conviction of even the guiltiest man.

For these reasons, there has been more and more thought about ways to stop the evil, not after it has had its effect, but before—to curtail indiscriminate, unfair publicity before criminal trials.

One course would be to move closer to the British system and curb irresponsible press or broadcast comments by contempt proceedings against those who make them. But that does not seem to be a practical solution for there is no discernible trend in the Supreme Court toward lessening the protections of freedom for the press. Some abuse goes along with freedom, the court might say, but it must be handled in ways that do not lead to restriction and timidity.

The idea endorsed by the Warren Commission was "the promulgation of a code of professional conduct governing representatives of all news media" in reporting on pending criminal cases. This idea has had a good deal of attention in newspaper and broadcast circles, too.

With all deference, the proposal for a self-promulgated code is not very promising. It is likely to be ignored by those who sin most. H. L. Mencken disposed of the idea a generation ago when he wrote:

"Journalistic codes of ethics are all moonshine. . . . If American journalism is to be purged of its present swinishness and brought up to a decent level of repute—and God knows that such an improvement is needed—it must be accomplished by the devices of morals, not by those of honor. That is to say, it must be accomplished by external forces, and through the medium of penalties exteriorly inflicted."

Another course, which has attracted growing support, is for the courts to crack down on those more clearly within their disciplinary jurisdiction than the press—the prosecutors and defense lawyers and police who are the sources of the material printed or broadcast.

The truth is that excessive pretrial publicity does flaw our generally civilized standards of criminal procedure. More of the press should recognize its responsibility and consider effective measures to prevent abuses instead of talking about "the right to know." Otherwise, there may come the external retribution of which Mencken spoke.

---

In the inscrutable ways of journalism, Anthony Lewis said farewell to the U.S. Supreme Court in 1965 and put his legal expertise behind him for the time being. His new post—the most cherished in the foreign service of journalism—was chief of the London bureau of the New York *Times*. In common with other American journalists, he had made a profession out of what had been accounted a mere trade fifty years ago.

If it was an increasingly important profession, the reason for it was that the journalists were more important to the people of this dark and dangerous age than the novelists, the dramatists, and perhaps even the poets. They wrote of life as it was, but they were not content with it. As the chief interpreters of their time, they did not shrink from the truth but they hoped eternally for a better world. This was the significance of their work. This was the meaning of the new front page.

# INDEX

# PERMISSIONS

I am indeed grateful to the following publications and organizations that kindly granted permission to use the material quoted in this book.

*I. The Civil Rights Struggle*
Linda Goes to School. Reprinted by permission of the Associated Press.
When Hate Filled Birmingham. Reprinted by permission of the Atlanta *Constitution* and the New York *Herald Tribune*.
"They Do Their Dirt at Night." Reprinted by permission of the St. Petersburg *Times*.
The Fighting Lady. Reprinted by permission of the St. Louis *Post-Dispatch*.
The Murder of Medgar Evers. Reprinted by permission of the Lexington *Advertiser*.
The March on Washington. Reprinted by permission of the New York *Herald Tribune*.
"Riders to the Blood-Red Wrath." Reprinted by permission of the author, the *Sunday Post-Dispatch*, and Harper & Row.
The Negro in America. Reprinted by permission of the St. Louis *Post-Dispatch*.
Civil Rights. Reprinted by permission of the Rochester *Times-Union*.

*II. Crime Reporters, New Style*
The Great Tank Mystery. Reprinted by permission of the Pecos *Independent* and the Houston *Chronicle*.
Outdoing Billie Sol. Reprinted by permission of the *Wall Street Journal*.
"Lay Off or Else . . ." Reprinted by permission of the Chicago *Tribune*.
Cosa Nostra. Reprinted by permission of the Washington *Star*.
Business and the Gangs. Reprinted by permission of the *Wall Street Journal*.
"I'll Get You!" Reprinted by permission of the Houston *Post*.

*III. The Diggers*
"The 101st Senator." Reprinted by permission of the Des Moines *Register-Tribune*.

Why Birth Control? Reprinted by permission of the Chicago *Daily News*.

A Favor for Joe. Reprinted by permission of the Washington *Post*.

"I Gotta Keep Pickin' Tomatoes . . ." Reprinted by permission of the New York *World-Telegram and Sun*.

Caught in a Paper Jungle. Reprinted by permission of the Buffalo *Evening News*.

IV. *This Is Public Service*

Milledgeville Revisited. Reprinted by permission of the Atlanta *Constitution*.

An Attack on Hatred. Reprinted by permission of the Santa Barbara *News-Press*.

"It Is a Fearsome Thing . . ." Reprinted by permission of the Hutchinson *News*.

"No Fuss, No Bother . . . Just Kicks." Reprinted by permission of the Los Angeles *Times*.

The Hustlers. Reprinted by permission of the Washington *Daily News*.

Just Above the Animal Level. Reprinted by permission of the Louisville *Times*.

V. *The Foreign Correspondents*

"There Is No News from Auschwitz." © 1958 by the New York Times Company. Reprinted by permission.

The Judgment. © 1961 by the New York Times Company. Reprinted by permission.

The Cuba Story. Reprinted by permission of the Miami *News*.

"A Hard Man to Find." Reprinted by permission of the New York *Herald Tribune*.

Birth of the Congo Republic. Reprinted by permission of the Associated Press.

Murder for a Small Fee. Reprinted by permission of the Associated Press.

The End of Diem. © 1963 by the New York Times Company. Reprinted by permission.

A Village Dies. Reprinted by permission of the Associated Press.

War Is Like That. Reprinted by permission of the Associated Press.

"Madman . . . but a Genius." Reprinted by permission of the Chicago *Daily News*.

John XXIII: A Great Pope. Reprinted by permission of the Detroit *News*.

Farewell to a Leader. Reprinted by permission of the *Christian Science Monitor*. © 1964. The Christian Science Publishing Society. All rights reserved.

A Picture Comes Down. © 1964 by the New York Times Company. Reprinted by permission.

Funeral for an Age. Reprinted by permission of the Chicago *Daily News*.

The Great Experiment. © 1959 by the New York Times Company. Reprinted by permission.

VI. *Specialists in the Space Age*
Samos. Reprinted by permission of the Washington *Post*.
"A Real Fireball of a Ride!" ⓒ 1962 by the New York Times Company. Reprinted by permission.
Dr. Kelsey's Story. Reprinted by permission of the Washington *Post*.
New Hope in Mental Health. Reprinted by permission of the Associated Press.
The Case Against Cigarettes. Reprinted by permission of the Minneapolis *Star-Tribune*.
In Darwin's Steps. Reprinted by permission of the San Francisco *Chronicle*.
What Is Life? Reprinted by permission of the Boston *Globe*.
"The Children Need Help." Reprinted by permission of the Charlotte *Observer*.

VII. *The Personal Touch*
Dallas, November 22, 1963. Reprinted by permission of United Press International.
The Finest Protect a President. Reprinted by permission of The Sterling Lord Agency and ⓒ 1965, New York Herald Tribune Inc.
My Life in Moscow. Reprinted by permission of United Press International.
Up Front in Viet Nam. Reprinted by permission of the Chicago *Sun-Times*.
Political Poll—1776. Reprinted by permission of the author and the Publishers Newspaper Syndicate.
A Californian Looks Up. Reprinted by permission of the San Francisco *Examiner*.
"The Good People." ⓒ 1964 by the New York Times Company. Reprinted by permission.
The Sickness Called Apathy. Reprinted by permission of the author. ⓒ 1964 by the New York Times Company.

VIII. *The Interpreters*
Portrait of a President. ⓒ 1965 by the New York Times Company. Reprinted by permission.
The Big Change. Reprinted by permission of the *Wall Street Journal*.
How Effective Is Congress? Reprinted by permission of the St. Louis *Post-Dispatch*.
The Sino-Soviet Crisis. Reprinted by permission of the Associated Press.
"There Will Be Profits . . ." Reprinted by permission of the Philadelphia *Bulletin*.
The UN Goes Home. Reprinted by permission of the Baltimore *Sun*.
The Future of the UN, ⓒ 1965 by the New York Times Company. Reprinted by permission.
The State of the World. Reprinted by permission of the Washington Post-Los Angeles Times Syndicate.
Morality in World Affairs. Reprinted by permission of the *Christian Science*

*Monitor.* © 1963. The Christian Science Publishing Society. All rights reserved.

## IX. *The Profession*

"The Golden Romance." Reprinted by permission of the author. © 1953 by the New York Times Company.

The Old, Old Herald. Reprinted by permission of the *Philippines Herald.*

The Best of Grantland Rice. Reprinted by permission of the author and of *Editor & Publisher.*

A Letter to Santa Claus. © 1962 by the New York Times Company. Reprinted by permission.

Fame and Robert Frost. Reprinted by permission of the Washington *Star.*

The Joy of O'Casey. © 1964 by the New York Times Company. Reprinted by permission.

What Price Television? Reprinted by permission of the author.

A Test for the Press. Reprinted by permission of the Los Angeles *Times.*

The Public Interest, © 1964 by the New York Times Company. Reprinted by permission.


*Illustrations*

A New Era in Communications. United Press International from NASA.

Civil Rights Marchers. Associated Press.

Paul Conrad on Civil Rights. Denver *Post.*

A Sad Day for Billie Sol. Associated Press.

For the Migratory Farm Worker. New York *World Telegram and Sun.*

Help Came Too Late. Minneapolis *Star.*

Serious Steps. Associated Press.

The New Face of War. Associated Press.

The Firing Squad. United Press International.

America's First Astronaut. United Press International from NASA.

The New Metropolis. New York *Times.*

LBJ at His Texas Ranch. United Press International.

A Comment on the Cold War. Des Moines *Register.*

Poet and President. United Press International.

The Murder of Lee Harvey Oswald. Dallas *Times-Herald.*